REFERENCE

A to Z of
WOMEN IN
SCIENCE
AND MATH

A to Z of
WOMEN IN
SCIENCE
AND MATH

LISA YOUNT

Facts On File, Inc.

A to Z of Women in Science and Math

Facts On File, Inc.
11 Penn Plaza
New York, NY 10001

Library of Congress Cataloging-in-Publication Data

Yount, Lisa.
   A to Z of women in science and math / Lisa Yount.
    p. cm.
   Includes bibliographical references and index.
   ISBN 0-8160-3797-3
   1. Women scientists—Biography—Encylopedias. 2. Women mathematicians—Biography—Encyclopedias.
  I. Title. II. Series.
  Q141.Y675   1999
  509.2'2—dc21 [b]
                                         98-46093

Facts On File books are available at special discounts when purchased in bulk quantities for businesses, associations, institutions, or sales promotions. Please call our Special Sales Department in New York at (212) 967-8800 or (800) 322-8755.

You can find Facts On File on the World Wide Web at http://www.factsonfile.com

Cover design by Cathy Rincon

Printed in the United States of America

MP FOF 10 9 8 7 6 5 4 3 2 1

This book is printed on acid-free paper.

To past women scientists
with admiration for all they have achieved
despite tremendous odds
and
To future women scientists
in the hope that the odds against them will be less
and their achievements even greater

CONTENTS

Acknowledgments ix
Author's Note xi
Introduction xiii

Entries:
Agnesi, Maria Gaetana 1
Agnodice 2
Ajakaiye, Deborah Enilo 2
Alexander, Hattie Elizabeth 3
Ancker-Johnson, Betsy 4
Andam, Aba A. Bentil 5
Anderson, Elda Emma 6
Anderson, Elizabeth Garrett 7
Anning, Mary 8
Apgar, Virginia 9
Ayrton, Hertha 10
Bailey, Florence Augusta
    Merriam 12
Bascom, Florence 13
Bassi, Laura Maria Catarina 14
Bechtereva, Natalia Petrovna 15
Bell Burnell, Susan Jocelyn 16
Benedict, Ruth Fulton 18
Bennett, Isobel 19
Blackwell, Elizabeth 20
Blodgett, Katharine Burr 22
Boden, Margaret 23
Brandegee, Mary Katharine
    Layne 24
Brooks, Harriet 25
Burbidge, Eleanor Margaret
    Peachey 26
Cannon, Annie Jump 29
Carr, Emma Perry 31
Carson, Rachel Louise 33

Châtelet, Emilie du 35
Clark, Eugenie 36
Cleopatra the Alchemist 37
Cobb, Jewel Plummer 38
Colborn, Theodora 39
Cori, Gerty Theresa Radnitz 40
Cremer, Erika 42
Curie, Marie 43
Daubechies, Ingrid 46
Dick, Gladys Rowena Henry 47
Dresselhaus, Mildred Spiewak 48
Duplaix, Nicole 49
Earle, Sylvia Alice 51
Eastwood, Alice 53
Eddy, Bernice 54
Edinger, Johanna Gabrielle
    Ottelie 55
Edlund, Sylvia 56
Elion, Gertrude Belle 57
Evans, Alice Catherine 60
Faber, Sandra Moore 63
Fawcett, Stella Grace Maisie 64
Fleming, Williamina Paton
    Stevens 65
Flügge-Lotz, Irmgard 67
Fossey, Dian 67
Franklin, Melissa Eve Bronwen
    69
Franklin, Rosalind Elsie 69
Frith, Uta Aunernhammer 72
Galdikas, Biruté M. F. 73
Gardner, Julia Anna 75
Geiringer, Hilda 76
Geller, Margaret Joan 76
Germain, Marie Sophie 78

Gilbreth, Lillian Evelyn Moller
    79
Goodall, Jane 80
Hamilton, Alice 83
Hawes, Harriet Ann Boyd 85
Hazen, Elizabeth Lee 86
Herschel, Caroline Lucretia 87
Hildegarde of Bingen 88
Hodgkin, Dorothy Crowfoot 89
Hopper, Grace Brewster Murray
    92
Horney, Karen Danielsen 94
Hrdy, Sarah Blaffer 95
Hyde, Ida Henrietta 97
Hyman, Libbie Henrietta 98
Hypatia 99
Ildstad, Suzanne 100
Jackson, Shirley Ann 102
Jacoba Felicie 103
Jemison, Mae Carol 103
Joliot-Curie, Irène 104
Jorge-Pádua, Maria Tereza 106
Kelsey, Frances Oldham 108
King, Mary-Claire 109
Kirch, Maria Winkelmann 112
Klein, Melanie Reizes 112
Kovalevskaia, Sofia Vasilyevna
    113
Ladd-Franklin, Christine 116
Leakey, Mary Douglas Nicol
    117
Leavitt, Henrietta Swan 118
Lehmann, Inge 120
Levi-Montalcini, Rita 121

Levy, Jerre   123
Levy, Julia   124
Lonsdale, Kathleen Yardley   125
Love, Susan   126
Lovelace, Augusta Ada Byron   127
Maathai, Wangari Muta   130
McClintock, Barbara   131
McNally, Karen Cook   134
Makhubu, Lydia Phindile   135
Margulis, Lynn Alexander   136
Maria the Jewess   138
Marrack, Philippa   138
Matzinger, Polly   139
Maury, Antonia Caetana   140
Mayer, Maria Gertrude Goeppert   141
Mead, Margaret   143
Meitner, Lise   146
Merian, Maria Sibylla   149
Mexia, Ynes Enriquetta Julietta   150
Mitchell, Maria   151
Morawetz, Cathleen Synge   153
Morgan, Ann Haven   154
Moss, Cynthia   156
Newton Turner, Helen Alma   159
Nice, Margaret Morse   160
Noether, Emmy   161

Noguchi, Constance Tom   162
Novello, Antonia Coello   164
Nuttall, Zelia Maria Magdalena   164
Ocampo-Friedmann, Roseli   166
Ohta, Tomoko   167
Patrick, Ruth   169
Patterson, Francine   171
Payne, Katharine Boynton   172
Payne-Gaposchkin, Cecilia Helena   173
Perey, Marguerite Catherine   174
Pert, Candace Beebe   175
Quimby, Edith Hinkley   177
Quinn, Helen Rhoda Arnold   178
Rajalakshmi, R.   179
Richards, Ellen Henrietta Swallow   180
Robinson, Julia Bowman   182
Rubin, Vera Cooper   183
Sabin, Florence Rena   186
Saruhashi, Katsuko   188
Scott, Charlotte Angas   189
Seibert, Florence Barbara   190
Simpson, Joanne Malkus   191
Sithole-Niang, Idah   192
Slye, Maud Caroline   192
Somerville, Mary Fairfax   193
Stevens, Nettie Maria   195

Stewart, Alice   196
Stewart, Sarah   197
Taussig, Helen   199
Trotula of Salerno   201
Van Dover, Cindy Lee   203
Vrba, Elisabeth   205
Wexler, Nancy Sabin   207
Wheeler, Anna Johnson Pell   209
Williams, Anna Wessels   210
Wong-Staal, Flossie   211
Wright, Jane Cooke   212
Wrinch, Dorothy Maud   213
Wu, Chien-shiung   214
Yalow, Rosalyn Sussman   217
Yener, Kutlu Aslihan   219
Zhao Yufen   222

Recommended Sources on Women Scientists and Mathematicians   223

Entries by Field   227

Entries by Country of Birth   229

Entries by Country of Major Scientific Activity   231

Entries by Year of Birth   233

Chronology   235

Index   239

ACKNOWLEDGMENTS

I would like to thank the following for their help:

The living women represented in this volume who took the time to read and correct their entries and, in some cases, send me additional material or speak with me by phone about their lives and work.

The staffs of the libraries, archives, and news bureaus of many universities, who assisted me in finding photographs.

The staff of the Richmond Public Library, who helped with interlibrary loans and other research.

Nicole Bowen, my editor at Facts On File, who proposed this project and provided many kinds of assistance along the way.

Last but never least, my husband, Harry Henderson, who provided extremely useful computer research, patiently sent endless faxes, and, above all, gave his love and support during this project, as he does for everything I do.

AUTHOR'S NOTE

There is no perfect way to decide on entrants for a volume such as this, particularly one that includes the contemporary period, in which (I am happy to say) a far larger number of talented women scientists are working than ever before. Inevitably, I will have included women whose importance some readers will question and excluded others for whose inclusion a good case could be made.

My choices were based primarily on the following three factors:

1. Importance of contribution to science. For the most part, I have chosen women who made a direct contribution through research rather than indirect ones through, say, teaching or writing. This factor has, however, been modified by two others:

2. Fame. I have included some women who are very well known or who have had a major social impact, such as Elizabeth Blackwell and Rachel Carson, even though they made few or no research advances.

3. Diversity. I have tried to include a diverse sampling of nationalities, ethnic groups, periods, and fields.

I apologize to all the women who deserve to be in this encyclopedia and are not. In most cases their exclusion does not represent my value judgment of their work but simply means that I did not encounter material about them when I was doing my research. I may be able to rectify some of these oversights in a future edition.

INTRODUCTION

Put on trial for daring to practice medicine even though she was a woman, 14th-century French physician Jacoba Felicie called several patients to testify to her skill. But proof of competence was no defense, her prosecutors noted, "since it is certain that a man approved in the aforesaid art [of medicine] could cure the sick better than any woman."

From ancient times to the present, scientifically inclined women in most cultures have had to battle against the notion that any man, no matter how incompetent, must be more adept at things of the mind than any woman, no matter how brilliant. Indeed, women were often barred, sometimes by law, from even attempting to gain an education or have an independent career. In Athens in the late fourth century B.C., a physician named Agnodice was put on trial for her life for the same "crime" as Jacoba Felicie. In A.D. 415, Hypatia did not even receive the courtesy of a trial for the crime of being one of Alexandria's most learned and powerful women; a Christian zealot mob simply pulled her from her coach and hacked her to pieces.

Physical violence or legal proscriptions usually were not necessary to keep women out of science, however. Social sanctions were enough. Even most women accepted the idea of their own inferiority. For instance, the 19th-century British science popularizer Mary Somerville, who might have done original research under better circumstances, wrote that she had "perseverance and intelligence but no genius. . . . That spark from heaven is not granted to the [female] sex."

Social opposition to women having a scientific education or intellectual life often came wrapped in the best of "protective" intentions. Many 19th- and even some early 20th-century American and European parents tried to prevent their daughters from studying because they believed that too much intellectual effort would make women physically or mentally ill. "We shall have Mary in a strait-jacket one of these days," Mary Somerville's father feared when he found her reading mathematics books.

Even parents who did not go quite that far believed that advanced education simply made women unhappy or, what they assumed amounted to the same thing, unmarriageable. Lise Meitner and Rita Levi-Montalcini both heard that line, and Barbara McClintock's mother expressed concern that going to a university would make Barbara "a strange person, a person that didn't belong to society . . . even . . . a college professor." In more subtle form, this message, of course, still exists; many a bright young woman's mother has warned her, "Brainy girls don't get dates."

Even subcultures that made some claim to admire women, such as the "courtly" aristocratic culture of late medieval Europe or the home-centered American and European middle class of the late 19th and early 20th centuries, confined that admiration to women in their proper "sphere"—social interaction and, above all, home and children. Any degree of learning that drew women beyond this sphere made them "unnatural" and was to be discouraged. Many groups both within and outside Western society still hold this belief. Ten eminent African women scientists who took part in a forum sponsored by the American Association for the Advancement of Science in 1993 unanimously decried the still-prevalent tradition among their peoples that educating girls is a waste of time and money because marrying and having children is a woman's only proper work. Population geneticist Tomoko Ohta has said that the same view is common in Japan. "How we think is very difficult to change," she noted.

A modern outgrowth of this "sphere" belief is many employers' and graduate schools' assumption that a woman scientist's career is only temporary. When looking for work as a physicist and engineer in the late 1950s and early 1960s, Betsy Ancker-Johnson was often turned down, even though she was highly qualified and physicists were much in demand. Although she says that "not one interviewer ever leveled with" her about the reason, she believes that it was because "I was in a . . . subset that employers had decided was not dependable, i.e. a woman will marry and quit, and what is invested in her goes down the drain." A graduate school adviser in the 1940s did level with Eugenie Clark, using almost exactly the same words. This belief that women have a "natural sphere" has also affected their choices and opportunities within science, making it much harder for them to enter and advance in "men's" fields such as physics and engineering than in fields such as medical and biological research, which are seen as closer to women's expected role as healers and nurturers.

Second only to general beliefs in the intellectual inferiority of women and the "naturalness" of their confinement to homemaking and child care as a barrier to women wishing to enter science has been lack of access to higher education. Until the late 19th century and often beyond, this hurdle was all but insurmountable. Women were frequently forbidden to enroll at universities or, at best, could attend lectures only as "special students" (often having to sit apart from men or even behind a screen) without receiving credit or a degree. Even when no official bar to enrollment existed, women usually had been sent to girls' schools that provided no academic preparation for a university. Thus those who, like Lise Meitner and Rita Levi-Montalcini, wished to pass stiff university entrance examinations had to hire tutors to make up their educational deficiencies.

Poverty made the problem worse for many women. Ellen Richards had to undergo several years of what she called "Purgatory" before saving enough money to enter Vassar. Other women, such as Nettie Stevens, worked as teachers or librarians for decades before finally becoming able to embark on a research career. The combination of poverty and traditional social biases still makes higher education and scientific careers impossible for all but a handful of women from developing nations. One American woman who worked in South America commented, "In the . . . countries where we served, girls were lucky to get through high school. Scientific careers would have been far beyond their reach."

Gaining a scientific education has been hard enough for women, but finding a job—especially a paying job—often has bordered on impossible. Even after women began to be admitted to most American and European universities as students, they were not allowed on university faculties. At best, they were taken on, frequently without pay, as "assistants" to their husbands or other male faculty members. This changed only slowly during the first half of the 20th century.

When women were hired, they were often much slower to be promoted than men of comparable or even lesser experience and qualifications. "You should know how many incompetent men I had to compete with—in vain," Danish seismologist Inge Lehmann once remarked. Around 1910, American mathematician Anna Pell Wheeler similarly wrote to a friend that in "good" universities, "there is such an objection to women that they prefer a man even if he is inferior both in training and in research." Clearly the automatic assumption of women's inferiority in science had changed little since Jacoba Felicie's day! Antidiscrimination laws have now driven such feelings underground, but there is little doubt that they still exist in some places.

One factor that has slowed hiring and promotion of women has been their exclusion from the social apparatus of science. Nineteenth-century women scientists had to have their husbands or other sympathetic men present their papers to key science organizations such as Britain's Royal Society because these groups did not allow women at their meetings. Even after science organizations began permitting woman speakers, many barred women from membership. The Royal Society, for instance, had no female full members until 1945. Most scientific societies now have women members, and many have even had women presidents, but women are still often denied access to the shadowy "old boys' network" that governs many promotion decisions. This is probably one of the chief reasons for the "glass ceiling"—that invisible level past which women are not allowed to advance—of which so many women professionals in science as well as business complain.

Another reason why so many women scientists have remained in the shadows is that when they worked closely with male scientists, the men usually received all the credit for their joint efforts. This occurred almost without exception until the 20th century. In more recent days, the danger of losing credit has been greatest when the men were heads of laboratories or other supervisors, but it has also existed when men and women research partners were more or less equal in age and qualification. Several women scientists whose lifelong research partners died in mid-career, including Marie Curie, Lillian Gilbreth, and Rosalyn Yalow, discovered that they had to deal with the loss of a beloved spouse or friend and at the same time reinvent their own scientific reputations because everyone assumed that the men had been "the brains of the outfit."

Until recently, most people expected that women scientists would not marry, or at least not have children, and conversely, that women who started families would give up their careers. Yet from the beginning, some brave women defied such expectations and insisted on "having it all." For

instance, the 18th-century Italian Laura Bassi, Europe's first woman physics professor, is said to have raised an incredible 12 children.

For achieving the double goal of family and career, women scientists have been forced to pay a steep price never demanded of men. First, finding work becomes infinitely more difficult when, as frequently happens, a woman scientist marries a man in the same field. Married scientists still struggle with the "two-body problem" of finding two decent research posts in the same geographic area. The struggle was far worse at mid-century, however, when antinepotism rules forbade a husband and wife from working in the same academic department or, often, even the same institution. These rules, which became widespread in the wake of Depression-era job shortages, were based on the dubious assumptions that married women did not really need (or deserve) jobs and that women who obtained work must have done so because of their husbands' influence rather than their own merits. Such rules, as Margaret Burbidge noted from personal experience, were "always used against the wife." For example, they kept Maria Mayer, whose talents eventually earned her a Nobel Prize, from having a paying faculty position for most of her career. Many institutions have now rescinded or at least modified these rules, but Joanne Simpson found them still in place in the U.S. government in the early 1970s.

Furthermore, as many modern women scientists have complained, their biological clocks and their professional clocks are forced to run side by side. The years that are best for childbearing and child rearing are also the ones that demand 80-hour weeks in the lab and a steady stream of published papers. Like other working mothers, women scientists who have children must arrange for child care and deal with the guilt of not being with their families full time. Hardest of l has been the lot of those whom death or divorce turned into single mothers.

Given all these obstacles, the incredible thing is not that so many women's actual or potential scientific work has been lost but that some women have achieved so much. What has set these successful women scientists apart from their less fortunate sisters?

First, some were lucky enough to live in times and places that did not share the prevailing denigration of women. Pagan Alexandria allowed Hypatia to achieve the public renown that made Christian Alexandria so jealous. The Christian Church, in turn, at least at some times and places during the Middle Ages, encouraged nuns such as Hildegarde of Bingen to pursue earthly as well as heavenly knowledge, provided they did so within an acceptable framework. Italy provided support to women academics to a degree unheard of in the rest of Europe, sponsoring Trotula and the other famous women physicians of Salerno in the 11th century and women scholars such as Maria Agnesi and Laura Bassi in the 18th century.

Whether or not they had such societal acceptance, many successful women scientists came from families who supported, or at least did not strongly oppose, education for women. Often this attitude was part of the Jewish tradition's respect for education. The immigrant parents of Mildred Dresselhaus and Rosalyn Yalow may have lacked money and education themselves, but they encouraged their daughters as well as their sons to pursue learning. Several African women scientists have mentioned that their parents opposed tradition by seeking education for their daughters.

Perhaps the most important external factor in women scientists' success before the late 20th century was the support—financial, emotional, or both—of a man. Since men held the keys to power, women's chances were greatly improved if some man was willing to share that power with them. The supporter could be a father, as with Hypatia, Maria Agnesi, or Elizabeth Garrett Anderson, or some other relative, such as Caroline Herschel's brother. It could be a mentor; Franklin Mall, head of Johns Hopkins Medical School's anatomy department, served this role for Florence Sabin, for instance, and Yasuo Miyake did the same for Katsuko Saruhashi. Most commonly, of course, it was a spouse. Women scientists have had their share of unhappy marriages, but their annals are also filled with stories of devoted couples who saw each other as full professional as well as personal equals, ranging from the famous Curies to today's Philippa Marrack and John W. Kappler, of whom Marrack says, "Scientifically we don't exist as individuals." Of course, as noted earlier, there was always a risk—to the woman—from such close collaboration; even if their mentors or husbands respected them, the scientific world often assumed that all the credit for their joint efforts really belonged to the men.

Women's support has also been influential. In ancient Athens, Agnodice's patients—who apparently included the wives of some of the most powerful men in the city—stormed the courthouse where her trial was being held and threatened mass suicide if she was put to death. As a result, not only was Agnodice freed, but the law under which she had been arrested was repealed. Well-to-do advocates of women's rights in the late 19th and 20th centuries provided financial support for women's science education, such as Ellen Richards's laboratory for women chemistry students at Massachussetts Institute of Technology (MIT) in the 1870s. In recent years, established women scientists have increasingly taken on the mentoring function formerly provided by men. Rosalyn Yalow, for instance, mentored Mildred Dresselhaus, and Dresselhaus, in turn, has helped a number of younger women at MIT.

Both men and women have helped women become scientists by providing sources of education. Surely one of the reasons why the number of women scientists began to increase in the late 19th century was the founding of women's colleges, such as Vassar and Mount Holyoke, that were determined to give women a higher education comparable to the best offered to men. Some coeducational institutions, too, liberalized their policies toward women much earlier than others. The "ladies of Baltimore" who donated the money to found Johns Hopkins University Medical School at the turn of the century, for instance, insisted from the start that women be admitted on a par with men.

For women scientists who have had children, a vital component of success has been the availability of regular, usually live-in, child care help. The helper might be a mother or other relative (Irène Joliot-Curie, Marie Curie's daughter, was raised largely by her grandfather) or might be hired. Most scientist-mothers have mentioned relying on such help at some time.

The biggest key to women scientists' success, however, has lain within themselves. Whatever the rest of their personalities, virtually all successful women scientists have possessed two qualities. One is a deep love of science—that is, of learning about the world—for its own sake. Joanne Simpson has told young women scientists that they must "love [their] work, for the sheer doing of it, as well as or more than anything else in life." Chien-shiung Wu said that "in physics . . . you must have total commitment. It is not just a job. It is a way of life." This commitment, however, is far from a joyless devotion to labor. Over and over, the best women scientists have emphasized that to them, science is "fun."

The other quality is determination, sometimes in what seems almost a superhuman degree. Whether the obstacles in their path came from poverty, physical handicap, family, social censure, or hide-bound laws and institutions, these women simply refused to take no for an answer. Quietly or stridently, they said and did whatever it took to put themselves in a position to do the work they loved. It is to be hoped that young women entering science today will not need to possess such an iron will. Changes in laws and institutions have made obtaining education and jobs easier, and changes in social attitudes are finally—perhaps—lowering the more subtle barriers to advancement and to combining career and family.

In the future, as their numbers grow, women scientists may come to be valued solely as Julia Robinson hoped she would be. "Rather than being remembered as the first woman this or that," she wrote, "I would prefer to be remembered, as a mathematician should, simply for the theorems I have proved and the problems I have solved." All the women in these pages certainly deserve to be remembered for their work alone, and pride of place is given to that work in the sketches that follow. However, it is also no more than just to honor these women—and all the many others of equal talent not included here or, perhaps, lost entirely to history—for the tremendous devotion and courage they showed in achieving it.

A

 ## AGNESI, MARIA GAETANA
(1718–1799) *Italian Mathematician*

Maria Gaetana Agnesi summarized the mathematics of her day in a textbook that was still popular 50 years after she wrote it. Born on May 16, 1718, in Milan, Italy, she was a child prodigy, and her father, Pietro, a mathematics professor at the University of Bologna, loved to show off her abilities. By age 11 she spoke French, Latin, Greek, German, Spanish, and Hebrew.

Agnesi's chief love was mathematics. She could solve difficult geometry problems at age 14. Beginning when she was 20, she spent 10 years writing a two-volume textbook that summarized European mathematical discoveries. The first volume covered algebra and geometry, while the second was devoted to calculus, a type of mathematics invented in the previous century by Isaac Newton and Gottfried von Leibniz. According to one biographer, Agnesi worked so hard on the book that she sometimes walked to her desk in her sleep and solved problems that had troubled her.

Agnesi's book, *Le Instituzioni Analitiche (Analytical Institutions)*, was published in 1748 to great praise. Empress Maria Theresa of Austria, to whom Agnesi dedicated the book, sent her a diamond ring

and a crystal box. M. Motigny of the French Academy of Sciences wrote to her, "I admire particularly the art with which you bring under uniform methods the divers [various] conclusions scattered among the works of geometers and reached by methods entirely different." Pope Benedict XIV offered Agnesi her father's old post at the University of Bologna in 1750, but she declined because she did not want to leave Milan. Science historian Margaret Alic calls Agnesi's book "the first systematic work of its kind" and states that "50 years later it was still the most complete mathematical text in existence."

Agnesi had never enjoyed public life, and after her father's death in 1752 she retired from the academic world. She headed a charitable institution and turned part of her home into a hospital. She died on January 9, 1799, as renowned for her good works as she had been for her learning.

In later centuries, Agnesi's name was remembered mainly in the form of a strange mistranslation. Because of a confusion between the Italian words for "curve" and "witch," a curve described in her book, called a versed sine curve, acquired the English name of "witch of Agnesi." Ironically, this saintly woman was sometimes referred to by the same name.

Further Reading

Alic, Margaret. *Hypatia's Heritage: A History of Women in Science from Antiquity Through the Nineteenth Century.* Boston: Beacon Press, 1986, 136–139.

Lauck, Mary R. Monaco. "Maria Gaetana Agnesi." In *Celebrating Women in Mathematics and Science,* edited by Miriam P. Cooney, 17–21. Reston, Va.: National Council of Teachers of Mathematics, 1996.

Osen, Lynn M. *Women in Mathematics.* Cambridge, Mass.: MIT Press, 33–48.

✳ AGNODICE
(late fourth century B.C.) *Greek Physician*

Women physicians were not uncommon in the ancient world, but in the Greek city-state of Athens around the fourth century B.C., women were forbidden on pain of death to practice medicine because they were thought to perform abortions. Agnodice defied the law and, with the help of her grateful patients, succeeded in having it changed.

Agnodice's story was recounted by the Roman historian Hyginus and translated into English in 1687. A wealthy young woman of Athens, she dressed herself in men's clothing and went to Alexandria, Egypt, around 300 B.C. to study medicine. Then, still disguised, she returned to Athens and began to treat women patients.

Many women died during childbirth or of "private diseases" because they were too embarrassed to visit male physicians. Speaking to one potential patient, Agnodice confessed her secret. The other woman then allowed Agnodice to treat her and was "cured . . . perfectly." Word spread, and "she became the successful and beloved physician of the whole sex."

Unfortunately, in time the male doctors also discovered the truth, and Agnodice was put on trial. Her patients, including the most influential women in Athens, stormed the courtroom. They told the judges that they would "no longer account them for husbands and friends, but for cruel enemies" if they killed Agnodice. They even threatened to die with her.

Bowing to the women's pressure, the men not only released Agnodice but changed the law. After that, any freeborn Athenian woman could become a physician, as long as she treated only women patients.

Further Reading

Alic, Margaret. *Hypatia's Heritage: A History of Women in Science from Antiquity Through the Nineteenth Century.* Boston: Beacon Press, 1986, 29–30.

Mozans, H. J. *Woman in Science.* Cambridge, Mass.: MIT Press, 1974, 268–269.

✳ AJAKAIYE, DEBORAH ENILO
(c. 1940–) *Nigerian Geologist*

Deborah Ajakaiye studies the geophysics of Nigeria, where she was born around 1940. Unlike many traditional African families, Ajakaiye's parents believed in education for girls as well as for boys and encouraged her to have a career. A primary school teacher awakened her interest in science. She received her bachelor's degree from University College in Ibadan, Nigeria, in 1962. She then went on to graduate training at the University of Birmingham in Britain, from which she received her master's degree, and Adhadu Bello University in Nigeria, from which she received her Ph.D. in 1970. "I chose . . . geophysics because I felt that this field could make possible significant contributions to the development of my country," she wrote in a 1993 paper for the American Association for the Advancement of Science.

Ajakaiye points out that geophysics can help a country identify valuable natural resources. For instance, she says, Africa is rich in several minerals needed by high-technology industries, and some parts of the continent, including Nigeria, possess large deposits of uranium, oil, natural gas, and coal. Selling these resources can give a country the money it needs to feed, house, and educate its people. Geophysics can also identify sources of precious groundwater and help to predict natural disasters.

Ajakaiye has looked for all these resources in Nigeria. In some studies she used a new technique called geovisualization, in which computers produce three-dimensional images of materials below the earth's surface. Ajakaiye and her students, including several women, also carried out a survey for a geophysical map of northern Nigeria. "By the end of the survey quite a few Nigerian men had changed their attitudes toward their female counterparts," she notes.

In addition to her research, Ajakaiye has taught at Adhadu Bello University and the University of Jos, both in Nigeria. She is presently professor of physics at the University of Jos and has been the dean of the university's natural science faculty. She was the first woman professor of physics in West Africa, the first woman dean of science in Nigeria, and the first female fellow of the Nigerian Academy of Science.

Further Reading

American Association for the Advancement of Science. *Science in Africa: Women Leading from Strength.* Washington, D.C.: American Association for the Advancement of Science, 1993, 101–111, 165.

 ALEXANDER, HATTIE ELIZABETH
(1901–1968) *American Microbiologist*

Hattie Alexander discovered a way to prevent most deaths caused by one form of meningitis, a devastating brain disease. Born on April 5, 1901, she grew up in Baltimore, Maryland. She was the second child of William Bain Alexander, a merchant, and his wife, Elsie.

Alexander preferred athletic activities to studying while at Goucher College in Towson, Maryland, and her grades were only Cs. After her graduation in 1923, however, she began working as a bacteriologist for state and national public health services, and she saved her money so that she could go to medical school. As a medical student at Johns Hopkins University she earned very high grades. She completed her M.D. in 1930.

Alexander spent her career at Babies Hospital, part of the Columbia-Presbyterian Medical Center in New York City. Eventually she headed its microbiology laboratory. She also taught in the Columbia University medical school, becoming a full professor in 1958. Her specialty was meningitis, a disease of the membranes around the brain that was almost always fatal, especially in children. Several types of microorganisms could cause meningitis, but Alexander concentrated on just one, a rod-shaped bacterium called *Hemophilus influenzae.*

When Alexander began her research, there was no effective treatment for *Hemophilus influenzae* meningitis. In the late 1930s, however, she heard of a technique in which rabbits were injected with bacteria. Reacting to the invaders, the rabbits' immune systems produced substances, collectively called antiserum, that could be used as a treatment for the disease caused by that kind of bacterium.

Working with Michael Heidelberger, Alexander injected rabbits with *Hemophilus influenzae* from children with meningitis. In 1939 she reported that the resulting antiserum had cured several infants. It dropped the disease's death rate by 80 percent by the end of its second year of use.

In the early 1940s, Alexander began treating meningitis with antibiotics, which had just come into use, as well as her antiserum. She noticed that bacteria sometimes developed resistance to the drugs and was one of the first to conclude that this resistance was due to mutations in the microorganisms' genes. In 1944, American researcher Oswald Avery claimed that the inherited information in genes was carried in a complex chemical called deoxyribonucleic acid (DNA) and reported that changing a bacterium's DNA changed the characteristics of future bacterial generations. Many researchers doubted these conclusions, but Alexander supported them by producing results like Avery's with *Hemophilus influenzae.*

Alexander won several prizes for her work, including the E. Mead Johnson Award for Research in Pediatrics (1942). She was the first woman president of the American Pediatric Society (1964) and one of the first to head any national medical society.

She retired in 1966 but continued to work almost until her death from cancer on June 24, 1968.

Further Reading

Dubos, Rene. "Alexander, Hattie Elizabeth." In *Notable American Women: The Modern Period,* edited by Barbara Sicherman and Carol Hurd Green, 10–11. Cambridge, Mass.: The Belknap Press of Harvard University Press, 1980.

Vare, Ethlie Ann, and Greg Ptacek. *Mothers of Invention.* New York: William Morrow, 1988, 121–122.

✳ ANCKER-JOHNSON, BETSY
(1927–) *American Physicist and Engineer*

Betsy Ancker-Johnson made important contributions to understanding the behavior of plasmas, called the "fourth state of matter," in solids as well as holding high-level posts in government and the automobile industry. She was born on April 29, 1927, to Clinton J. and Fern Ancker, in St. Louis, Missouri. After living in many places as a child, she spent what she has called "idyllic" years studying physics at Wellesley College, graduating in 1949 with high honors.

The happy times ended when Ancker decided to follow her "love of adventure" and interest in other cultures and do her graduate work at Tübingen University in Germany. Her German professors "told me that women can't think analytically and I must, therefore, be husband-hunting" rather than being serious about a career, Ancker-Johnson recalled in a 1971 talk. Nonetheless, she obtained her Ph.D. with high honors in 1953.

On returning to the United States, Ancker encountered equal disbelief when she tried to find a job. She discovered that "a woman in physics must be at least twice as determined as a man with the same competence, in order to achieve as much as he does." Physicists were much in demand, but she was offered only second-rate jobs. "Not one interviewer ever leveled with me" about the reason, but she believes it was because "I was in a . . . subset that employers had decided was not dependable; i.e., a

woman will marry and quit, and what is invested in her goes down the drain."

Ancker finally took a minor academic post at the University of California in Berkeley. There, through the Inter-Varsity Christian Fellowship, for which she did volunteer work, she met a mathematician named Harold Johnson. "My husband is man enough not to be threatened by his wife's awareness of electrons," she said later. They married in 1958, after which she used the name Ancker-Johnson.

Ancker-Johnson did research in solid state physics for Sylvania from 1956 to 1958 and for RCA from 1958 to 1961. After her marriage she encountered a new prejudice: employers' fear that she would soon quit to raise a family. She informed them that she did plan to have children but would hire live-in help to care for them while she continued to work. During her first pregnancy, she has said, male executives seemed to view her condition as something like "an advanced case of leprosy." For three months before her first daughter's birth she was not even allowed to enter the laboratory building without the director's permission. By the time she had her second child, Ancker-Johnson was working for Boeing, a "more enlightened" company. This time company officials merely stopped her salary eight weeks before the baby's birth and started it again six weeks afterward, even though she continued working during all but two weeks of that period.

Ancker-Johnson made her chief contributions to plasma and solid state physics while working for Boeing in Seattle, which she did from 1961 to 1973. (She was also an affiliate professor of electrical engineering at the University of Washington during this time.) In the early 1970s she was supervisor of the company's solid state and plasma electronics laboratory and manager of their advanced energy systems. She identified several types of instabilities that can occur in plasmas in solids, including oscillation, pinching, and microwave emission. She produced the microwaves by applying an external electric field, but she showed that the field did not have to be present when they appeared, a new discovery. Building on her work, other scientists have suggested that solid state plasmas may be useful sources of microwave radiation. Other applications of her work potentially affect computer technology and extraction of aluminum and other elements from low-grade ore.

Betsy Ancker-Johnson holds several patents in solid state physics and semiconductor electronics. She is a member of the National Academy of Engineering and fellow of several professional societies, including the Institute of Electrical and Electronic Engineers and the American Physical Society. She won excellence awards from Boeing and the Carborundum Company and the Chairman's Award from the American Association of Engineering Societies. She has been a member of the Board of Directors of the Society of Automotive Engineers, the Motor Vehicle Manufacturers Association, Varian Associates, and General Mills.

From 1973 to 1977, Ancker-Johnson served as the assistant secretary of commerce in charge of science and technology. In this job she controlled six organizations with a $230 million total annual budget. In contrast to the prejudice she faced earlier—but equally irritating to her—she feels she got this job primarily because she was a woman; she was the first woman to be appointed by a president to the Department of Commerce.

After her time in government ended, Ancker-Johnson worked for 14 months as director for physical research at Argonne National Laboratory, near Chicago. Then, in 1979, General Motors made her a vice president in charge of environmental activities. She was the first woman in the auto industry to achieve such a high rank. "Environmental activities" included such things as pollution controls, automobile safety, and fuel economy. Ancker-Johnson retired from this job in 1992, but she is still active on many committees and is director of the World Environment Center.

Further Reading

Ancker-Johnson, Betsy. "Physicist: Betsy Ancker-Johnson." In *Women and Success: The Anatomy of Achievement*, edited by Ruth B. Kundsin, 44–49. New York: William Morrow, 1973.

"Ancker-Johnson, Betsy," CWP at physics.UCLA.edu. Available online. URL: http://www.physics.ucla.edu/~cwp.html. Downloaded on May 22, 1998.

Gleasner, Diana C. *Breakthrough: Women in Science*. New York: Walker, 1983, 75–96.

Vare, Ethlie Ann, and Greg Ptacek. *Mothers of Invention*. New York: Morrow, 1988, 187–190.

✳ ANDAM, ABA A. BENTIL
(c. 1960–) *Ghanaian Physicist*

Aba A. Bentil Andam's research is helping to shield the people of Ghana from possible dangerous radiation. She was born around 1960 and did her undergraduate training at the University of Cape Coast in Ghana, where she was the only woman in the physics department. She earned her master's degree from the University of Birmingham and her Ph.D. from the University of Durham, both in Britain.

In 1986 and 1987, Andam studied subatomic particles called charmed mesons at the Deutsches Elektronen-Synchrotron in Hamburg, Germany. Since then she has devoted most of her research to radon, a gas produced when the element radium decays. Radon is given off naturally by soil or minerals that contain radium or uranium. It blows away harmlessly in open air, but people in closed, air-conditioned buildings on sites where large amounts of radon are given off can receive significant exposure to the gas. Because radon is radioactive, exposure to it can increase the chance of developing cancer.

Andam and her coworkers have surveyed radon levels in different parts of Ghana. They sampled the insides of homes and office buildings, the soil on which buildings stood, clays used for making bricks, gold mines deep in the earth, and earthquake faults through which radon might rise to the surface. They used the "closed can technique," in which plastic detector sheets inside small sealed cans pick up tracks created by subatomic particles. The particles come from the radon in air trapped inside the cans.

Andam's survey is a first step toward determining how much radiation from radon Ghana's citizens are exposed to and toward reducing that exposure if necessary. Andam has also pursued the basic goal of protecting people from radiation in other ways, for example, by working out safety standards for equipment used in medical X-ray tests.

Today Andam teaches at the University of Science and Technology in Kumasi, Ghana. She also does research in applied nuclear physics at the Nuclear Research Laboratory in that city. She shares her experience and love of science with girls in secondary school through a program called Science Clinics, first organized in 1987, in which girl students meet with women scientists who act as role models. Afterward, Andam says, they "say to themselves that what one woman has done, another woman can do."

Further Reading

American Association for the Advancement of Science. *Science in Africa: Women Leading from Strength.* Washington, D.C.: American Association for the Advancement of Science, 1993, 81–88, 166.

 ## ANDERSON, ELDA EMMA
(1899–1961) *American Physicist and Medical Researcher*

Elda Emma Anderson worked on the atomic bomb, then helped to develop a new scientific field that tries to minimize harm from radiation. She was born on October 5, 1899, in Green Lake, Wisconsin, the middle one of Edwin A. and Lena Anderson's three children. Her older sister, who became a chemistry teacher, interested her in science. She received her bachelor's degree from Ripon College in 1922, then went to the University of Wisconsin, where she earned a master's degree in physics in 1924. In 1941 she returned to the university to obtain her Ph.D.

Anderson was dean of physics and mathematics at Estherville Junior College in Iowa from 1924 to 1927, where she also taught chemistry. Then, starting in

1929, she was a professor in the new physics department of Milwaukee-Downer College. She became head of the department in 1934.

In late 1941, Anderson took a vacation from teaching to work in the Office of Scientific Research and Development at Princeton University. There she became involved with the Manhattan Project, the code name for the secret project to develop an atomic bomb. She moved to the project's headquarters at Los Alamos, New Mexico, in 1943. She worked—sometimes for 18 hours a day—measuring subatomic particles produced in cyclotrons, or atom smashers. This work proved vital to both the development of the bomb and the design of nuclear power reactors.

Anderson returned to teaching in 1947, but her old life seemed dull after the Manhattan Project days. Her research in atomic physics had also stirred her concern about the harm that radiation could do to living things. A new field of science called health physics had been established toward the end of the war to study and try to prevent such effects. Anderson left Milwaukee-Downer College in 1949 and devoted the rest of her life to developing health physics and making other scientists recognize its importance.

Anderson became the first chief of education and training for the Health Physics Division at Tennessee's Oak Ridge National Laboratory. She also set up the American Board of Health Physics, a professional certifying agency. Perhaps as a result of her work with radiation, Anderson developed leukemia, a blood cell cancer, in 1956. She died on April 17, 1961.

Further Reading

Bailey, Brooke. *The Remarkable Lives of 100 Women Healers and Scientists.* Holbrook, Mass.: Bob Adams, 1994, 8–9.

Kathren, Ronald L. "Anderson, Elda Emma." *In Notable American Women: The Modern Period*, edited by Barbara Sicherman and Carol Hurd Green, 20–21. Cambridge, Mass.: The Belknap Press of Harvard University Press, 1980.

✳ ANDERSON, ELIZABETH GARRETT
(1836–1917) *British Physician*

Inspired by ELIZABETH BLACKWELL, Elizabeth Garrett Anderson opened the medical profession to women in Britain, just as Blackwell had done in the United States. Garrett was born in Whitechapel, a poor section of London, in 1836. Her father, Newson Garrett, soon became successful in business, however, and moved his family to a large house in the village of Aldeburgh. Elizabeth and her eight brothers and sisters thus grew up in comfort.

In 1859, when Elizabeth Garrett was 23 years old, a friend told her that Elizabeth Blackwell was going to speak in London. She obtained a personal introduction to Blackwell, who assumed that Garrett must be planning to be a physician like herself. That idea had never crossed Garrett's mind until that meeting, but suddenly it began to seem a real possibility. Still, she wrote later, "I remember feeling as if I had been thrust into work that was too big for me."

When Garrett told her parents about her new plans, Louisa Garrett predicted that the "disgrace" of her daughter's action would kill her, and Newson Garrett pronounced the idea of a woman doctor "disgusting." Nonetheless, he agreed to go with her to talk to London physicians.

What Miss Garrett wanted, the doctors said, was impossible. The Medical Act of 1858 said that no physician could be placed on the Medical Register, Britain's list of approved physicians, without a license from a qualified examining board—and no board would allow a woman to take its examinations. Newson Garrett did not take kindly to being told no, on his daughter's behalf any more than his own. The physicians' opposition turned him into Elizabeth's strongest supporter.

Obtaining a physician's license by getting an M.D. degree seemed out of the question, because no British medical school admitted women. However, the charter of the Society of Apothecaries—medical practitioners who made and distributed drugs—said that the society would grant a license to "all persons" who completed five years of training with a qualified doctor or doctors, took certain required classes, and passed its examination. An apothecary's license was not as prestigious as an M.D., but it would get Garrett onto the Medical Register.

Facing the Garrett father-daughter team in August 1861, the society directors had to admit that Elizabeth Garrett was a person and therefore could potentially qualify for a license. They told her to return when she had completed their requirements—hoping, no doubt, never to see her again.

Bit by bit, Garrett accumulated the training she needed, and in 1865 she returned to the apothecaries with proof in hand. The society tried to back out of its earlier promise, but after Newson Garrett threatened a lawsuit, it let Elizabeth take the examinations. She found them "too easy to feel elated about" and earned a higher score than anyone else. By 1866 she had her apothecary's license and her spot on the Medical Register.

Once Garrett set up her medical practice, friends and acquaintances flocked to her. One, women's rights advocate Josephine Butler, commented, "I gained more from her than [from] any other doctor; for she . . . entered much more into my mental state and way of life than they could." In addition, Garrett opened a small clinic, St. Mary's Dispensary for Women and Children, in a poor part of London. In 1872 the clinic would become the New Hospital for Women. It was renamed the Elizabeth Garrett Anderson Hospital at the time of its founder's death in 1917.

Meanwhile, Garrett wanted to spend more time in a hospital to add to the practical side of her medical training. In 1869 she applied for a post at London's Shadwell Hospital for Children. One director on the hospital board who was sure he did not want her to work there was James George Skelton Anderson, the Scottish head of a large shipping company. Once he met the young woman doctor, however, he changed his mind. Garrett and Anderson were married in 1871 and later had three children. Their daughter, Louisa, also became a physician and during World War I headed the first group of British women doctors to serve in active duty in wartime.

Elizabeth Anderson was still determined to obtain an M.D. degree. In 1868 the University of Paris had opened its doors to women, and Anderson got permission to take the school's examinations for physicians even though she had not actually studied there. She passed the test and obtained her M.D. at last on June 15, 1870. The British medical journal *Lancet* reported, "All the [French] judges are complimenting Miss Garrett [and have] . . . expressed liberal opinions on the subject of lady doctors."

Working as a physician was only part of Elizabeth Garrett Anderson's busy life. She taught at and was dean and, later, president of the London School of Medicine for Women, the teaching arm of her New Hospital for Women, from 1886 to 1902. She was elected to the London school board and, at the age of 71, became mayor of Aldeburgh, to which she and her husband had retired in 1902. She was the first woman mayor elected in Britain.

Elizabeth Garrett Anderson died on December 17, 1917, at the age of 81. A fellow physician said of her, "She did more for the cause of women in medicine in England than any other person."

Further Reading

Anderson, Louisa Garrett. *Elizabeth Garrett Anderson.* London: Faber and Faber, 1919.

Hume, Ruth Fox. *Great Women of Medicine.* New York: Random House, 1964, 84–123.

Manton, Jo. *Elizabeth Garrett Anderson.* London: Adam and Charles Black, 1958.

Ogilvie, Marilyn Bailey. *Women in Science: Antiquity Through the Nineteenth Century.* Cambridge, Mass.: MIT Press, 1986, 28–31.

✳ ANNING, MARY
(1799–1847) *British Paleontologist*

Mary Anning discovered fossils that helped give British scientists their first understanding of prehistoric life. Born in 1799, she grew up in Lyme Regis, on a part of Britain's southwest coast that had been a sea bottom 200 million years before. People in Lyme Regis often found bones, shells, or other remains of the creatures that had lived in that long-ago ocean, now turned to rock and sticking out of the cliffs or washed down onto the beach.

Lyme Regis became a popular resort in the late 18th century, and some townsfolk with an eye for business began collecting fossils to display or sell to visitors. One was Richard Anning, who earned most of his living from cabinetmaking. He taught his wife, Molly, and children, Joseph and Mary, how to look for fossils during walks beside the cliffs. When he died in 1810, leaving his family with little money, they tried to support themselves through their fossil business.

In 1811, Joseph made the family's first important find, a huge skull with a long snout and rows of sharp teeth embedded in a rock on the beach. He thought the skull belonged to a crocodile, but in fact it came from an ancient, dolphinlike sea reptile called an ichthyosaur, or "fish-lizard." A year later, 12-year-old Mary found the rest of the animal's 30-foot-long skeleton projecting from a cliff. The two fossils added up to one of the first ichthyosaurs ever discovered.

Mary Anning, whom one visitor described as "a strong, energetic spinster . . . tanned and masculine in expression," continued to find and sell prize fossils all her life. In addition to several more ichthyosaurs, she found the first complete skeletons of plesiosaurs, nine-foot-long sea reptiles with small heads, long necks, and paddlelike fins. She found her first plesiosaur in 1821. In 1828 she found the first British pterosaur, a flying reptile.

Anning corresponded with scientists and collectors all over England. Her fossils provided important study material for researchers in the new field of paleontology, and if she had belonged to a time and class in which women were educated, she herself might have become a paleontologist. As it was, she was merely a fairly successful businessperson and a local curiosity. When she died in 1847, a guidebook commented that her "death was in a pecuniary [financial] sense a great loss to the place, as her presence attracted a large number of distinguished visitors." More flattering, the scientists whom she had served paid to have a stained-glass window added to a town church in her honor.

Further Reading

Cole, Sheila. *The Dragon in the Cliff.* New York: Lothrop, Lee, and Shepard, 1991.

Taylor, Michael, and Hugh S. Torrens. "Fossils by the Sea." *Natural History,* October 1995, 67–71.

✳ APGAR, VIRGINIA
(1909–1974) *American Physician*

"Every baby born in a modern hospital anywhere in the world is looked at first through the eyes of Virginia Apgar," a fellow physician once said. He meant that the quick tests of a newborn infant's health that Apgar developed are now used almost everywhere.

Virginia Apgar was born to Charles and Helen Apgar in Westfield, New Jersey, on June 7, 1909. She shared a love of music with her family, playing the violin during family concerts and, as an adult, even making her own instruments. Her family also taught her to appreciate science; her businessman father's hobbies included astronomy and wireless telegraphy.

During her undergraduate years at Mount Holyoke College, Apgar helped to pay for her schooling by waiting on tables and working in the school library and laboratories. She also reported for the college newspaper, won prizes in tennis and other sports, acted, and played in the orchestra.

After graduating from Mount Holyoke in 1929, Apgar went to medical school at Columbia University, earning her M.D. in 1933. She wanted to be a surgeon, but her professors convinced her that she could never earn a living in this male-dominated field. "Even women won't go to a woman surgeon," she remarked later. When asked why, she sighed, "Only the Lord can answer that one."

Apgar turned her attention to the new specialty of anesthesiology instead. She was only the 50th physician to be certified as a specialist in giving painkilling and sleep-inducing drugs during surgery. Being a woman was no problem in this field, since anesthesia had previously been given by nurses, most of whom were women. Apgar began teaching at Columbia's medical school in 1936, and she became the school's first full professor of anes-

thesiology and first woman full professor in 1949. Beginning in 1938, she was also clinical director of Presbyterian Hospital's anesthesiology department. She was the hospital's first woman department head. She helped to establish anesthesiology as a medical specialty.

Within anesthesiology, Apgar focused on anesthesia given during birth. In the process of assisting at some 17,000 births, she came to the conclusion that, as she wrote in a 1972 book called *Is My Baby All Right?*, "Birth is the most hazardous time of life . . . It's urgently important to evaluate quickly the status of a just-born baby and to identify immediately those who need emergency care." Yet, she noticed, a newborn baby was often simply wrapped up and hustled off to the hospital nursery. Serious problems sometimes went undetected for hours or days, and by the time they were found, it was too late to treat them.

"I kept wondering who was really responsible for the newborn," Apgar later told a reporter, and apparently she decided that she was. "I began putting down all the signs about the newborn babies that could be observed without special equipment and that helped spot the ones that needed emergency help." The result was the Apgar Score System, five tests that a doctor or nurse could perform in a few seconds during the first minute or so after a birth. The tests, which Apgar introduced in 1952, rate a baby's color, muscle tone, breathing, heart rate, and reflexes on a scale of 0 to 2. The combined results are the Apgar Score. A score of 10 means a very healthy baby, while a low score warns of problems needing immediate treatment.

After 33 years at Columbia, Virginia Apgar surprised her colleagues by going back to school. In 1959, at the age of 49, she earned a master's degree in public health from Johns Hopkins University. At this same time the charity organization called the National Foundation-March of Dimes, founded to help children with polio, was changing its focus to birth defects, which affect 500,000 children born in the United States each year. The charity asked Apgar to direct its department of birth defects. "They said they were looking for someone with enthusiasm, who likes to travel and talk," Apgar recalled. "I love to see new places, and I certainly can chatter." She knew little about birth defects, but she learned.

Apgar's work for the foundation included writing, distributing research grants, fund-raising, and public speaking around the world. She traveled some 100,000 miles a year for the group. It was said to be largely due to her efforts that the foundation's annual income rose from $19 million when she joined them to $46 million at the time of her death. She became director of the foundation's basic research department in 1967. In 1965, Apgar also became the first person to lecture on birth defects as a medical subspecialty.

Apgar received many honors for her work, including the ELIZABETH BLACKWELL Citation from the New York Infirmary in 1960 and the American Society of Anesthesiologists' Distinguished Service Award in 1961. The *Ladies' Home Journal* named her their Woman of the Year in science in 1973. The Alumni Association of the Columbia College of Physicians and Surgeons awarded her its Gold Medal for Distinguished Achievement in Medicine in 1973; she was the first woman to win this prize. Apgar died of liver disease on August 7, 1974, at the age of 65.

Further Reading

"Apgar, Virginia." *Current Biography Yearbook 1968.* New York: H. W. Wilson, 1968, 25–27.

Bailey, Brooke. *The Remarkable Lives of 100 Women Healers and Scientists.* Holbrook, Mass.: Bob Adams, 1994, 10–11.

Vare, Ethlie Ann, and Greg Ptacek. *Mothers of Invention.* New York: William Morrow, 1988, 133–134.

Waldinger, Robert J. "Apgar, Virginia." In *Notable American Women: The Modern Period,* edited by Barbara Sicherman and Carol Hurd Green, 27–28. Cambridge, Mass.: The Belknap Press of Harvard University Press, 1980.

✳ AYRTON, HERTHA (Phoebe Sarah Marks)
(1854–1923) *British Physicist and Engineer*

One of the first woman electrical engineers, Hertha Ayrton improved the working of the electric arc, used in lighting of her time, and invented a fan to clear poisonous gases from mines and soldiers' bunkers. She was the first woman to gain an award from Britain's prestigious Royal Society.

At her birth, Hertha Ayrton was named Phoebe Sarah Marks. She was born in 1854 in Portsea, England, into the large family of Levi Marks, a Jewish refugee from Poland. Marks, a jeweler and clockmaker, died in 1861, leaving his wife, Alice, in poverty with eight children to support. While Alice worked as a seamstress, Sarah, the oldest girl, took care of her brothers and sisters. She did not go to school until she was nine.

Sarah's aunt ran a school in London, and in time Sarah was allowed to study there. While at school she met Barbara Bodichon, a wealthy women's rights advocate and philanthropist who became her friend and supporter. Bodichon helped Sarah enter Girton, a women's college connected with Cambridge University, in 1876. Sarah changed her name to Hertha while at college.

After graduating from Girton in 1880, Marks turned a cousin's idea into her first invention, a tool that divided a line into equal parts. She obtained a patent on it in 1884, and it proved useful to engineers, architects, and artists. Encouraged by this success, Marks began studying at Finbury Technical College, where one of her teachers was physicist W. E. Ayrton. Ayrton admired Marks's intelligence and energy, and the two married in 1885. They later had a daughter, Barbara. Hertha helped her husband in his work, but he encouraged her to do her own research as well, letting her use his laboratory and calling her his "beautiful genius."

Some of Hertha Ayrton's most important work began in 1893 as a continuation of a project her husband was doing on electric arcs, which were used in streetlights, searchlights, and, later, movie projectors. She became determined to "solve the whole mystery of the arc from the beginning to the end." The arc, a glowing stream of electrons that flowed between two carbon electrodes separated by a pit or crater, often degenerated into rainbow flickers accompanied by a hissing noise; early movies were nicknamed "flickers" or "flicks" because of this failing. Hertha showed that these problems occurred because oxygen from the air got into the crater and combined with the carbon in the electrodes. Drawing on her research, engineers worked out a way to protect the arc from the air and thus increase its power and reliability.

These and other experiments made Hertha Ayrton a national authority on the electric arc. In 1895 the magazine *Electrician* asked her to write a series of articles on the subject, which she expanded into a book in 1902. The Institute of Electrical Engineers was so impressed with her paper explaining the hissing of the electric arc, which she read to them in March 1899, that the group made her its first woman member two months later. A reviewer called the paper "a model of the scientific method of research." Ayrton's paper on the electric arc was also presented to Britain's premier organization of scientists, the Royal Society, in 1901, but this time a man had to read it because the society did not permit women at its meetings.

W. E. Ayrton's health began to fail in 1901, and he and Hertha moved to the coast in an attempt to improve it. Unable to continue her electrical experiments because she now lacked a laboratory, Hertha became curious about the sandy beaches covered with what she later described as "innumerable ridges and furrows, as if combed by a giant comb." To learn how waves shaped the sand, she built glass tanks in her attic, put a layer of sand in the bottom, and filled them with water. She put the tanks on rollers to imitate wave motion. She found that when waves moved constantly back and forth over the same spot, they created regular ripples that eventually pushed the sand into two mounds between the crests of the waves. Ayrton believed that this kind of wave action formed both sand dunes on the shore and underwater sandbanks that often wrecked ships. She hoped other engineers could use her research to keep sandbanks from forming.

Ayrton presented a paper about her sand research to the Royal Society in 1904. This time she was allowed to read it herself, becoming the first woman to read a paper before the group. The society awarded her its Hughes Medal in 1906 for her work on electric arcs and sand. She was the first woman to win an award from the Royal Society. Commenting on the award, the *London Times* wrote, "It seems that the time has now come when woman should be permitted to take her place in . . . all our learned bodies."

Several of Hertha Ayrton's inventions helped her country during wartime. She made improvements in searchlights that made night spotting of aircraft easier. She also used what she had learned in her beach experiments to design a fan that drove poison gas out of bunkers and trenches and brought in fresh air. One soldier whom it helped during World War I wrote to her: "There are thousands and thousands of inarticulate soldier persons who are extremely grateful to you." The Ayrton fan was later modified to drive dangerous gases out of factories and mines.

Hertha Ayrton once said, "Personally I do not agree with sex being brought into science at all. . . . Either a woman is a good scientist, or she is not." She expressed her belief in women's equality in another way by joining the Women's Social and Political Union, one of the most militant organizations seeking votes for women. Ayrton's gender denied her some of the scientific recognition she deserved, but she did live to see British women gain the right to vote in 1918. She died five years later.

Further Reading

Ogilvie, Marilyn Bailey. "Marital Collaboration: An Approach to Science." In *Uneasy Careers and Intimate Lives: Women in Science 1789–1979*, edited by Pnina G. Abir-Am and Dorinda Outram, 104–125. New Brunswick, N.J.: Rutgers University Press, 1987.

———. *Women in Science: Antiquity Through the Nineteenth Century*. Cambridge, Mass.: MIT Press, 1986, 32–34.

Sharp, Evelyn. *Hertha Ayrton: A Memoir*. London: E. Arnold, 1926.

B

✳ BAILEY, FLORENCE AUGUSTA MERRIAM
(1863–1948)   *American Zoologist*

Many people in the late 19th and early 20th centuries learned about birds from the writings of Florence Merriam Bailey. Born on August 8, 1863, in Locust Grove, New York, Florence grew up on Homewood, the Merriam family's country estate. Her father, Clinton, a New York businessperson, took her on camping trips to collect wildlife specimens. She learned about stars from her mother, Caroline, and about birds and mammals from her older brother, Hart. Of all these she liked birds the best.

Merriam entered Smith College in 1882 but earned only a certificate instead of a degree. (Smith finally awarded her a B.A. in 1921.) She then returned to Homewood, where she observed and wrote about birds by "sit[ting] down, pull[ing] the timothy [a kind of plant] stems over my dress, [and] make[ing] myself look as much as possible like a meadow." She made her notes into articles for *Audubon Magazine,* and these in turn grew into her first book, *Birds Through an Opera Glass,* published as a book for young people in 1889.

Merriam made her first trip to the Southwest in 1893. She went for health reasons, but the bird-watching she did there provided material for two

more books. Meanwhile, her brother, C. Hart Merriam, became the first chief of the U.S. Biological Survey, and when Florence returned to the East in late 1895, she moved to Washington, D.C., to live with him. There she continued to write. Her book *Birds of Village and Field,* published in 1898, became one of the first popular American guides for amateur birders. In it she said that bird-watchers needed only four things: "a scrupulous conscience, unlimited patience, a notebook, and an opera glass [an equivalent of binoculars]."

Merriam's brother introduced her to Vernon Bailey, the Biological Survey's chief field naturalist. Merriam and Bailey married in 1899 and thereafter spent part of each year camping in the West, observing wildlife and gathering specimens. Vernon Bailey specialized in mammals, reptiles, and plants, while Florence continued to focus on birds.

Florence Bailey's writing became more scientific after her marriage. In 1902 she published the *Handbook of Birds of the Western United States,* which became a standard field guide for 50 years. Her most monumental work was *Birds of New Mexico,* published in 1928. Because of this book the American Ornithological Union not only made Bailey its first woman member in 1929 but awarded her its Brewster Medal in 1931.

Florence Merriam Bailey studied birds during camping trips in the Southwest in the early 1900s.
(Courtesy Smithsonian Institution Archives, Record Unit 7150, Records of the American Ornithological Union)

Bailey's last book, *Among the Birds in the Grand Canyon Country,* appeared in 1939, when she was 76. She died on September 22, 1948.

Further Reading

Bonta, Marcia Myers. *Women in the Field: America's Pioneering Women Naturalists.* College Station Tex.: Texas A&M University, 1991, 186–196.

Oehser, Paul H. "Bailey, Florence Augusta Merriam." In *Notable American Women, 1607–1950, vol. I: A–F,* edited by Edward T. James, 82–83. Cambridge, Mass.: Belknap Press of Harvard University Press, 1971.

Ogilvie, Marilyn Bailey. *Women in Science: Antiquity Through the Nineteenth Century.* Cambridge, Mass.: MIT Press, 1986, 34–35.

✳ BASCOM, FLORENCE
(1862–1945) *American Geologist*

Florence Bascom, America's first professional woman geologist, trained other women geologists and revealed new facts about how mountains are built. She was born on July 14, 1862, to John Bascom, a professor of philosophy at Williams College in Williamstown, Massachusetts, and his wife, Emma, a teacher and women's rights crusader. When Florence was 12, the family moved to Madison, where John Bascom became president of the University of Wisconsin.

Bascom herself attended that university. She graduated in 1882 with two bachelor's degrees, one in literature and one in arts. She received a B.S. degree in 1884, then earned a master's degree in geology in 1887. She specialized in petrography, the study of rocks, focusing on the complex layers of rocks that make up mountains. In 1891 she became one of the first women permitted to attend classes at Johns Hopkins University. She earned her Ph.D. in 1893, the first woman to receive the degree from Johns Hopkins. She was also the first woman in the United States to receive a doctor's degree in geology.

Bascom went to Bryn Mawr in 1895 and remained there for the rest of her career, becoming a full professor in 1906. She set up the college's geology department almost single-handedly, starting with only a storage area in the science building, and established programs that earned international respect. When President M. Carey Thomas tried to reduce geology from a major to an elective in 1899, Bascom threatened to resign, and rather than lose her, the college trustees made Thomas back down.

In 1896, Bascom became the first woman hired as an assistant geologist by the U.S. Geological Survey (USGS). She was promoted to geologist in 1909. Every summer she climbed through the Piedmont Mountains in Pennsylvania, Maryland, and New Jersey, noting their layers of rocks and collecting specimens. Her reports, which appeared between 1909 and 1938, became part of the USGS's

Florence Bascom, shown here in 1910, mapped the geology of the Piedmont mountain range in Pennsylvania and New Jersey and founded Bryn Mawr's geology department.
(Courtesy Sophia Smith Collection, Smith College Library)

extensive mapping of the country. They helped to explain how the Piedmonts, part of the Appalachian range, had formed.

Bascom became the first woman fellow of the Geological Society of America in 1894. She served as the organization's vice-president in 1930. She retired from Bryn Mawr in 1928 but kept on working until her death from a stroke on June 18, 1945, at age 82.

Further Reading

Arnold, Lois. *Four Lives in Science: Women's Education in the Nineteenth Century.* New York: Schocken Books, 1984.

Ogilvie, Marilyn Bailey. *Women in Science: Antiquity Through the Nineteenth Century.* Cambridge, Mass.: MIT Press, 1986, 36–37.

Rosenberg, Carroll S. "Bascom, Florence." In *Notable American Women, 1607–1950, vol. I: A–F,* edited by Edward T. James, 108–110. Cambridge, Mass.: The Belknap Press of Harvard University Press, 1971.

✳ BASSI, LAURA MARIA CATARINA
(1711–1788) *Italian Physicist*

Laura Bassi was the first woman to hold a professorship in physics in a European university. Born in

Bologna, Italy, in 1711, she became fluent in French and Latin while still a child. In 1733, at age 21, she debated philosophy publicly with five of the city's most renowned scholars. She was made a doctor of philosophy less than a month later in an elaborate ceremony, during which she made a speech in Latin and was crowned with a silver laurel wreath. After passing a stiff oral examination, she became a physics professor at the University of Bologna. Italian universities, unlike those elsewhere in Europe, occasionally had women professors, but there had never been one in physics.

Students and scholars from all over Europe attended Bassi's lectures. One reported, "She con-

After receiving her doctorate in an elaborate ceremony in 1733, Laura Bassi became a professor of physics at Italy's Bologna University—the first woman physics professor in Europe.
(Courtesy The Schlesinger Library, Radcliffe College)

versed fluently with me in Latin for an hour with grace and precision. She is very proficient in metaphysics [philosophy]; but she prefers modern physics, particularly that of [Isaac] Newton." In addition to her specialty, mechanics, and other aspects of physics, Bassi spoke on mathematics and even anatomy, the structure of the body.

Bassi must have had tremendous energy. She not only taught but prepared papers such as "On the compression of air" and "On the bubbles observed in freely flowing fluids" and invented equipment for experiments on electricity. Furthermore, she married Giuseppe Veratti, another professor, in 1738 and raised 12 children. She also helped the poor, wrote poetry, corresponded with scientists and thinkers throughout Europe, and attended meetings of the Bologna Academy of Science. She died in 1788.

Further Reading

Mozans, H. J. *Woman in Science.* Cambridge, Mass.: MIT Press, 1974, 203–210.

Schiebinger, Londa. *The Mind Has No Sex? Women in the Origins of Modern Science.* Cambridge, Mass.: Harvard University Press, 1989, 14–16.

 BECHTEREVA, NATALIA PETROVNA
(c. 1918–) *Russian Brain Researcher*

Natalia Bechtereva developed techniques to study electrical signals from the brain in action, providing information about the way nerve cells work when people think. She grew up in St. Petersburg, then called Leningrad. Her chief interests in college were mathematics and chemistry, but a desire to help her country during World War II made her decide to become a physician.

Bechtereva did most of her research at the Institute of Experimental Medicine, part of the Academy of Medical Sciences in Leningrad. She eventually became head of the institute's department of human neurophysiology (brain function). Her first work, in the 1950s and 1960s, aided surgeons who operated on the brain to treat severe epilepsy and other disorders that did not respond to drugs. She improved other researchers' techniques for recording electrical signals from cells in different parts of the brain, letting surgeons identify diseased areas by their abnormal signals.

Bechtereva slowly realized that using electrodes to record signals from brain cells provided "small windows looking into the cosmic world of the brain." She decided to use the technique to study normal brain function, which had never been done before. Her subjects were people scheduled to have brain surgery or electrode stimulation because of illness. Implanting electrodes temporarily in their brains did not harm them or cause pain.

Bechtereva and her coworkers found that one type of signal, called slow electrical processes, reflected emotions. She worked out an "alphabet" of signal patterns associated with different emotions and matched them to the kind of electrical change in the skin, also caused by emotion, that is measured by lie detectors.

In the mid-1960s Bechtereva extended her research to thinking. While electrodes were in place, her team asked patients to carry out simple mental tasks such as saying what several words related in meaning had in common. The researchers found that some areas of the brain were always active during certain tasks, while others were sometimes active and sometimes not. "We developed the hypothesis that mental activity is maintained by a system with rigid links and flexible ones," Bechtereva says. The rigid links are necessary for brain functions. The flexible links are probably reserves used when the brain learns or compensates for damage.

Bechtereva's research also showed that thinking takes place in networks of interconnected nerve cells, which she calls working assemblies. The cells involved in a working assembly may change from task to task and day to day. "Assemblies are very dynamic— . . . incessantly 'breathing,'" she says.

Further Reading

Bechtereva, Natalia P. "A Little About Myself—and More About a More Important Matter, the Brain." In *Women Scientists: The Road to Liberation*, edited by Derek Richter, 136–157. London: Macmillan, 1982.

✳ BELL BURNELL, SUSAN JOCELYN
(1943–) *British Astronomer*

While she was still a graduate student, Jocelyn Bell Burnell spotted a "bit of scruff" on a paper tape carrying recorded signals from space. As a result, she found a new kind of star. *Current Biography* called this discovery "one of the most exciting events in the history of astrophysics."

Susan Jocelyn Bell was born on July 15, 1943, in Belfast, Northern Ireland. She and her sisters and brother grew up in Solitude, their family's large country house. When Jocelyn was about 11 years old, her father, Philip, an architect, helped to rebuild Armagh Observatory. Jocelyn came along, met the observatory's astronomers, and learned to love their science.

At the University of Glasgow, Bell was the only woman among her class's 50 physics majors. She earned a B.S. with honors in 1965 and moved on to Cambridge University, where she studied radio astronomy. Radio astronomers map the sky by recording radio waves that stars and other objects in space give off, just as conventional astronomers record and use light. Other astronomers can also study the sky through other parts of the electromagnetic spectrum, such as microwaves, X rays, and gamma rays. Each type of radiation provides a different "picture" of the universe.

Bell's first task was to help build a new radio telescope, which sometimes meant swinging a 20-pound sledgehammer to drive in the poles that would hold up its antenna wire. Once the telescope was operating, Antony Hewish, the head of the radio astronomy project, gave her the painstaking job of analyzing the 100 feet of tape that its recorders spewed out each day. One day in October 1967, after Bell had been doing this for several months, she saw an unusual signal—what she called a "bit of scruff." As she said later, "I . . . remember[ed] that I had seen this particular bit of scruff before, and from the same part of the sky."

When Bell checked back, she found that the strange signal appeared once every 23 hours and 56 minutes. This meant that it was keeping sidereal time, or "star time," rather than sun time. The earth rotates with respect to the sun once every 24 hours, but its rotation time with respect to the stars is slightly less. The fact that the signal recurred on a star-time schedule meant that it almost surely came from outside the solar system.

The signals pulsed once every 1.3 seconds. Since no natural object that could make such rapidly pulsing signals was known, Hewish's group began to wonder whether the signals could be communications from another solar system. They joked about "little green men." At the end of 1967, however, Bell disproved this idea by finding another signal, pulsing even faster than first, in a different part of the sky. "It was highly unlikely that there were two lots of little green men signaling to us from opposite sides of the universe," she concluded. She soon found two more such signals.

Hewish published an article about the discovery on February 9, 1968. The new objects were dubbed pulsars, and astronomers speculated that they might be neutron stars, a strange kind of star predicted by theory but never observed before. They knew that when a large star runs out of nuclear fuel, it blows up in a colossal explosion called a supernova. The core left after a supernova explosion was expected to be only 6.2 to 9.3 miles (10 to 15 km) across, yet heavier than the sun. Its tremendous gravity would probably smash electrons into protons in the atoms' nuclei, leaving a soup of neutrons. Only something as small and heavy as a neutron star could spin as fast as the pulsars were doing without being torn apart. Astronomers guessed that powerful radio waves streamed from the star's magnetic poles and "flashed" at earth once each time the object rotated, just as the turning light in a lighthouse seems to flash each time its beam passes an observer.

Jocelyn Bell received her Ph.D. in 1969. She then married Martin Burnell, a government official, and moved with him whenever he was transferred to a new town, which happened often. They had a son in 1973, and Bell Burnell, as she now called herself, decided to work only part-time so she could care for him. "I am very conscious that having worked part-time, having had a rather disrupted career, my

research record is a good deal patchier than any man's of a comparable age," she says. On the plus side, her peripatetic career has produced a breadth of experience that few other astronomers can equal. For instance, she has done gamma-ray astronomy at Southampton University, done X-ray astronomy with the Mullard Space Science Laboratory of University College, London, and managed a telescope in Hawaii for the Scottish Royal Observatory.

Antony Hewish was awarded the Nobel Prize in physics in 1974, partly for his "decisive role in the discovery of pulsars." Jocelyn Bell Burnell did not share the award. This angered one of Britain's foremost astronomers, Sir Fred Hoyle, who claimed that Hewish had "pinch[ed] [stolen] the discovery from the girl." He praised Bell Burnell's "willingness to contemplate as a serious possibility a phenomenon that all past experience suggested was impossible." Bell Burnell said that Hoyle's accusation was "overstated," but some other astronomers agree with it at least in part. In any case, Bell Burnell has received plenty of other awards, including the Franklin Institute of Philadelphia's Michelson Medal (1973), the Herschel Medal from the Royal Astronomical Society of London (1989), and the Jansky Award of the National Radio Astronomy Observatory (1995).

Since 1991, Bell Burnell, now divorced, has been a professor and chairperson of the physics department at the Open University, which offers classes to adults all over Europe through correspondence, television, and computer. She calls herself "a role model, a spokeswoman, a representative, and a promoter of women in science in the U.K." She continues research as well, some of it on pulsars, the mysterious stars she helped to discover.

Further Reading

"Bell Burnell, Jocelyn." *Current Biography Yearbook 1995.* New York: H. W. Wilson, 1995, 42–46.

Irwin, Aisling. "Jocelyn Bell Burnell." In *Beyond the Glass Ceiling: Forty Women Whose Ideas Shape the Modern World,* edited by Sian Griffiths, 18–22. Manchester, England: Manchester University Press, 1996.

McGrayne, Sharon Bertsch. *Nobel Prize Women in Science: Their Lives, Struggles, and Momentous Discoveries.* New York: Birch Lane Press, 1993, 359–379.

Wade, Nicholas. "Discovery of Pulsars: A Graduate Student's Story." *Science,* August 1, 1975, 358–364.

✳ BENEDICT, RUTH FULTON
(1887–1948) *American Anthropologist*

Ruth Benedict was one of the first American women to become a professional anthropologist. She proposed the idea that each of the world's cultures has its own "personality." She fought against racism, a term she coined, and wrote books that helped different cultures understand one another. She was one of the first to combine anthropology with psychology and sociology to gain a multifaceted understanding of human culture. She also pioneered in using anthropology to study major modern cultures.

Ruth Fulton was born on June 5, 1887, in New York City. Her childhood was scarred by the death of her father, Frederick, a surgeon, when she was less than two years old. Reaction to this loss and to her mother's continuing grief made her depressed and lonely throughout the first half of her life. Hardness of hearing, the result of a childhood attack of measles, also helped to isolate her. She and her younger sister, Margery, grew up partly on their grandparents' farm and partly in the cities where their mother, Bertrice, found teaching jobs. Money was always scarce.

Fulton graduated from Vassar College in 1909, but she had little idea of what she wanted to do with her life. She taught school and also wrote poetry, some of which appeared in national magazines under the name Anne Singleton. In 1914 she married Stanley Benedict, a biochemist. They slowly drifted apart, however, and separated permanently in 1930.

To fill time, Ruth Benedict began taking classes in the New School for Social Research in New York City in 1919. Teachers there introduced her to Columbia University's Franz Boas, the "grand old man" of anthropology. Benedict soon began studying anthropology full-time and earned her doctorate in 1923. Columbia immediately hired her and, according to *Current Biography,* "eventually she became, next to Dr. Boas himself, the key figure in the Department of Anthropology." Her teaching inspired such students as MARGARET MEAD, and her fieldwork among the Native Americans of the Southwest resulted in two books, *Tales of the Cochiti Indians* (1931) and a two-volume work on Zuñi mythology (1935). She also edited the *Journal of American Folklore* between 1925 and 1940.

Benedict came to believe that each culture forms a basic pattern into which it tries to integrate all the random details of daily life. It honors only certain human traits, rejecting others that might be respected by other groups. Taken together, she said, the traits a culture honors form a sort of collective personality of that culture. She described these ideas in her best-known book, *Patterns of Culture,* published in 1934. Benedict was one of the first to link culture and individual personality, combining findings from anthropology and psychology. Later scholars have doubted that a single cultural pattern dominates daily life as much as Benedict believed, but her book remained a popular introduction to anthropology for more than 25 years.

Although still only an associate professor, a title she had been given in 1931, Benedict became acting head of Columbia's anthropology department after Franz Boas's retirement in 1936. In 1940, when the belief that some races were superior to others was tearing the world apart, she published a book called *Race: Science and Politics* to disprove this poisonous myth, which she called racism. "All the arguments are on the side of the Founding Fathers [of the United States], who urged no discrimination on the basis of race, creed, or color," she wrote. The army's Morale Division arranged for the distribution of 750,000 copies of *The Races of Mankind,* a pamphlet with the same message that she coauthored.

Benedict worked for the Office of War Information in Washington, D.C., from 1943 to 1945, advising the agency about dealing with people in occupied and enemy territories. After the war she extended her idea of cultural patterns into a detailed study of Japanese culture called *The Chrysanthemum and the Sword*. Most Americans thought of Japan only as an enemy that they had fought during World War II, but Benedict's book, published in 1946, helped them understand and respect the Japanese.

In 1947 the U.S. Office of Naval Research gave Columbia a grant to carry out research on contemporary cultures and chose Ruth Benedict to head this huge endeavor, the most ambitious anthropology project yet seen in the United States. She also served as president of the American Anthropological Association in 1947–48. Most people in the field had considered Benedict the leading American anthropologist since Franz Boas's death in 1942, but Columbia waited until 1948 to make her a full professor. Unfortunately, she did not have long to enjoy her new status. Benedict died of a heart attack on September 17, 1948.

Further Reading

Caffrey, Margaret M. *Ruth Benedict: Stranger in This Land*. Austin: University of Texas Press, 1989.

Fleming, Donald. "Benedict, Ruth Fulton." In *Notable American Women, 1607–1950, vol. I: A–F*, edited by Edward T. James, 128–131. Cambridge, Mass.: The Belknap Press of Harvard University Press, 1971.

Mead, Margaret. *Ruth Benedict*. New York: Columbia University Press, 1974.

Modell, Judith Schachter. *Ruth Benedict: Patterns of a Life*. Philadelphia: University of Pennsylvania Press, 1983.

✳ BENNETT, ISOBEL
(1909–) *Australian Marine Biologist*

Isobel Bennett gained an international reputation as a marine biologist even though she lacked formal training and never achieved an academic's status at the University of Sydney, where she worked most of her life. She was born in Brisbane in 1909, the oldest of four children. Her mother died when she was nine years old. Her family's money ran out when Bennett was just 16, and she had to leave school and earn a living. She worked at secretarial jobs, but in 1932 the Great Depression caused the last of these to vanish.

Refusing to let their spirits be dampened, Bennett and one of her sisters spent the remainder of their savings on a cruise to Norfolk Island. As luck had it, another passenger on the cruise was William J. Dakin, professor of zoology at the University of Sydney. Dakin became friends with the two young women and offered Isobel Bennett a job helping with his research on the history of whaling. Bennett took him up on the offer.

Dakin's specialty was marine biology, and Bennett too became interested in the subject. Dakin trained her and gave her increasingly challenging assignments. For instance, she became a regular crew member on the university's research ship, *Thistle*, sorting through nets full of plankton (tiny, floating marine life) and, later, giving informal instruction to the students who came on the ship's expeditions. She took on other jobs herself, such as cataloging and reorganizing the department's library. "When she saw something that should be done, she simply did it," writes her biographer, Nessy Allen.

In time, Bennett became almost as expert as Dakin. Her specialty was the ecology of the intertidal area, a world of constant change alternating between wet and dry and battered by wind and waves. She studied intertidal shore life in Australia and in Antarctica, which she was one of the first four Australian women scientists to visit (in 1957). She wrote many scientific papers and nine books, some of which became widely used textbooks.

The University of Sydney never paid Bennett what it would have paid someone with an M.S. or Ph.D., even though she did similar work. In 1962, however, the university did award her an honorary master's degree. Bennett also received other awards, including the Order of Australia and, in 1982, the Mueller Medal from the Australia and New Zealand Association for the Advancement of Science. She was only the second woman to receive this latter award. The Royal Zoological Society of New South Wales gave awards to two of her books.

Although she officially retired in 1971, Isobel Bennett was still working in 1992 at the age of 83. Other scientists have called her "one of Australia's foremost marine scientists."

Further Reading

Allen, Nessy. "Australian Women in Science: Two Unorthodox Careers." In *Women's Studies International Forum.* New York: Pergamon Press, 1992, 551–562.

✳ BLACKWELL, ELIZABETH
(1821–1910) *British/American Physician*

The one medical school that admitted her thought Elizabeth Blackwell's application was a joke, but to her, becoming a physician was a "moral crusade." She became the first woman to obtain an M.D. degree.

Elizabeth was born on February 23, 1821, in Bristol, England, the third of what were to be 12 children born to Samuel and Hannah Blackwell. Samuel, the well-to-do owner of a sugar refinery, filled his house with visitors who, like him, supported rights for women, the abolition of slavery, and similar social causes. He hired tutors to educate his children and insisted that his daughters be taught the same subjects as his sons.

Samuel Blackwell moved his family to the United States in 1832, when Elizabeth was 11 years old, after a fire destroyed his British refinery. They settled first in New York City, where Samuel established another sugar refinery. He lost most of his wealth in a financial panic in 1837, however. The Blackwells moved to Cincinnati, Ohio, in May 1838, hoping for a new start, but their hopes ended when Samuel died of a fever that August. He left his family with tremendous grief and no money.

Hannah Blackwell and her three oldest daughters, including Elizabeth, tried to earn a living by teaching. Teaching did not really appeal to Elizabeth, nor did marriage, but she was not sure what else to do with her life until a dying friend, Mary Donaldson, urged her to become a physician. Donaldson said she might have sought treatment sooner if she could have seen a woman doctor.

Elizabeth Blackwell had never dreamed of such a thing. Not only were no women physicians known, but, she wrote later, she had always been "filled . . . with disgust . . . [by] the physical structure of the body and its various ailments." Nonetheless, after "many a severe [internal] battle . . . the idea of winning a doctor's degree gradually assumed the aspect of a great moral struggle, and the moral fight possessed immense attraction for me."

Most of the physicians Blackwell talked to tried to discourage her, and 29 medical schools turned down her application—but the 30th did not. The dean of Geneva Medical College, a small college in upstate New York, wrote on behalf of his students, "In extending our unanimous invitation to Elizabeth Blackwell, we pledge ourselves that [she shall never] regret her attendance at this institution."

Blackwell didn't know it, but the letter had been meant as a joke. When the dean read her application to the students, they thought it was a prank from a rival college, and they replied in the same spirit. They were flabbergasted when a real and serious young woman appeared at their school on November 6, 1847. To their credit, however, they kept the pledge in the dean's letter. The Geneva townspeople were less understanding. They assumed that a woman who said she wanted to be a doctor was either a person of ill repute, probably an abortionist, or insane. They often crossed the street to avoid speaking to her.

Blackwell had her first practical experience in caring for the sick in 1848 at the hospital attached to the huge, grim Blocksley Almshouse in Philadelphia. Her patients were Irish immigrants felled by an epidemic of typhus fever, an infectious disease carried by lice. She wrote her thesis on the illness, emphasizing the importance of sanitation in preventing it.

Elizabeth Blackwell received her M.D. degree on January 23, 1849. "It shall be the effort of my life to shed honor on this diploma," she said. The crowd at the graduation ceremony burst into cheers.

Blackwell knew she needed to add more practical training to her classroom work. Doctors normally spend their first year after medical school obtaining such experience in a hospital. No American hospital would accept a woman doctor, so she decided to go to Paris.

French hospital administrators told Blackwell that the only training she could take was that of a student midwife at La Maternité, the state-run maternity hospital. Midwives provide assistance and nursing care to women giving birth. Blackwell accepted this choice and even came to enjoy it, in spite of 12-hour work shifts—until the day when she was treating a baby with an infected eye, and germ-laden matter from the eye splashed into her own. By the next day, her eye was swollen shut and terribly inflamed. Before long she had to face the fact that the sight in that eye was lost and, with it, her hope of becoming a surgeon.

Blackwell finally obtained the experience she needed at St. Bartholomew's, a huge and famous teaching hospital in London. After about a year there, she returned to the United States in August 1851. She rented rooms in New York City and put a notice in the newspaper stating that she was "prepared to practice in every department of her profession," but no patients came. She was desperately lonely. She wrote to one of her sisters: "I understand now why this life has never been lived before. It is hard, with no support but a high purpose, to live against every species of social opposition. I should like a little fun now and then. Life is altogether too sober."

In the hope of improving her finances, Blackwell gave lectures in which, among other things, she suggested that girls should take regular exercise in the open air and should be taught how their bodies worked. These novel ideas shocked many, but they appealed to a group of wealthy women who belonged to the Religious Society of Friends, or Quakers. These Quaker women became Blackwell's first patients and provided her with much-needed financial support. Blackwell's lectures were published in 1852 as a book, *The Laws of Life, with Special Reference to the Physical Education of Girls.*

Now that she had a few paying patients, Blackwell also began helping people who could not pay. In March 1853 she set up a one-room dispensary, or clinic, for women and children near Tompkins Square, one of the worst slums in New York. The clinic was open just three afternoons a week, but it treated 200 women in its first year.

Two other pioneering women physicians, Blackwell's younger sister Emily and a Polish immigrant, Marie Zakrzewska, arrived in 1856 to help her at the clinic. With their labor and money from her Quaker friends, Blackwell transformed a run-down building into a hospital, the New York Infirmary for Women and Children. It opened on May 12, 1857, becoming the first hospital to be staffed entirely by women.

Leaving the new hospital in the other two doctors' capable hands, Blackwell went to England again in 1858 and gave lectures on medical education for women. One young woman she inspired was ELIZABETH GARRETT (ANDERSON), who would later become the first British woman M.D. The Civil War started soon after Blackwell returned to the United States, and Elizabeth and Emily trained battlefield nurses during the war.

After the war ended, Blackwell went to work on a second dream, a medical school for women as good as those for men. The Women's Medical College of the New York Infirmary opened on November 2, 1868. It had entrance examinations, a rarity in those days. It also offered three years of training instead of the usual two, plus extensive practice in the hospital.

In 1869, Blackwell returned to England, this time for good. In addition to treating a large number of patients, she gave lectures on the need for improved sanitation and wrote two more books, *Counsel to Parents on the Moral Education of Their Children* (1878) and *The Human Element in Sex* (1884). She was ahead of her time in her stress on preventive medicine ("prevention is better than cure," she wrote) and her willingness to discuss taboo subjects such as sex. She eventually retired to Hastings, on England's southern coast. She died there on May 31, 1910, at the age of 89.

Further Reading

Blackwell, Elizabeth. *Opening the Medical Profession to Women*. New York: Schocken Books, 1977. (Reprint of 1895 ed.)

Hays, Elinor Rice. *Those Extraordinary Blackwells*. New York: Harcourt, Brace, and World, 1967.

Ross, Ishbel. *Child of Destiny*. New York: Harper, 1949.

Thomson, Elizabeth. "Blackwell, Elizabeth." In *Notable American Women, 1607–1950, vol. I: A–F*, edited by Edward T. James, 161–165. Cambridge, Mass.: The Belknap Press of Harvard University Press, 1971.

Truman, Margaret. *Women of Courage*. New York: Morrow, 1976, 129–144.

✳ BLODGETT, KATHARINE BURR
(1898–1979) *American Physicist*

Katharine Burr Blodgett was one of the first women scientists to win a major reputation in industry, creating several techniques relating to films on a surface that are still used. She was born in 1898 in Schenectady, New York, home of the giant General Electric Corporation (GE). Her father was GE's head patent attorney. Unfortunately, he died just before Katharine's birth. Her mother then embarked on years of travel, taking Katharine and her older brother to live for a while in France and then in Germany.

After graduating from Bryn Mawr in 1917, Blodgett followed her father's footsteps back to General Electric and applied for a research job. She was told that she needed more science background, so she spent a year at the University of Chicago earning a master's degree in physics. Even that might not have been enough if World War I had not taken so many young men out of the country. As it was, however, GE hired her in 1918 as an assistant to Irving Langmuir, who would later (1932) win a Nobel Prize in chemistry. Blodgett was the first woman to work in GE's laboratories and virtually the only woman physicist working for industry at the time.

Langmuir helped Blodgett get into the Cavendish Laboratory at Britain's Cambridge University, an almost unheard-of feat for a woman. She earned her Ph.D. in 1926, becoming the first woman to receive that degree from Cambridge. She then returned to Langmuir's laboratory.

Langmuir had invented a way to deposit oil onto the surface of water so that it formed a film just one molecule thick. Blodgett discovered in December 1933 that, by dipping a flat surface into such a film, she could deposit an equally thin layer onto the surface. The technique could be repeated to build up as many layers as were desired. "You keep barking up so many wrong trees in research," she later told writer Edna Yost. "This time I . . . barked up one that held what I was looking for."

Blodgett developed two applications of her technique. First, she noticed that when oily layers built up on a surface, they reflected different colors under white light, just as a film of oil on a puddle shows a rainbow reflection. She made a gauge that showed the colors of different thicknesses of film. By matching the color of an unknown film with a color on the gauge, a scientist could measure the thickness of the film with an accuracy of millionths of an inch.

In 1938, Blodgett found that if a film exactly four millionths of an inch thick was put on glass, the light waves reflected from the bottom of the coating and those reflected from the top canceled each other out. As a result, no light was reflected, and the glass in effect became invisible. Her "invisible" coated glass was used to make lenses for cameras, telescopes, and other optical instruments because it stopped the 8 to 10 percent loss of gathered light that was normally caused by reflection. This cut down on the exposure time needed to produce a good image.

Katharine Blodgett received several awards for her work, including the American Chemical Society's Garvan Medal (1951) and the Progress Medal of the Photographic Society of America (1972). She retired from GE in 1963 and died in 1979. The techniques she discovered are still used in physics, chemistry, and metallurgy.

Further Reading

Jones, L. M. "Intellectual Contributions of Women to Physics." In *Women of Science: Righting the Record*, edited by

G. Kass-Simon and Patricia Farnes, 198–199. Bloomington: Indiana University Press, 1990.

Vare, Ethlie Ann, and Greg Ptaceck. *Mothers of Invention.* New York: William Morrow, 1988, 193–195.

Yost, Edna. *American Women of Science.* Philadelphia: Frederick A. Stokes, 1943, 196–213.

BODEN, MARGARET
(1936–) *British Psychologist*

Margaret Boden has popularized the idea that the computer programming involved in so-called artificial intelligence (AI) can explain much about how the human mind works. She was born on November 26, 1936, to a lower middle-class British family. "I'd never expected to go to university," she told reporter Celia Kitzinger in 1992. "Neither of my parents did." Nonetheless, she won a scholarship to prestigious Cambridge University in 1955. She found Cambridge "like being born anew. . . . So many doors opened—intellectual doors, social doors, cultural doors."

Boden studied medicine and philosophy at Cambridge, but she was not happy with her postgraduate experience in either working with mental patients or teaching philosophy (from 1959 to 1962 she was a lecturer in philosophy at the University of Birmingham). Soon after going to Harvard University in 1962 to work on a doctorate in social and cognitive psychology, she happened to pick up a book called *Plans and the Structure of Behavior.* "Just leafing through it in the bookshop . . . change[d] my life," she recalls. "It was the first book that tried . . . to apply the notion of a . . . computer program to the whole of psychology." This idea struck her "like a flash of lightning."

Boden's doctoral thesis considered how the idea of intention or purpose for actions was applied in various theories of psychology and how it could be understood in terms of actions taken by a computer. This thesis grew into her first book, Purposive Explanation in Psychology, published in 1972. She says that book contained all her basic ideas and that her later, more popular books are mere "footnotes" to it.

In 1965 Boden began teaching at Sussex University. She married two years later (she divorced in 1981) and soon had two young children. She wrote her first two books in snatches while they napped. Her second book, *Artificial Intelligence and Natural Man,* (1977) used comparisons drawn from subjects including knitting and baking to explain the complex computer programming involved in artificial intelligence and show how it could be used to explore human thinking. She followed this book with one on Swiss psychologist Jean Piaget, first published in 1979, which discussed his biology and philosophy as well as his famous theories about children's psychological development. She related his ideas to AI and, in the book's second edition, to artificial life (A-Life).

Boden's fourth major book, published in 1990, was called *The Creative Mind.* It extended the links between computer programs and human thinking into the realm of creativity. Boden maintained that insights into human creativity can be gained by studying the results of attempts to program computers to be creative.

As of 1998, Boden, a fellow of the British Academy and of the American Association for Artificial Intelligence, was professor of psychology and philosophy at the University of Sussex, where in 1987 she had become the founding dean of the School of Cognitive and Computing Sciences. The department's interdisciplinary courses echo her own ability to combine insights from many disciplines. "I'm interested in the human mind, not computers," she emphasizes, "but I use computers as a way of thinking about the mind."

Further Reading

Boden, Margaret. *The Creative Mind: Myths and Mechanisms.* London: Weidenfeld and Nicolson (and Abacus), 1990.

Irwin, Aisling. "Margaret Boden." In *Beyond the Glass Ceiling: Forty Women Whose Ideas Shape the Modern World,* edited by Sian Griffiths, 11–17. Manchester, England: Manchester University Press, 1996.

Kitzinger, Celia. "The Thinking Woman's Guide to the Mind." *New Scientist,* January 18, 1992, 30–33.

✳ BRANDEGEE, MARY KATHARINE LAYNE ("Kate")
(1844–1920) *American Botanist*

Katharine Brandegee was curator of botany at the California Academy of Sciences for 22 years and also made major contributions to the University of California at Berkeley's herbarium (dried plant collection). She was born Mary Katharine Layne in Tennessee on October 28, 1844. Her father, Marshall, whom she called "an impractical genius," moved his family from place to place, finally settling near Folsom, California, when Kate, as she was always known, was nine. Growing up in California's beautiful Gold Rush country, she wrote later that "biology always attracted me greatly."

In 1866, Kate Layne married Hugh Curran, an Irish police constable. Eight years later he died of alcoholism, in 1874. Seeking a new life, Kate Curran enrolled at the medical school of the University of California at Berkeley in 1875, only the third woman to do so. She earned her M.D. in 1878. She was "not overrun with patients," however, so she decided to pursue an interest in plants begun when

In spite of poor health, Kate Brandegee thrived on the rough life of a plant collector in turn-of-the-century California.

(Courtesy Archives, University and Jepson Herbaria, University of California, Berkeley)

she learned about them in medical school as sources for drugs.

Curran studied botany under two experts at the Academy of Sciences in San Francisco and was soon helping them organize the academy's plant collection. When the curator of the collection retired in 1883, the academy, whose charter stated that it "highly approve[d] the aid of females in every department of natural history," took the very unusual step of giving her his job. Fellow botanist Marcus Jones wrote that she "was a model in thoroughness in her botanical work."

Curran fell "insanely in love" (as she wrote to her sister) with a plant collector named Townshend Stith Brandegee when he visited the academy in 1886. They married in San Diego on May 29, 1889, and spent their honeymoon walking from there to San Francisco, gathering plant specimens all the way. In 1895 they left the academy's herbarium in the capable hands of ALICE EASTWOOD, whom Brandegee had trained, and moved back to San Diego, where they set up a home, herbarium, and garden that one visitor called "a botanical paradise."

The Brandegees, traveling sometimes together and sometimes separately, made collecting trips all over California, including Baja California, as well as to parts of Arizona and Mexico. In spite of poor overall health, Kate Brandegee enjoyed these arduous journeys. "I am going to walk from Placerville to Truckee," she wrote to her husband in 1908, when she was 64 years old. "I have had considerable hardship in botanizing and perhaps in consequence—I am unusually strong and well."

When the herbarium at the University of California's Berkeley campus was destroyed in the huge earthquake of 1906, the Brandegees not only gave the university their collection (numbering some 100,000 plants) and library but moved to Berkeley to manage them. They remained there the rest of their lives, working without pay.

Marcus Jones wrote that Kate Brandegee "was the one botanist competent to publish a real flora of California [book describing all California plants]," but she never did so. "Her worst sin was caution, which led her to put off publication too long," Jones lamented. Brandegee died on April 3, 1920.

Further Reading

Bonta, Marcia Myers. *Women in the Field: America's Pioneering Women Naturalists*. College Station, Tex.: Texas A&M University Press, 1991, 85–92.

Dupree, Hunter, and Marian L. Gade. "Brandegee, Mary Katharine Layne Curran." In *Notable American Women 1607–1950, vol. I: A–F*, edited by Edward T. James, 228–229. Cambridge, Mass.: The Belknap Press of Harvard University Press, 1971.

Rush, Elizabeth. "On Her Terms." *Pacific Discovery*, Winter 1997, 22–27.

✳ BROOKS, HARRIET
(1876–1933) *Canadian Physicist*

In 1907, Nobel-winning British physicist Ernest Rutherford, for whom she had worked, called Harriet Brooks "next to Mme. [Marie] Curie, . . . the most prominent woman physicist in the department of radioactivity." Harriet was born in Exeter, Ontario, on July 2, 1876, the second of George and Elizabeth Brooks's eight children. Her father was a traveling salesman for a flour company, and the family moved frequently during her childhood.

Brooks won a scholarship to McGill University in Montreal, where she studied mathematics, languages, and physics. She graduated with honors in 1898 and then began work in the laboratory of Rutherford, who had just come to Canada. She also taught at the Royal Victoria College, a new women's college associated with McGill. In 1901 she earned a master's degree, the first one McGill gave to a woman.

Brooks discovered that strange "emanations" given off when radium broke down were not a form of that element but instead were a new element, a gas later called radon. Her paper on the subject, published in 1901, provided the first proof that one element could change into another. She also discovered a quality of radioactive atoms called recoil that helped in identifying the radioactive forms of elements, and she made important studies of the radioactive decay process in radium and actinium.

While spending a year of postgraduate study at the Cavendish Laboratory of Britain's Cambridge University in 1902–1903, Brooks met and fell in love with a physicist from Columbia University named Bergen Davis. She followed him to the United States in 1905 and took a teaching post at Barnard, a women's college at Columbia. She and Davis soon became engaged. When she announced the fact, she was shocked to receive a letter from Barnard's dean, Laura Gill, saying: "I feel very strongly that . . . your marriage . . . ought to end your official relationship with the college." Brooks snapped back, "I think . . . it is a duty I owe to my profession and to my sex to show that a woman has a right to the practice of her profession and cannot be condemned to abandon it merely because she marries."

As it happened, the engagement broke off, but perhaps not surprisingly, Brooks soon left Barnard. She traveled to Italy, where she met MARIE CURIE, and then to France, where she studied the element actinium at the Radium Institute. In 1907 she married Frank Pitcher, a physicist whom she had met earlier at McGill, and they returned to Montreal. Brooks then retired from science to raise two children. She died on April 17, 1933.

Further Reading

Rayner-Canham, Marelene F., and Geoffrey W. Rayner-Canham. *Harriet Brooks, Pioneer Nuclear Scientist.* Toronto: University of Toronto Press, 1992.
———. "Canada's First Woman Nuclear Physicist, Harriet Brooks, 1876–1933." In *Despite the Odds: Essays on Canadian Women and Science*, edited by Marianne Gosztonyi Ainley, 195–203. Montreal: Vehicule Press, 1990.

✳ BURBIDGE, ELEANOR MARGARET PEACHEY
(1919–) *British/American Astronomer*

Margaret Burbidge helped to explain how chemical elements are created inside stars. She has also headed Britain's most famous astronomical observatory. A 1974 *Smithsonian* article called her "probably . . . the foremost woman astronomer in the world."

Eleanor Margaret Peachey was born on August 12, 1919, in Davenport, England. Her father, Stanley, was a chemistry teacher at the Manchester School of Technology. Marjorie, her mother, had been one of his few woman students. Margaret first became interested in the stars at age four, when she saw them through a porthole during a trip across the English Channel. "They are so beautifully clear at night from a ship," she recalls. When she was 12, she was delighted to learn that astronomy involved not only stars but her other favorite thing, large numbers. "I decided then and there that the occupation I most wanted to engage in 'when I was grown up' was to determine the distances of the stars."

Margaret Peachey majored in astronomy at University College, London, earning a bachelor's degree in 1939 and a Ph.D. in 1943. In 1945 she applied for a grant to work at California's Mount Wilson telescope but was turned down because the telescope's administrators did not permit women to use it. She returned to University College two years later to take an advanced course in physics and met another student named Geoffrey Burbidge. They married on April 2, 1948. Geoff, as he was known, started out as a physicist, but he, too, became an astronomer.

After two years of work in the United States, the Burbidges returned to Britain in 1953 and began working with British astronomer Fred Hoyle and nuclear physicist William Fowler on a theory that explained how elements were made inside stars. The theory came to be called the B^2FH theory from the first letters of its creators' last names. (Other astronomers referred to the

Burbidges, who often worked together, as B^2, or "B squared.") It said that as stars age and exhaust their nuclear fuel, they go through a series of reactions that make heavier and heavier elements by fusing the atomic nuclei of the elements made in the previous reaction. Finally, if a star is large, it destroys itself in a violent explosion called a supernova, creating the heaviest elements in the process. Gas from the supernova, containing all the elements that the star produced, drifts out into space and is eventually captured and reused by other stars and planets.

To gather data to support their theory, the Burbidges braved Mount Wilson again in 1955. They got Margaret in by pretending that she was Geoff's assistant. She actually did most of the telescope work, spending nights high in the unheated observatory dome while pregnant with the couple's only child, Sarah. She photographed the light of stars and analyzed it to show what elements the stars contained. The four astronomers presented the B^2FH theory in 1957, and the Burbidges won the Warner Prize in 1959 for helping to devise and prove it. Writer Dennis Overbye says that the theory "laid out a new view of the galaxy as a dynamic evolving organism, of stars that were . . . an interacting community."

In the late 1950s the Burbidges worked at the University of Chicago's Yerkes Observatory in Wisconsin, studying different kinds of galaxies. The university hired Geoff as an associate professor, but antinepotism rules forbade hiring Margaret as well. (Such rules "are always used against the wife," she says.) The most she could get was a research fellowship. It was little wonder that, when the newly established University of California at San Diego offered to hire both Burbidges in 1962, they accepted. Margaret Burbidge became a full professor of astronomy there in 1964. At San Diego the Burbidges studied quasars, or quasi-stellar radio sources. Astronomers still do not know exactly what these strange starlike objects are.

When the Burbidges visited Britain in 1971, the head of the country's Science Research Council (SRC) asked a startled Margaret to become the director of the Royal Greenwich Observatory, Brit-

Margaret Burbidge helped to devise and test a theory of how elements were made inside stars and was the first woman to head Britain's prestigious Royal Greenwich Observatory. (Photo by Pat Gifford, courtesy E. Margaret Burbidge)

ain's most famous observatory. No woman had ever held this post. Geoff was offered a job there as well. The Burbidges accepted and moved back to England in 1972.

Unfortunately, being head of the Greenwich Observatory proved to include as much frustration as honor. For instance, the observatory director was normally given the title of astronomer royal, but Margaret, for unknown reasons, was not. The Burbidges also became involved in a dispute over whether the observatory's largest telescope should be moved out of the country. Geoffrey published a blunt letter on the subject in the science journal *Nature*, which angered the SRC. After what

Margaret calls a "bitter confrontation," she resigned, after heading Greenwich for just 15 months. The Burbidges then returned to San Diego.

Margaret Burbidge became the first woman president of the American Astronomical Society in 1976. She was president of the American Association for the Advancement of Science in 1981 as well. She headed a team that designed a faint object spectrograph, one of the instruments attached to the Hubble Space Telescope. She also directed San Diego's Center for Astrophysics and Space Sciences from the early 1980s, when it was founded, until 1988. As of 1998, Burbidge was still continuing her investigation of quasars, using the spectrograph she helped to design. She had retired as a university professor, but she still worked as a research professor.

Further Reading

Burbidge, E. Margaret. "Watcher of the Skies." *Annual Review of Astronomy and Astrophysics*, 1994, 1–36.

Green, Timothy. "A Great Woman Astronomer Leaves England—Again." *Smithsonian*, January 1974, 34–40.

Wade, Nicholas. "Astronomy in Britain: Fogged Up by Cloudy Skies and Schisms." *Science*, November 30, 1973, 900–901.

Yount, Lisa. *Twentieth-Century Woman Scientists*. New York: Facts On File, 1996, 38–49.

CANNON, ANNIE JUMP
 (1863–1941) *American Astronomer*

Annie Jump Cannon studied more stars than any other person—some 350,000 of them. She perfected a system for classifying stars according to patterns in their light and produced a giant star catalogue that astronomers still consult. Harlow Shapley, director of the Harvard Observatory, called her "one of the leading women astronomers of all time."

Annie Cannon, born on December 11, 1863, spent a happy childhood in a large family in Dover, Delaware. Her father, Wilson, was a wealthy shipbuilder. Her mother, Mary, taught her to recognize constellations, using a textbook from her own school days. The two built a makeshift observatory in their attic, and Annie sometimes climbed through the attic's trapdoor to watch the stars from the house's roof. She then returned to bed to read by candlelight, making her father afraid she would start a fire.

Even though college education for women was a new and rather shocking idea, Wilson Cannon recognized his daughter's intelligence and encouraged her to go to Wellesley, a new women's college in Massachusetts. Annie enjoyed her years there, but she was not prepared for the chilly New England winters. During her first year she had one cold after another. The illnesses damaged her eardrums, producing deafness that became worse as she grew older.

After graduating in 1884, Cannon returned to her home in Delaware and led a carefree social life. That life ended abruptly when her mother died in 1893. The two had been very close, and Cannon could not bear to stay in the places they had shared. She decided to go back to Wellesley instead. She took a year of graduate courses there, then enrolled in 1895 as a special student in astronomy at Radcliffe, the women's college connected with Harvard University, so she could use Harvard's observatory.

To Cannon's surprise, she found a number of other women working at the observatory, including WILLIAMINA FLEMING and ANTONIA MAURY. Edward C. Pickering, the observatory's director, was making a gigantic survey of all the stars in the sky, and he made a point of hiring women to help him. His publicly stated reason for preferring women was his belief that they had more patience than men, a better eye for detail, and smaller hands that could more easily manipulate delicate equipment. However, he also pointed out to the Harvard trustees in 1898 that women "were capable of doing as much good routine work as [male] astronomers who would receive much larger salaries. Three or four times as many assistants can thus be employed . . . for a given expenditure."

Pickering's survey depended on a device called a spectroscope, which converted light from stars or other sources into rainbowlike patterns called spectra. Astronomers had learned to combine a spectroscope, a camera, and a telescope to take pictures of the spectrum made by each star's light. By studying these spectrograms, as the pictures were called, a trained observer with a magnifying glass could find out what elements the star con-

tained, how hot it was, how big it was, and how fast it moved through space.

Annie Cannon joined the Harvard Observatory staff in 1896. Pickering by then had accumulated 10 years' worth of spectrograms, each of which contained the spectra of hundreds of stars, and analyzing them became Cannon's job. No two stars' spectra were exactly alike, so she used each star's spectrum to identify it. She also grouped stars with similar spectra together. She refined a classification system that Williamina Fleming had devised, eventually dividing stars into classes that, in order of their surface temperature from hottest to coolest,

Around the turn of the century, Harvard Observatory astronomer Annie Jump Cannon worked out a new system for classifying stars according to qualities of their light as shown in spectrograms, or photographs taken through a prism. Here she examines a star photograph on a light table.

(Courtesy Harvard College Observatory)

are designated O, B, A, F, G, K, and M. (Generations of astronomy students have memorized this list by means of the rather sexist sentence, "O Be a Fine Girl, Kiss Me.") By 1910 astronomers everywhere were using her system.

Cannon examined the spectra of an unbelievable 350,000 stars during her lifetime. "Each new spectrum is the gateway to a wonderful new world," she once said. She grew so expert that she could classify three spectra a minute. She also calculated each star's position. Her work became the core of the giant *Henry Draper Star Catalogue*, issued in nine volumes between 1918 and 1924, and its two extension volumes, issued in 1925 and 1949. Harlow Shapley, who became director of the Harvard Observatory after Pickering, said that Cannon's contributions to astronomy make "a structure that probably will never be duplicated . . . by a single individual." It is still a standard reference for astronomers all over the world.

Cannon earned her master's degree from Wellesley in 1907. In 1911 she took over Williamina Fleming's job as curator of photographs at the Harvard Observatory, a post she kept for 27 years. She was also named the William Cranch Bond Astronomer at Harvard in 1938, becoming one of the first women to be given a titled appointment by the university. She was elected an honorary member of Britain's Royal Astronomical Society.

Cannon won many awards, including the first honorary doctorate given to a woman by Britain's prestigious Oxford University (1925). She won the Draper Medal of the National Academy of Sciences in 1931 (the first gold medal ever awarded to a woman by this group) and the Ellen Richards prize of the Society to Aid Scientific Research by Women in 1932. She used the money that came with the Richards Prize to fund an award of her own, the Annie Jump Cannon Prize, to be given every third year by the American Astronomical Society to a woman who had given distinguished service to astronomy. Cannon died of heart disease on April 13, 1941, at the age of 77.

Further Reading

Hoffleit, Dorrit. "Cannon, Annie Jump." In *Notable American Women, 1607–1950, vol. I: A–F*, edited by Edward T. James, 281–283. Cambridge, Mass.: The Belknap Press of Harvard University Press, 1971.

Rubin, Vera. "Women's Work." *Science 86*, July–August 1986, 58–65.

Veglahn, Nancy. *Women Scientists*. New York: Facts On File, 1991, 26–35.

Yost, Edna. *American Women of Science*. Philadelphia: Frederick A. Stokes, 1943, 27–43.

✳ CARR, EMMA PERRY
(1880–1972)   *American Chemist*

Emma Carr provided groundbreaking information about the complex structure of certain organic chemicals, or carbon-containing compounds. She was born on July 23, 1880, in Holmesville, Ohio, the third of Edmund and Mary Carr's five children. Her father was a physician. The Carrs moved to Coshocton, Ohio, before Emma was a year old, and she grew up there.

After attending Ohio State University in 1898–99, Emma Carr transferred to Mount Holyoke, a women's college in Hadley, Massachusetts. In 1905 she went to the University of Chicago to finish her B.S. degree. She also obtained her Ph.D. in physical chemistry from that university in 1910. She spent the rest of her life at Mount Holyoke, where she became a full professor and head of the chemistry department in 1913.

The qualities of organic compounds depend largely on the arrangement of atoms within their molecules. One way to find out the structure of organic molecules is to analyze them with a spectroscope, which breaks up light into a pattern of rainbow colors overlaid by dark lines (a spectrum). Using a new form of spectroscopy developed in Europe, Carr focused on the way organic compounds absorb ultraviolet light.

During the early 1920s, Carr and her coworkers (who included undergraduates as well as graduate students and professors) synthesized a wide variety

Mount Holyoke chemist Emma Perry Carr worked out key features of the molecular structure of important organic (carbon-containing) compounds from the 1920s to the 1940s.
(Courtesy Mount Holyoke College Archives and Special Collections)

of compounds and analyzed their light. In the late 1920s, however, they began examining one group, the hydrocarbons, more systematically. They studied hydrocarbons that differed only in the numbers and placement of a key feature, double bonds between carbon atoms. They began with simple hydrocarbons, then extended their work to more complex ones in the 1930s and 1940s. They received large grants from the National Research Council and the Rockefeller Foundation for their work. Carr called her research "an exciting adventure."

Carr was a consultant on spectra for the group preparing the International Critical Tables, a set of references intended to be used by chemists worldwide. She became the first recipient of the American Chemical Society's Francis Garvan Medal in 1937. She retired in 1946 but remained active in college affairs until 1964. She died on January 7, 1972.

Further Reading

"Carr, Emma P(erry)." *Current Biography Yearbook 1959.* New York: H. W. Wilson, 1959, 55–57.

Miller, Jane A. "Women in Chemistry." In *Women of Science: Righting the Record,* edited by G. Kass-Simon and Patricia Farnes, 312–313. Bloomington: Indiana University Press, 1990.

Verbrugge, Martha H. "Carr, Emma Perry." In *Notable American Women: The Modern Period,* edited by Barbara Sicherman and Carol Hurd Green, 136–138. Cambridge, Mass.: The Belknap Press of Harvard University Press, 1980.

 ## CARSON, RACHEL LOUISE
(1907–1964)   *American Marine Biologist and Ecologist*

Rachel Carson combined a professional knowledge of science (she trained as a marine biologist) with poetic writing skill to write best-selling books about the sea. Her impact on history, however, came from a book she did not really want to write: a warning that unless human exploitation of the environment was curbed, much of nature might be destroyed. Carson's book *Silent Spring* introduced the idea of ecology to the American public and almost single-handedly spawned the environmental movement.

Rachel Carson was born in Springdale, western Pennsylvania, on May 27, 1907. Her father, Robert, sold insurance and real estate. Her family never had much money, but the 65 acres of land around their home near the Alleghany Mountains was rich in natural beauty, which her mother, Maria, taught her to love. "I can remember no time when I wasn't interested in the out-of-doors and the whole world of nature," Carson once said.

Before she become famous as the writer-ecologist who warned of the harm that pesticides could do to the environment, Rachel Carson worked as a biologist for the U.S. Fish and Wildlife Service.
(Courtesy Yale Collection of American Literature, the Beinecke Rare Book and Manuscript Library, Yale University)

When Carson entered Pennsylvania College for Women (later Chatham College) on a scholarship, she planned to become a writer. A biology class from an inspired teacher made her change her major to zoology, however. She graduated magna cum laude in 1929 and obtained another scholarship to do graduate work at Johns Hopkins University. She also began summer work at the Marine Biological Laboratory in Woods Hole, Massachusetts. Carson had always loved reading about the sea, and Woods Hole gave her a long-awaited chance not only to see the ocean but to work in it. She obtained a master's degree in zoology from Johns Hopkins in 1932.

Carson taught part-time at Johns Hopkins and at the University of Maryland for several years. Then, in 1935, her father died suddenly and her mother moved in with her. A year later her older sister also died, orphaning Carson's two young nieces, Virginia and Marjorie. Carson and her mother adopted the girls.

Needing a full-time job to support her family, Carson applied to the U.S. Bureau of Fisheries. In August 1936 she was hired as a junior aquatic biologist—one of the first two women employed there for anything except clerical work. Elmer Higgins, Carson's supervisor, recognized her writing ability and steered most of her work in that direction. He rejected one of her radio scripts, however, saying it was too literary for his purposes. He suggested that she make it into an article for *Atlantic Monthly,* and it appeared as "Undersea" in the magazine's September 1937 issue.

An editor at Simon & Schuster asked Carson to expand her article into a book. The result, *Under the Sea Wind,* appeared in November 1941. Critics liked it, but the United States entered World War II a month later, and book buyers found themselves with little interest to spare for poetic descriptions of nature. The book sold poorly.

Carson continued her writing for the U.S. Fish and Wildlife Service, created in 1940 when the Bureau of Fisheries and the Biological Survey merged. She became editor in chief of the agency's publications division in 1947. In 1948 she began work on another book, drawing on information about oceanography that the government had obtained during the war. That book, *The Sea Around Us,* described the physical nature of the oceans. It was more scientific and less poetic than Carson's first book. Published in 1951, it became an immediate best-seller, remaining on the *New York Times* list of top-selling books for a year and a half. It also received many awards, including the National Book Award and the John Burroughs Medal.

Suddenly Rachel Carson found herself famous and, for the first time, relatively free from money worries. In June 1952 she quit her U.S. Fish and Wildlife Service job to write full time. A year later she built a home on the Maine coast, surrounded by "salt smell and the sound of water, and the softness of fog." She shared it with her mother, her niece, Marjorie, and Marjorie's baby son, Roger. Later, when Marjorie died in 1957, Carson adopted Roger and raised him.

Carson's third book, *The Edge of the Sea,* described seashore life. Published in 1955, it sold almost as well as *The Sea Around Us* and garnered its own share of awards, including the Achievement Award of the American Association of University Women.

The book that gave Rachel Carson a place in history, however, was yet to be written. It grew out of an urgent letter that a friend, Olga Owens Huckins, sent to her in 1957 after a plane sprayed clouds of the pesticide DDT over the bird sanctuary that Huckins and her husband owned near Duxbury, Massachusetts. Government officials told Huckins that the spray was a "harmless shower" that would kill only mosquitoes, but the morning after the plane passed over, Huckins found seven dead songbirds. "All of these birds died horribly," she wrote. "Their bills were gaping open, and their splayed claws were drawn up to their breasts in agony." Huckins asked Carson's help in alerting the public to the dangers of pesticides.

Carson had been concerned about these widely used chemicals for years, and she now began researching their effects in earnest. "The more I learned about pesticides, the more appalled I became," she wrote later. "Everything which meant most to me as a naturalist was being threatened." The evidence suggested to her that the compounds were doing terrible damage to wildlife and perhaps to people as well. She did not want to be a crusader, but, she felt, "there would be no peace for me if I kept silent." She spent four years amassing scientific data to support her ideas. She told her editor that her book would be "a synthesis of widely scattered facts that have heretofore not been considered in relationship to each other. It is now possible to build up, step by step, a really damning case against the use of these chemicals as they are now inflicted on us."

Silent Spring, the book that grew out of Carson's research, appeared in 1962. It took its title from the "fable" at the book's beginning, which pictured a spring that was silent because pesticides had destroyed singing birds and much other wildlife. The health of the human beings in her scenario was imperiled as well. This was the only fiction in the book.

Carson's book did more than condemn pesticides. These toxic chemicals, she said, were just one example of humans' greed, misunderstanding, and exploitation of nature. "The 'control of nature' is a phrase conceived in arrogance born of the . . . [belief] . . . that nature exists for the convenience of man." People failed to understand that all things in nature, including human beings, are interconnected and that damage to one meant damage to all. Carson used the word *ecology*, from a Greek word meaning "household," to describe this relatedness. She said that people needed to respect and work with nature rather than trying to conquer it.

Reporter Adela Rogers St. Johns wrote that *Silent Spring* "caused more uproar . . . than any book by a woman author since *Uncle Tom's Cabin* started a great war." The powerful pesticide industry claimed that if Carson's supposed demand to ban all pesticides—a demand she never actually made—were followed, the country would plunge into a new Dark Age because pest insects would devour its food supplies and insect carriers such as mosquitoes would spread disease everywhere. Publicity pictured Carson as an emotional female with

no scientific background, ignoring her M.S. degree and years as a U.S. Fish and Wildlife Service biologist. A *Time* magazine review called her book "unfair, one-sided, and hysterically overemphatic." Many scientists took Carson's side, however. President John F. Kennedy appointed a special panel of his Science Advisory Committee to study the issue, and the panel's 1963 report supported most of Carson's conclusions.

Rachel Carson died of breast cancer on April 14, 1964. The trend she started, however, did not die. It resulted in the banning of DDT in the United States and the creation of the Environmental Protection Agency (EPA). Most important, it reshaped the way that the American public viewed nature. As one newspaper editorial put it, "A few thousand words from her, and the world took a new direction." Today's environmental protection movement is Rachel Carson's legacy.

Further Reading

Brooks, Paul. *The House of Life: Rachel Carson at Work.* Boston: Houghton Mifflin, 1972.

Carson, Rachel. *The Sea Around Us.* New York: Oxford University Press, 1951.

———. *Silent Spring.* Boston: Houghton Mifflin, 1962.

Graham, Frank Jr. *Since Silent Spring.* Boston: Houghton Mifflin, 1972.

Lear, Linda J. *Rachel Carson: Witness for Nature.* New York: Holt, 1997.

✳ CHÂTELET, EMILIE DU (Gabrielle-Emilie Le Tonnelier de Breteuil)
(1706–1749) *French Mathematician and Physicist*

Emilie du Châtelet went from decadent court lady to scientist, producing a French translation of Isaac Newton's *Principia* that is still used. She was born Gabrielle-Emilie Le Tonnelier de Breteuil in 1706. Her father, the baron de Breteuil, was chief of protocol to Louis XIV. He gave her an education, fearing she was too tall and clumsy ever to get a husband, but by the time she was presented to the

French court at age 16, she had become a beauty. In 1725 she married the marquis Florent-Claude du Châtelet-Lomont, who had the advantages of being frequently away from home and not caring what his wife did while he was gone. They had three children.

Emilie, now the marquise du Châtelet, for the most part was a typical court lady until 1733, when she met François Marie Arouet, better known as Voltaire. She and this poet, playwright, and philosopher soon became more than friends. When the government threatened to arrest Voltaire for some of his writings in 1734, the couple fled to Cirey, a distant castle belonging to du Châtelet's husband. With the marquis's permission and Voltaire's money they remodeled the castle, bringing in thousands of books for their library and turning the great hall into a physics laboratory.

In the 10 years they spent at Cirey, Voltaire and du Châtelet entertained thinkers from all over Europe. (Everyone, including du Châtelet, worked in their rooms all day and partied half the night.) From Voltaire and some of their visitors du Châtelet learned about the new discoveries in physics and mathematics made by the English scientist Isaac Newton. She became very interested in these and in the science-related philosophy of the German Gottfried von Leibniz. In 1740 she anonymously published the *Institutions de Physique,* a simplified description of Newton's physics and Leibniz's philosophy. Science historian Margaret Alic says that in this book du Châtelet "summarize[d] almost all of 17th-century science and philosophy."

Du Châtelet began her most important writing, a translation into French of Isaac Newton's massive *Principia Mathematica* plus her own commentaries, around 1744. Soon afterward she discovered that she was pregnant—at age 42. Fearing that she would not survive the birth, she worked night and day to finish her translation before the child was due. She died of childbirth fever in September 1749, just after completing the *Principia.* Published 10 years after her death, it is still the only French translation of this work. It is a fitting memorial to the woman whom one admirer, Frederick II of Prussia, nicknamed "Venus-Newton."

Further Reading

Alic, Margaret. *Hypatia's Heritage: A History of Women in Science from Antiquity Through the Nineteenth Century.* Boston: Beacon Press, 1986, 139–147.

Osen, Lynn M. *Women in Mathematics.* Cambridge, Mass.: MIT Press, 1974, 49–70.

Schiebinger, Londa. *The Mind Has No Sex? Women in the Origins of Modern Science.* Cambridge, Mass.: Harvard University Press, 1989, 59–65.

✳ CLARK, EUGENIE
(1922–) *American Marine Biologist*

Eugenie Clark has done so much research on sharks that she has been called the "shark lady." Sharks, however, are just one form of ocean life she has studied. Eugenie was born in New York City on May 4, 1922. Her father, Charles, died a year after she was born, and her mother, Yumico, had to work to support herself and her daughter. When Yumico worked on Saturdays, she left Eugenie at the New York Aquarium. "I brought my face as close as possible to the glass [of the largest aquarium tank] and pretended I was walking on the bottom of the sea," Eugenie Clark recalls.

Clark majored in zoology at Hunter College in New York City, graduating in 1942. She then took graduate science courses from New York University at night while working at a plastics factory in the daytime. She finished her master's degree in 1949 and her Ph.D. in 1950.

In June 1949 the U.S. Navy and the Pacific Science Board awarded Clark a scholarship to investigate poisonous fish in the South Pacific. She then went to the Red Sea, between Africa and the Arabian Peninsula, to collect other poisonous fish. She married Ilias Papaconstantinou, a Greek-born physician whom she had met in New York, in June 1951, and they spent their honeymoon diving in the Red Sea. They later had four children.

Clark wrote a book about her experiences in the Pacific and the Red Sea called *Lady with a Spear.* Published in 1953, it attracted a wide audience, including a wealthy couple who asked Clark to start

Eugenie Clark, shown here in a jumpsuit she wore on the Russian submersible *Mir*, has dived all over the world to study sharks and other marine animals. (Courtesy Andreas Rechnitzer)

a marine biology laboratory on land they owned in Florida. The facility, which opened in 1955, was called the Cape Haze Marine Laboratory.

One of Clark's chief projects during her years at Cape Haze was a study of the intelligence of sharks. She found that they were much smarter than biologists had thought. She calls sharks "magnificent and misunderstood."

Clark and her husband divorced in 1967. She left Florida and joined the University of Maryland the following year. Since then she has done underwater research all over the world. She has studied fish that can change sex in 10 seconds, a flatfish that exudes a poison that make even a big shark back off in disgust, and sharks that "sleep" in underwater caves while

smaller fish pick parasites off their skins. She has also worked to preserve the ocean habitat she loves, for instance helping to make Ras Muhammad, a favorite diving site, into Egypt's first national park. She retired from the university in 1992, but as of 1998 was still active there as a senior research scientist and professor emerita. She was also still diving. "I plan to keep on diving and researching and conserving until I'm at least ninety years old," she says.

Further Reading

Clark, Eugenie. *The Lady and the Sharks.* New York: Harper and Row, 1969.

———. *Lady with a Spear.* New York: Harper and Row, 1953.

McGovern, Ann. *Adventures of the Shark Lady: Eugenie Clark Around the World.* New York: Scholastic Book Services, 1998.

Yount, Lisa. *Contemporary Women Scientists.* New York: Facts On File, 1994, 59–71.

✳ CLEOPATRA THE ALCHEMIST
(c. fourth century)   *Egyptian Chemist*

The ancient science called alchemy was the ancestor of chemistry. It combined magic, mystical symbols, and experimental study of chemical elements and compounds. Cleopatra was one of several women who contributed to the early development of alchemy.

Almost nothing is known of Cleopatra's life. She is thought to have lived in the Egyptian city of Alexandria in the fourth or fifth century, when Alexandria was a world center of learning. Early Christian zealots destroyed many books on alchemy, which they held to be evil magic. Islamic scholars copied or preserved some alchemy books, however, and one was Cleopatra's *Chrysopoeia,* or "Gold-making."

Cleopatra's book, like most books written by alchemists, blended the poetic and the practical. It compared the making of metals to the process of pregnancy and birth. It also used, perhaps for the first time, images that became popular in Western poetry and art, such as a snake that forms a ring by swallowing its own tail. One modern scholar has called Cleopatra's book "the most imaginative and deeply felt document left by the alchemists."

Cleopatra's gold-making book also contained descriptions of equipment used in alchemy. One device distilled substances, or purified them by boiling them and cooling the vapor. Another softened and colored metals by heating them over a flame in an enclosed chamber. For Cleopatra, as for MARIA THE JEWESS, who probably created some of the devices Cleopatra described, alchemy was an experimental science as well as a mystical art.

Further Reading

Alic, Margaret. *Hypatia's Heritage: A History of Women in Science from Antiquity Through the Nineteenth Century.* Boston: Beacon Press, 1986, 39–41.

✳ COBB, JEWEL PLUMMER
(1924–) *American Cancer Researcher*

Jewel Plummer Cobb has excelled in research, teaching, and college administration. Born on January 17, 1924, in Chicago, she grew up in a family who discussed "science things at the dinner table." Her father, Frank, was a physician. Carriebel, her mother, taught physical education. Jewel became interested in biology in high school, when she first looked through a microscope. "It was really awe inspiring," she says.

Plummer earned her B.A. at Talladega College in Alabama in 1944 and her master's degree (1947) and Ph.D. (1950) at New York University. She then joined the Cancer Research Foundation of Harlem Hospital in New York City, where she worked under another African-American woman scientist, JANE WRIGHT. Wright and Plummer tried to develop a way to test anticancer drugs on cells from a patient's tumor in the laboratory to determine the best dose to give to the patient. Plummer did the lab work, studying cells under the microscope and making time-lapse films to show how they changed after drugs were added. The project did not succeed,

Jewel Plummer Cobb did research on cancer and anticancer drugs, then become president of the California State University campus at Fullerton in 1981, the first African-American woman to head a large public university on the West Coast.
(Courtesy Jewel Plummer Cobb)

but the researchers learned much about how the drugs affected cancer cells.

Plummer left full-time research in 1952 and began teaching at the University of Illinois. In 1954 she married Roy Cobb, an insurance salesman, and they had a son, Jonathan. She moved to Sarah Lawrence College in 1960. There, in addition to teaching, she did research on skin cells, both normal and cancerous, that contain the dark pigment melanin.

The Cobbs were divorced in 1967, leaving Jewel Cobb with a young son to raise alone. In 1969, nonetheless, she became dean of Connecticut College and thus began a third career, that of college administrator. She eventually had to give up research because it took too much time.

Cobb became dean of Douglass College, the women's college of Rutgers University, in 1976. Then, in 1981, she became president of the California State University campus at Fullerton. No other African-American woman had headed such a large public university on the West Coast. While there, she established schools of communication and of engineering and computer science as well as the campus's first residence hall.

Cobb retired from Cal State Fullerton in 1990. She is a trustee professor of the state university system. From her office in Los Angeles she oversees a center that improves science education for minority students. She once told an interviewer that she wanted to be remembered as "a black woman who cared very much about what happens to young folks."

Further Reading

Irvin, Dona L. "Jewell Plummer Cobb." In *Epic Lives: One Hundred Black Women Who Made a Difference,* edited by Jessie Carney Smith, 90–96. Detroit: Visible Ink Press/ Gale Research Inc., 1993.

"Shaper of Young Minds." *Ebony,* August 1982, 97–100.

Yount, Lisa. *Contemporary Women Scientists.* New York: Facts On File, 1994, 72–82.

✳ COLBORN, THEODORA ("Theo")
(1927–) *American Zoologist and Ecologist*

Like RACHEL CARSON, Theodora Colborn has sounded a warning about poisons in our environment. Born on March 28, 1927, she worked as a pharmacist in New Jersey and then, starting in 1964, as a sheep rancher in Colorado. Her love of nature, especially birds, led her to become involved with the environmental movement. At age 51, she went back to college. She earned a Ph.D. in zoology from the University of Wisconsin, Madison, in 1985.

In 1987, Colborn went to work for the Conservation Foundation, a think tank in Washington, D.C. While coauthoring a book about the condition of the Great Lakes, she reviewed vast numbers of scientific papers on the health of wildlife and people in the region. Although pollution in the lakes, once heavy, had decreased considerably, she discovered that 16 kinds of animals that ate fish from the lakes were still having problems reproducing. Often the adult animals appeared healthy, but they either bore deformed or sickly young that did not live long or else had no young at all.

Colborn became convinced that substances in the lake water were acting as "hand-me-down poisons," somehow derailing the development of young animals. After further research, she suggested that certain pollutants might cause these problems by imitating or modifying the action of hormones, chemicals made in one part of the body that affect actions in another. Hormones control many body processes, including reproduction and most important, how a baby develops in the womb.

In 1991, Colborn set up a meeting of scientists to discuss the possible dangers of pollutants that affect the hormones that control the development of living things, both wildlife and humans. They found that hormone-related abnormalities in both animals and humans were being reported all over the world. Researchers have since found at least 51 types of chemicals in pesticides, plastics, and other common substances that act like or interfere with the hormones that control body processes and development. Colborn, now a senior researcher with the World Wildlife Fund, continues to push for investigation of these pollutants.

Not all scientists think low doses of hormone-mimicking substances are as dangerous as Colborn and her supporters say they are. More research will be needed to show whether Theo Colborn is correct and, like Rachel Carson, the issuer of a timely warning about a major danger to life on this planet.

Further Reading

Colborn, Theo, Dianne Dumanoski, and John Peterson Myers. *Our Stolen Future.* New York: Dutton Signet/Penguin, 1996.

Nash, J. Madeleine. "Not So Fertile Ground." *Time,* September 19, 1994, 68–70.

✳ CORI, GERTY THERESA RADNITZ
(1896–1957) *American Biochemist*

The bodies of living things constantly store, use, and recycle the energy that they get from food. Gerty Radnitz Cori and her husband, Carl Cori, worked out the steps in this energy cycle and discovered several chemicals and reactions involved in it. Gerty Cori also showed that certain inherited diseases are caused by the absence of key chemicals in this cycle. Her work earned her a share of a Nobel Prize in 1947.

Gerty Theresa Radnitz was born on August 15, 1896, in Prague, then part of the empire of Austria-Hungary and later the capital of Czechoslovakia. She was the oldest of the three daughters of Otto Radnitz, a well-to-do businessperson and chemist who owned several beet sugar refineries, and his wife, Martha. Gerty's early education did not prepare her for medical school, so she had to master years of missed subjects in a short time in order to pass the school's entrance exam. She later said that it was "the hardest examination I was ever called upon to take." She enrolled in the Carl Ferdinand Medical School in Prague in 1914.

Gerty met Carl Cori, the son of a marine biologist, in her freshman anatomy class. He admired her "charm, vitality, intelligence, . . . sense of humor, and love of the outdoors." Joint work on a research project convinced them that they were ideal partners, and they married on August 5, 1920, two months after they earned their M.D. degrees. They had a son, Tom Carl, in 1936.

After a year of working separately in Vienna, the Coris moved to the United States. Carl was offered a post at the New York State Institute for the Study of Malignant Diseases (later the Roswell Park Memorial Institute) in Buffalo early in 1922, and after six months he was able to arrange for a job there for Gerty as well. The pair stayed in Buffalo for the next nine years, becoming American citizens in 1928. Gerty later said, "I believe the benefits of two civilizations, a European education followed by the freedom and opportunities of this country, have been essential to whatever contributions I have been able to make in science."

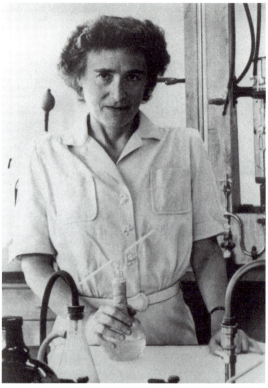

At Washington University School of Medicine in St. Louis, Gerty Cori and her husband, Carl, worked out the steps and compounds in the cycle by which the body metabolizes carbohydrates, food substances that provide energy. Cori also discovered the biochemical defects involved in certain inherited diseases. The Coris won the 1947 Nobel Prize in physiology or medicine.
(Courtesy the Bernard Becker Medical Library, Washington University School of Medicine)

One project the Coris worked on concerned the way cancerous tumors use carbohydrates. Carbohydrates are sugars and starches, the chief foods that living things break down to get energy. This project interested the pair in the way the healthy body uses carbohydrates, and through years of painstaking experiments they worked out the basic cycle of carbohydrate use in the bodies of mammals. They first described this cycle, which came to be called the Cori cycle, in 1929. The two forms of carbohydrate in the Cori cycle are glucose, a simple sugar, and glycogen, the "sugar maker," a complex carbohydrate made of hundreds of glucose molecules bonded together. Glucose is the form that the muscles break down to get energy. Glycogen is the form in which carbohydrate energy is stored.

The Cori cycle goes into action every time a human or animal exercises. When a lion runs, for instance, its muscles break down glycogen stored there to form glucose. They then break down most of the glucose into carbon dioxide and water, releasing energy in the process. A little unused energy remains in the form of a chemical called lactic acid. The blood carries the lactic acid to the liver, which converts it back into glycogen and stores it there. When a new supply of energy is needed, glycogen from the liver is released into the blood as glucose. The muscles take up this glucose, convert it to glycogen once more, and use it again. The supply of energy is constantly replenished by carbohydrates from food.

Although the Buffalo institute gave the Coris a free hand with their work, they decided that they should work for an institution more devoted to basic research. The problem was finding a place that would hire both of them. Most universities at the time had rules forbidding two family members to work for the same department or, often, even the same university. In practice this meant that a man would be hired but his wife would not or, at best, would have to work for little or no pay as his "assistant." One university interviewer even pulled Gerty aside and told her that it was un-American for a man to work with his wife.

The Coris refused to be separated because they knew what a good professional as well as personal team they made. Their collaboration was so close that, as a *New York Post* reporter wrote: "It is hard to tell where the work of one leaves off and that of the other begins." They had different strengths that enhanced each other. William Daughaday, who worked in their lab, said, "Carl was the visionary. Gerty was the lab genius." In his Nobel Prize acceptance speech, Carl Cori said that his

and Gerty's "efforts have been . . . complementary, and one without the other would not have gone as far as in combination."

Finally, in 1931, the Coris found a university that would take both of them—though not at equal rank. The Washington University School of Medicine in St. Louis, Missouri, accepted Carl as a professor and head of its pharmacology department. It hired Gerty only as a research associate, a sort of glorified lab technician, for a fifth of the pay offered to Carl. She was not made an associate professor until 1944. She became a full professor in 1947, the same year she won the Nobel Prize.

At Washington University the Coris continued their work on the carbohydrate cycle, figuring out the details of the process they had described in broad outline before. They discovered several key compounds involved in the cycle, including glucose-1-phosphate, a new form of glucose that came to be called the Cori ester. They first found this substance in 1936. The Cori ester is the product of the first step in the process of breaking down glycogen to form glucose and, at the other end of the cycle, the last step in converting glucose to glycogen.

Beginning in 1938, the Coris focused their attention on a poorly understood group of substances called enzymes. Enzymes make most chemical reactions in the body take place. One enzyme the pair discovered was phosphorylase, which tears the bonds of the glycogen molecule apart to form glucose-1-phosphate. The Coris also found out how enzymes' structure helps them turn particular reactions on and off.

The year 1947 brought both disaster and triumph to the Coris. Some of the bad news came first. While on a hiking trip with Carl in the Rocky Mountains, Gerty Cori fainted. Medical tests showed that her blood contained far fewer red blood cells than it should. At the time, no one knew what caused this anemia.

The triumph came while the Coris were still worrying about this incident. On October 24, 1947, they learned that they had been awarded shares of that year's Nobel Prize in physiology or medicine for their discovery of the enzymes involved in the carbohydrate cycle. Arne Tiselius, vice president of the Nobel Foundation, said, "The intricate pattern of chemical reactions in the living cells, where everything appears to depend on everything else, requires for its study an unusual intuition and a technical skill of which the Coris are masters." They shared the prize with Bernardo A. Houssay, a researcher from Argentina who had done research on a hormone involved in the same cycle. Gerty Cori was the third woman, and the first American woman, to win a Nobel Prize in science.

Before the Coris left for Sweden, they learned that Gerty had an incurable disease of the bone marrow, which makes all the cells in the blood. Over the next 10 years the illness slowly became worse, sapping her strength and requiring blood transfusions to keep her alive. She continued doing research, however, and even branched out in a new direction. She showed that several rare, inherited diseases that usually killed their victims in early childhood were caused by the lack of certain enzymes in the carbohydrate cycle. Without these enzymes, the body could not break down glycogen, and it accumulated in the liver and other organs with fatal results. This was the first time an inherited disease was shown to be due to the lack of a particular enzyme. A coworker, Herman Kalckar, called Cori's discovery "an unmatched scientific achievement."

Gerty Cori died on October 26, 1957. Her memorial service included the playing of a speech she had made on a recording called *This I Believe*. She said in part, "For a research worker, the unforgotten moments of his life are those rare ones, which come after years of plodding work, when . . . what was dark and chaotic appears in a clear and beautiful light and pattern." Gerty Cori's work revealed many such patterns.

Further Reading

"Cori, Carl F(erdinand); Cori, Gerty T(heresa Radnitz)." *Current Biography Yearbook 1947*. New York: H. W. Wilson, 1947, 135–137.

McGrayne, Sharon Bertsch. *Nobel Prize Women in Science: Their Lives, Struggles, and Momentous Discoveries*. New York: Birch Lane Press, 1993, 93–116.

Opfell, Olga. *The Lady Laureates: Women Who Have Won the Nobel Prize*. Metuchen, N.J.: The Scarecrow Press, 1986, 213–223.

Parascandola, John. "Cori, Gerty Theresa Radnitz." In *Notable American Women: The Modern Period*, edited by Barbara Sicherman and Carol Hurd Green, 165–167. Cambridge, Mass.: The Belknap Press of Harvard University Press, 1980.

Veglahn, Nancy. *Women Scientists*. New York: Facts On File, 1991, 57–65.

✳ CREMER, ERIKA
(1900–1996) *Austrian Chemist and Physicist*

Working in a bombed-out laboratory during World War II, Erika Cremer created the first gas chromatograph, a device still used in laboratories worldwide. Cremer, born in 1900 in Munich, grew up in a family that had included four generations of professors. She obtained her Ph.D. in physical chemistry from the University of Berlin in 1924 and worked with fellow chemist Otto Hahn on some of the experiments that led to the discovery of atomic fission by LISE MEITNER. Universities refused to hire her, however, until labor shortages caused by the war helped her gain a "temporary" teaching post at the University of Innsbruck in Austria.

Beginning around 1940, Cremer became interested in chromatography, a technique first invented by Michael S. Tswett, a Russian scientist, in 1906. Tswett had used it to separate pigments in leaves, which appeared as differently colored bands when he poured them through a column of chalk. Other chemists' reactions were "fairly skeptical and negative" when Cremer claimed that chromatography was a useful way to separate compounds in mixtures, but she persisted. Even though an air raid had damaged the Innsbruck University and research there had officially ceased, Cremer and a coworker, Fritz Prior, constructed the first modern gas chromatograph there during the war. It separated chemicals by their different rates of movement in a stream of compressed gas flowing over the coated walls of a long glass tube.

Cremer continued to develop chromatography at Innsbruck after the war ended. In 1945 she became head of the Institute of Physical Chemistry, but she was not made a professor at the university for another six years. Gas chromatography, the form of chromatography she invented, is used today to measure, for instance, oxygen and other gases in blood and pollution in air. Cremer has been called the "mother of chromatography." She died in 1996.

Further Reading

Aquamarin Documentary Films. "Ein Leben Für die Wissenschaft" (A Life in Science"). Film in German in two parts. Vienna, Austria: Aquamarin Documentary Films, 1998.

Miller, Jane A. "Women in Chemistry." In *Women in Science: Righting the Record*, edited by G. Kass-Simon and Patricia Farnes, 326–327. Bloomington: Indiana University Press, 1990.

✳ CURIE, MARIE (Marya Sklodowka, "Manya")
(1867–1934) *French Physicist and Chemist*

When people are asked to name a woman scientist, the one person sure to be mentioned is Marie Curie. With her husband, Pierre, Curie discovered two chemical elements and proved that atoms, once thought indivisible, could break down. She coined the term *radioactivity* to describe this process. Curie was the first woman to receive a Nobel Prize and the first person to receive two of the prestigious prizes.

Marie Curie was born Marya Sklodowska in Warsaw, Poland, on November 7, 1867. Her parents, Vladislav and Bronislawa Sklodowski, were schoolteachers. Her mother died of tuberculosis when Manya, as she was called, was just nine years old. Russia controlled the part of Poland the Sklodowskis lived in and punished any sign of Polish nationalism, but many Poles, including the Sklo-

dowskis, retained a powerful love of their culture. In avoiding Russian punishment, Manya learned early to hide her feelings.

Manya and her older sister Bronya helped each other gain an education. From 1885 to 1891, Manya worked as a governess, or live-in tutor, for the children of well-to-do families. Her salary paid Bronya's tuition at the Sorbonne in Paris, the nearest place where a woman could train to be a physician. Once she obtained her medical degree, Bronya sent for Manya.

Arriving in 1891, 24-year-old Manya changed her first name to its French form, Marie, and began studying science and mathematics at the University of Paris. In spite of Bronya's financial help, Marie at times had so little money that she had to live in an attic with no heat and survive on only bread, butter, and tea. Her family later jokingly called this her "heroic period." Still, she wrote: "This life, painful from certain points of view, . . . gave me a very precious sense of liberty and independence." Living became a little easier in 1893, when she won a fellowship that paid most of her expenses. By then she had earned the equivalent of a master's degree in physics, and the next year she earned a similar degree in mathematics.

In 1894, Sklodowska met Pierre Curie, the laboratory director of the Municipal School of Industrial Physics and Chemistry in Paris. Curie, eight years older than Sklodowska, was already recognized as an important physicist. He persuaded Sklowdowska to stay in France, rather than returning to Poland as she had originally planned, and join him in a life of research. They married in 1895, just after Pierre had earned his doctorate and obtained a position as a full professor. Their first daughter, Irène (later IRÈNE JOLIOT-CURIE), was born in 1897 and a second, Eve, in 1904.

French physicist Henri Becquerel discovered in 1896 that pitchblende, a mineral that contained uranium, gave off mysterious radiation that darkened photographic film and made nearby air conduct electricity. For her doctoral research, Marie Curie set out to learn whether any other elements gave off similar radiation. Within a few days of starting her research, she found that thorium also made air conduct measurable electricity.

Curie next measured the amount of electricity produced by different compounds of uranium and of thorium. To her surprise, she found that the amount of radiation depended only on the amount of uranium or thorium in the compounds. In a stroke of genius, she concluded that the radiation arose, not from the molecules that formed the compounds, but from the elements' atoms. If atoms

Working in France with her husband, Pierre, Marie Curie, probably the best known of all women scientists, codiscovered two radioactive elements and helped to found the study of radioactivity. The Curies shared the 1903 Nobel Prize in physics with Henri Becquerel, and in 1911, after Pierre's death, Marie won a solo Nobel Prize in chemistry as well. (Courtesy Radium Institute and Emilio Segrè Visual Archives, American Institute of Physics)

could give off energy in the form of radiation, then they could change. This was a revolutionary idea.

When Curie tested minerals that contained uranium or thorium, she discovered that pitchblende gave off four times as much radiation as would be expected from the amount of uranium it contained. She guessed that the mineral must contain another, unknown element that could also give off radiation, a power she called radioactivity. She published a paper in April 1898 announcing the radioactivity of thorium and her guess that an even more strongly radioactive element awaited discovery.

At this point Pierre Curie abandoned his own physics projects and joined Marie's research. Later in 1898, the Curies isolated a substance from pitchblende that was 400 times more radioactive than uranium. Marie called it polonium in honor of her native country. They soon found a second element even more radioactive than polonium, which they named radium.

The Curies' next task was to purify the new elements. Lacking a proper laboratory, they did the work in a dilapidated shed with a dirt floor, a leaky roof, no heat, and poor ventilation. A visiting German chemist described it as "a cross between a stable and a potato cellar." They had to break down tons of pitchblende to extract a tiny amount of radium. "Sometimes," Marie wrote, "I had to spend a whole day mixing a boiling mass with a heavy iron rod nearly as large as myself. I would be broken with fatigue at the day's end." And yet, she concluded, "it was in this miserable old shed that the best and happiest years of our life were spent." The Curies loved to go back to their shed after dark to see the firefly-like bluish glow from their tubes of radioactive compounds. Describing one such night, Marie Curie wrote that she would "remember forever this evening of glowworms, this magic."

Finally, in September 1902, the Curies produced 0.0035 ounce (0.1 g) of pure radium chloride. Marie described her research in her doctoral thesis in June 1903, and her examining committee told her that her paper was the greatest contribution to science ever made by a doctoral dissertation. That fall she won a far more important honor, the 1903 Nobel Prize in physics. Pierre Curie insisted that Marie share the prize with him and Henri Becquerel.

Radium caught the public's fancy, and the Curies found themselves famous. Much more important to their minds, the Sorbonne hired Pierre as a professor in 1904 and promised him a decent laboratory. Sadly, he was never to see it. Crossing a rainy Paris street on April 19, 1906, he absentmindedly walked in front of a horse-drawn wagon. It knocked him down, and one of its wheels passed over his head, killing him instantly. When Marie heard the news, her daughter Eve wrote later, "a cape of solitude and secrecy fell upon her shoulders forever."

With two young daughters to support, Marie Curie pushed aside her grief and, within weeks of Pierre's death, convinced the Sorbonne to hire her as an assistant lecturer—its first woman professor. (She was made a full professor of physics in 1908.) She then set out to uphold her reputation as a scientist by refuting critics' claim that radium was not really an element. After four years of hard work, she produced radium as a pure metal.

The year 1911 found Curie in newspaper headlines again when the wife of Paul Langevin, a physicist friend of the Curies, published love letters (possibly misinterpreted or faked) that she said Langevin had exchanged with Curie. Tabloids called the former "Vestal Virgin of Radium" a homewrecker. The scandal depressed Curie so much that she considered returning to Poland or even killing herself. More happily, on November 4 other headlines announced that Curie had won a second Nobel Prize, this one in chemistry, for her discovery and isolation of radium and polonium.

Curie helped her adopted country during World War I by organizing a fleet of wagons, which came to be called "little Curies," to carry portable X-ray equipment to battle sites. They helped doctors set fractures or extract bullets on the spot rather than having to transport soldiers to hospitals. She eventually opened 200 X-ray stations that examined over a million soldiers.

Curie's lifelong dream of a research institute devoted to radioactivity was fulfilled in 1918, when the Radium Institute opened in Paris. At first it had no money to buy equipment or radioactive materials, but here, for once, publicity came to Curie's rescue. In 1920 she became friends with an American magazine writer named Marie (Missy) Meloney, and Meloney arranged a fund-raising tour of the United States for her. At the end of it, the Radium Institute had the $100,000 it needed to buy one precious gram of radium. A second tour in 1929 brought money for another gram of radium to be sent to Poland, where Curie also established a research institute.

Marie Curie suffered increasingly from ailments caused by her years of exposure to radiation, and one of them, blood cancer, finally killed her on July 4, 1934. Her life had illustrated the advice she once gave to others: "We must have perseverance and above all confidence in ourselves. We must believe that we are gifted for something, and that this thing, at whatever cost, must be attained."

Further Reading

Curie, Eve (tr. Vincent Sheehan). *Madame Curie.* New York: Doubleday, 1937.

Curie, Marie (tr. Charlotte and Vernon Kellogg). *Pierre Curie.* New York: Macmillan, 1923.

Pflaum, Rosalynd. *Grand Obsession: Madame Curie and Her World.* New York: Doubleday, 1989.

Quinn, Susan. *Marie Curie: A Life.* New York: Simon & Schuster, 1995.

Reid, Robert. *Marie Curie.* New York: New American Library, 1975.

D

✳ **DAUBECHIES, INGRID**
(1954–) *Belgian/American Mathematician*

Ingrid Daubechies has worked on mathematical constructs called wavelets which are used, among other things, to solve the problem of separating a signal—useful information—from surrounding noise, or random data. She was born in Houthalen, Belgium, on August 17, 1954. She earned a bachelor's degree in physics from the Free University of Brussels in 1975, followed by a Ph.D. in 1980, and remained at that university, rising to the rank of tenured assistant professor, until 1987. In 1984 she won the Luis Empain Prize for Physics, given once every five years to a Belgian scientist on the basis of work done before age 29. Her early work was on the application of mathematics to physics, especially to quantum mechanics, the laws that govern physics at very small (atomic) scales.

Daubechies's career changed direction in 1985, when she first became interested in wavelets. She was thinking about ways in which to reconcile different requirements for wavelet constructions at the time she attended a conference in Montreal,

Canada, in February 1987. She had hoped to tour the city, but it was too cold to go out much. "I was kind of forced to stay in my hotel room—and calculate," she told *Discover* magazine writer Hans Christian von Baeyer in 1995. "It was a period of incredibly intense concentration." Even her wedding, scheduled to take place in a few weeks, took a back seat to the ideas she was having about ways to process information.

Nineteenth-century mathematician and physicist Jean-Baptiste Fourier worked out a method of breaking down signals into groups of regular, repeating waves in order to analyze them, and scientists have used his method ever since. Unfortunately, this method, which determines the pitch of a note, cannot at the same time determine when it was struck. Compromise techniques must be used if someone wants to have both types of information, and none of these has been completely satisfactory. During her chilly stay in Canada, Ingrid Daubechies found a way to construct wavelets that has proved particularly effective in helping computers solve this type of problem. Her method has set wavelets to work in astronomy, physics, computer science, and more.

For instance, it can be used to analyze the complex patterns in air streaming over a plane's wing.

Daubechies moved to the United States soon after her discovery about wavelets and has since become a naturalized citizen. From 1987 to 1994 she worked primarily at AT&T Bell Laboratories. She then came to Princeton University, where she is now a full professor. She was a fellow of the John D. and Catherine T. MacArthur Foundation from 1992 to 1997 and has won two prizes from the American Mathematical Society. She was elected to the American Academy of Arts and Sciences in 1993 and the National Academy of Sciences in 1998. She continues to research wavelets and their applications, for instance working out a program to apply them to signals from biomedical devices.

Further Reading

von Baeyer, Hans Christian. "Waves of the Future." *Discover*, May 1995, 69–74.

✳ DICK, GLADYS ROWENA HENRY
(1881–1963) *American Microbiologist*

Working with her husband, Gladys Dick discovered the microbe that caused a serious childhood disease called scarlet fever. The Dicks also developed a test and a treatment for the illness.

Gladys Rowena Henry was born in Pawnee City, Nebraska, on December 18, 1881, but grew up in Lincoln. She became interested in medicine while attending the University of Nebraska, from which she graduated with a B.S. in 1900, but her mother, Azelia, forbade her to go to medical school. Henry taught high school biology and took graduate courses at the university until she finally wore down her mother's resistance. She enrolled at Johns Hopkins Medical School in 1903, received her M.D. in 1907, and remained at Hopkins for several years afterward.

Henry's mother moved to Chicago, and Henry followed her there in 1911. She began doing medical research for the University of Chicago and became interested in scarlet fever, a disease named

for the red rash that broke out on its victims' skins. On January 28, 1914, she married George Frederick Dick, whose research specialty was also scarlet fever. The Dicks continued their work at the John R. McCormick Memorial Institute for Infectious Diseases, named after a child who had died of the disease.

Scarlet fever was contagious, so scientists knew it must be caused by a microorganism, but no one had been able to discover which one. In 1923, after 10 years of struggle, the Dicks proved that the illness was caused by a bacterium called hemolytic streptococcus. They went on to show that the bacteria did most of their damage by means of a toxin, or poisonous substance. The Dicks used this toxin to create a test that quickly identified people with the disease. They also developed an antitoxin, which was the first successful treatment for scarlet fever.

The Dicks received the Mickle Prize of the University of Toronto in 1926 and the Cameron Prize of the University of Edinburgh in 1933 for their discoveries. They were considered for a medicine Nobel Prize in 1925, but no prize was given that year. Their fame turned to notoriety when they took out patents on their toxin and antitoxin in 1924 and 1926, causing accusations of greed. They claimed that they made no money from the products and took out the patents simply to guarantee their quality.

In her later years, Gladys Dick did research on polio. She also helped to found the Cradle Society, probably the first professional adoption agency in the United States. Dick died of a stroke on August 21, 1963.

Further Reading

Bailey, Brooke. *The Remarkable Lives of 100 Women Healers and Scientists.* Holbrook, Mass.: Bob Adams, 1994, 52–53.

Rubin, Lewis P. "Dick, Gladys Henry Rowena." In *Notable American Women: The Modern Period,* edited by Barbara Sicherman and Carol Hurd Green, 191–192. Cambridge, Mass.: The Belknap Press of Harvard University Press, 1980.

✴ DRESSELHAUS, MILDRED SPIEWAK
(1930–) *American Physicist and Engineer*

Mildred Dresselhaus raised herself from poverty to become head of the Massachusetts Institute of Technology's Materials Science Laboratory and one of the university's 12 Institute Professors. She was born Mildred Spiewak on November 11, 1930, in a Brooklyn slum. Her parents were immigrants with no money or education, but they taught their two children that the United States was a land of opportunity. Dresselhaus says, "I found out that opportunities did present themselves [but] one had to take the initiative to find these opportunities and exploit them."

Mildred realized that education was the key to a better life, and she determined to enter Hunter College High School, which prepared talented girls in New York City for college. (The school later become co-ed.) That meant passing a rigorous entrance exam, a task that seemed hopeless. She studied in every spare moment, however, and not only passed but made a perfect score in mathematics. "Passing the entrance examination to Hunter College High School is the greatest achievement of my life," Dresselhaus says.

Mildred Spiewak went on to Hunter College, which offered free tuition. At first she planned to become an elementary school teacher, but her physics teacher, later Nobel winner ROSALYN YALOW, steered her toward that subject. After Spiewak graduated in 1951, Yalow helped her obtain a Fulbright Fellowship to study for a year at Britain's Cambridge University.

Spiewak went to Radcliffe for her master's degree in physics, which she earned in 1953, and to the University of Chicago for her Ph.D. She decided to specialize in the physics of solids. For her thesis project she studied how magnetic fields affect superconductors, unusual materials that conduct electricity without converting any of it to heat. She married fellow physicist Gene Dresselhaus soon after both received their Ph.D.s in 1958.

After two years at Cornell University and the birth of their first child, the Dresselhauses moved to the Lincoln Laboratory at the Massachusetts

Physicist and engineer Mildred Dresselhaus worked her way up from poverty to become an Institute Professor, the highest faculty designation, at the Massachusetts Institute of Technology. She has explored the properties of unusual materials ranging from semiconductors to buckyballs.
(Courtesy Donna Coveney/MIT News Service)

Institute of Technology in 1960. Mildred switched her research to semiconductors, her husband's specialty. Semiconductors, crystalline materials such as silicon that can be treated so that they conduct electricity somewhat the way metals do, are used in transistors and computer chips. As she had with superconductors, Mildred studied how magnetic fields affected these materials. She also studied so-called semimetals—elements such as arsenic, graphite (a form of carbon), and bismuth, which act like semiconductors in some ways and superconductors in others.

Dresselhaus says that her seven years at the Lincoln Laboratory were "the most productive years of my research career," even though she had three more children during this time. A live-in nanny cared for the children in the daytime, and the Dresselhauses spent time with them in the evenings. "My children have gained more than they have lost because of my professional career," Dresselhaus believes.

In 1967 the Dresselhauses began working for MIT's National Magnet Laboratory, where Mildred continued her research on the effects of magnetic fields on semiconductors. She became a full professor in the university's electrical engineering department a year later. She was associate head of the Electronic Science and Engineering department between 1972 and 1974, and between 1973 and 1985 she was the Abby Rockefeller Mauze Professor, an endowed position for a woman professor interested in furthering the careers of women undergraduates. She was director of the university's Center of Materials Science and Engineering from 1977 to 1983. Since 1985 she has been one of 12 Institute Professors, MIT's highest faculty designation—the first woman given this honor. She has also been a visiting professor at universities from Brazil to Japan.

Dresselhaus has won many awards for her work, including the Hunter College Hall of Fame Award (1972), the Society of Women Engineers' Achievement Award (1977), and the National Medal of Science (1990). She was the second woman to be made a member of the National Academy of Engineers. In 1984 she became the first woman president of the American Physical Society, and in 1998 she became president of the American Association for the Advancement of Science.

Dresselhaus's work today involves another unusual material—carbon molecules made up of 60 atoms arranged in a structure like a soccer ball. These molecules have been nicknamed "buckyballs" because they also resemble the dome-shaped houses popularized by architect Buckminster Fuller in the 1950s. Buckyballs, part of a larger class of similarly shaped carbon molecules called fullerenes, may prove useful for making industrial diamonds and materials that conduct light. In this work, as in her other research, Dresselhaus has been more interested in discovering the qualities of materials than in developing practical uses for them. "We tend to be . . . 10 years in advance of commercial applications," she told writer Iris Noble.

Mildred Dresselhaus has made a point of mentoring young women scientists, just as Rosalyn Yalow once did for her. She helps them find or make the opportunities they need, the way she herself did. "If you go into science and engineering," she tells them, "you go in to succeed."

Further Reading

Dresselhaus, Mildred. "Electrical Engineer: Mildred S. Dresselhaus." In *Women and Success: The Anatomy of Achievement*, edited by Ruth B. Kundsin, 38–43. New York: William Morrow, 1973.

Noble, Iris. *Contemporary Women Scientists of America.* New York: Julian Messner, 1979, 138–152.

Veglahn, Nancy. *Women Scientists.* New York: Facts On File, 1991, 117–127.

Zinberg, Dorothy. "Mildred Dresselhaus." In *Beyond the Glass Ceiling: Forty Women Whose Ideas Shape the Modern World*, edited by Sian Griffiths, 92–98. Manchester, England: Manchester University Press, 1996.

✳ DUPLAIX, NICOLE
(1942–) *French/American Zoologist and Ecologist*

Nicole Duplaix drifted down piranha-infested rivers in South America to study endangered giant river otters, which local people called "big water dogs." Born in 1942 to Georges and Lily Duplaix, wealthy artists and writers, she grew up in New York, Paris, and Palm Beach, Florida. "My childhood was marvelous, and I was spoiled rotten," she says.

In 1964 and 1965, while studying at Manhattanville College, Duplaix did volunteer work at the Bronx Zoo. The zoo's curator of mammals, "an otter freak," introduced her to these playful, often endangered sea and river animals. She studied animal ecology at the University of Paris in 1965 and 1966, earning the equivalent of a master's degree.

After four years in London as the wife of a commodities broker, Duplaix divorced and returned to the Bronx Zoo in 1974. Here she worked out her plan for studying giant Brazilian river otters. Once common throughout much of South America, these 60-pound, 6-foot animals had become rare or extinct through most of their range. They were still common only in Suriname, a country on the northeast coast of South America.

Arriving in Suriname in 1976, Duplaix traveled down rivers with her dog and a crew of Bush Negroes, descendants of escaped slaves. Impressed by her ability to catch fish and repair their canoe's cranky outboard motor, the crew's leader once said, "That Mrs. Otter knows everything!"

Duplaix finally found a large population of otters on Kapoeri Creek, near Suriname's western boundary. She identified 249 different animals during over a year of study. Among other things, she learned that each extended otter family claimed a territory about a mile long. The family cleared semicircular "campsites" on the riverbank and visited them repeatedly, marking them with a distinctive scent to warn other otters away.

Duplaix's discoveries became the subject of her doctoral thesis for the University of Paris, which she presented in 1980. They also helped officials in Suriname plan how to preserve the river otters. The otters remain endangered by development projects, however.

Duplaix worked as a fund-raiser and speaker for the World Wildlife Fund during the 1980s. In the early 1990s she lived in Florida, but as of 1998 she had moved back to Paris.

Further Reading

Duplaix, Nicole. "Giant Otters: 'Big Water Dogs' in Peril." *National Geographic*, July 1980, 130–142.

LaBastille, Anne. *Women and Wilderness.* San Francisco: Sierra Club Books, 1980, 263–273.

E

 EARLE, SYLVIA ALICE
(1935–) *American Botanist and Marine Biologist*

Sylvia Earle has spent more than 6,000 hours underwater, including living in an undersea "habitat" for two weeks, and has dived deeper than any other solo diver. Admiring colleagues call her "Her Royal Deepness."

Sylvia was born on August 30, 1935, in Gibbstown, New Jersey, and spent her childhood on a farm near Camden. Her mother, Alice, a former nurse, taught Sylvia and her brother and sister to love nature. "I think I always knew I would work [as a scientist] with plants and animals," Earle once told an interviewer. Her favorite spot was a pond in her backyard.

In 1948, when Sylvia was 12 years old, her father, Lewis, an electrical engineer, moved the family to Dunedin, Florida. Now the "pond" in Sylvia's backyard was the Gulf of Mexico. She made her first ocean dive when she was 17 and "practically had to be pried out of the water."

Earle earned a B.S. from Florida State University in 1955 and an M.S. in botany from Duke University in 1956. She married a zoologist named John Taylor around 1957 (they divorced in 1966) and had two children, Elizabeth and John (Richie). She began full-time undersea research in 1964. Among other things, she collected algae (seaweeds and related plants) in the Gulf of Mexico for her Ph.D. project at Duke, which she finished in 1966. Unlike most marine biologists of the time, she dived to study undersea life in its own habitat rather than dragging it up to the deck of a ship in nets.

In 1970, Earle lived underwater for two weeks as part of a NASA-sponsored project called Tektite. The name came from a type of glassy meteoric rock often found on the seafloor. She headed a crew consisting of four other women scientists. Their "habitat," 50 feet under the Caribbean Sea, consisted of two tanks connected by a passageway. It included not only beds and a kitchen but even hot showers and television. The women spent up to 10 hours a day in the water, studying ocean life.

The group did nothing that all-male Tektite crews had not also done, but they emerged into a blizzard of publicity, hailed as "aquababes." They also received the Conservation Service Award, the Department of the Interior's highest civilian award. The fuss irritated Earle, who saw it as reverse discrimination, but it also made her realize that, as a woman scientist, she had a unique opportunity to reach and educate the public.

Ironically, a greater achievement of Earle's won much less attention. In September 1979 she donned a heavy plastic and metal "Jim suit" (named after a diver who tested an early version of it), a sort of underwater space suit, and dived 1,250 feet into the water near Hawaii. A submarine lowered and then released her. No other diver had gone this deep without being attached to a cable. *Current Biography* called this "possibly the most daring dive ever made." Earle remained submerged for two and a half hours under water pressure of 600 pounds per square inch, observing such creatures as "an 18-inch-long shark with glowing green eyes" and "a lantern fish . . . with lights along its sides, looking like a miniature passenger liner."

While preparing for the Jim suit dive, Earle met British engineer Graham Hawkes, who had designed the suit. The two found that they shared a love of diving and a desire to improve diving technology. They formed two companies, Deep Ocean Technology and Deep Ocean Engineering, in 1981. One of their products was a one-person submersible called *Deep Rover*, which Earle piloted down to about 3,000 feet in 1985, the deepest any solo diver had gone. The couple also married in 1986. (This was Earle's third marriage; between 1966 and 1975 she was married to Giles Mead and had a third child, Gale.) Earle and Hawkes have since divorced. In 1992, Earle founded her own undersea technology company, Deep Ocean Exploration and Research (DOER). DOER consults on, operates, and designs manned and robotic underwater systems.

Earle took part in many research projects during the 1970s and 1980s, including diving with humpback whales as part of a study done by Roger and KATHARINE PAYNE. She was also curator of phycology (the study of algae, or seaweeds) at the California Academy of Sciences in San Francisco from 1979 to 1986.

During her long career, Earle has led more than 50 oceanic expeditions and won many awards for her work. They include the John M. Olguin Marine Environment Award (1998), the Kilby Award (1997), the Director's Award of the Natural Re-

sources Council (1992), and the Society of Women Geographers Gold Medal (1990). She is a fellow of the American Association for the Advancement of Science, the Marine Technology Society, the California Academy of Sciences, the World Academy of Arts and Sciences, and the Explorers Club.

Earle served on the President's Advisory Committee on Oceans and Atmosphere from 1980 to 1984. Then, in 1990, President George Bush chose her to be the chief scientist of the National Oceanic and Atmospheric Administration (NOAA). She was the first woman to hold this post. She hoped to use the position to push for ocean conservation projects, "put[ting] the O back in NOAA," but the Gulf War broke out just after her appointment, and she spent most of her time assessing the damage done to Persian Gulf sea life by the oil spills and fires in Kuwait. She resigned from NOAA in February 1992, saying, "I think I can be more effective [in preserving the oceans] if I am on the loose."

In 1998, Earle's major project was the Sustainable Sea Expeditions, a five-year study of the National Marine Sanctuaries sponsored by the National Geographic Society and funded by the Goldman Foundation. Earle hopes in future to explore the deepest parts of the sea, including the Marianas Trench, near Guam, which contains the deepest water in the world.

Meanwhile, Earle speaks and writes to warn people about overfishing, pollution, and other human activities that threaten ocean life. "We're strip-mining the sea," she says. "If we don't wake up soon to the damage we are doing, it may be too late."

Further Reading

"Earle, Sylvia A." *Current Biography Yearbook 1992*. New York: H. W. Wilson, 1992, 174–178.

Earle, Sylvia A. *Sea Change: A Message of the Oceans*. New York: Putnam, 1995.

———. and Al Giddings. *Exploring the Deep Frontier*. Washington, D.C.: National Geographic Society, 1980.

White, Wallace. "Her Deepness." *The New Yorker*, July 3, 1989, 41–65.

✳ EASTWOOD, ALICE

(1859–1953) *American Botanist*

Continuing the work of KATHARINE BRANDEGEE, Alice Eastwood was curator of the herbarium, or dried plant collection, of the California Academy of Sciences in San Francisco for 57 years. Alice was born on January 19, 1859, in Toronto, Canada. Her mother died when she was six, and she and her brother and sister were raised by relatives until 1873, when Colin, her father, sent for them to join him at the store he then ran in Denver, Colorado. Her schooling was often interrupted by work, so she graduated from East Denver High School only in 1879, when she was 20.

Eastwood began teaching at the high school, but her happiest times were the summers, when she climbed into the Rockies to collect plants. By 1890 income from lucky investments let her devote all her time to botany. She visited the California Academy and became friends with Katharine Brandegee, then its curator of botany. In 1892, Brandegee persuaded her to move to San Francisco and become joint curator. When Brandegee moved to San Diego a year later, Eastwood took over her position. In addition to improving the organization of the plant collection,

Alice Eastwood succeeded Katharine Brandegee as curator of the herbarium (dried plant collection) of the California Academy of Sciences in San Francisco in 1893. She helped to save the most valuable specimens during the 1906 earthquake and to rebuild the collection afterward, eventually adding over 340,000 specimens to it. Here she gathers specimens of a type of grass named after her, *Festuca eastwoodae*.

(Courtesy Special Collections, California Academy of Sciences)

Eastwood personally added many specimens to it, sometimes hiking 20 miles a day through the Sierras with her heavy wooden plant presses on her back.

On April 18, 1906, a huge earthquake shook San Francisco, followed by a citywide fire. Eastwood found the academy building partly in ruins and the fire approaching. She had stored her most valuable plants in her sixth-floor office, but the building's staircase had collapsed. As she wrote later in *Science* magazine, she and a friend "went up chiefly by holding on to the iron railing and putting our feet between the rungs. Porter helped me to tie up the plant types, and we lowered them to the floor . . . by ropes and strings." She got out with her plants just as flames reached the building.

For the next six years the academy had no home, so Eastwood visited herbaria in the East and Europe. She rejoined the academy in 1912, when it built a new headquarters in Golden Gate Park. She spent the rest of her life rebuilding and improving its plant collection, adding over 340,000 specimens to it. Of the work represented by the many plants lost in the 1906 fire, she said only, "It was a joy to me when I did it, and I can still have the same joy in starting it again."

Eastwood finally retired in 1949, when she was 90. The next year, the Eighth International Botanical Congress in Sweden recognized her lifetime of work by electing her its honorary president. As a mark of its respect, the group seated her in a wooden chair once used by Carl Linnaeus, the 18th-century Swedish scientist who had designed the system of naming plants and animals that all biologists use. Eastwood died on October 30, 1953.

Further Reading

Bonta, Marcia Myers. *Women in the Field: America's Pioneering Women Naturalists.* College Station Tex.: Texas A&M University Press, 1991, 93–102.

Hollingworth, Buckner. *Her Garden Was Her Delight.* New York: Macmillan, 1962.

Wilson, Carol. *Alice Eastwood's Wonderland: The Adventures of a Botanist.* San Francisco: California Academy of Sciences, 1955.

✳ EDDY, BERNICE
(1903–)   *American Medical Microbiologist*

Bernice Eddy had a knack for discovering facts that her superiors didn't want to know or have others know. She warned of, but was unable to prevent, a disaster that struck in the early days of making polio vaccines. She also codiscovered the first virus shown to cause cancer in mammals.

Bernice was born in Glendale, West Virginia, in 1903. She grew up in nearby Auburn. Her father, Nathan Eddy, was a physician. Bernice went to college in Marietta, Ohio, where her mother moved after her father's death, and graduated in 1924. She earned a master's degree in 1925 and a Ph.D. in 1927 in bacteriology from the University of Cincinnati.

After remaining at the University of Cincinnati for several years, Eddy joined the Public Health Service in 1930. Five years later she transferred to the Biologics Control Division of the National Institutes of Health (NIH) in Bethesda, Maryland. This department of NIH checks the quality of vaccines that the government distributes.

Soon after she joined NIH, Eddy married Jerald G. Wooley, a physician who worked for the Public Health Service. They had two daughters, Bernice and Sarah. Unfortunately, Wooley died while the girls were still young. Eddy's mother helped her raise the children.

Beginning at the start of World War II and continuing for 16 years, Eddy checked army influenza vaccines. She became chief of the flu virus vaccine testing unit in 1944. In 1952 she also began doing research on possible treatments for polio. She received an NIH Superior Accomplishment Award in 1953 for this work.

In 1954, Eddy was asked to perform safety tests on batches of a killed-virus vaccine for polio that Jonas Salk had just invented. A huge national program using the vaccine was about to begin, and Eddy and her staff had to work around the clock. "We had eighteen monkeys," Eddy said later. "We inoculated these monkeys with each vaccine [batch] that came in. And we started getting paralyzed monkeys." This meant that some of the virus in the vaccine was still able to cause disease. Alarmed, Eddy told her supervisors about her results, but they ignored her and went ahead with the vaccination program. Shortly afterward, live virus in a few batches of the vaccine gave polio to about 200 children.

Eddy was taken off polio research and assigned to test a vaccine that was supposed to prevent colds. Meanwhile, she began working with fellow NIH scientist SARAH STEWART on a virus that Stewart had discovered, which seemed to cause leukemia (a blood cell cancer) in mice. Eddy worked out a way to grow the virus dependably in the laboratory.

Eddy and Stewart began publishing papers about their virus in 1957, reporting that it produced a bizarre collection of tumors in every animal that received it. They named it the SE polyoma virus, SE for Stewart and Eddy and polyoma meaning "many tumors." Viruses that caused cancer in birds had been known, but polyoma was one of the first viruses shown to cause tumors in mammals and the first to cause the disease in a wide range of animals. "It was a major, major discovery," says NIH's Alan Rabson.

Both the cold vaccine and the polio vaccine contained viruses that were grown in monkey kidney cells in the laboratory. Around 1959, Eddy noticed that the monkey cells sometimes died for no obvious reason. She suspected that they were being killed by an unknown virus. When she injected ground-up monkey cells into newborn hamsters, the animals developed tumors, suggesting that the virus could cause cancer.

Once again Bernice Eddy had disturbing news for her superiors. On July 6, 1969, she told her boss, Joseph Smadel, about the hamster tumors and suggested that steps be taken to keep the virus out of future lots of vaccine. Smadel did not want to hear that vaccines already in widespread use might contain a cancer-causing virus. He dismissed the tumors as mere "lumps."

Undaunted, Eddy described her experiments with the mystery virus at a meeting of the New York Cancer Society in the fall of 1960. Smadel heard about her speech and telephoned her in a fury. "I never saw anybody so mad," Eddy said later. Smadel ordered her not to speak in public again without clearing the contents of her speeches with him.

Shortly afterward another researcher, Maurice Hilleman, reported the same discovery Eddy had made. He called the virus SV40 (the 40th simian, or monkey, virus to be discovered). It proved to be very similar to the polyoma virus that Eddy and Stewart had described. Fortunately, it did not appear to cause cancer in humans.

During her remaining years at NIH, Bernice Eddy was pushed into smaller and smaller laboratories and denied permission to attend professional meetings and publish papers. She continued her work as best she could until her retirement in 1973, at age 70. She received several awards at or after the time of her retirement, including a Special Citation from the secretary of the Department of Health, Education, and Welfare in 1973 and the NIH Director's Award in 1977. Her biographer, Elizabeth O'Hern, writes of her: "Tenacious under siege, she maintained a steady course and suffered harassment with remarkably good grace."

Further Reading

O'Hern, Elizabeth. *Profiles of Pioneer Women Scientists.* Washington, D.C.: Acropolis Books, 1985, 151–160.
Shorter, Edward. *The Health Century.* New York: Doubleday, 1987, 68–69, 195–204.

✳ EDINGER, JOHANNA GABRIELLE OTTELIE ("Tilly")
(1897–1967) *German/American Paleontologist*

Tilly Edinger was the first person to make a systematic study of the brains of long-extinct animals. She was born Johanna Gabrielle Ottelie Edinger on November 13, 1897, in Frankfurt, Germany. Her father, Ludwig, was a wealthy medical researcher who compared the brain structure of different animals. Anna, her mother, was active in social causes. Tilly, as she was called, surely must have gotten her interest in the brain from her father, but he did not believe in careers for women and did not encourage her.

Edinger studied at the universities of Heidelberg and Munich from 1916 to 1918 and then at the University of Frankfurt, from which she received a doctorate in 1921. Unlike her father, who examined the brains of kinds of animals now living, Edinger studied fossils. She worked at the university for six years as a research assistant in paleontology.

In 1927, Edinger became curator of the vertebrate collection at the Senckenberg Museum in Frankfurt. Her first book, *Die Fossilen Gehirne* (Fossil Brains), was published two years later. Edinger essentially invented the field of paleoneurology, the study of fossil brains. Brains themselves are too soft to form fossils, but she discovered that plaster casts of the inside of fossil skulls revealed the shape of the long-vanished organs because mammals' brains fit very tightly against their skulls.

Because Tilly Edinger was Jewish, her quiet days in Frankfurt ended in 1933, when the violently anti-Semitic Nazis took control of Germany. The museum had to make her continued employment a secret. The director removed her name from her office door, and she sneaked in each day by a side entrance. When the secret was revealed in 1938, Edinger decided to leave the country. She fled Germany in May 1939 and came to the United States the next year. She joined the Harvard Museum of Comparative Zoology, becoming a U.S. citizen in 1945. In her new country, Edinger maintained her reputation as one of the top figures in vertebrate paleontology, and the Society of Vertebrate Paleontology made her its president in 1963–1964.

In 1948, Edinger published a second monumental book, *The Evolution of the Horse Brain*. In it, she showed that advances in brain structure such as an enlarged forebrain had evolved independently in several groups of mammals. Many scientists pictured evolution as a steady advance along a single "chain of creation," but Edinger showed that evolution was more like a many-branched tree. Edinger died after a car accident on May 27, 1967.

Further Reading

Bailey, Brooke. *The Remarkable Lives of 100 Women Healers and Scientists.* Holbrook, Mass.: Bob Adams, 1994, 66–67.
Gould, Stephen Jay. "Edinger, Tilly." In *Notable American Women: The Modern Period,* edited by Barbara Sicherman and Carol Hurd Green, 218–219. Cambridge, Mass.: The Belknap Press of Harvard University Press, 1980.

✳ EDLUND, SYLVIA
(1945–) *Canadian Botanist*

Sylvia Edlund overcame physical disability to become an expert on Arctic plants. She was born in Pittsburgh on August 15, 1945, and grew up there and in Ontario, Canada. She always liked nature. "I was the kind of kid who'd stop and pet every caterpillar," she says.

Chronically ill as a child and teenager, Sylvia was often confined to her bed and, when she did walk, she used crutches. Her doctor helped her get into Case Western Reserve University in Cleveland, Ohio. At first she planned to be a physician, but she came to like biology better than medicine. Finding that she was the only student who signed up for one course, the professor turned it into a personal tutorial, taking Edlund on field trips, crutches and all. As she exercised more, she became stronger. By the time she finished college she could walk without help.

Edlund took graduate training in botany at the University of Chicago, obtaining her Ph.D. in 1970. She chose this field partly because her illness still sometimes caused difficulty, and "I figured I shouldn't study anything I'd have to chase." Later an active outdoor life cleared up her remaining health problems.

Edlund's first important job, working with a United Nations team to list all the plants and animals of the Far North, introduced her to the Arctic. She worked with the Geological Survey of Canada from 1974 to 1994, mapping plant communities in relation to Arctic geology and "trying to convince geologists that plants are important." She says she sometimes got in trouble with her superiors because she insisted on going beyond a mere inventory of plants, gathering information from different scientific disciplines to try to find out why certain plants grew where they did. Her work helped scientists understand the climate zones in which different kinds of vegetation grow and may shed light on effects of global warming. An illness unrelated to her childhood ones affected her memory and forced her to retire, but she says she is "having a blast" sewing and writing about recovering memory.

Further Reading

May, Elizabeth. *Claiming the Future: The Inspiring Lives of Twelve Canadian Women Scientists and Scholars.* Markham, Ontario: Pembroke Publishers, 1991, 9–12.

✳ ELION, GERTRUDE BELLE ("Trudy")
(1918–1999) *American Chemist and Medical Researcher*

Although Nobel science prizes are usually awarded for basic research, the 1988 prize in physiology or medicine went to three people in applied science—drug developers. "Rarely has scientific experimentation been so intimately linked to the reduction of human suffering," the 1988 *Nobel Prize Annual* said of their work. One of the researchers was Gertrude Elion.

Gertrude, whom everyone called Trudy, was born on January 23, 1918, to immigrant parents in New York City. Her father, Robert, was a dentist. The family moved to the Bronx, then a suburb, in 1924. Trudy spent much of her childhood reading, especially about "people who discovered things."

In 1933, the same year Trudy graduated from high school at age 15, her beloved grandfather died painfully of stomach cancer, and she determined to find a cure for this terrible disease. There was no money to send her to college, however, because her family had lost its savings in the 1929 stock market crash. Trudy enrolled at New York City's Hunter College, which offered free tuition to qualified women. She graduated from Hunter with a B.A. in chemistry and the highest honors in 1937.

Elion failed to win a scholarship to graduate school, so she set out to find a job—not easy for anyone during the depression, let alone for a woman chemist. One interviewer turned her down because he feared she would be a "distracting influence" on male workers. She took several short-term jobs and also went to New York University for a year, beginning in 1939, to take courses for her master's degree. She then did her degree research on evenings and weekends while teaching high school and finally completed the degree in 1941.

World War II removed many men from workplaces, making employers more willing to hire women, and in 1944 it finally opened the doors of a research laboratory to Gertrude Elion. Burroughs Wellcome, a New York drug company, hired her as an assistant to researcher George Hitchings. Most drugs in those days were developed by trial and error, but Hitchings had a different approach. His lab looked systematically for differences between the ways that normal body cells and undesirable cells such as cancer cells, bacteria, and viruses used key chemicals as they grew and reproduced. The researchers then tried to find or make chemicals that interfered with these processes in undesirable cells but not in normal ones.

Elion at first worked mostly as a chemist, synthesizing compounds that closely resembled the building blocks of nucleic acids. The nucleic acids, DNA and RNA, carry inherited information and are essential for cell reproduction. Scientists had theorized around 1940 that an antibiotic called sulfanilamide killed bacteria by "tricking" them into taking it up instead of a nutrient that the bacteria needed, thus starving them to death, and Hitchings thought that a similar "antimetabolite" therapy might work against cancer. If a cancer cell took up compounds similar but not identical to parts of nucleic acids, he reasoned, the chemicals would keep the cell from reproducing and eventually kill it, much as a badly fitting part can jam the works of a machine. He and Elion set out to create such compounds.

In 1950, Elion invented 6-mercaptopurine (6-MP), which became one of the first successful

Gertrude Elion, winner of a share of the 1988 Nobel Prize in physiology or medicine, helped to develop drugs that treat cancer and other diseases and prevent rejection of organ grafts. Here she poses with a high-pressure liquid chromatograph, which separates a solution into its chemical components. (Courtesy Gertrude B. Elion)

drugs to fight cancer by interfering with cancer cells' nucleic acid. It worked especially well against childhood leukemia, a blood cell cancer that had formerly had killed its victims within a few months. When combined with other anti-cancer drugs, 6-MP now cures about 80 percent of children with some forms of leukemia.

Meanwhile, Robert Schwartz, a scientist at the Tufts University Medical Center in Boston, noticed that 6-MP kept rabbits' immune systems from reacting to injected "foreign" substances and wondered if it could fight autoimmune diseases

such as rheumatoid arthritis, in which the immune system attacks the body's own tissues as if they were foreign. British surgeon Roy Calne read about Schwartz's work and, in turn, thought 6-MP might help people who needed organ transplants. Such transplants (except between identical twins) had always failed because recipients' immune systems destroyed the transplanted organs. Wiping out the recipients' immune systems with radiation saved the transplants but left the people defenseless against disease-causing microbes. Calne tried the drug on dogs to whom he had given experimental kidney transplants. Such dogs usually rejected the kidneys within 10 days, but a dog treated with 6-MP kept its transplanted kidney healthy for 44 days.

Calne came to the United States to work for a year with Boston surgeon Joseph Murray, and on the way he visited Hitchings and Elion and told them of his results. They suggested that he test another drug of theirs called azathioprine, a relative of 6-MP that, at least in mice, suppressed the immune system even better than 6-MP did. In 1960, working in Murray's laboratory, Calne used azathioprine to keep a dog with a transplanted kidney from an unrelated donor alive for eight months. Soon thereafter, Murray used the same drug in the first successful kidney transplant between unrelated humans. Azathioprine proved to be the breakthrough drug that made organ transplants possible.

Another compound Elion developed in her cancer research that proved to have other uses was called allopurinol. Because it can prevent the formation of uric acid, allopurinol has become the standard treatment for a painful disease called gout, in which crystals of uric acid are deposited in a person's joints.

Still another breakthrough began in 1969, when Elion sent John Bauer, a researcher at the Burroughs Wellcome Laboratories in England, a new drug she had created that was related to a known virus-killing compound. She suggested that he test her drug against a dangerous group of viruses called herpesviruses, and he found that it stopped their growth. Elion and her coworkers then launched a search for variants of the drug that would kill herpesviruses even better than the original compound. In 1974, Burroughs Wellcome researcher Howard Schaeffer synthesized a drug called acyclovir, which was 100 times more effective against herpesviruses than Elion's first drug. Elion's lab then did four years of research to find out exactly how acyclovir worked. Acyclovir was the first drug that treated herpesvirus infections successfully, and it is still one of Glaxo Wellcome's (previously Burroughs Wellcome) best-selling drugs.

As Hitchings and Elion developed drug after drug, they advanced together within Burroughs Wellcome. Finally, in 1967, Elion was made head of her own laboratory, the newly created Department of Experimental Therapy. Although she had always enjoyed working with Hitchings, she was glad to have more independence. When Burroughs Wellcome moved to Research Triangle Park, North Carolina, in 1970, Elion moved with it. Her laboratory became a "mini-institute" with many sections.

Gertrude Elion officially retired in 1983, but she has remained as busy as ever. In addition to acting as a consultant to other scientists engaged in drug research, she speaks to a wide variety of groups and is involved in several programs that encourage young people, especially minorities and women, to enter science. "We've got to tell them how much fun it is," she says, "how exciting it is to go in to work every day, and how you really don't want the weekend to come."

Elion's scientific legacy has lived on as well. Workers from her team, using approaches she had developed, discovered AZT, the first drug approved for the treatment of AIDS. Approved in 1986, the drug does not cure the disease, but it slows its progress. Today AZT is usually used in combination with other drugs.

Elion's greatest honors came after her retirement. On October 17, 1988, she learned that she had won the greatest scientific award of all, the Nobel Prize. In 1991 she was given a place in the Inventors' Hall of Fame, the first woman to be so honored. She also received the National Medal of Science that year. She is included in the National Women's Hall of Fame and the Engineering and Science Hall of Fame as well. As the years passed, the awards kept coming: In 1997, Elion received the Lemelson/MIT Lifetime Achievement Award. Although she was glad to have these prizes, Elion said: "My rewards had already come in seeing children with leukemia survive, meeting patients with long-term kidney transplants, and watching acyclovir save lives and reduce suffering." Elion died on February 21, 1999.

Further Reading

Bouton, Katherine. "The Nobel Pair." *New York Times Magazine*, January 29, 1989.

"Elion, Gertrude B." *Current Biography Yearbook 1995.* New York: H. W. Wilson, 1995, 139–144.

Holloway, Marguerite. "The Satisfaction of Delayed Gratification." *Scientific American,* October 1991, 40–44.

McGrayne, Sharon Bertsch. *Nobel Prize Women in Science: Their Lives, Struggles, and Momentous Discoveries.* New York: Birch Lane Press, 1993, 280–303.

St. Pierre, Stephanie. *Gertrude Elion: Master Chemist.* Vero Beach, Fla.: Rourke Enterprises, 1993.

✳ EVANS, ALICE CATHERINE
(1881–1975) *American Microbiologist*

Alice Evans showed that a dangerous disease was transmitted in fresh milk, forcing the dairy industry to begin heat-treating milk to kill bacteria. She was born in Neath, Pennsylvania, on January 29, 1881. Her father, William, was a farmer, surveyor, and teacher. Alice obtained a minimal education at the Susquehanna Institute in Tonawanda, then taught school for four years. A Cornell University nature study course for teachers turned her interest toward science, and she enrolled in the Cornell College of Agriculture, from which she earned a B.S. in 1909. She chose bacteriology as her specialty.

Evans won a scholarship to do graduate work at the University of Wisconsin at Madison, from which she earned a master's degree in 1910. She then joined the Dairy Division of the Bureau of Animal Industry of the U.S. Department of Agriculture, working at first at its branch on the Madison campus. When the division gained permanent research laboratories in Washington, D.C., in 1913, Evans transferred there. She was the first woman given permanent employment in the Dairy Division.

Evans worked with a group looking for ways to keep disease-causing bacteria from contaminating fresh milk. On her own, she also studied the bacteria in uncontaminated milk, which was thought to be safe to drink. She was especially interested in two types of supposedly unrelated bacteria. One, *Bacillus abortus,* caused a contagious disease that made pregnant cattle miscarry. The other, *Micrococcus melitensis,* produced a debilitating and sometimes fatal human illness that was called undulant fever because of its pattern of rising and falling body temperature. It had first been identified in British soldiers on Malta who drank milk from infected goats.

Evans discovered that *B. abortus* was common in the milk of apparently healthy cows. She also found that *B. abortus, M. melitensis,* and a third microbe from pigs were almost identical. Together, these facts suggested to her that a germ often found in fresh cow's milk could cause human disease.

When Evans presented her findings at a meeting of the Society of American Bacteriologists (now the American Society of Microbiology) in 1917, other bacteriologists were skeptical. (Evans commented later that at least one may have opposed her because he "was not accustomed to considering a scientific idea proposed by a woman.") In 1920, however, some other bacteriologists confirmed her work, reclassifying her goat, cow, and pig bacteria into a new genus, *Brucella.* The disease they caused was renamed brucellosis. By the end of the decade, reports from all over the world proved Evans's claim that humans could catch brucellosis by drinking fresh cows' milk.

Evans showed in the 1930s that brucellosis had a chronic or long-lasting form that had previously been unknown because it mimicked other diseases. This explained why the number of human brucellosis cases had appeared to be small even though infection in cows was common. It turned out that there were 10 times as many cases of brucellosis in the United States as had been thought. Evans herself contracted chronic brucellosis in 1922 and suffered from it for 23 years, until it became treatable with antibiotics.

Evans had pointed out from the start that the threat of brucellosis and other diseases carried in milk could be removed by a heat treatment called pasteurization, invented by French bacteriologist Louis Pasteur in the 1860s. Dairies had resisted pasteurization because it meant buying new equipment, but by the 1930s they were finally persuaded to begin using it. Pasteurization is required for all milk sold in the United States today.

Evans's work won recognition and awards, including several honorary degrees. In 1928 she became the

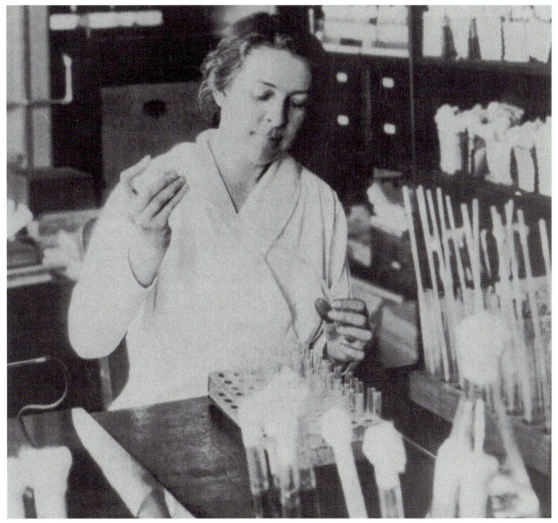

Alice Evans analyzed milk for the U.S. Department of Agriculture and the Public Health Service and showed in the 1920s and 1930s that fresh milk from apparently healthy cows could carry the microorganisms that caused a serious disease of humans and cattle called brucellosis. Her work pushed dairy farmers to begin pasteurizing (heat-treating) all milk to kill dangerous microbes.
(Courtesy National Library of Medicine)

first woman to be elected president of the American Society for Microbiology. Around 1939 she turned to research on streptococci, a type of bacteria that infects wounds, and continued this work until her retirement in 1945. She died on September 5, 1975. According to science historian Elizabeth O'Hern, Evans's work on brucellosis "has been cited as one of the outstanding achievements in medical science in the first quarter of the 20th century."

Further Reading

Burns, Virginia L. *Gentle Hunter: Biography of Alice Evans, Bacteriologist.* Laingsburg, Mich.: Enterprise Press, 1993.

O'Hern, Elizabeth M. "Evans, Alice Catherine." *In Notable American Women: The Modern Period*, edited by Barbara Sicherman and Carol Hurd Green, 219–221. Cambridge, Mass.: The Belknap Press of Harvard University Press, 1980.

———. *Profiles of Pioneer Women Scientists*. Washington, D.C.: Acropolis Books, 1985, 127–140.

Vare, Ethlie Ann, and Greg Ptacek. *Mothers of Invention*. New York: William Morrow, 1988, 128–130.

F

※ FABER, SANDRA MOORE
(1944–) *American Astronomer*

Sandra Faber has provided groundbreaking new infomation about how galaxies formed and the material of which they are made. She has helped to show that the universe is "lumpy," with clusters of galaxies drawing together to form still larger aggregates. She has also played a major role in the repair of the Hubble Space Telescope and the construction of the earth's largest optical telescopes, the twin 400-inch Keck telescopes in Hawaii.

Sandra Moore was born in Boston on December 28, 1944, but grew up in Cleveland, Ohio. As a child, she told *Omni* interviewer Paul Bagne, "Science was as natural to me as breathing." Her father, a civil engineer, encouraged her interest in astronomy by buying her a pair of binoculars to help her observe the stars.

A favorite teacher at Swarthmore College inspired Moore to make astronomy her career. Moore graduated from Swarthmore with high honors in physics in 1966 and a year later married Andrew Faber, a physicist she had met at college (he later became an attorney). She earned her Ph.D. in astronomy from Harvard in 1972. The Fabers then moved to northern California, where Sandra joined the Lick Observatory of the University of California at Santa Cruz, becoming the observatory's first female member. Soon afterward she gave birth to a daughter, the first of two. In 1975 she and fellow Lick astronomer Robert Jackson discovered the Faber-Jackson relation, a relationship between the size and brightness of elliptical galaxies and the speeds of stars orbiting within them. This was the first of several major research advances by Faber.

Around 1979, Faber and other astronomers proved that about 90 percent of the matter in the universe is dark, or invisible. She and two Santa Cruz colleagues proposed in 1984 that this dark matter was "cold" and consisted of relatively massive subatomic particles. Their theory also stated that galaxies developed from relatively dense "seeds" that were formed soon after the Big Bang, the gigantic explosion believed to have given birth to the universe. This was the first compehensive theory of how galaxies evolved, and although some details of it are being modified, Faber says the theory is still "the current working paradigm for structure formation in the Universe." She now believes that galaxies may consist of a mixture of cold dark matter and ordinary matter.

Ever since the Big Bang, all objects in space have been streaming away from each other. While measuring the motion of certain galaxies in the late 1980s, Faber and six coworkers, later nicknamed the "Seven Samurai," found other "peculiar" kinds of motion occurring as well, causing nearby galaxies to move faster than expected. They concluded that gravity is pulling our local supercluster of galaxies toward a section of the sky that they called the Great Attractor. This area, about 150 million light-years from earth and 300 million light-years across, has the mass of 10s of thousands of galaxies. Faber now thinks the Great Attractor and its attendant galaxies, in turn, are flowing toward a still larger mass somewhere else. The discovery of the Great Attractor, like the work of VERA RUBIN and MARGARET GELLER, suggests that the universe is far "lumpier" than had been thought.

Faber has also improved in the technology with which she and other astronomers study the universe. In the late 1980s she was one of three scientists who diagnosed the flaw in the mirror of the Hubble Space Telescope, and she also helped to design the procedure that repaired it. That project was exhausting but was also, she has written, "the most exhilarating phase of her career" so far. She has also played a major part in managing the construction of the Keck telescopes, built in the 1990s. She is currently building a new spectrograph for the second Keck, which will increase its power to observe distant galaxies by 13 times.

Faber has received many awards for her work, including the Bok Prize of Harvard University (1978) and the Heineman Prize of the American Astronomical Society (1986). She has been elected to both the National Academy of Sciences (1985) and the American Academy of Arts and Sciences (1986). Since 1996 she has been one of the three University Professors of the University of California.

Today, Faber is using the Hubble Space Telescope to study the centers of galaxies, which, according to evidence she and others have gathered, often hide massive black holes. She is also observing extremely distant galaxies, which date from early in the formation of the universe. As she expected, they are smaller and less organized than later galaxies, but she does not yet know why they changed in exactly the way they have. She hopes her work will help her discover how galaxies developed in the early universe.

Further Reading

Bagne, Paul. "Interview: Sandra Faber," *Omni*, July 1990, 62–64, 88–92.

Lightman, Alan, and Roberta Brawer. *Origins: The Lives and Worlds of Modern Cosmologists.* Cambridge, Mass.: Harvard University Press, 1990, 324–340.

Vogel, Shawna. "Star Attraction." *Discover*, November 1989, 20–23.

✳ FAWCETT, STELLA GRACE MAISIE
(1902–1988) *Australian Botanist*

In pioneering fieldwork on Australia's high plains, Maisie Fawcett showed how overgrazing affected plant life and led to soil erosion. Stella Grace Maisie Fawcett was born in 1902 in Footscray, a suburb of Melbourne, and grew up there. After several years of teaching school, she won a scholarship to the University of Melbourne at age 20. Told that her first career choice, geology, was "not for women," she changed to botany. She earned a M.S. in 1936 and remained at the university as a demonstrator and researcher.

Cattle and sometimes sheep had grazed on the high plains of the Australian state of Victoria since the mid-19th century. By the early 1940s, the toll they had taken on the land was becoming clear. Victoria's Soil Conservation Board (SCB) asked John Turner, head of the University of Melbourne's botany department, to find a "suitable man" to study the effect of grazing on the plant life of the plains. World War II made men scarce, so Turner suggested that the best "man" for the job was Maisie Fawcett.

The 29-year-old Fawcett reached the Bogong High Plains in September 1941 and fenced off two study areas on the steep, forest-covered slopes. The fences kept grazing animals out, so she could note which plants sprang up there. Linden Gillbank describes some of the hardships of Fawcett's work: "Thistles ripped through her clothes, it poured

[rain] non-stop for days, fences were damaged, and she was absolutely physically exhausted from riding and recording."

Dealing with the ranchers was difficult, too. Fawcett wrote: "The Board will never realize the amount of charm, pasture wisdom, and general knowledge I have expended on the locals to get them to . . . stir themselves." The ranchers at first were amused by Fawcett, nicknaming her "Washaway Woman" (a washaway was an erosion gully) or "Erosion Girl," but in time they became fond of her.

During the early 1940s, Fawcett showed that overgrazing was causing erosion in both lower and higher pastures. She recommended allowing fewer cattle on the land, bringing them to the high pastures later in the year (which gave plants a head start on their growing season), and completely banning sheep, which graze down to the ground. The government backed her proposals, and the soil situation improved.

Fawcett moved back to Melbourne in 1949 and became a temporary lecturer in ecology at the university. She was made a permanent senior lecturer in 1952. She started a massive book on the plant life of Victoria, which the botany students who helped her with it dubbed "the Monster."

Fawcett married Denis Carr, a fellow professor, in the 1950s. They moved to Canberra in 1967. Fawcett was a visiting fellow at Australian National University until her death in 1988.

Further Reading

Gillbank, Linden. "Into the Land of the Mountain Cattlemen." In *On the Edge of Discovery*, edited by Farley Kelly, 133–154. Melbourne, Australia: Text Publishing, 1993.

✳ FLEMING, WILLIAMINA PATON STEVENS ("Mina")
(1857–1911) *American Astronomer*

Going from housemaid to astronomer, Williamina Fleming helped to devise a way to classify stars according to patterns in their light. She also identified a number of unusual stars. She was born Williamina Paton Stevens on May 15, 1857, in Dundee,

Scotland. Her father, Robert, carved and gilded picture frames and furniture. He died when Mina, as people called her, was seven.

Mina did so well in school that she became a student teacher at age 14. She married James Fleming in 1877, and they sailed for Boston the next year. There Fleming abandoned his pregnant bride. Mina looked for domestic work and was hired by Edward C. Pickering, head of the Harvard Observatory.

Pickering was starting a huge project that classified stars according to their spectra, the patterns revealed when their light was broken up into a rainbow (by passing it through a crystal called a prism) and photographed. Differences in spectra reflect such characteristics as a star's surface temperature and the chemical elements in it. According to legend, Mina Fleming got her start in astronomy when Pickering lost patience with a young man hired to analyze the spectra and snapped, "My Scottish maid could do better!" He brought the Scottish maid—Fleming—to the observatory and found that indeed she could.

Whether or not her introduction really happened like this, Pickering did eventually show Fleming how to study spectra with a magnifying glass and found that she had a knack for sorting them according to similarities and making the calculations necessary to determine the stars' position. She was hired as a permanent employee of the observatory in 1881 and put in charge of the star project in 1886. She and Pickering devised the system (later improved by ANNIE JUMP CANNON) used to classify the spectra of 10,351 stars in the massive *Draper Catalogue of Stellar Spectra*, published in 1890, and she did most of the classification. When Pickering began work on an even larger star catalogue and hired a "harem" (as people joked) of young women as "computers" on the project, Fleming supervised them with a kindly but stern eye. They included Annie Cannon, HENRIETTA LEAVITT, ANTONIA MAURY, and CECILIA PAYNE-GAPOSCHKIN.

In addition to her work on the star catalogues, Fleming made some original contributions to

Williamina Fleming (standing) went from being the maid of Harvard Observatory director Edward Pickering to being the supervisor of his "harem" of women "computers," which included such talented astronomers as Antonia Maury (left rear). She and Pickering worked out a system for classifying stars according to features of their light, and she also studied variable stars, whose light brightens and dims in a regular cycle. This photo shows Fleming and her charges analyzing photographs of stars at the observatory around 1890.
(Courtesy Harvard College Observatory)

astronomy. She was the first to notice, for instance, that variable stars, whose light regularly brightened and dimmed, could be identified by bright lines in their spectra. In 1907 she published a list of 222 variable stars, most of which she had discovered.

Despite her humble beginnings and lack of formal training, Williamina Fleming became the foremost American woman astronomer of her time. In 1898 the Harvard Corporation, which ran the university, made her the observatory's curator of photographs, the first appointment the corporation gave to a woman. In 1906, Fleming became the sixth woman, and the first American woman, to be elected to Britain's prestigious Royal Astronomical Society. Fleming died of pneumonia on May 21, 1911, at the age of 54.

Further Reading

Hoffleit, Dorrit. "Fleming, Williamina Paton Stevens." In *Notable American Women, 1607–1950, vol. I: A–F,* edited by Edward T. James, 623–630. Cambridge, Mass.: The Belknap Press of Harvard University Press, 1971.

Mack, Pamela E. "Straying from Their Orbits: Women in Astronomy in America." In *Women of Science: Righting the Record*, edited by G. Kass-Simon and Patricia Farnes, 92–94. Bloomington: Indiana University Press, 1990.

Ogilvie, Marilyn Bailey. *Women in Science: Antiquity Through the Nineteenth Century.* Cambridge, Mass.: MIT Press, 1986, 85–86.

✺ FLÜGGE-LOTZ, IRMGARD
(1903–1974) *German/American Engineer and Mathematician*

Irmgard Flügge-Lotz's improvements in the design of aircraft included the automatic controls that made jet aircraft possible. She was born Irmgard Lotz on July 16, 1903, in Hameln, Germany. Irmgard became interested in building things at an early age, thanks both to her father, Oscar, a mathematician, and her mother, Dora, whose family had worked in construction for generations. She liked to go with her uncle to watch construction projects. She once said that she became an engineer because she "wanted a life which would never be boring."

Lotz studied applied mathematics and fluid dynamics at the Technische Hochschule of Hanover, graduating with the equivalent of a bachelor's degree in 1927 and earning a doctorate in engineering in 1929. She then became a junior research engineer at the Aerodynamische Versuchsanstalt (AVA) at Göttingen, one of Europe's most respected aeronautical research centers. In 1931 she worked out a formula for determining the distribution of lift over the span of a plane's wings, from wingtip to wingtip. She also fell in love with a fellow engineer, Wilhelm Flügge, and they married on June 4, 1938. Irmgard thereafter used the last name Flügge-Lotz.

Just after their marriage, the Flügges joined the German government's chief aeronautics research institute, the Deutsche Versuchsanstalt für Luftfahrt. Hermann Göring, the head of the air force and aeronautical research, hired them in spite of their open anti-Nazi views because he respected their technical skill, but the couple never knew how

long they would be safe. Wilhelm Flügge said later, "The balance of power was … always precarious."

The Flügges immigrated to the United States in 1948. Stanford University hired Flügge as a professor of engineering but accepted Flügge-Lotz only as a lecturer and research supervisor. While at Stanford, Flügge-Lotz perfected the research on automatic aircraft controls that she had begun in Germany. Her book on the subject, *Discontinuous Automatic Control*, was published in 1953. Stanford finally made her a full professor in 1960—the university's first woman professor of engineering.

Flügge-Lotz published a second book, *Discontinuous and Optimal Control*, in 1968 and retired the same year. Two years later she became the second woman to be made a fellow of the American Institute of Aeronautics and Astronautics and also won the Achievement Award of the Society of Women Engineers. She died on May 22, 1974.

Further Reading

Hallion, Richard P. "Flügge-Lotz, Irmgard." In *Notable American Women: The Modern Period*, edited by Barbara Sicherman and Carol Hurd Green, 241–242. Cambridge, Mass.: The Belknap Press of Harvard University Press, 1980.

Vare, Ethlie Ann, and Greg Ptacek. *Mothers of Invention.* New York: Morrow, 1988, 197–198.

✺ FOSSEY, DIAN
(1932–1985) *American Zoologist*

Living like a hermit in a mountain rain forest in Africa, Dian Fossey learned more about the endangered mountain gorilla than had ever been known. As more and more gorillas were killed by poachers, she turned from scientist to fierce conservationist. She finally gave her life for the animals she loved.

Dian Fossey was born in San Francisco, California, in 1932 and grew up there. Her father, George, taught her to love nature, but her parents divorced when she was six, and her mother, Kitty, and stepfather, Richard Price, did not let her have pets. She loved animals anyway, and in 1950 she entered the University of California at Davis with plans to become

67

a veterinarian. After two years, however, she transferred to San Jose State College, where she trained as an occupational therapist. She obtained her B.A. in 1954. In 1956 she moved to Louisville, Kentucky, and became head of the occupational therapy department at Kosair Crippled Children's Hospital.

"I had this great urge, this *need* to go to Africa," Fossey once told a *Chicago Tribune* interviewer. In 1963 she borrowed money to finance a seven-week safari to the continent. She met British anthropologist Louis Leakey and saw her first mountain gorillas during this trip. When she saw Leakey again in Louisville in 1966 and he said he was looking for a woman to do a long-term study of mountain gorillas like the one his protégée JANE GOODALL was doing with chimpanzees, Fossey eagerly volunteered. She even followed Leakey's half-joking suggestion that she have her appendix removed before going to Africa because, camping in the rain forest, she would be so far from medical help.

Mountain gorillas are much rarer than lowland gorillas. They live only in the Virunga Mountains, a group of volcanoes in east central Africa shared among the countries of Rwanda, Uganda, and the Democratic Republic of Congo. Fossey began her research in Congo in early 1967, but the country was involved in a civil war, and soldiers drove her out of her camp and imprisoned her after she had been there only six months. She escaped and fled to Rwanda, where she set up a new camp on Mount Visoke near another mountain, Karisimbi. She named the camp Karisoke and settled down at last to her research. Local people soon began calling her *Nyirmachabelli*, "the woman who lives alone in the forest."

Contrary to their fearsome "King Kong" image, the gorillas were very shy. Fossey finally learned to sooth the animals' fears by imitating the loud belches and other sounds they made while eating. She observed nine groups, each consisting of five to 19 members, and made close contact with four. She gave the animals in these groups whimsical names such as Digit (because of the animal's twisted finger), Uncle Bert, and Beethoven. Her studies uncovered many details of the gorillas' family life, mating, diet, and communication that had never

been observed before. For instance, she noted that the "gentle giants," as she called them, were almost never truly aggressive. To gain more scientific validation for her work, she wrote it up as a thesis for a doctorate in zoology, which she obtained from Cambridge University in 1974.

In a census she did in 1970, Fossey found that there were only 375 gorillas left in the Virunga Mountains. She became increasingly determined to protect the animals, which was no easy task. The people of Rwanda, then the most heavily populated country in Africa, needed more land for themselves, and they often invaded what was supposed to be parkland. Cattle herders and woodcutters damaged the gorillas' forest habitat. Worse still, poachers killed the animals themselves—sometimes accidentally and at other times deliberately—in order to obtain body parts that could be sold as trophies or for magic.

When poachers killed Digit, Fossey's favorite gorilla, in 1977, she felt as if a beloved family member had been murdered. The following year she established a fund in Digit's name to pay Rwandan guards to track and drive off poachers. She also began a personal war against the intruders, using tactics that ranged from scaring them with a Halloween mask to kidnapping their children. Her approach angered local people, Rwandan government officials, and even some wildlife protection groups.

Desperate for funds to continue her work, Fossey went to the United States in 1980 and stayed for three years, teaching and lecturing at Cornell University and writing a popular book about her experiences called *Gorillas in the Mist*. The book, published in 1983, became a best-seller and earned enough money to let her return to Rwanda.

Fossey now suffered from emphysema and other health problems and had to abandon her gorilla research to assistants. Growing moodiness and her obsession with fighting poachers isolated her from those around her. In mid-1985 she said, "I have no friends. The more you learn about the dignity of the gorilla, the more you want to avoid people."

Unfortunately, she was not able to do so. On December 27, 1985, one of her Rwandan guards found Fossey in her hut, slashed to death by a machete. The murderer was never identified. Fossey's friends buried her in the graveyard she had set up for the slain gorillas, under a tombstone that reads: "No one loved gorillas more. Rest in peace, dear friend, eternally protected in this sacred ground, for you are home where you belong."

Further Reading

Fossey, Dian. *Gorillas in the Mist.* Boston: Houghton Mifflin, 1983.

Hayes, Harold T. P. *The Dark Romance of Dian Fossey.* New York: Simon & Schuster, 1990.

Montgomery, Sy. *Walking with the Great Apes.* Boston: Houghton Mifflin, 1991.

Mowat, Farley. *Woman in the Mists.* New York: Warner, 1987.

 FRANKLIN, MELISSA EVE BRONWEN
(1956–) *American Physicist*

Melissa Franklin led the group that discovered the top quark, the last subatomic particle predicted by theory that had remained unknown to science. She was born in Canada in 1956 and is still a Canadian citizen. She showed her independence early by dropping out of high school and joining friends to form an alternative school. She eventually entered the University of Toronto, where she studied physics and graduated in 1977. She obtained her Ph.D. from Stanford University in 1982 after working at the university's Linear Accelerator Center (SLAC) and did postdoctoral study at the Lawrence Berkeley Laboratory, part of the University of California at Berkeley. From 1986 to 1988 she was an assistant professor at the University of Illinois and worked at Fermilab, near Chicago. She joined Harvard University in 1987 and is now a full professor there, the first tenured woman professor in the physics department.

Physicists believe that subatomic particles such as protons and neutrons are made up of other particles called quarks, which are thought to be the ultimate building blocks of matter. The six kinds of quarks predicted by theory have been given the whimsical names of top, bottom, up, down, strange, and charmed. Five of the six were identified in

debris produced by atom smashers in the 1970s, but the top quark remained elusive because it breaks down within a trillionth of a trillionth of a second. It could be detected only by finding its breakdown products, some of which last long enough to leave evidence in particle detectors. Unfortunately, it could produce many possible assortments of particles. Determining whether any pattern of particles was really produced by the top quark was therefore difficult.

Franklin, who became a fellow of the American Physical Society in 1994, heads a small Harvard group that built and maintains two particle detectors attached to the Tevatron, a giant atom smasher at Fermilab, where the hunt for the top quark took place. For more than a decade, Franklin has flown to Chicago every few weeks to check on and fix problems. "I want to be with the equipment," she says. "I need to stroke it." Franklin's industry paid off when her group finally proved the existence of the top quark in 1995. Fellow Harvard professor Isaac Silvera calls her an "unconventional thinker" who is "going to be one of the bright stars of the high energy future."

Further Reading

Freedman, David H. "Over the Top." *Discover*, February 1995, 75–81.

 FRANKLIN, ROSALIND ELSIE
(1920–1962) *British Chemist*

Deoxyribonucleic acid, or DNA, carries the inherited information in the genes of most living things. In the early 1950s, scientists realized that the key to finding out how this information was stored and reproduced lay in the structure of DNA's complex molecules. Rosalind Franklin took X-ray photographs that gave two rival scientists, James Watson and Francis Crick, the clues they needed to work out the structure of DNA.

Rosalind Franklin was born on July 25, 1920, in London. Her father, Ellis, was a well-to-do banker, and her mother, Muriel, did volunteer social work as well as raising five children. Rosalind decided at age 15 that she wanted to be a scientist. Her father objected, believing like many people of the time that higher education and careers made women unhappy, but she finally overcame his resistance. She studied chemistry at Newnham, a women's college at Cambridge University, and graduated in 1941.

As a way of helping her country during World War II, Franklin became assistant research officer at the Coal Utilization Research Association (CURA). She did research on the structure of carbon molecules, bringing, according to one professor, "order into a field which had previously been in chaos." She turned some of this work into the thesis for her Ph.D., which she earned from Cambridge in 1945.

Seeking new challenges, Franklin went to work for the French government's central chemical research laboratory in 1947. Friends later said that her three years there were the happiest of her life. She enjoyed an easy cameraderie with her coworkers, chatting at cafés and on picnics. She also learned a technique called X-ray crystallography, to which she would devote the rest of her career.

Many solid materials form crystals, in which molecules are arranged in regular patterns. In 1912 a German scientist named Max von Laue found that if a beam of X rays is shone through a crystal, some of the rays bounce off the crystal's atoms, while others pass straight through. When photographic film, which is sensitive to X rays, is placed on the far side of the crystal, the resulting photograph shows a pattern of black dots that can reveal important facts about the three-dimensional structure of the molecules in the crystal.

Chemists eventually also found ways to use X-ray crystallography on amorphous compounds, which did not form obvious crystals. Most of the complex chemicals in the bodies of living things are amorphous compounds. Molecular biologists were beginning to realize that the structure of these compounds revealed much about their function, and crystallography was a promising tool for revealing that structure. One of the molecules about whose structure scientists were most curious was DNA, which is found in every cell of the body and had been shown in the late 1940s to be a carrier of inherited information.

Franklin became expert at taking X-ray photos of amorphous compounds, and she was eager to try her skill on biological molecules. In 1950 she joined a group of researchers at King's College, part of the University of London, who were trying to work out the structure of DNA. Unfortunately, Franklin and the group's leader, Maurice Wilkins, disliked each other on sight. The problem may have been their genders but more likely lay in their different personalities. Wilkins was a retiring man who disliked conflict, whereas Franklin loved a good verbal fight. Raymond Gosling, a graduate student who worked with Franklin at King's College, commented, "You had to argue strongly with Rosalind if she thought you were wrong, whereas Maurice [Wilkins] would simply shut up." Another cause of trouble was that Wilkins thought of Franklin as his assistant, whereas Franklin believed she had been hired as an independent researcher within his group.

Scientists knew that the DNA molecule consisted of several smaller molecules. It had a long chain, or "backbone," made of alternating molecules of sugar and phosphate (a phosphorus-containing compound). Four different kinds of other molecules called bases were attached to the backbone. No one knew, however, whether the chain was straight or twisted, how the bases were arranged on it, or how many chains were in each molecule. Franklin and Wilkins hoped that Franklin's X-ray photographs would provide this information.

Franklin photographed two forms of DNA, a "dry," or crystalline, form and a "wet" form that contained extra water molecules. No one had photographed the wet form before. At the time, Franklin was not sure which type gave the more useful information. She took an excellent photograph of the wet form in May 1952, but she put it aside in a drawer and continued working with the dry form.

Franklin believed that there was more than one chain in each DNA molecule and that, at least in the wet form, each chain had the twisted shape of a helix, like the threads of a screw. She also believed that the phosphate backbone was on the outside of the chain and the bases on the inside. She did not follow up on these ideas, however. Some of her friends think she might have done so and discovered the structure of DNA herself if she had had a scientist of her own caliber with whom to talk over ideas. Aaron Klug, who worked with her later, wrote: "She needed a collaborator, . . . somebody to break the pattern of her thinking, to show her what was right in front of her, to push her up and over."

Two Cambridge scientists, a brash young American named James Watson and a somewhat older Britisher, Francis Crick, were also trying to work out the structure of DNA. Although Watson saw himself and Crick as competitors of the King's College group, he and Wilkins became friends, and on January 30, 1953, he visited Wilkins at King's College. Without asking Franklin's permission, Wilkins showed Watson the photograph of "wet" DNA that she had made in May 1952. When he saw the photo, Watson wrote later, "my mouth fell open and my pulse began to race." He hurried back to Cambridge to describe the photo to Crick.

To Watson, the X-shaped pattern of dots in Franklin's photo showed clearly that the DNA molecule had the shape of a helix. On the basis of this and other evidence, he and Crick concluded, as by this time Franklin also had, that the molecule consisted of two helices twined around each other. The backbones were on the outside and the bases stretched across the center. In other words, the molecule was shaped like a spiral staircase or a twisted ladder with the bases as steps or rungs.

After further discussion, Watson and Crick had two key insights that went beyond the evidence in Franklin's photo. Two of the four kinds of bases were larger than the other two, and Watson realized that one large base plus one small one made a pair exactly the right size to fit in the space between the backbones indicated in Franklin's photograph. Crick, in turn, realized that the two backbones coiled in opposite directions, so the molecule looked the same from either end.

Watson and Crick published a groundbreaking paper on the structure of DNA in Britain's chief science journal, *Nature*, on April 25, 1953. Neither then nor later did they fully credit Franklin for the important part her photograph had played in their

discovery, and Franklin herself probably never realized its role. By the time the Cambridge scientists' paper appeared, she was no longer working on DNA. She had moved from King's College to Birkbeck, another college in the University of London, and was beginning an X-ray study of a common plant virus called tobacco mosaic virus. Almost nothing was known about the structure of viruses at that time. Franklin drew on her crystallography studies to make a model of the tobacco mosaic virus that was exhibited at the 1957 World's Fair in Brussels. The virus's inherited information was carried in RNA, a chemical similar to DNA. Franklin showed that the RNA molecule was also a helix.

In 1956, Rosalind Franklin discovered that she had ovarian cancer. The cancer proved untreatable, and she died of it on April 16, 1958. Four years later, Watson, Crick, and Wilkins shared the 1962 Nobel Prize in physiology or medicine for their work on DNA. Nobel Prizes are never awarded after a person's death, so there was no question of including Franklin. Supporters and critics still debate whether she would or should have been included if she had lived. As it was, she was remembered in the high praise of some of her colleagues. For instance, crystallography pioneer J. D. Bernal, under whom Franklin worked at Birkbeck, wrote of her, "As a scientist Miss Franklin was distinguished by extreme clarity and perfection in everything she undertook. Her photographs are among the most beautiful X-ray photographs . . . ever taken."

Further Reading

Bernstein, Jeremy. *Experiencing Science.* New York: E.P. Dutton, 1978, 143–162.

Judson, Horace Freeland. "The Legend of Rosalind Franklin." *Science Digest*, January 1986, 56–59, 78–84.

McGrayne, Sharon Bertsch. *Nobel Prize Women in Science: Their Lives, Struggles, and Momentous Discoveries.* New York: Birch Lane Press, 1993, 304–332.

Sayre, Anne. *Rosalind Franklin and DNA.* New York: Norton, 1975.

Watson, James. D. *The Double Helix.* New York: New American Library, 1959.

✳ FRITH, UTA AUERNHAMMER
(1941–) *British Psychologist and Brain Researcher*

Uta Frith has provided new understanding of several brain disorders and also of the normal brain. She was born Uta Auernhammer in Rockenhausen, Germany, on May 25, 1941, to an artist father and a writer mother. She started her elementary education in a girls' school, but at age 12 she insisted on going to the more demanding boys' school instead.

At college in Saarbrucken, Auernhammer decided on psychology as a career. She came to Britain in 1964 and earned a Ph.D. in psychology from the Institute of Psychiatry at London University in 1968. She then took a job at the Medical Research Council's Developmental Psychology Unit. Until 1998 she was a senior scientist with its successor, the Cognitive Development Unit. She moved to the Institute of Cognitive Neuroscience at University College, London (UCL), when the Cognitive Development Unit closed. She has been an honorary professor at UCL since 1996. She is married to Christopher Frith.

One of Uta Frith's specialties is a brain disorder called autism, which isolates people emotionally. It is probably caused by brain damage or failure of development at or before birth. Frith believes that the main kind of thinking defect in autism is a lack of ability to form what psychologists have called a theory of mind. Autistic people cannot understand that other people's perceptions, thoughts, beliefs, and feelings differ from their own. "Autism [is] a kind of . . . mindblindness," Frith told writer Karen Gold in 1996.

Frith and coworkers Alan Leslie and Simon Baron-Cohen demonstrated the theory-of-mind defect in 1986 by telling autistic and normal children a story about two girls, Sally and Anne, who were playing with a marble. Frith explained that Sally put the marble in a basket and left the room. While she was gone, Anne put the marble in a box. Frith then asked the children where Sally would look for the marble when she returned. Normal children as young as four years old said that Sally would look for the marble in the basket because she would not know that Anne had moved it. Autistic children, however—even teenagers of normal

or superior intelligence—said that Sally would look for the marble in the box. They could not grasp the fact that even though *they* knew the marble had been moved, Sally didn't. In more recent years, Frith and her coworkers have used imaging techniques to tie this inability to "mind-read" to lack of activity in a particular small area of the brain.

Frith has also studied dyslexia. This brain disorder is best known for its ability to cause trouble in reading and spelling by making people see groups of letters in words as reversed, but Frith believes that it is a basic disorder of speech processing that can reveal itself long before a child attempts to read. It may be inherited. In 1995, Frith and her husband used an imaging technique called PET (positron emission tomography) to show that when normal people took language tests, two brain areas just above the ear and a third part called the insula (island), which connects them, were all active. The insula, however, was not active in dyslexics. "Each of the language areas deals with a specific aspect of word processing and in normal people the insula synchronizes this work," Frith told the magazine *New Scientist*. "In dyslexics the areas are disconnected."

Frith has received several honors for her work on autism and dyslexia, including the British Psychological Society's President's Award in 1990. She was made a fellow of the British Psychological Society in 1991 and a member of the Academia Europa in 1992. She and collaborator John Morton are working on a general framework within which to explain developmental disorders such as autism and dyslexia that will combine the biological, cognitive (mental), and behavioral aspects of the defects. "Making links between these levels continues to be my main objective in the future," Frith wrote in 1998.

Further Reading

"Dyslexia's Broken Bridge." *New Scientist*, March 23, 1996, 19.

Gold, Karen. "Uta Frith" in *Beyond the Glass Ceiling: Forty Women Whose Ideas Shape the Modern World*, edited by Sian Griffiths, 99–104. Manchester, England: Manchester University Press, 1996.

G

 ## GALDIKAS, BIRUTÉ M. F.
(1946–)   *Canadian Zoologist*

Biruté M. F. Galdikas studies and protects one of humanity's closest cousins, the red-haired Asian ape called the orangutan. She has discovered much of what is known about this solitary animal. She believes she inherited her love of nature from her ancestors in Lithuania, the heavily forested central European country where her parents, Antanas and Filomena Galdikas, grew up. They fled the country separately during World War II and met in a refugee camp. They were married in 1945, and Biruté, their oldest child, was born in Wiesbaden, Germany, on May 10, 1946.

After the war the Galdikases immigrated to Canada, where Antanas Galdikas worked as a miner. Biruté grew up in Toronto with two brothers and a sister. In high school she first read about orangutans, whose name means "people of the forest" in the language of their homeland, Indonesia.

Biruté's family moved to the United States in 1965, and she went to college at the University of California at Los Angeles (UCLA). She stayed there to do graduate work in anthropology, the study of humankind.

While at UCLA, Galdikas heard about two young women, JANE GOODALL and DIAN FOSSEY, who were doing groundbreaking studies of chimpanzees and gorillas by observing the animals in their natural habitat for years at a time. Galdikas became "obsessed" with the idea of doing similar work with orangutans. "I was born to study orangutans," she writes.

Galdikas knew that the great apes—chimpanzees, gorillas, and orangutans—are humans' closest living relatives. All shared an ancestor millions of years ago. Orangutans are the only apes that still live in trees, as human ancestors did 15 million years ago. Galdikas thought that learning more about these apes might help people understand their own origins. In her autobiography she writes: "Orangutans reflect, to some degree, the innocence we humans left behind in Eden."

Galdikas found a path to her dream in 1969, when she attended a lecture given by British anthropologist Louis S. B. Leakey. Leakey had sponsored the work of Goodall and Fossey. Galdikas introduced herself to him and begged him to help her as well. After some discussion, he agreed.

Galdikas finally reached Indonesia, a string of islands off the southeast Asian coast, in September 1971. Rod Brindamour, a fellow Canadian whom she had met at UCLA and married in 1969, came with her. Officials sent them to Tanjung Puting, a forest reserve on the southern coast of the country's largest island, Borneo.

Galdikas and Brindamour set up camp in a bug-infested hut with a grass roof and bark walls, an old hunters' shelter. Honoring Galdikas's mentor, they named it Camp Leakey. Temperatures averaged 90°F (32°C), humidity hovered around 100 percent, and bloodsucking leeches "dropped out of our socks and off our necks and fell out of our underwear" when the couple undressed each night. Nonetheless, Galdikas loved the rain forest, which she calls "a great cathedral."

At first the couple seldom saw the orangutans, which moved silently through the trees far above their heads. With time and patience, however, Galdikas learned to spot the orange apes and follow their progress. The orangutans, in turn, slowly came to ignore the intruders. Galdikas took notes as the apes searched for fruit, their chief food, during the day and made sleeping nests in the trees at night. She saw adult males, built like wrestlers, fight over a female. She watched females care for their babies, who clung constantly to their mothers during their first years. She verified that, unlike gorillas and chimpanzees, adult orangutans usually lived alone.

Galdikas and Brindamour remained in the forest for four years without a break, spending 6,804 hours observing 58 individual orangutans. After an additional three years, Galdikas wrote up her research as her Ph.D. thesis for UCLA. It described details of orangutans' daily lives that had never been reported before. Galdikas has said, "My main contribution [to science] is . . . following one population longer than anyone."

Almost as soon as she began observing wild orangutans, Galdikas also started rehabilitating young orangutans that had been seized from people who captured them illegally to sell to zoos or keep as pets. Forestry officials asked Galdikas and Brindamour to provide a haven for these repossessed babies and help them return to life in the wild.

Galdikas did most of her research with orphan orangutans clinging to her body. As they grew

Biruté Galdikas, seen here in 1972, made many of her observations of wild orangutans in the Indonesian rain forest while orphaned ex-captive baby orangutans clung to her body. Her long-term study has revealed much new information about these endangered apes.
(Courtesy Orangutan Foundation International)

older, the "unruly children in orange suits," as she called them, tore up or tried to eat almost everything in camp. Seeing them slowly go back to forest life was worth the struggle, however. Galdikas has returned more than 80 ex-captive orangutans to the wilderness.

Meanwhile, Galdikas was also raising her own son, Binti Paul, born in 1976. Binti's life in the forest ended in 1979 when Rod Brindamour divorced Galdikas, remarried, and returned to Canada, taking the boy with him. Galdikas herself married again in 1981. Her second husband, Pak Bohap bin Jalan, is a Dayak, one of the aboriginal people of Borneo. He and Galdikas have two children, Frederick and Jane.

Galdikas today divides her time between overseeing research and rehabilitation work at her camp—now much enlarged—and raising funds for Orangutan Foundation International (OFI), a group she founded in 1986. OFI works to protect the world's 10,000 to 20,000 remaining orangutans, most of which live on Borneo or another Indonesian island, Sumatra. Galdikas tries to educate people both locally and worldwide about the need to preserve these gentle, intelligent animals and their forest home, "a world which is in grave danger of vanishing forever." In 1997 her work earned the Tyler Prize for Environmental Achievement.

Further Reading

Galdikas, Biruté M. F. *Reflections of Eden*. Boston: Little, Brown, 1995.

Gallardo, Evelyn. *Among the Orangutans: The Biruté Galdikas Story*. San Francisco: Chronicle Books, 1993.

Montgomery, Sy. *Walking with the Great Apes*. Boston: Houghton Mifflin, 1991.

Yount, Lisa. *Twentieth-Century Women Scientists*. New York: Facts On File, 1996, 94–105.

 ## GARDNER, JULIA ANNA
(1882–1960)   *American Geologist and Paleontologist*

Julia Gardner used the fossils of snail-like ocean animals to identify rocks that contained oil. She was born on January 26, 1882, in Chamberlain, South Dakota. Her father, Charles, a physician, died when she was just four months old. She and her schoolteacher mother, also named Julia, moved several times as she grew up.

Gardner went to college at Bryn Mawr, where pioneer geologist FLORENCE BASCOM interested her in that subject and became her mentor and friend. Gardner also studied paleontology, the science of fossils. She graduated in 1905 and, after a year of teaching school, returned to Bryn Mawr to earn her master's degree in 1907. Bascom helped her obtain a scholarship to Johns Hopkins University, where she earned her Ph.D. in paleontology in 1911. She

stayed on to teach at Hopkins, sometimes without pay, until 1917. She also began to work as a contractor for the U.S. Geological Survey (USGS). Her specialty was identifying certain kinds of rocks, formed when ancient seabeds turned to stone, by identifying the fossils of mollusks (shelled sea creatures) embedded in them.

Gardner joined the USGS full-time as an assistant geologist in 1920. She worked in the coastal plain section on a survey of part of Texas and then, starting in 1936, in the paleontology and stratigraphy section. She became an associate geologist in 1924 and a geologist in 1928. The kinds of rocks she mapped were important because many of them contained oil. Writing in *Notable American Women: The Modern Period*, Clifford M. Nelson and Mary Ellen Williams say that "by the 1940s, Gardner's work . . . was of national and international importance."

During World War II, Gardner worked for the Military Geology Unit of the USGS, which analyzed maps, aerial photographs, and other sources for information that might be helpful in the war. When Japan sent firebombs to America's northwest coast, Gardner used shells in recovered bombs' sand ballast to identify the beaches from which the sand and the bombs came.

Gardner's war work aroused her interest in the geology of the Pacific, and after the war she began work on geological maps of Western Pacific islands. She retired from the USGS in 1952 but was immediately rehired as a contractor to continue her study of fossil mollusks on the islands. In the year she retired, she received the Interior Department's Distinguished Service Award and served as president of the Paleontological Society. She was also a vice president of the Geological Society of America in 1953. A stroke ended her career in 1954, and she died on November 15, 1960.

Further Reading

Bailey, Brooke. *The Remarkable Lives of 100 Women Healers and Scientists*. Holbrook, Mass.; Bob Adams, 1994, 86–87.

Nelson, Clifford M., and Mary Ellen Williams. "Gardner, Julia Anna." In *Notable American Women: The Modern Period*, edited by Barbara Sicherman and Carol Hurd Green, 260–262. Cambridge, Mass.: The Belknap Press of Harvard University Press, 1980.

 GEIRINGER, HILDA
(1893–1973) *German/American Mathematician*

Hilda Geiringer's research in applied mathematics has helped scientists understand subjects as diverse as flexible surfaces and genetics. She was born on September 28, 1893, in Vienna, Austria, to Ludwig Geiringer, a cloth manufacturer, and his wife, Martha. She had an amazing memory and a talent for mathematics, which her parents encouraged her to pursue. She studied mathematics at the University of Vienna, earning a Ph.D. in 1917.

In 1921, Geiringer moved to the University of Berlin, where she became an assistant to Richard von Mises, a professor at the university's Institute of Applied Mathematics. She also married mathematician Felix Polaczek, but the marriage failed after three years and she was left with a daughter, Magda, to bring up alone. She became a lecturer at the university in 1927. She did research on probability theory and on the mathematics governing the bending of plastic (flexible) materials.

Geiringer was being considered for promotion to professor in 1933, when the Nazis took over Germany. Instead, like other Jewish academics, she abruptly lost her job. She and Magda fled to Turkey in 1934, where she became professor of mathematics at Istanbul University. When World War II began in 1939, she moved to the United States.

Geiringer lectured at Bryn Mawr College from 1939 to 1944 and became a U.S. citizen in 1945. She also became reacquainted with Richard von Mises, who was now teaching at Harvard. The two married on November 5, 1943. They saw each other only on weekends, however, after Geiringer became professor and chairman of the mathematics depart-

ment at Wheaton College in Norton, Massachusetts, in 1944.

In addition to teaching, Geiringer continued to do research in applied mathematics. In 1953 she wrote that research "is a necessity for me; I never stopped it since my student days, it is the deepest need in my life." In addition to further work on flexible materials, she studied statistics, especially the mathematics underlying genetic inheritance. After von Mises died in 1953, she extended his research in probability theory and statistics.

Geiringer retired from Wheaton University in 1959, and the university awarded her an honorary degree a year later. The University of Berlin made her a paid professor emeritus in 1957, and the University of Vienna made a special presentation to her in 1967. She died on March 22, 1973.

Further Reading

Bailey, Brooke. *The Remarkable Lives of 100 Women Healers and Scientists.* Holbrook, Mass.; Bob Adams, 1994, 88–89.

Richards, Joan L. "Geiringer, Hilda." In *Notable American Women: The Modern Period*, edited by Barbara Sicherman and Carol Hurd Green, 267–268. Cambridge, Mass.: The Belknap Press of Harvard University Press, 1980.

✳ GELLER, MARGARET JOAN
(1947–) *American Astronomer*

Astronomers used to believe that the universe was as smooth as pudding, with galaxies scattered through it evenly like raisins. Margaret Geller, however, has shown that it is more like a dishpan full of soap bubbles. She has helped to make the most extensive existing maps of the nearby universe. The largest of the structures shown in Geller's maps, the Great Wall, contains thousands of galaxies and is at least half a billion light-years across.

Margaret Geller was born on December 8, 1947, in Ithaca, New York. Her father was a crystallographer at Bell Laboratories and sometimes took her to work with him. "I got the idea that science was an exciting thing to do," she says. He also gave her toys that helped her visualize in three dimensions, a skill that proved essential in her later work. Her mother encouraged her interest in language and art; Geller has said that if she hadn't become a scientist, she probably would have been an artist. These two interests combine in Geller's fondness for patterns in nature.

At the University of California at Berkeley, Geller changed her major from mathematics to physics. She graduated in 1970. Then, excited by new findings in astronomy, she specialized in astrophysics in graduate school. She obtained her master's degree in 1972 and her Ph.D. in 1975 from Princeton University. She was not comfortable with the scientific atmosphere there, however, and she often considered dropping out.

After several years of postdoctoral work at the Harvard-Smithsonian Center for Astrophysics, Geller spent a year and a half at Britain's Cambridge University, mostly thinking over her career. "I realized that if I was going to stay in science, I was going to have to make some changes and do problems because I was interested in them," she says. What interested her, she decided, was the large-scale structure of the universe—a subject which she came to realize was largely unexplored. She returned to the Harvard-Smithsonian Center in 1980, continuing her affiliation with both it and Harvard University, at which she became a professor in 1988.

In 1985, Geller and fellow Harvard-Smithsonian astronomer John Huchra decided to map the distribution of galaxies in a given volume of space. They examined a pie-slice-shaped segment of the sky with a 60-inch telescope on Mount Hopkins, Arizona. Huchra and a French graduate student, Valerie de Lapparent, gathered data at the telescope, scanning the sky in a strip and measuring about 20 galaxies a night. Geller worked to interpret the results.

The researchers expected the galaxies to be more or less evenly distributed. When de Lapparent plotted a computer-generated map showing the location of the galaxies in the pie slice, however, it revealed a remarkable pattern. "A lot of science is really . . . mapping," Geller says. "You have to make a map before you understand."

When Geller, Huchra, and de Lapparent looked at the map of about 1,000 galaxies in the fall of 1986, they were astounded. Instead of an even distribution of galaxies, the map showed clusters of these star systems curving around dark voids almost bare of visible matter. Geller said that their slice of the universe looked like a "kitchen-sink-full of soapsuds."

Astronomers had seen clusters of galaxies before, but, Geller says, "nobody had seen *sharp* structures . . . The pattern is so striking." Most striking of all was the strange shape in the center of the map, which looked like a child's sketch of a person and has been nicknamed the stickman. In 1989, as the group's survey continued, they discovered another structure, now called the Great Wall.

Geller and Huchra's discoveries have "changed our understanding of the universe," *Discover* writer Gary Taubes wrote in 1997. They showed that the universe did not have the smooth structure that everyone had expected. Geller believes that the patterns she and her coworkers see are explained by the action of gravity. She agrees that the distribution of matter in the universe was even just after the Big Bang, 10 to 15 billion years ago, but says that the details of the universe's formation and evolution to its present structure remain to be discovered.

Today, Geller and another Smithsonian astrophysicist, Dan Fabricant, are preparing to make an even deeper map that they hope will allow them to see the evolution of the distribution of galaxies directly. They plan to begin the project in 1999, using improved technology to survey thousands of galaxies a night. They expect to survey over 50,000 galaxies, reaching out to a distance of 5 billion light-years from earth.

Geller, in 1998 a professor of astronomy at Harvard and a senior scientist at the Harvard-Smithsonian Center for Astrophysics, has won several awards, including the MacArthur "genius" award (1990) and the Newcomb-Cleveland Award of the American Association for the Advancement of Science (1991). Even more than awards, however,

Geller loves the process of discovery. She says that her long-range scientific goals are "to discover what the universe looks like and to understand how it came to have the rich patterns we observe today."

Further Reading

Bartusiak, Marcia. "Mapping the Universe." *Discover*, August 1990, 60-63.

Geller, Margaret J. "A Voyage Through Space . . . and Time: Mapping the Universe." *Mercator's World*, November-December 1997, 35-39.

Lightman, Alan, and Roberta Brawer. *Origins: The Lives and Worlds of Modern Cosmologists.* Cambridge, Mass.: Harvard University Press, 1990, 359-377.

✳ GERMAIN, MARIE SOPHIE
(1776–1831) *French Mathematician*

Because Sophie Germain taught herself, she saw mathematical problems in a fresh way and solved some of them better than any man of her time. She is considered one of the founders of mathematical physics.

Marie Sophie Germain was born in Paris on April 1, 1776, to Ambrose Germain, a silk merchant, and his wife. Although the family was comfortably off financially, the bloody chaos of the French Revolution surrounded Sophie's childhood, and she retreated to her father's library.

Sophie's parents, like most at the time, feared that mental effort would harm their daughter's health, so they tried to stop her from studying. When she was 13, they took away her clothing, candles, and the fire that warmed her room so that she would not get out of bed at night. Sophie got up anyway, wrapped quilts around herself, lit candles that she had hidden, and went on with her math, even though the room was so cold that her ink froze.

In 1798, Germain wanted to hear Joseph Lagrange's mathematics lectures at the Ecole Polytechnique in Paris, but the school did not admit women. Undaunted, Germain borrowed the notes of men friends who went to the lectures. To escape "the ridicule attached to a woman devoted to science," she submitted an end-of-term paper under the name of Monsieur Leblanc. Lagrange praised the paper and was astounded when Germain revealed her identity.

Lagrange became Germain's mentor and helped her meet or correspond with other mathematicians, such as the German Karl Friedrich Gauss. Gauss exchanged letters with Germain under her Leblanc pseudonym for several years before learning that she was a woman. When he found out, he wrote to her that since she had learned mathematics in spite of all the obstacles that society put in the way of female education, she must possess "the most noble courage, extraordinary talent, and superior genius."

Germain made contributions in both pure and applied mathematics. Her studies in pure mathematics involved number theory, Gauss's field. At the age of 25, she offered a proof of part of an equation called Fermat's Last Theorem. No one else of her time was able to prove even a part of the theorem, and no one proved the whole theorem until 1993.

Physicist Ernest Chladni inspired Germain's contribution to applied mathematics. Chladni caused a sensation in 1808 by placing sand on a metal or glass plate on a stand and making the plate vibrate by drawing a violin bow along its edge. Lagrange, for one, believed that mathematics was not advanced enough to produce equations that could describe the curving patterns the sand formed on this flexible, or elastic, surface. When the French Academy of Sciences announced a competition to attempt that task in 1809, Sophie Germain was the only person brave—or naive—enough to enter. Lagrange and two other mathematicians reviewed her paper, which she submitted anonymously. They found serious flaws in it, thanks mostly to gaps in her home-grown education, but praised her effort.

The academy held the contest again in 1813 and 1815, and each time Germain was the best entrant, although her work was still far from perfect. She finally was awarded a prize in a public ceremony on January 8, 1816. When her paper was published in 1821, French mathematician Claude Navier said of it, "It is a work which few men are able to read and which only one woman was able to write." In 1822 the Academy of Sciences formally admitted Germain to its meetings, an unusual honor for a woman.

Germain died of breast cancer in 1831.

Further Reading

Alic, Margaret. *Hypatia's Heritage: A History of Women in Science from Antiquity Through the Nineteenth Century.* Boston: Beacon Press, 1986, 148–157.

Osen, Lynn M. *Women in Mathematics.* Cambridge, Mass.: MIT Press, 1974, 83–93.

Throm, Elaine Bertolozzi. "Sophie Germain." In *Celebrating Women in Mathematics and Science*, edited by Miriam P. Cooney, 37–45. Reston, Va.: National Council of Teachers of Mathematics, 1996.

✳ GILBRETH, LILLIAN EVELYN MOLLER
(1878–1972) *American Psychologist and Engineer*

Working with her husband, Frank, Lillian Gilbreth studied workers' movements and redesigned workplaces and homes to make labor both more efficient and easier. She also made managers see the importance of workers' psychological needs. In an essay in *Women of Science*, Martha Trescott calls Gilbreth "probably the best-known woman engineer in history."

Lillian Evelyn Moller was born into a prosperous family in Oakland, California, on May 24, 1878. Her father, William, owned a large hardware business. As the oldest of eight children, Lillian often cared for the younger ones when her mother, Annie, was sick or pregnant. Although a shy girl, she insisted on the unusual step of going to college. She earned a B.A. in literature from the nearby University of California at Berkeley in 1900 and became the first woman to speak at the university's commencement.

Moller obtained a master's degree from UC Berkeley and planned to go on to a doctorate, but her plans changed after she met Frank Bunker Gilbreth while visiting friends in Boston in 1903. The energetic Gilbreth had taught himself con-

struction skills and engineering and become one of the country's leading building contractors. His specialty was "speed building," using techniques and devices that helped workers do their jobs more efficiently. He and Moller married at her home on October 19, 1904.

The Gilbreth marriage was a partnership in every sense. Lillian edited Frank's writing, learned the construction business, and even devised new building techniques. The couple had 12 children, and Frank, for his part, took a full share in raising them. Applying their efficiency techniques to the household, the Gilbreths taught their children to take responsibility for themselves and each other. Two of the brood described the family's happy if eccentric life in a humorous memoir called *Cheaper by the Dozen*, which later became a movie. The family lived first in New York City, then in Providence, Rhode Island, and finally in Montclair, New Jersey.

Frank Gilbreth admired the ideas of Frederick Taylor, who had developed a concept called time and motion study. By analyzing workers' movements, Taylor said, managers could eliminate unnecessary motion and thus increase the amount of work done in a given length of time. Gilbreth insisted that workers' comfort as well as their efficiency be considered. After filming workers on the job, he redesigned workplaces so that, for instance, tools could be reached without stretching or bending. In both his own business and in others that hired him as a consultant, he looked for the "one best way"—the way that required the least effort—to do each task. He became a pioneer in what was called scientific management.

Lillian Gilbreth, in turn, went beyond Frank's ideas, pointing out that changes that improved physical efficiency but psychologically stressed or isolated workers would fail to improve production in the long run. The Society of Industrial Engineers said in 1921 that Lillian was "the first to recognize that management is a problem of psychology and . . . to show this fact to both the managers and the psychologists." She helped managers and workers find ways to cooperate rather than opposing each other.

The Gilbreths began doing management consulting full time in 1914, and their company, Gilbreth, Inc., soon earned an international reputation. Besides lecturing and visiting factories, they held summer classes in their home. They wrote many articles and books about their ideas, including *A Primer of Scientific Management* (1912) and *Applied Motion Study* (1917).

At Frank's urging, Lillian studied for a Ph.D. in psychology at Brown University, obtaining it in 1915. Her doctoral thesis grew into a book, *Psychology of Management,* which was published in 1914. Martha Trescott says that this book "open[ed] whole new areas to scientific management. . . . [It] formed a basis for much modern management theory."

Frank Gilbreth died of a heart attack on June 14, 1924. As recounted in *Belles on Their Toes,* the sequel to *Cheaper by the Dozen,* life was hard for his family for a while. Managers who had hired the Gilbreths doubted that Lillian Gilbreth could be a useful consultant on her own. Gilbreth, however, continued teaching and speaking as well as running Gilbreth, Inc., and in time she persuaded clients that she was more than competent.

Gilbreth also took over her husband's position as visiting lecturer at Purdue University in Indiana after his death. From 1935 to 1948 she was a professor of management in Purdue's School of Mechanical Engineering, the first woman to be a full professor in an engineering school. She was also Purdue's consultant on careers for women from 1939 until her death. In addition to teaching at Purdue, she became head of the new Department of Personnel Relations at the Newark School of Engineering in 1941.

Beginning in the late 1920s, Gilbreth extended her ideas about efficient work into the home, taking industrial engineering "through the kitchen door." She pointed out that homemakers lost time and effort to badly designed room layouts and appliances, just as factory workers did. She designed an "efficiency kitchen" for the Brooklyn Gas Company that was featured in women's magazines. She also worked out kitchen and household arrangements for disabled people that helped them achieve greater

independence. Her books on these subjects include *Normal Lives for the Disabled* (1944, with Edna Yost) and *Management in the Home* (1954).

Lillian Gilbreth continued writing, teaching, and lecturing well into her eighties. She received many awards, including over 20 honorary degrees and commendations. She was made an honorary member of the Society of Industrial Engineers in 1920. In 1966 she became the first woman to win the Hoover Medal for distinguished public service by an engineer. She also was awarded the National Institute of Social Science's medal "for distinguished service to humanity." She died on January 2, 1972, at 93.

Further Reading

Cowan, Ruth Schwartz. "Gilbreth, Lillian Evelyn Moller," in *Notable American Women: The Modern Period*, edited by Barbara Sicherman and Carol Hurd Green, 271–273. Cambridge, Mass.: The Belknap Press of Harvard University Press, 1980.

Gilbreth, Frank B., Jr. *Time Out for Happiness.* New York: Crowell, 1970.

———. and Ernestine Gilbreth Carey. *Belles on Their Toes.* New York: Crowell, 1950.

Yost, Edna. *Frank and Lillian Gilbreth: Partners for Life.* New Brunswick, N.J.: Rutgers University Press, 1949.

GOODALL, JANE
(1934–) *British Zoologist*

Jane Goodall's research on chimpanzees in Africa is the longest continuous study of animals in the wild and, according to naturalist Stephen Jay Gould, "one of the Western world's great scientific achievements." For it she was named a commander of the British Empire, given the U.S. National Geographic Society's Hubbard Medal, and awarded the Kyoto Prize, Japan's equivalent of the Nobel Prize. Today she educates people about chimpanzees, works to rescue captive chimpanzees and save the habitat of wild ones, and sponsors a program that teaches children to care about animals, the environment, and their home communities.

Jane, the older of Mortimer and Vanne Morris-Goodall's two daughters, was born in London on April 3, 1934. Her father was an engineer, her mother a housewife and writer. Her favorite toy as a baby was a stuffed chimpanzee named Jubilee, which she still owns.

An incident that happened when Jane was just five years old showed her patience and determination as well as her interest in animals. One day, while on a farm, she vanished for more then five hours. Vanne Goodall called the police, but before a search could be launched, Jane reappeared. She explained that she had been sitting in the henhouse, waiting for a hen to lay an egg. "I had always wondered where on a hen was an opening big enough for an egg to come out," Goodall recalled later. "I hid in the straw at the back of the stuffy little hen house. And I waited and waited."

Jane's family moved to the seaside town of Bournemouth at about that time, and she stayed there with her mother and sister after her parents divorced several years later. They had no money for college, so she went to work as a secretary. Then, in 1957, a former school friend invited Jane to visit her in Kenya. The invitation revived a childhood dream of going to Africa that Jane had formed after reading books such as Hugh Lofting's fantasies about Dr. Doolittle, who lived in Africa and could talk with animals. Jane began saving her money and left as soon as she could pay the fare.

While in Kenya, Jane Goodall met famed British anthropologist Louis S. B. Leakey, who had made pioneering discoveries about early humans. Leakey, then the head of Kenya's National Museum of Natural History, liked Goodall and hired her as an assistant secretary. In time he told her about his belief that the best way to learn how human ancestors might have lived was to study the natural behavior of their closest cousins, the great apes—chimpanzees, gorillas, and orangutans—over long periods of time. He wanted to start with chimpanzees, and he asked Goodall if she would like to do the research. "Of course I accepted," she says.

Following Leakey's recommendation, Goodall decided to work at Gombe Stream, a protected area on the shores of Lake Tanganyika in the neighboring country of Tanzania. When British officials informed her that they could not let her live alone in the wilderness, her mother agreed to stay with her for a few months. The Goodalls and their African assistants set up camp at Gombe in July 1960. Goodall could not get anywhere near the chimpanzees at first, but as the months passed, they grew used to the "peculiar, white-skinned ape." She, in turn, learned to recognize them as individuals. She gave them names such as Flo and David Graybeard.

In the first year of her research, Goodall made several observations that overturned long-held beliefs about chimpanzees. Scientists had thought that the animals ate only plants, insects, and perhaps an occasional rodent, but Goodall saw them eating meat from larger animals. Later she saw groups of them hunt young baboons. Even more amazing, Goodall one day watched David Graybeard lower a grass stem into the hard-packed open tower of a termite mound. After a few moments he pulled it out with several of the antlike insects clinging to it, then ate them. She later saw other chimps do the same thing. The animals were clearly using the grass blades as tools to get the insects, contradicting the common belief that only humans used tools. Goodall even saw the chimps make tools by selecting twigs and stripping the leaves from them. She observed other kinds of tool use as well. "Chimpanzees are so inventive," Goodall told writer Peter Miller.

In 1961, Goodall enrolled in the Ph.D. program in ethology, the study of animal behavior, at Britain's prestigious Cambridge University. She was only the eighth student in the university's long history to be admitted to a Ph.D. program without having first obtained a bachelor's degree. She wrote up her chimpanzee studies as her thesis and obtained her degree in 1965.

In 1962 the National Geographic Society sent a Dutch photographer, Baron Hugo van Lawick, to take pictures of Goodall at work. Van Lawick and Goodall fell in love and married on March 28, 1964. Their wedding cake was topped by a statue of a chimpanzee. In 1967 they had a son, whom they named Hugo after his father, but everyone called the blond youngster Grub, Swahili for "bush baby." Imitating the behavior of good chimpanzee mothers, Goodall kept the child close to her and showered him with affection. Goodall and van Lawick divorced in 1974. Grub later attended boarding school in England, but he returned to Africa as an adult.

As Goodall's observations continued, she discovered dark sides to chimpanzee behavior. For instance, she saw the animals wage war. One group staged repeated sneak attacks on a neighboring group over a period of four years, eventually wiping them out. "When I first started at Gombe, I thought the chimps were nicer than we are," she said in a 1995 *National Geographic* article. "But time has revealed that they are not."

In 1975, Goodall married Derek Bryceson, who was in charge of Kenya's national parks. He was the only white official in the country's cabinet. Unfortunately, Bryceson developed cancer in 1980 and died within a few months.

Another tragedy struck Goodall soon after her marriage. Her camp had grown to include students from the United States and Europe, and on May 19, 1975, rebel soldiers from nearby Zaire invaded the camp and seized four of the students. The soldiers demanded ransom for the students' return. After two months of negotiations, money was paid and the students were released unharmed, but the Edenlike peace of Gombe had been permanently damaged.

About this time, Goodall decided that "I had to use the knowledge the chimps gave me in the fight to save them." She left the continuing observation of the Gombe chimps to her students and began to travel the world as a spokesperson for the animals. In 1977 a nonprofit organization, the Jane Goodall Institute, was formed to help with her work. In 1998 its headquarters were in Silver Spring, Maryland.

The greatest danger to wild chimpanzees, Goodall says, is loss of their forest habitat, which is shrinking their populations greatly. Over a million chimps once ranged across 25 countries in central Africa, but only about 200,000 remain. She is equally concerned about captive chimpanzees, which are often confined under miserable conditions. She rescued her first captive, Whiskey, in 1989 and since then has established several sanctuaries where the animals can live, since they cannot be returned to the wild.

Chimpanzees used in medical research are a third source of distress for Goodall. She claims that chimps in many labs are kept in conditions "not unlike [those in] concentration camps." Goodall belives it is wrong for humans to use chimpanzees or other animals in any way they see fit. She would like to see experimentation on animals made illegal in cases where the experiments are unnecessary or alternative methods exist. When chimpanzees must be used in laboratory experimentation, they should be kept in large enclosures with other chimps, climbing equipment and platforms, and toys or puzzles to occupy their minds.

The ultimate way to help chimpanzees and other animals, Goodall believes, is to teach people—especially children—to respect them. In 1991 she developed a program called Roots & Shoots, now implemented worldwide, that educates children about nature. "Teaching [children] to care for the earth, and each other, is our hope for the future," she says. In 1998 she published a book for children entitled *With Love: Ten Heartwarming Stories of Chimpanzees in the Wild.*

Further Reading

Goodall, Jane. *The Chimpanzees of Gombe.* Cambridge, Mass.: Harvard University Press, 1986.

———. *Through a Window: My Thirty Years with the Chimpanzees of Gombe.* Boston: Houghton Mifflin, 1991.

———. and Dale Peterson. *Visions of Caliban: On Chimpanzees and People.* Boston: Houghton Mifflin, 1993.

Miller, Peter. "Jane Goodall." *National Geographic*, December 1995, 104–129.

Montgomery, Sy. *Walking with the Great Apes.* Boston: Houghton Mifflin, 1990.

H

 HAMILTON, ALICE
(1869–1970) *American Physician*

When Alice Hamilton began investigating industry in the early years of this century, no laws protected workers on the job. Many lost their health or even their lives to poisoning or accidents. Hamilton almost singlehandedly established industrial medicine in the United States, and her research helped persuade employers and legislators to make workplaces safer.

Alice was born in New York City on February 27, 1869, the second of Montgomery and Gertrude Hamilton's four children. She grew up with other members of the large Hamilton clan on her grandmother's estate in Fort Wayne, Indiana. Montgomery was part owner of a wholesale grocery firm, though he had little love for business. Gertrude schooled her children at home, teaching them not only languages, literature, and history but also responsibility and independence. Alice said later that she had learned from her mother that "personal liberty was the most precious thing in life."

Following family tradition, Alice was sent to Miss Porter's School for Girls in Farmington, Vermont, when she was 17. Because Montgomery Hamilton's business had failed the year before, she knew that,

unlike most of Miss Porter's students, she would soon have to earn a living. To the surprise of those who knew her, Alice decided to become a doctor. She had never felt any interest in science, but she chose medicine, she said later, "because as a doctor I could go anywhere I pleased and be of use."

After taking classes at the Fort Wayne College of Medicine to gain the science background that Miss Porter's school had not provided, Alice Hamilton entered the University of Michigan medical school in 1892 and earned her M.D. degree in 1893. She then took practical training at two hospitals, plus a year of graduate study in Germany and another at Johns Hopkins University. Beginning in 1897, she taught at the Women's Medical School of Northwestern University, near Chicago, but lost that job when the school closed in 1902. She then began research at the Memorial Institute of Infectious Diseases, also near Chicago.

The move to Chicago allowed Hamilton to fulfill a longtime dream by becoming a member of Hull House, the famous settlement house that Jane Addams had founded in 1889. The house, located in one of the city's worst slums, was staffed by young women who worked without pay to help the immigrant families who crowded into the area. Hamilton took on several health-related jobs at Hull House, including teaching mothers about nutrition and health care and holding a well-baby clinic in the house's basement washroom. She later said that washing those babies was the most satisfying work she ever did. Nonetheless, after 10 years at Hull House, Hamilton, by then almost 40, was dissatisfied with her life. Her laboratory research seemed "remote and useless," and her settlement work left her feeling "pulled about and tired and yet never doing anything definite." She felt that neither made much difference in the world.

In the course of her work at Hull House, Hamilton often met laborers who were severely ill. A British book called *The Dangerous Trades* opened her eyes to the fact that many of these illnesses could be caused by lead or other poisons that the workers were exposed to on the job. She learned that Britain and Germany had tried to reduce poisoning in workplaces, but no such attempts had been made in the United States.

Hamilton was not the only American concerned about workplace safety. In 1908 the governor of Illinois appointed a commission to make a survey of work-related illness, something no state had done before. Hamilton applied for a place on the commission and was put in charge of the survey, which began in 1910.

The survey focused on poisoning by lead, which was used in over 70 industries. Hamilton found workers breathing lead-laden dust and fumes in many factories, but proving that individuals had been poisoned was not easy. She wrote later that most company doctors "knew little and cared less" about the health risks workers ran, and many seemed to feel that the whole subject of industrial medicine was "tainted with Socialism or feminine sentimentality for the poor." Their badly kept records gave her little help. Workers themselves often refused to talk to her out of fear that they or family members would lose their jobs. Nonetheless, Hamilton's survey finally documented 578 cases of work-related lead poisoning. Her commission published its report, *A Survey of Occupational Diseases,* late in 1910, and a year later Illinois passed a law requiring safety measures, regular medical check-

ups, and payments for workers who became ill or injured on the job.

While still working on the Illinois survey, Hamilton attended an international meeting on occupational accidents and diseases in Belgium. There she met Charles O'Neill, commissioner of labor in the U.S. Commerce Department, who asked her to conduct a similar survey that would cover the whole country. She said later that this meeting "resulted in the taking up of this new specialty as my life's work."

Hamilton began the national survey in 1911 and continued it through the years of World War I. She and her assistants visited factories, mills, quarries, mines, and construction sites, looking not only for lead poisoning but also poisoning from arsenic, mercury, and organic compounds such as benzene. In many cases, her blend of politeness and persistence persuaded employers to correct the problems she uncovered.

Hamilton was one of the world's chief authorities on industrial diseases and virtually the only expert in the United States when, in 1919, Harvard University—which did not yet take women students and had never had a woman on its faculty before—asked her to teach industrial medicine in its School of Public Health. Hamilton took the position (part-time, so she could continue her survey work), but Harvard hardly went out of its way to make her welcome. She was kept at the lowly rank of assistant professor during all 16 years she taught there. She was also slighted in small ways, such as being forbidden to enter the faculty club or march in the commencement procession.

In the wider world, Hamilton could see that her work was making a difference. In the 1920s, after she finished her national survey, one state after another passed laws requiring safety measures in workplaces and payments to workers who suffered illness or injury on the job. All states had such laws by the end of the 1930s. Hamilton herself made a few investigations of new industrial poisons after 1920, such as the tetraethyl lead added to gasoline, but for the most part she acted as a consultant to employers and governments. In 1925 she summarized her work in *Industrial Poisons in the United States,* the first American textbook on the subject. She published another textbook, *Industrial Toxicology,* in 1934.

Hamilton worked for many social causes besides industrial safety. She joined Jane Addams and other women on an international mission to try to stop World War I. After the war she raised money for starving German children. She served two terms on the Health Committee of the League of Nations, the forerunner of the United Nations, in the 1920s. On the national front, she supported birth control and opposed capital punishment. In 1963, at the age of 94, she wrote an open letter demanding withdrawal of U.S. troops from Vietnam.

After Hamilton retired from Harvard in 1935, she became a consultant for the Division of Labor Standards in the U.S. Department of Labor, testifying before many congressional committees. She died on September 22, 1970, at the age of 101, knowing that the "dangerous trades" were no longer as dangerous because of her. Near the end of her life she said, "For me the satisfaction is that things are better now, and I had some part in it."

Further Reading

Grant, Madeline. *Alice Hamilton: Pioneer Doctor in Industrial Medicine.* New York: Abelard-Schuman, 1967.

Hamilton, Alice. *Exploring the Dangerous Trades.* Boston: Little, Brown, 1943.

Sicherman, Barbara. *Alice Hamilton: A Life in Letters.* Cambridge, Mass.: Harvard University Press, 1984.

———. "Hamilton, Alice." In *Notable American Women: The Modern Period,* edited by Barbara Sicherman and Carol Hurd Green, 303–306. Cambridge, Mass.: The Belknap Press of Harvard University Press, 1980.

Veglahn, Nancy. *Women Scientists.* New York: Facts On File, 1991, 36–47.

✳ HAWES, HARRIET ANN BOYD
(1871–1945) *American Archaeologist*

When she led a group excavating a 3,000-year-old Cretan town in 1901, Harriet Hawes became the first woman to head a large archaeological dig. She was born in Boston on October 11, 1871, to Alexander Boyd, who owned a leather business, and his wife, also named Harriet. Harriet's mother died when she was a baby, so she grew up in a household of men—her father and four older brothers. Her second brother, Alexander, passed on to her his interest in ancient civilizations.

Boyd studied classics at Smith College, from which she graduated in 1892. She did four years of graduate work at the American School of Classical Studies in Athens, Greece. Her professors told her to stick to library research, but, as she wrote to her family, "I was not cut out for a library student."

In 1900, using money from a fellowship plus her own savings, Boyd and a woman friend traveled to the island of Crete, home of a spectacular ancient civilization whose remains archaeologists were just beginning to study. Boyd was the first American archaeologist to go there. An account by the Archaeological Institute of America pictured her "daring to travel—as few women had yet done—through rugged mountains . . . riding on muleback in Victorian attire . . . Here we have all the elements of romance and danger." At a spot called Kavousi, on the eastern side of the island, Boyd uncovered several Iron Age tombs. She wrote up this discovery as the thesis for her master's degree, which she received from Smith in 1901.

To Boyd's delight, a grant from the American Exploration Society let her return to Kavousi that same year. This time, at a nearby site named Gournia, she discovered the remains of an entire town. Dating to the early Bronze Age, it was even older than the tombs she had found before. Because Gournia had been occupied chiefly by workers, it offered valuable glimpses of the era's ordinary people. Boyd led further expeditions to Gournia in 1903 and 1904, supervising over a hundred villagers. It was the first Bronze Age Cretan city to be fully excavated. She described the excavation in a report published by the exploration society in 1908.

Boyd married Charles Henry Hawes, a British anthropologist whom she had met on Crete, on March 3, 1906. They collaborated on a popular book, *Crete: The Forerunner of Greece,* which was published in 1909. They later had a son and a daughter, and Harriet spent most of her time caring for them. Eventually the family moved to Boston, where Charles Hawes became assistant director of the Museum of Fine Arts. In 1920, Harriet resumed her career, teaching pre-Christian art at Wellesley College until 1936. She died on March 31, 1945.

Further Reading

Allsebrook, Mary N. *Born to Rebel: The Life of Harriet Boyd Hawes.* Oxford: Oxbow Books, 1992.

Kohler, Ellen L., and Paul S. Boyer. "Hawes, Harriet Ann Boyd." In *Notable American Women, vol. II: G–O,* edited by Edward T. James, 160–161. Cambridge, Mass.: The Belknap Press of Harvard University Press, 1971.

Ogilvie, Marilyn Bailey. *Women in Science: Antiquity Through the Nineteenth Century.* Cambridge, Mass.: MIT Press, 1986, 95.

 ## HAZEN, ELIZABETH LEE
(1885–1975) *American Medical Researcher*

Elizabeth Lee Hazen improved methods for identifying human diseases caused by fungi and, with chemist Rachel Brown, discovered a drug that became the first successful treatment for many of them. She was born to William and Maggie Hazen on a cotton farm in Rich, Mississippi, on August 24, 1885. Her parents died when she was a child, and an aunt and uncle in nearby Lula raised her and her sister.

Hazen graduated from the State College for Women (later Mississippi University for Women) in Columbus in 1910. After several years of teaching high school science, she went to Columbia University and obtained a master's degree in bacteriology in 1917. She worked for a West Virginia hospital for years before finally going back to Columbia for a Ph.D., which she received in 1927, at age 42. After four years of teaching at the university, she joined the New York City branch laboratory of the New York State Department of Health's Division of Laboratories and Research. She became an expert in identifying disease-causing fungi, which few other researchers had studied.

Penicillin and other antibiotics developed in the 1940s had no effect on fungi, so Hazen decided to search for a drug that would kill these stubborn microbes. Soil, the source of several antibiotics, seemed a likely place to look. Hazen traveled around the country gathering samples of soil, which she took back to to her laboratory and sprinkled in nutrient-filled dishes so that microorganisms in them would form colonies. She sent these cultures to Rachel Brown at the Department of Health's laboratory in Albany, and Brown extracted substances that the microbes made and sent them back to Hazen. Hazen tested them to see which ones killed disease-causing fungi.

In 1948, Hazen collected a soil sample near Warrenton, Virginia, which proved to contain a microbe that produced two fungus-killing substances. One was new to science, and Hazen and Brown announced its discovery late in 1950. The drug made from this substance, named Nystatin in honor of the New York State Health Department, was first marketed in 1954. The women patented the drug but gave the $13 million profit from it to a foundation that endowed medical research. Hazen and Brown received several awards for their discovery, including the Squibb Award (1955) and Chemical Pioneer Awards from the American Institute of Chemists (1975). The New York Department of Health gave Hazen a Distinguished Service Award in 1968.

Nystatin proved to have a surprising range of uses. In addition to attacking fungi that caused human illnesses, it destroyed the fungus that caused Dutch elm disease, a widespread killer of trees. It killed molds that spoiled stored fruit, livestock feed, and meat. It saved priceless paintings and manuscripts from mold damage after a flood in Florence, Italy, in 1966.

After the New York City branch laboratory closed in 1954, Hazen worked at the central laboratory in Albany. In 1955 she wrote a textbook called *Identification of Pathogenic Fungi Simplified.* She was an associate professor at Albany Medical College from 1958 until her retirement from both this position and the one at the Department of Health in 1960. After that she became a guest investigator at Columbia's Medical Mycology (study of fungi) Laboratory. She died on June 24, 1975.

Further Reading

Baldwin, Richard S. *The Fungus Fighters: Two Women Scientists and Their Discovery.* Ithaca, N.Y.: Cornell University Press, 1981.

O'Hern, Elizabeth Moot. *Profiles of Pioneer Women Scientists.* Washington, D.C.: Acropolis Books, 1985, 95–100.

Rubin, Lewis P. "Hazen, Elizabeth Lee." In *Notable American Women: The Modern Period,* edited by Barbara Sicherman and Carol Hurd Green, 326–328. Cambridge, Mass.: The Belknap Press of Harvard University Press, 1980.

✳ HERSCHEL, CAROLINE LUCRETIA
(1750–1848) *British Astronomer*

Caroline Herschel not only assisted her famous astronomer brother William but "swept the skies" on her own, spotting at least five comets for the first time. The youngest of Isaac and Anna Herschel's 10 children, she was born in Hanover, later a part of Germany, on March 16, 1750. She wrote later that her father, a musician, was also a "great admirer" of astronomy and once took her "on a clear and frosty night into the street, to make me acquainted with several of the beautiful constellations." Isaac wanted to see all his children educated, but Anna opposed this, believing that girls should be taught only household skills.

Caroline's brothers William and Alexander moved to England in 1758, and William became a music teacher and organist at Bath, a popular resort. Caroline remained behind as a sort of household slave until William rescued her in 1772. In Bath he helped her train as a singer and taught her English, mathematics, and above all, astronomy, which he loved more than music.

Unlike most astronomers, William made his own telescopes. His devotion—and Caroline's—to this painstaking task resulted in instruments much better than average. William polished his telescope mirrors by hand, once for 16 hours straight, while Caroline read to him and fed him. When he built a 40-foot telescope in the 1780s, Caroline pounded up horse manure and forced it through a seive to make molds for the device's giant mirrors.

In 1779 the Herschels began the first round of a project to map all the objects in the night sky. They made several "sweeps," each more extensive than the last, between this year and 1802. Night after night, William looked through his telescope and called out his observations to Caroline, who wrote them down. Next day she made a clean copy of her notes and calculated each object's position. It is not clear when she found time to sleep.

William Herschel's first sky sweep uncovered nothing less than a new planet, now known as Uranus, in 1781. King George III was so impressed that he named Herschel the Royal Astronomer the following year and gave him a salary of 200 pounds a year. That meant that Herschel could quit music and work full-time on astronomy. William's quitting meant that Caroline quit too, since she refused to sing under the direction of anyone else. She felt "anything but cheerful" about it, but she did not protest.

In 1786 the Herschels settled in Slough, where they found a house with a yard big enough for their telescopes. William had taught Caroline how to use a telescope by this time and had even built small telescopes for her, but she could do concentrated work or observe through his big telescopes only when he was away on trips. On August 1, 1786, during one such absence, she found her first new comet. She sent a letter about it to Britain's chief scientific body, the Royal Society, and it was published in their journal.

Caroline Herschel's find made her famous in the scientific world. Soon afterward, when George III gave William extra money to help pay for the 40-foot telescope, he also granted a yearly allowance of 50 pounds to Caroline, officially acknowledging her as William's assistant. The amount was small, but the recognition was unusual. Caroline proudly wrote in her diary that this was "the first money I ever in all my lifetime thought myself to be at liberty to spend to my liking."

William married Mary Pitt in 1788, and his bride insisted that Caroline live separately from the couple. Caroline was grieved at first, but eventually she realized that the situation left her more time to "mind the heavens." Between 1788 and 1797, in addition to helping William, she spotted seven more new comets, as well as other heavenly objects such as star clusters.

Caroline's most important works were the *Index to the Catalogue of 860 Stars Observed by Flamsteed but Not Included in the British Catalogue* and *Index to Every Observation of Every Star in the British Catalogue*, published by the Royal Society in 1798. These books resolved discrepancies between unpublished notes left by Flamsteed, the first Royal Astronomer, and a catalogue he had published in 1725.

William Herschel died in 1822. Desolate, Caroline moved back to Hanover. She became a family drudge again, but she also continued William's work, assembling a catalogue of 2,500 nebulae (cloudlike star formations) and star clusters that he (and she) had observed. In 1825 she sent the finished catalogue to William's son, John, who had also become a famous astronomer. When John presented it to the Royal Astronomical Society in 1828, the group awarded Caroline a gold medal, calling the book "the completion of a series of exertions probably unparalleled either in magnitude or importance, in the annals [history] of astronomical labour." The society made Caroline an honorary member in 1835.

In 1846, on her 96th birthday, the king of Prussia gave Caroline another gold medal. Awards meant little to her, however; she always insisted that she had done no more for William than "a well-trained puppy-dog" could have done. She died on January 9, 1848, never guessing that she would later be called "the most famous and admired woman astronomer in history."

Further Reading

Alic, Margaret. *Hypatia's Heritage: A History of Women in Science from Antiquity Through the Nineteenth Century.* Boston: Beacon Press, 1986, 125–133.

Murray, James G. "Caroline Lucretia Herschel." In *Celebrating Women in Mathematics and Science*, edited by Miriam P. Cooney, 25–34. Reston, Va.: National Council of Teachers of Mathematics, 1996.

Ogilvie, Marilyn Bailey. *Women in Science: Antiquity Through the Nineteenth Century.* Cambridge, Mass.: MIT Press, 1986, 96–99.

Osen, Lynn M. *Women in Mathematics.* Cambridge, Mass.: MIT Press, 1974, 71–81.

✳ HILDEGARDE OF BINGEN
(1098–1179)   *German Botanist and Physician*

Head of a prosperous convent on Germany's Rhine River, Hildegarde of Bingen was known throughout Europe for her writings on both religious and natural subjects. She was called "the Sibyl of the Rhine," and some people considered her a saint. She recorded accurate descriptions of plants and described their use in medicine, as well as listing other treatments for illness. She is the earliest woman scientist whose major works have survived intact.

Hildegarde was born in 1098, the 10th and youngest child of Mechtilde and Hildebert, a knight who lived at Bockelheim, near what is now Mainz. She wrote later that she began having "secret and wonderful" visions at age 15. Some modern scholars think her visions may have been caused by migraine headaches or epilepsy. Hildegarde believed they came from God.

When she was just eight years old, Hildegarde's parents sent her to the convent of Disibodenberg, which her aunt Jutta headed. In a ceremony signifying their complete withdrawal from the world, Jutta, Hildegarde, and a serving woman were given the rites for the dead and sealed into cells that they were supposed to occupy for the rest of their lives.

Luckily, the reality of Hildegarde's later life was much less grim. Jutta gave her niece a good education, and as for isolation, so many nuns eventually joined the convent (which was unwalled to allow for expansion) that it became too crowded for Hildegarde's taste. She took Jutta's place as head of Disibodenberg when Jutta died in 1136, but in the late 1140s she started her own convent with 18 other nuns at Rupertsberg, near the town of Bingen.

Bingen, located where the Nahe River flowed into the Rhine, was a prosperous medieval trading center.

As an abbess, or head of a convent, Hildegarde was a powerful woman. In those days the head of a German religious order controlled lands just as a noble did. Hildegarde kept up a lifelong correspondence with emperors, kings, and popes, and she did not hesitate to tell them what she thought they should do in matters of politics as well as religion.

Hildegarde wrote 14 books, as well as a large amount of outstanding music and a play. She made or at least designed the art that illustrated some of her books. She traveled widely and taught as well. Most of her writings concern religion, but she can be counted among scientists because of one book that described the natural world and another that provided medical information. Monks and nuns were the chief practitioners of medicine (and science in general) in the Middle Ages, and most of Hildegarde's medical descriptions were probably based on her own experiences as a healer.

Hildegarde presented her picture of the natural world and some of her medical ideas in a book later called *Physica,* written between 1150 and 1160. The book described 230 plants, 60 trees, and a variety of stones, metals, mammals, birds, reptiles, and fish. These included some creatures that the learned abbess had never seen, such as the lion and the unicorn, but most of her work was based on observation and the folklore of the people around her. Germans still use the names she listed for many common plants. Her book described medicinal uses of plants, animals, and minerals.

Hildegarde's last major book, *Causae et Curae* (*Causes and Cures*), was devoted completely to medicine. Its recipes for healing, like the descriptions of nature in *Physica*, were a mixture of fantasy and accurate observation. Some, such as a powder to be used against "poison and magic words," were strictly magical. Others were down-to-earth recommendations for a healthy life that included fresh air, a moderate diet, exercise, rest, and cleanliness (she was far ahead of her time in suggesting that water from doubtful sources be boiled before drinking). Hildegarde discussed mental as well as physical illness. Her book even contained some surprisingly frank descriptions of sex.

Hildegarde lived to be 81 years old, an incredible age for her time. Following her death in 1179, three different popes considered whether she should be declared a saint. Although she never quite met the Church's standards for canonization, she is often referred to as St. Hildegarde. She was something of a saint of science, too, in that she was one of the few who kept scientific knowledge alive during a period when such knowledge was not encouraged in people of either gender.

Further Reading

Alic, Margaret. *Hypatia's Heritage: A History of Women and Science from Antiquity Through the Nineteenth Century.* Boston: Beacon Press, 1986, 62–74.

Brooke, Elisabeth. *Women Healers.* Rochester, Vt.: Healing Arts Press, 1995, 40–53.

Ogilvie, Marilyn Bailey. *Women in Science: Antiquity Through the Nineteenth Century.* Cambridge, Mass.: MIT Press, 1986, 99–101.

Strehlow, Wighard, and Hertzka, Gottfried. *Hildegarde of Bingen's Medicine.* Santa Fe, N.M.: Bear & Co., 1987.

✳ HODGKIN, DOROTHY CROWFOOT
(1910–1994) *British Crystallographer*

By interpreting X-ray photographs of crystals, Dorothy Hodgkin worked out the three-dimensional structure of the vital and complex molecules of penicillin, vitamin B12, and insulin. Her work won a Nobel Prize in 1964.

Dorothy Mary Crowfoot was a globe-trotter from birth. She was born on May 12, 1910, in Cairo, Egypt, where her father, John Crowfoot, worked for the Ministry of Education, part of the British government that controlled Egypt at the time. Dorothy's mother, Molly, was an expert on ancient cloth and a keen student of plants.

World War I broke out when four-year-old Dorothy was visiting England with her family. Her parents felt they had to go back to Egypt but thought it too dangerous to take their three daughters with them, so they left them in England under the care of a maid, Katie, and their grandmother. The girls saw their mother only once during the next four years.

As a teenager, Dorothy became interested in chemistry, especially the study of crystals—solids whose molecules are arranged in regular patterns. For her 16th birthday her mother gave her a book by William Henry Bragg, a pioneer in the new field of X-ray crystallography. The book explained that in 1912, German physicist Max von Laue had discovered that a beam of X rays shone through a crystal bounced off the atoms in its molecules, becoming bent or diffracted as a result. Bragg and his son found that if photographic film was placed on the far side of the crystal, the X-ray beam produced a pattern of dark dots on the film. Trained observers could figure out the three-dimensional arrangement of atoms within the crystal's molecules by analyzing the size, brightness, and position of the dots, a task that author Sharon McGrayne compares to "analyzing a jungle gym from its shadows." Bragg wrote that "the discovery of X-rays has increased the keenness of our vision over ten thousand times. We can now 'see' the individual atoms and molecules." Dorothy decided that she, too, wanted to "see" molecules with X-ray crystallography.

Dorothy Crowfoot entered Somerville, a women's college at Oxford University, in 1928. She graduated with a bachelor's degree in chemistry in 1932, then began working at Cambridge, Britain's other most famous university, with J. D. Bernal, who was among the first to use X-ray crystallography to study the complex molecules made in the bodies of living things. She made a habit of "clearing Bernal's desk," analyzing the crystals that scientists from all over the world sent to him for study. These included vitamin D, vitamin B_1, sex hormones, and the digestive enzyme pepsin. "My research with Bernal formed the foundation for the work I was to do during the rest of my career," she said later.

Somerville persuaded Crowfoot to return as a researcher and teacher in 1934, but it failed to provide her with a decent laboratory. She had to work in the basement of the Oxford Museum, surrounded by dinosaur bones and cases of dead beetles. A far more serious difficulty was the rheumatoid arthritis that Crowfoot developed around 1934. This painful disease twisted and deformed the joints of her hands and feet.

Throughout her career, Dorothy Crowfoot chose tasks that everyone else believed could not be done, then developed techniques to make them possible. One of the first molecules for which she did this was cholesterol, a fat best known today for its role in heart disease. To discover cholesterol's structure, Crowfoot first applied a method that used thousands of calculations to produce a diagram something like a topographical map. Instead of showing the elevation of hills and valleys, the map showed the density of electrons struck by the X-ray beam, which in turn revealed where atoms were located. She supplemented this technique with another that she developed herself, which involved making crystals that were just like natural ones except that they contained an extra atom of a heavy element such as mercury. She filled in missing parts of a crystal's structure by comparing X-ray photos of natural and artificial crystals.

Crowfoot was so excited when she finally figured out the structure of cholesterol that she literally danced around her lab. She used this work as her Ph.D. thesis, receiving her degree in 1937. Cholesterol was the most complex molecule yet analyzed by crystallography and the first to have its structure worked out by this technique alone.

In that same year, Crowfoot met Thomas L. Hodgkin, a cheerful, outgoing man who seemed to balance her own quiet nature. They married on December 16, 1937. For eight years they could spend only weekends together because Thomas taught in the north of England, while Dorothy taught at Oxford. In 1945, however, he too obtained a post at Oxford. They had three children, raised partly by family members and live-in helpers.

As World War II began, several scientists were trying to find ways to make the antibiotic penicillin in large quantities, and Dorothy Hodgkin met one of them, Ernst Chain. Penicillin, discovered by

Scottish bacteriologist Alexander Fleming in 1928, was made naturally by a mold, but no one then knew how to grow the mold in large amounts. Chain hoped to make the drug artificially instead. He told Hodgkin that knowing the exact structure of its molecules would help in this task.

Even penicillin's chemical formula was unknown at the time, but Hodgkin said she might still be able to determine the penicillin molecule's structure if Chain could get her some crystals of the compound. Soon afterward, some of the first penicillin crystals ever made were flown to her. Hodgkin and graduate student Barbara Rogers-Low solved the penicillin puzzle in 1946 after four years of hard work. Making the drug naturally in vats of mold turned out to be the best way to mass produce it after all, but Hodgkin's work helped chemists create synthetic penicillins that were better than the natural form at attacking certain kinds of bacteria.

Hodgkin's work on penicillin made her internationally famous. Britain's top scientific body, the Royal Society, elected her to membership in 1947; she was only the third woman to receive this honor. By that time she had a larger laboratory and an official post and salary as a lecturer and demonstrator, but Oxford did not make her a reader, the equivalent of an American full professor, until 1957 or give her a fully modern laboratory until 1958.

In 1948 a scientist from the drug company Glaxo gave Hodgkin a vial of wine-colored crystals that he had just made and asked her to work out the structure of the molecules in them. The crystals were vitamin B_{12}, a compound essential for healthy blood. Some people could not extract the vitamin from their food and needed to take it as a drug. As with penicillin, Glaxo wanted to learn B_{12}'s structure so it could make it in large quantities.

Even less was known about B_{12} than about penicillin, and it was a much larger molecule. Hodgkin's research team gathered data about the molecule for six years before even trying to analyze it. When they did start analyzing, they got some welcome help. In 1953, Hodgkin met a scientist named Kenneth Trueblood, who had programmed an early computer at the University of California at Los Angeles

(UCLA) to do crystallography calculations. Hodgkin said later that she deciphered the B_{12} molecule "by post and cable," sending her data to be analyzed by Trueblood's computer. J. D. Bernal called this work, which she finished in 1956, "the greatest triumph of crystallographic technique that has yet occurred."

Dorothy and Thomas Hodgkin once again developed a commuting marriage when Thomas, an expert on African history, became the director of the Institute of African Studies at the University of Ghana in 1962. Dorothy was visiting him there in October 1964 when she learned that she had won that year's Nobel Prize in chemistry. She was the first British woman to win a science Nobel. The following year she also received the Order of Merit, one of Britain's highest awards. Only one other British woman, Florence Nightingale, had received this honor.

Hodgkin's next big project was insulin, a hormone (substance made in one part of the body that affects the action of other parts) that helps cells turn sugar into energy. A lack of it produces diabetes. Hodgkin had wanted to find out the structure of the insulin molecule since the mid-1930s, but its 777 atoms defeated even her until 1969. Working out insulin's structure required analysis of 70,000 X-ray spots—no mean feat even with a computer. Her work helped scientists understand how insulin functions.

Dorothy Hodgkin retired in 1977 and died on July 30, 1994, at the age of 84. All those who knew her mourned the woman whom a scientist friend, Max Perutz, called the "gentle genius."

Further Reading

Julian, Maureen M. "Women in Crystallography." In *Women of Science: Righting the Record*, edited by G. Kass-Simon and Patricia Farnes, 371–376. Bloomington: Indiana University Press, 1990.

McGrayne, Sharon Bertsch. *Nobel Prize Women in Science: Their Lives, Struggles, and Momentous Discoveries.* New York: Birch Lane Press, 225–254.

Opfell, Olga S. *The Lady Laureates: Women Who Have Won the Nobel Prize.* Metuchen, N.J.: Scarecrow Press, 1986, 239–253.

Shiels, Barbara. *Winners: Women and the Nobel Prize.* Minneapolis, Minn.: Dillon Press, 1985, 147–166.

✳ HOPPER, GRACE BREWSTER MURRAY
(1906–1992) *American Computer Scientist*

Grace Hopper knew computers almost from their birth, when the hulking machines filled a room and could do only three calculations a second. She helped make them practical for businesses and individuals to use by devising ways for them to do some of their own programming and helping to develop a programming language that used English words.

Grace Brewster Murray was born in New York City on December 9, 1906, to Walter Murray, an insurance broker, and his wife, Mary. She was inspired both by her great-grandfather, an admiral in the navy ("a very impressive gentleman," she recalled), and her grandfather, a civil engineer, who sometimes took her with him on surveying trips. She tried her own first engineering project at age seven, when she took apart seven of the family's clocks but failed to put them back together.

Murray graduated from Vassar College with a B.A. in mathematics and physics in 1928. She earned a master's degree at Yale in 1930 and shortly afterward married Vincent Foster Hopper, a teacher of English and literature. The next year she began teaching mathematics at Vassar. She continued with her graduate studies as well, earning a Ph.D. from Yale in 1934.

In December 1943, the height of World War II, Grace Hopper left her post as an associate professor at Vassar and enlisted in the Naval Reserve. By that time she had separated from her husband (they divorced in 1945). She was assigned to the Bureau of Ordnance (gunnery) computing project at Harvard University. She reported to Howard Aiken, the head of the project, on July 2, 1944, and got her first look at the Mark I, 51 feet long and 8 feet high—the country's first modern computer. Aiken's instructions for using this monster consisted of telling Hopper, "That's a computing engine." Hopper said later that she was "scared to death" by

the machine, but she also thought it was "the prettiest gadget I ever saw."

During the war, the Mark I and its successors, Marks II and III, performed the calculations needed to aim complex navy guns and rockets accurately. The machines worked night and day, and so did Hopper and the rest of the crew who ran them. The computer operators sometimes slept on their desks so they could spring into instant action when one of the machine's thousands of mechanical switches failed, which happened often. The most unusual cause of a failure was a moth that was caught in a switch and beaten to death. After the moth incident, Hopper and the others began to call finding and correcting failures "debugging." Computer programmers still use this term.

While Hopper and her cohorts were debugging the Marks, a pair of inventors named John Mauchly and J. Prosper Eckert built ENIAC, the world's first general-purpose electronic computer. They were among the few people at the time who believed that computers would eventually be useful to ordinary businesses, and Hopper came to share their enthusiasm. She joined their fledgling company in 1949.

The company built UNIVAC, the first mass-produced commercial computer, in 1951. UNIVAC could calculate 1,000 times faster than the Mark I, but it was still too big, too expensive, and, above all, too difficult to use to appeal to any but the largest businesses. For instance, each new program had to be entered into the machine, even though parts of many programs were the same. In 1952, Hopper devised a new type of program called a compiler, which allowed a computer to assemble its own programs from shorter routines stored in its memory. This not only saved time but eliminated errors introduced during retyping.

Another problem was that the "languages" in which computer instructions had to be written were complex and required special training to understand. In 1957, Hopper designed a new language called Flowmatic, which used English words in both its data and its instructions. Flowmatic became one of the ancestors of COBOL (Common Business-Oriented Language), which Hopper and

Grace Hopper helped to make computers practical for businesses and individuals to use by inventing compiler programs and helping to design a computer language called COBOL, which resembles English. She worked both for private industry and for the U.S. Navy, of which she became the only woman admiral in 1985. She is seen here in the 1950s with the Uniservo IIA for the Univac II, one of the earliest mass-produced commercial computers.

(Courtesy Unisys Corporation)

other computer experts designed in 1959. COBOL used English words in structures that resembled ordinary sentences and aided greatly in making computers acceptable to business.

During all her years in business, Hopper had kept her position in the Naval Reserve. When she reached the age of 60 and was told that she had to retire from the navy, she called it "the saddest day of my life." Her sadness lasted only seven months, however. She was then called back to "temporary active duty"—for 19 years. Her hardest task was persuading navy bureaucrats around the country to use COBOL and teaching them how to do it. She performed similar work for businesses and also taught at several universities. She once said that her students were her greatest achievement.

Hopper received many awards during her career, including the Naval Ordnance Development Award (1946), the Legion of Merit (1973), induction into the Engineering and Science Hall of Fame (1984), and the National Medal of Technology (1991). The award she treasured most, however, came on November 8, 1985, when the navy raised her to the rank of rear admiral—the only woman admiral in the country's history.

Hopper retired from the Sperry Corporation (the descendant of Eckert and Mauchly's firm) in 1971, and she finally retired from the navy for good in 1979. At that time she received the Distinguished Service Medal, the Department of Defense's highest honor. She went on working as a consultant, however. "I seem to do an awful lot of retiring, but I don't think I will ever be able to really retire," she once said. "Amazing Grace," as she was lovingly called, died at the age of 85 on January 1, 1992.

Further Reading

Billings, Charlene W. *Grace Hopper*. Hillside, N.J.: Enslow, 1989.

Rausa, Captain Rosario M. "Grace Murray Hopper." *Naval History*, Fall 1992, 58–60.

Slater, Robert. *Portraits in Silicon*. Cambridge, Mass.: MIT Press, 1987, 219–229.

Yount, Lisa. *Contemporary Women Scientists*. New York: Facts On File, 1994, 26–37.

✳ **HORNEY, KAREN DANIELSEN**
(1885–1952)   *German/American Psychologist*

Karen Horney was what one biographer called a "gentle rebel." As a child she rebelled against her father's authoritarian discipline. As an adult she rebelled against Sigmund Freud's equally authoritarian ideas about how the mind works, especially his negative view of women.

Karen Danielsen was born in Blankenese, near Hamburg, Germany, on September 16, 1885. Her father, Norwegian-born Berndt Danielsen, was a ship captain. She admired him in some ways but disliked his sternness and his belief that women should confine themselves to the home. When her parents separated in 1904, Karen remained with her mother, Clotilde.

While still a teenager, Karen decided to be a doctor. She persuaded her mother, who in turn persuaded her father, to help her get the education she needed. She studied medicine at the universities of Freiburg, Göttingen, and Berlin, obtaining her M.D. from the University of Berlin in 1911. In 1909, while still a student, she married Oskar Horney, a lawyer and businessperson. They had three daughters, then separated in 1926 and later divorced.

Karen Horney decided to specialize in psychoanalysis, the form of psychiatry created by Sigmund Freud. She began seeing patients around 1912, obtained a Ph.D. in 1915, and worked at a psychiatric hospital for several years. Then, in 1919, she joined the highly respected Berlin Psychoanalytic Clinic and Institute. She was a lecturer, analyst, and trainer of other analysts there until 1932.

From the beginning, Horney's ideas caused controversy. Freud had claimed that women envied and felt inferior to men, but Horney claimed that the idea "that one half of the human race is discontented with the sex assigned to it . . . is decidedly unsatisfying, not only to feminine narcissism but also to biological science." She said it was just as likely that men envied women their ability to give birth and nurture children. If women envied anything about men, it was their social and economic power. These views pleased feminists but shocked many of Horney's Berlin colleagues.

In 1932, Franz Alexander, a former student of Horney's who had become the director of the Chicago Institute for Psychoanalysis, invited her to be the institute's assistant director. Horney accepted, glad to leave the increasing power of the Nazis, who had labeled psychoanalysis a "Jewish science" and therefore liable to persecution. Once in Chicago, however, she found that she and Alexander had different ideas, and they parted in 1934.

Horney moved to New York City and began lecturing at the New School for Social Research, teaching at the New York Psychoanalytic Institute, and carrying on a thriving private practice. She then once again rebelled against her colleagues' ideas. Freud and his followers blamed most mental illness on instinctive sexual conflicts with parents during infancy, but Horney believed that social and cultural factors were more important. She presented her views in lectures and in books such as *The Neurotic Personality of Our Time* (1937) and *New Ways in Psychoanalysis* (1939).

According to Horney's theory, social factors often put a strain on parents, who responded by becoming less affectionate or more controlling toward their children. The children, in turn, developed behaviors that they hoped would protect them from their parents. These behaviors usually continued into adulthood. If they failed to provide protection or conflicted with each other, the people developed the form of mental illness called neurosis. "The genesis [cause] of a neurosis," Horney wrote, "is . . . all those adverse influences which make a child feel helpless . . . and which make him conceive the world as potentially menacing."

The traditional psychoanalysts who dominated the New York Institute resented Horney's departure from Freud's theories and her introduction of ideas from sociology and anthropology into psychoanalysis. In 1941 they voted to bar her from training other analysts. Horney, four supporters, and 14 students responded by resigning. "Reverence for dogma has replaced free inquiry," they complained. The group formed its own professional organization, the Association for the Advancement of Psychoanalysis, and training center, the American Institute for Psychoanalysis. Horney was dean of the institute and editor of its journal for the rest of her life.

In the 1940s, Horney presented other new ideas in her lectures and in several books, including *Self-Analysis* (1942), *Our Inner Conflicts* (1945), and *Neurosis and Human Growth* (1950). She said that people had a natural tendency to improve themselves and develop their full potential. Unlike Freud and his followers, who felt that most neurotic people could improve only after a lengthy series of sessions with an analyst, Horney thought that people often could learn to analyze themselves. She "encourage[d] people to make the attempt to do something with their own problems." When people did undertake psychoanalysis with a professional, Horney recommended that the analyst take a nonjudgmental approach and focus on present problems and solutions rather than dwelling on the patient's early childhood, as traditional Freudians did.

Horney died of cancer on December 4, 1952, but many of her ideas live on as accepted parts of psychiatry. The Karen Horney Foundation in New York, founded in 1955, carries on her work.

Further Reading

Paris, Bernard J. *Karen Horney: A Psychoanalyst's Search for Self-Understanding.* New Haven, Conn.: Yale University Press, 1994.

Quinn, Susan. *A Mind of Her Own: The Life of Karen Horney.* New York: Summit Books, 1987.

Rubins, Jack L. *Karen Horney: Gentle Rebel of Psychoanalysis.* New York: Dial Press, 1978.

Sayers, Janet. *Mothers of Psychoanalysis.* New York: Norton, 1991, 85–141.

✳ HRDY, SARAH BLAFFER
(1946–) *American Anthropologist*

Sarah Hrdy has shown that the needs, strategies, and behaviors of female animals are just as important as those of males in shaping the way a species evolves. The daughter of an oil-rich Texas family, she was born Sarah Blaffer on July 11, 1946, in Dallas, but she grew up in Houston. Although her mother encouraged her desire to get an education and have a career, the society around her did not. When she went to a girls' boarding school in Maryland at age 16, "it was the first time in my life when the things I loved were valued and vindicated," she told interviewer Lucy Hodges.

At Wellesley College, Blaffer majored in philosophy but also took creative writing courses. She decided to write a novel about the Maya culture of South America and began researching the folklore of the Maya as background. Finding the research more interesting than the novel, she transferred to Radcliffe and changed her major to anthropology. For her undergraduate thesis, Blaffer wrote about the demon H'ik'al, who took the form of either a bat or a black man and punished women who violated sexual taboos. Her research earned her a B.A. in 1969 and was published as a book, *The Black-man of Zinacantan,* in 1972.

"This is a lot of fun," Sarah Hrdy said later that she thought, "but I want to do something relevant to the world." Deciding to learn how to make films that could teach people from developing nations about subjects such as health care, she signed up for filmmaking courses at Stanford University. The courses were disappointing, but while at Stanford she attended a class by Paul Ehrlich, who taught about problems caused by overpopulation. This suggested an idea for her Ph.D. thesis. She had heard that black-faced Indian monkeys called langurs sometimes lived in overcrowded colonies and that male langurs often killed infants in their groups. Blaffer decided to test the hypothesis that overcrowding caused the infanticide.

In 1972, Blaffer married Daniel Hrdy, then a fellow anthropologist, whose unusual name reflected his Czech ancestry. They later had three children. Daniel Hrdy went with Sarah to study the langurs living on Mount Abu in Rajasthan.

To her surprise, Sarah Hrdy found that under certain conditions, langur males killed infants whether the monkeys were overcrowded or not. Each langur troop consists of one male and several females, plus a number of other males that swarm around the central group. Every 28 months or so, one of these outside males ousts a troop leader and takes over his harem. The new leader then usually kills all the infants in the troop. Hrdy concluded that, far from being the "sick" response to environmental stress that other observers had thought it was, this behavior made evolutionary sense from the killer's point of view. Killing the infants made the females receptive to mating, so the new male could sire offspring that would pass on his own genes instead of wasting his energy raising babies sired by another male.

Hrdy wrote up her langur research for her Ph.D., which she received from Harvard in 1975. Two years later she published her findings in a book called *The Langurs of Abu.* When her work first appeared, Hrdy told interviewer Thomas Bass, "I was attacked by some of the most eminent anthropologists in the country. . . . [They] couldn't believe [that what she reported] was happening." Her discoveries challenged the common belief that primates (monkeys and apes) acted for the good of their group. Instead, it fitted with a new evolutionary doctrine called sociobiology, which stated that animals act in ways that maximize the chances of passing on their genes. The pattern of infanticide Hrdy described was later found not only in other primates but in animals ranging from hippos to wolves.

Like most researchers of the time, Hrdy began by watching the males in the langur troops. After a while, though, she began to pay more attention to the females. She noticed that they mated not only with their troop leader, old or new, but with as many of the outside males as possible, even when they were already pregnant. Hrdy concluded that the females did this as a strategy to protect their babies, since a male would not kill babies that might be his own. Her evidence that female primates had evolved important sexual strategies helped to change the way anthropologists thought.

Hrdy's interest in the behavior and strategies of female primates, including human females, has expanded over the years. She published a book on the subject, called *The Woman That Never Evolved*, in 1981. Much behavior of female primates, she believes, evolved because of competition between females, which she calls an "evolutionary trap." Human women, however, can resist evolutionary pressures and cooperate. "The female with 'equal rights' never evolved," Hrdy wrote. "She was invented and fought for consciously with intelligence, stubbornness, and courage."

Hrdy has been a full professor of anthropology at the University of California at Davis since 1984. In the late 1990s she was investigating animal motherhood. She wants to know whether the amounts of resources that mothers invest in male and female offspring are equal and, if not, what conditions produce more investment in either sons or daughters. "Mother nature," she is learning, is more complex than anyone has dreamed.

Further Reading

Bass, Thomas A. *Reinventing the Future*. Reading, Mass.: Addison-Wesley, 1994, 6–25.

Hodges, Lucy. "Sarah Hrdy." In *Beyond the Glass Ceiling: Forty Women Whose Ideas Shape the Modern World*, edited by Sian Griffiths, 137–144. Manchester, England: Manchester University Press, 1996.

Hrdy, Sarah. *The Langurs of Abu: Female and Male Strategies of Reproduction*. Cambridge, Mass.: Harvard University Press, 1977.

———. *The Woman That Never Evolved*. Cambridge, Mass.: Harvard University Press, 1981.

✳ HYDE, IDA HENRIETTA
(1857–1945) *American Physiologist*

Ida Hyde invented the microelectrode, an essential tool for research on nerve cells. She was born on September 8, 1857, in Davenport, Iowa, to Meyer and Babette Heidenheimer, both immigrants from Germany. Meyer Heidenheimer, a merchant, changed the family name to Hyde soon after his arrival in the United States.

Young Ida's future seemed to hold nothing more ambitious than her job in a hat shop, but she attended night classes and at age 24 won a scholarship to the University of Illinois. She was there only a year before she had to go to work as a teacher to help her family. She finally obtained a B.S. from Cornell in 1891, when she was 34 years old. Her specialty was physiology, the way the body and its parts function.

Hyde's first job as a researcher was at Bryn Mawr College. An eminent German professor was so impressed by her published work that he invited her to study in that country, but her experience there was best described in the title she later chose for an article about it: "Before Women Were Human Beings." She finally obtained a Ph.D. from the University of Heidelberg—the first woman to do so—in 1896.

Back in the United States, Hyde worked and taught at several schools and universities, including Harvard Medical School, at which she was the first woman researcher. In 1898 she moved to the University of Kansas, where she spent most of the rest of her career. The university created a separate department of physiology in 1905 and chose Hyde to head it, making her a full professor. She wrote two textbooks on physiology, which were published in 1905 and 1910.

Hyde investigated the circulatory, respiratory, and nervous systems of a variety of animals, but her greatest contribution to science was the microelectrode. Science historian G. Kass-Simon calls this device the "most useful and powerful tool in electrophysiology." To understand how nerve and muscle cells work, scientists need to be able to stimulate individual cells electrically or chemically and record the resulting changes in the tiny electric current that the cells produce. Devices that added chemicals to a cell or recorded its current had been created earlier, but Hyde, in 1920, was the first to make a single tool that could do both at once. Unfortunately, her work was not well known, and other scientists later unwittingly repeated it and received credit for her invention.

Hyde was elected to the American Physiological Society in 1902, its first woman member. She endowed several scholarships for women science students but insisted that women meet the highest academic standards. She retired in 1920 and then moved to California. She died on August 22, 1945.

Further Reading

Deyrup, Ingrith J. "Hyde, Ida Henrietta." In *Notable American Women. 1607–1950, vol. II: G–O,* edited by Edward T. James, 247–249. Cambridge, Mass.: The Belknap Press of Harvard University Press, 1971.

Kass-Simon, G. "Biology Is Destiny." In *Women of Science: Righting the Record,* edited by G. Kass-Simon and Patricia Farnes, 238–244. Bloomington: Indiana University Press, 1990.

Ogilvie, Marilyn Bailey. *Women in Science: Antiquity Through the Nineteenth Century.* Cambridge, Mass.: MIT Press, 1986, 103–104.

 ## HYMAN, LIBBIE HENRIETTA
(1888–1969) *American Zoologist*

Libbie Hyman produced a multivolume study of invertebrates, or animals without backbones, that is still a standard reference. She was born in Des Moines, Iowa, on December 6, 1888, but grew up in Fort Dodge. Both her parents were immigrants; her father, Joseph, came from Poland and her mother, Sabina, from Russia. Libbie escaped from her father's poverty and her mother's bossiness by exploring the woods and fields near her home.

Hyman graduated in 1905 as both the youngest member of her high school class and its valedictorian. A teacher helped her get a scholarship to the University of Chicago, and she obtained a B.S. in zoology in 1910 and a Ph.D. in 1915. One of her professors, Charles Manning Child, then invited her to stay on as his research assistant. She did experiments to provide support for his theories about the way certain animals regenerated lost limbs or other tissues. Her knowledge of chemistry proved especially helpful. She also taught and wrote two books, *Laboratory Manual for Elementary Zoology* (1919) and *Laboratory Manual for Comparative Vertebrate Anatomy* (1922), which became standard works.

Even though one of her books dealt with vertebrates, Hyman once said, "I just can't get excited about [vertebrates]. . . . I like invertebrates . . . [especially] the soft delicate ones, the jellyfishes and corals and the beautiful microscopic organisms." She became an expert on the taxonomy, or scientific classification, of invertebrates and grew used to receiving parcels from all over the world containing odd creatures for her to identify. Her specialty was worms, which few other biologists studied.

In 1931, when she was over 40, Hyman found herself truly on her own for the first time. Her mother had recently died, Child was on leave, and royalties from her books brought her enough money to live on. She left the University of Chicago and eventually settled in New York City, where, working first in her apartment and then, after 1937, at the American Museum of Natural History, she began a massive reference work on the biology and classification of all million known invertebrates. The first volume of *The Invertebrates* appeared in 1940 and the fourth, the last on which she worked, in 1967, two years before her death on August 3, 1969. A fifth volume was added later.

Hyman received several awards for her work, including gold medals from the Linnean Society in 1960 and from the American Museum of Natural History in 1969. She was elected to the National Academy of Science in 1954. Her books are still the primary reference source for scientists who study invertebrates.

Further Reading

Kass-Simon, G. "Biology Is Destiny." In *Women of Science: Righting the Record,* edited by G. Kass-Simon and Patricia Farnes, 222–224. Bloomington: Indiana University Press, 1990.

Winsor, Mary P. "Hyman, Libbie Henrietta." In *Notable American Women: The Modern Period,* edited by Barbara Sicherman and Carol Hurd Green, 365–367. Cambridge, Mass.: The Belknap Press of Harvard University Press, 1980.

Yost, Edna. *American Women of Science.* Philadelphia: Frederic Stokes, 1943, 122–138.

✳ HYPATIA
(370–415) *Egyptian Mathematician, Astronomer, and Physicist*

Hypatia is the earliest woman scientist about whom much is known and is one of the most famous women scientists of all time. She was born around A.D. 370 in Alexandria, Egypt. Her father, Theon, a mathematician and astronomer, headed the famous Museum of Alexandria, which was the equivalent of a large university. Wanting his daughter to be a "perfect human being," Theon taught Hypatia mathematics, philosophy, and astronomy. He then sent her to Italy and Athens for further study, where she impressed everyone with her beauty as well as her intelligence.

After returning to Alexandria, Hypatia lectured and wrote about mathematics, astronomy, philosophy, and mechanics. Her students called her "The Muse" and "The Philosopher." Her writings have been lost, but historians know about her from the writings of some of these students, such as Synesius of Cyrene, later Bishop of Ptolemais in Libya. According to one account, Hypatia took over her father's leadership of the museum at age 31.

Hypatia is believed to have written a 13-volume commentary on the *Arithmetica* of Diophantus, an Alexandrian mathematician who had recently invented algebra. She also wrote an eight-book popularization of a work on conic sections by another Alexandrian, Apollonius. Conic sections are the geometric figures formed when a plane passes through a cone. Hypatia worked in astronomy as well, compiling the *Astronomical Canon*, a set of tables describing the movements of heavenly bodies.

According to Synesius, Hypatia invented a device for removing salt from seawater as well as a plane astrolabe, which determined the positions of the sun, stars, and planets and was useful for navigation and telling time. She also invented a planisphere for identifying stars and their movements, a device for measuring the level of water, and a hydrometer for determining the density or specific gravity of liquids.

Hypatia was a close friend of Orestes, the Roman prefect (political leader) of Egypt, and, as one of her students wrote: "The magistrates were wont to consult her first in their administration of the affairs of the city." Cyril, the head of the powerful Christian church in Alexandria, denounced Orestes, Hypatia, and other non-Christians as evil. In March 415, inspired by Cyril and possibly following his orders, a mob attacked Hypatia's chariot, dragged her into a nearby church, cut her to pieces with sharpened oyster shells, and publicly burned her remains. Many historians have seen her brutal murder as the start of an eclipse of both science and women's rights that lasted more than a thousand years.

Further Reading

Alic, Margaret. *Hypatia's Heritage: A History of Women in Science from Antiquity Through the Nineteenth Century.* Boston: Beacon Press, 1986, 41–46.

Ogilvie, Marilyn Bailey. *Women in Science: Antiquity Through the Nineteenth Century.* Cambridge, Mass.: MIT Press, 1986, 104–5.

Osen, Lynn M. *Women in Mathematics.* Cambridge, Mass.: MIT Press, 1974, 21–32.

✳ ILDSTAD, SUZANNE
(1952–) *American Immunologist*

The discoveries of Suzanne Ildstad, a surgeon turned researcher, may lead to breakthroughs in organ transplantation and new treatments for AIDS, diabetes, and other diseases. She was born in Minneapolis on May 20, 1952. Both her mother, Jane, and her grandmother were nurses; her grandmother was a scrub nurse for the famous Mayo brothers, who founded the Mayo Clinic and Medical School in Rochester, Minnesota. After receiving a B.S. in biology, summa cum laude, from the University of Minnesota in 1974, Suzanne, in turn, earned her M.D. from the Mayo Medical School in 1978.

Ildstad became a surgeon, specializing in transplanting organs in children. She found surgery exciting, but she knew that it was the easy part of the transplant process. The hard parts were waiting for an organ to be found—far more people need organs than donate them—and then fighting a lifelong battle to keep the recipient's immune system from destroying the transplant. This can be done only with the help of drugs that partly suppress the immune system, leaving the patient vulnerable to cancer and infections. In transplants of bone mar-

row, from which almost all blood and immune cells come, an opposite but equally deadly problem occurs unless donor and recipient are carefully chosen to be genetically very similar: Immune cells from the grafted marrow attack the recipient.

To fight these problems, Ildstad turned from the operating room to the laboratory, beginning at the National Institutes of Health in the early 1980s and continuing at the University of Pittsburgh, which she joined in 1988. She found that removing a certain type of immune cells, called T cells, kept marrow grafts from attacking the body, but very similar but much rarer cells (she calls them facilitating cells), which she was the first to see, had to remain if the graft was to survive. After years of work, Ildstad succeeded in removing T cells from grafts while preserving the facilitating cells. Marrow treated in this way survived in mice without attacking them, even if it came from rats. The result was a chimera, a mouse with an immune system that was partly mouse and partly rat. Such an animal could accept organ grafts from rats without needing drugs.

Ildstad also designed a procedure for transplanting bone marrow from baboons, which cannot get AIDS, into humans. Surgeons used this procedure on a man named Jeff Getty in December 1995 after destroying Getty's own AIDS-weakened marrow with radiation. Although Getty had been expected to die in a few months without treatment, his health improved considerably in the year after he received the baboon marrow. The baboon cells apparently survived for only two weeks, however, so it is unclear whether or how the transplant helped him. In 1998, three years after his transplant, he was still in relatively good health.

Ildstad, now an elected member of the prestigious Institute of Medicine, moved to the Allegheny University of the Health Sciences in Philadelphia in September 1997 and became head of its new Institute for Cellular Therapeutics. Her husband, public health physician David J. Tollerud, directs another center there. (They married in 1972 and have two children.) She continues to refine her human bone marrow transfer. In an initial test in which five people with advanced leukemia were given marrow from unmatched donors, minus T cells but with facilitating cells, the marrow transplants survived and did not attack the recipients. If Ildstad's treatment proves dependable, it could be a transplant breakthrough. Marrow transplants from people who are naturally resistant to AIDS, she believes, could treat those who have the disease. Marrow transplants could also help people who suffer from diabetes, arthritis, or other conditions in which the immune system attacks the body's own tissues. Blending marrow from potential donors and recipients, as she did with the rats and mice, could make subsequent organ transplants—even, perhaps, between animals and humans—possible without immune-suppressing drugs. "It's a very exciting time," Ildstad said in 1998.

Further Reading

Caldwell, Mark. "The Transplanted Self." *Discover*, April 1992, 62–68.
Whitcomb, Claire. "Doctor Suzanne Ildstad: The Science of Making a Difference." *Victoria*, October 1997, 14, 16.

J

JACKSON, SHIRLEY ANN
(1946–) *American Physicist*

Shirley Jackson, the first black woman to earn a Ph.D. from the Massachusetts Institute of Technology, has researched solid state physics at AT&T Bell Laboratories and has headed the federal Nuclear Regulatory Commission (NRC) since 1995. She was born on August 5, 1946, in Washington, D.C., the second daughter of George and Beatrice Jackson. Her father encouraged her interest in science by helping her with school science projects.

Jackson went to college at the Massachusetts Institute of Technology, earning a B.S. in 1968 and a Ph.D. in 1973 in theoretical elementary particle physics. After research on strongly interacting subatomic particles at the Fermi National Accelerator Laboratory and the European Center for Nuclear Research, she joined AT&T Bell Laboratories in Murray Hill, New Jersey, in 1976 and remained there until 1991. There she did research in theoretical, solid state, quantum, and optical physics, especially on the behavior of subatomic particles in solid material. From 1991 to 1995, in addition to serving Bell Labs as a consultant in semiconductor theory, she was a professor of physics at New Jersey's Rutgers University. Jackson has won honors including

the New Jersey Governor's Award in Science and MIT's Karl Taylor Compton Award, and she has been elected a fellow of the American Physical Society and of the American Academy of Arts and Sciences. She is married to physicist Morris A. Washington and has one son, Alan.

Jackson was a member of the New Jersey Commission on Science and Technology in the late 1980s and early 1990s. Then, in 1995, President Bill Clinton appointed her to head the Nuclear Regulatory Commission (NRC). She was the first woman and first African American to chair this federal agency. The NRC oversees safety in the nuclear industry, including preventing accidents at nuclear power plants and ensuring safe disposal of nuclear waste. "My job is public service at a very high level," Jackson says.

Ten months after Jackson took over the NRC, a whistleblower revealed many violations of NRC rules at the nuclear division of Northeast Utilities, which operates nuclear power plants in New England, and accused the NRC of failing to enforce safety codes. Jackson admitted that "there is truth in . . . those charges" and called the scandal "a wake-up call." She vowed to toughen up her agency, stating that "We must demonstrate vigilance, objectivity and consistency." Since then, in addition to shutting down several Northeast Utilities plants, Jackson has added eight other plants to the NRC's "watch list" of places with possible problems. Bill Megavern, director of the Critical Mass Energy Project at Ralph Nader's Public Citizen group, said in 1997 that she "is the toughest [NRC] chairman we've seen."

Further Reading

Mickens, Ronald E. "Shirley Ann Jackson." In *Epic Lives: One Hundred Black Women Who Made a Difference,* edited by Jessie Carney Smith. Detroit: Gale Research, 1993, 291–292.

Pooley, Eric. "Nuclear Safety Fallout." *Time,* March 17, 1997, 34–36.

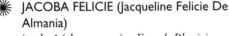 JACOBA FELICIE (Jacqueline Felicie De Almania)

(early 14th century)   *French Physician*

Jacoba Felicie, like AGNODICE, was a woman who tried to practice medicine at a time when men controlled the profession completely. Both women were put on trial for their "crimes," but with opposite results.

Jacoba Felicie came from a Jewish family and was probably of aristocratic birth. She practiced medicine in Paris in the early 1300s, treating patients of both sexes. In doing so, she violated a law that said all physicians in the city must be licensed by the medical faculty of Paris University. Such licenses usually were given only to those who had been named Masters of Medicine by the university—which admitted only men.

On August 11, 1322, Jacoba Felicie was put on trial for practicing medicine. Rather than denying the charges, her lawyer called patients who testified to her skill. The women among them said they would have remained untreated if they had not been able to go to a woman doctor. In her own defense, Jacoba Felicie said, "It is better . . . that a wise woman learned in the art [of medicine] should visit the sick woman and inquire into the secrets of . . . her hidden parts, than

a man should do so, for whom it is not lawful to see . . . the aforesaid parts. . . . A woman before now would allow herself to die rather than reveal the secret of her infirmities to a man."

None of that mattered to the prosecutors. "Her plea that she cured many sick persons whom the . . . [male physicians] could not cure, ought not to stand," they said, "since it is certain that a man approved in the aforesaid art could cure the sick better than any woman." The judges found Jacoba Felicie guilty and charged her a heavy fine. Her punishment discouraged women from practicing medicine in France for the next 550 years.

Further Reading

Brooke, Elisabeth. *Women Healers: Portraits of Herbalists, Physicians, and Midwives.* Rochester, Vt.: Healing Arts Press, 1995, 60–65.

Marks, Geoffrey, and William K. Beatty. *Women in White.* New York: Charles Scribner's Sons, 1972, 53–55.

✳ JEMISON, MAE CAROL
(1956–)   *American Physician*

Mae Jemison has taken her skills as a physician around the world and was the first African-American woman astronaut. She was born in Decatur, Alabama, on October 17, 1956, but grew up in Chicago. Her father, Charlie Jemison, was a roofer, carpenter, and maintenance supervisor, and her mother, Dorothy, was a teacher. From childhood, Mae planned to be a scientist. To her, as she wrote in *Odyssey* magazine, being a scientist "meant that I wondered about the universe around me and wanted to devote a significant part of my life to exploring it." She also was determined to be an astronaut, even though until she was almost through college, all astronauts, like most scientists, were white and male.

Jemison entered California's prestigious Stanford University at age 16 and graduated in 1977 with a B.S. in chemical engineering and a B.A. in African and Afro-American Studies. When asked why she studied such different fields, she told interviewer Maria Johnson, "Someone interested in science is interested in understanding what's going on in the world. That means you have to find out about social science, art, and politics."

In 1981, Jemison earned her M.D. from Cornell University Medical College in New York City. While still in medical school she began working in Cuba, Kenya, and a Cambodian refugee camp in Thailand, and in 1983 she joined the Peace Corps to continue her overseas work. She was the medical officer for the West African nations of Sierra Leone and Liberia for two and a half years.

When Jemison returned to the United States in 1985, she began working for CIGNA, a health maintenance organization in Los Angeles. She also applied to NASA to become an astronaut candidate. In June 1987 she learned that she was one of 15 people accepted from among 2,000 applicants. After a year of grueling training, she was qualified as a "mission specialist" (scientist) astronaut.

Jemison achieved her dream of going into space on September 12, 1992, as one of a seven-person crew aboard the shuttle *Endeavour*. During her eight days in space as part of a U.S./Japan joint mission called Specelab J, she fertilized frog eggs and found that the resulting embryos developed into normal tadpoles under weightless conditions. She also designed and carried out an experiment to study calcium loss from astronauts' bones during their time in space. Jemison has emphasized that space travel "is a birthright of everyone who is on this planet" and that space and its resources "belong to all of us." She told Constance Green, "This is one area where we [African Americans and women] can get in on the ground floor and . . . help to direct where space exploration will go."

Mae Jemison resigned from the astronaut program in March 1993 and formed a Houston company called the Jemison Group, which develops advanced technology for export to developing nations. In 1998 she was still the company's president as well as serving as a professor in environmental studies and the director of the Jemison Institute for Advancing Technology in Developing Countries at Dartmouth College. The institute researches, de-

signs, implements, and evaluates "cutting-edge" technology to ensure that such technology works to the benefit of people in developing countries.

Honors given to Jemison include induction into the Women's Hall of Fame and the Kilby Science Award. The Mae Jemison Academy, a Detroit school that focuses on science and technology, is named after her. In 1998, Jemison wrote that her aim was to "focus on the beneficial integration of science and technology into our everyday lives—culture, health, environment and education—for all on this planet."

Further Reading

"Jemison, Mae C." *Current Biography Yearbook 1993*. New York: H. W. Wilson, 1993, 277–281.

Lindop, Laurie. *Dynamic Modern Women: Scientists and Doctors*. New York: Holt, 1997, 29–38.

Reef, Catherine. "Mae C. Jemison." *Black Explorers*. New York: Facts On File, 1996.

Smith, Jessie Carney. "Mae C. Jemison." In *Epic Lives: One Hundred Black Women Who Made a Difference*, edited by Jessie Carney Smith, 295–298. Detroit: Visible Ink, 1993.

✳ JOLIOT-CURIE, IRÈNE
(1897–1956) *French Physicist and Chemist*

Daughter of Nobel Prize winners Pierre and MARIE CURIE, Irène Joliot-Curie won her own Nobel (with her husband, Frédéric Joliot-Curie) for discovering artificial radioactivity. She was born in Paris on September 12, 1897, just as her parents were beginning their groundbreaking research on radioactivity. She was their first child. Marie Curie doted on the baby, calling her "my little Queen," but she was often busy in the laboratory, so Irène's grandfather, Eugène Curie, took over most of the child's care.

World War I broke out in 1914, when Irène was just 17 years old. Marie organized a fleet of wagons (nicknamed "little curies") to carry portable X-ray equipment to battlefields, and Irène traveled to hospitals near the battlefront to teach surgeons how to use the machines. Neither Marie nor Irène questioned the young woman's fitness for this mission.

"My mother had no more doubts about me than she doubted herself," Irène said later.

When Marie Curie's new Radium Institute opened in Paris after the war, Irène became her mother's laboratory assistant. Studying chemistry, physics, and mathematics, she published her first research paper in 1921. She did her Ph.D. project on the alpha particles (nuclei of helium atoms) given off by the nuclei of polonium atoms as they broke down. She received her degree from the Sorbonne in 1925.

That same year, Irène Curie met another laboratory assistant at the Radium Institute, a young army officer named Frédéric Joliot. The charming, outgoing Joliot was very different from Curie in personality, but they shared many interests. Fred, as everyone called him, later said of Irène, "I discovered in this girl, whom other people regarded . . . as a block of ice, an extraordinary person, sensitive and poetic." They married on October 9, 1926, and thereafter both used the hyphenated last name Joliot-Curie. They had a daughter, Hélène, born in 1927, and a son, Pierre, born in 1932.

Much of the Joliot-Curies' research at the Radium Institute resulted in frustrating near misses to great discoveries. In 1931, for instance, they showed that when beryllium, a lightweight metal, was bombarded with alpha particles from polonium, it gave off powerful rays that could make protons burst at high speed from the atomic nuclei in paraffin wax. They concluded that the rays were a new type of gamma ray, the most powerful form of atomic radiation then known. When British physicist James Chadwick repeated their experiment, however, he realized that the rays included a new kind of massive subatomic particle, which he called a neutron. He later won a Nobel Prize for this insight.

Finally, however, it was the Joliot-Curies' turn for success. Early in 1933 they found that when they placed polonium next to aluminum foil, neutrons and positrons (electrons with a positive charge—another particle they had just missed discovering) flew out of the foil instead of the protons they expected. Furthermore, when they moved the polonium away, the positrons kept streaming from the aluminum. A Gei-

ger counter, which detects radioactive particles, kept ticking for several minutes when placed next to the aluminum. Somehow the alpha particles from the polonium had made the aluminum radioactive.

The Joliot-Curies concluded that the nuclei of the aluminum atoms had absorbed alpha particles from the polonium, ejecting a neutron in the process and changing to a radioactive form of phosphorus that did not exist in nature. The phosphorus nuclei broke down in a few minutes, emitting a positron and changing to a stable, nonradioactive form of silicon. The couple had created the first artificial radioactive isotope, or variant form of an element. Irène used her chemical expertise to devise a test that proved that the short-lived phosphorus actually existed.

The aging Marie Curie was thrilled when her daughter and son-in-law showed her their experiment early in 1934, about the time they published their results. She was sure they would win a Nobel Prize for it, and she was right, though she did not live to see their triumph. The Joliot-Curies received the chemistry prize in 1935, when Irène was 37 years old. Their work led to the creation of radioactive isotopes of many other elements, which proved useful in physics, chemistry, industry, and medicine. The Joliot-Curies also won other prizes for their discovery, including America's Bernard Gold Medal for Meritorious Service to Science (1940), the Henri Wilde Prize, and the Marquet Prize of the French Academy of Sciences.

Although they remained as close as ever in private life, the Joliot-Curies stopped doing research together after they won the Nobel Prize. Fred became a professor at the Collège de France, the country's foremost research institution. Irène, meanwhile, continued to direct research at the Radium Institute, as she had since 1932, and also became a professor at the University of Paris.

When the Popular Front was elected to political power in France in 1936, it asked Irène to become the undersecretary of state for scientific research. She thus became one of France's first woman cabinet ministers. By prearrangement she gave up the post after three months, however, and returned to her beloved laboratory, where she continued to work in spite of ill health caused by tuberculosis and radiation exposure.

Irène Joliot-Curie's research included one more important near miss, which, if it had succeeded, might have allowed her to duplicate her mother's record of two Nobel Prizes. Like several other eminent scientists in the late 1930s, she studied what happened when neutrons bombarded uranium, the heaviest natural element. All expected that when the neutrons penetrated the uranium atoms' nuclei, they would create artificial elements, probably short-lived and radioactive, that were heavier than uranium. In 1938, therefore, when Joliot-Curie detected what appeared to be lanthanum, an element lighter than uranium, in the wake of such an experiment, she assumed she had made a mistake. German scientists Otto Hahn and Fritz Strassmann also disbelieved their results when, soon afterward, they obtained another lightweight element, barium, from a similar experient. They, however, had an advantage that Joliot-Curie did not have: the imagination of LISE MEITNER, who guessed after hearing of their experiment that they had split the nuclei into two parts.

After Germany invaded France in 1940, Fred joined the Resistance, the underground movement that opposed the Germans. Fearing danger to Irène and their two children because of this work, he helped them flee the country by hiking across the Jura Mountains to Switzerland on June 6, 1944—D day—when the Germans were preoccupied with the Allied invasion of France. The family was reunited after France was freed in 1945.

Fred was considered a war hero, and the new French president, Charles de Gaulle, made him head of the National Center for Scientific Research in 1945 and the Atomic Energy Commission in 1946. Irène was made a member of the commission as well. However, Fred's opposition to research on the hydrogen bomb and his Communist sympathies made him unpopular in a world increasingly dominated by cold war tension between the United States and Soviet Russia. The American government persuaded France to relieve Fred of his post in 1950. Irène served out her five-year term but was not reappointed when it expired.

Irène became the head of the Radium Institute in 1949. Her health had improved after the war when an antibiotic cured her tuberculosis, but in the mid-1950s she became ill again. Early in 1956 she learned that she had leukemia, the same cancer that had killed her mother. "I am not afraid of death," she told a longtime friend. "I have had such a thrilling life!" Irène Joliot-Curie died on March 17, 1956, at the age of 58.

Further Reading

"Joliot-Curie, Irène." *Current Biography Yearbook 1940.* New York: H. W. Wilson, 1940, 141–142.

McGrayne, Sharon Bertsch. *Nobel Prize Women in Science: Their Lives, Struggles, and Momentous Discoveries.* New York: Birch Lane Press, 117–143.

McKown, Robin. *She Lived for Science: Irène Joliot-Curie.* New York: Julian Messner, 1961.

Opfell, Olga S. *The Lady Laureates: Women Who Have Won the Nobel Prize.* Metuchen, N.J.: Scarecrow Press, 1986, 195–212.

Pflaum, Rosalind. *Marie Curie and Her Daughter Irène.* Windsor, Calif.: National Women's History Project, 1992.

✳ JORGE PÁDUA, MARIA TEREZA
(1943–) *Brazilian Ecologist*

Ecologist Maria Tereza Jorge Pádua has been called "the Mother of Brazil's National Parks." Born on May 8, 1943, in São José do Rio Pardo, Brazil, she learned to love nature when visiting her grandparents' farm and picnicking with her parents.

Jorge Pádua studied agronomical engineering as an undergraduate and went on to earn a master's degree in ecology from the University of Rio de Janeiro in 1972. She married a fellow ecologist and had three children. (The couple later divorced.) She joined Brazil's new national park system in 1968 and became one of the system's directors in 1970. She proved that she was more than a bureaucrat. "I had to show the men in the field that women can ride a horse like them, drive heavy machines and walk for hours in the jungle," she told writer Anne Labastille.

Jorge Pádua worked to extend Brazil's areas of protected wilderness. During the 1970s, for in-

Maria Tereza Jorge Pádua has helped to establish parks and reserves in her native Brazil and, as president of FUNATURA, works for nature conservation worldwide.
(Courtesy Maria Tereza Jorge Pádua)

stance, she helped to establish parks and reserves totaling almost 20 million acres in Amazonia, the Brazilian state that includes much of the Amazon rain forest. Her determination made her unpopular with people who wanted to exploit the forest or its products, including some members of the government, and she received threats of death to both herself and her family. "If you are honest, you receive threats," she says, adding, "I never thought of quitting. I never was afraid." Her courage earned her a share of the John Paul Getty Prize from the World Wildlife Fund in 1982.

Jorge Pádua founded an organization called Fundação Pró-Natureza (Foundation for the Protection of Nature), or FUNATURA, in 1986. It works to increase the number of Brazilian parks and protected areas and to devise plans that permit development of the country's resources without major damage to the environment. Jorge Pádua has worked full-time for the group since 1993 and as of 1998 was its president. She writes and speaks on conservation and related topics for an international audience and serves on many committees and groups concerned with the protection of nature.

In her roles as a director in the national park system and president of FUNATURA, Jorge Pádua has preserved more natural areas than anyone else in the world. "People in the environmental world know who I am, and I am proud of that," she says. Thomas Lovejoy of the Smithsonian Institution calls her "one of the leaders of her generation."

Further Reading

Brooke, Elizabeth Heilman. "Maria Tereza Jorge Pádua: Brazil's Nature Savior." *Nature Conservancy*, May/June 1993, 10–14.

Labastille, Anne. "Eight Women in the Wild." *International Wildlife*, January-February 1983, 36–43.

K

✳ KELSEY, FRANCES OLDHAM
(1914–) *American Physician*

Only the "stubbornness" of Food and Drug Administration medical officer Frances Oldham Kelsey kept an epidemic of deformed babies that swept Europe in the early 1960s from striking in the United States as well. Frances Oldham was born on July 14, 1914, to Katherine and Frank Oldham, a retired British army officer. She grew up in Cobble Hill on Vancouver Island, part of the Canadian province of British Columbia. She received a bachelor's degree in 1934 and a master of science degree in 1935 from McGill University in Montreal.

Oldham studied pharmacology at the University of Chicago, obtaining a Ph.D. in 1938. She then joined the university's faculty. In 1943 she and another pharmacologist, Fremont Ellis Kelsey, discovered that the fetuses in pregnant rabbits' wombs could not break down a common drug that adult rabbits' bodies were able to detoxify. This was one of the first explanations for the fact that the effects of drugs on the unborn could be very different from the effects on adults.

Oldham and Kelsey married near the end of 1943. That decision cost Frances Kelsey her job, since the university, like many others, did not permit a husband and wife to work in the same department. Kelsey went to medical school instead, meanwhile giving birth to two daughters. She obtained her M.D. from the University of Chicago in 1950.

After eight years at the University of South Dakota, during which (in 1956) Frances became a U.S. citizen, the Kelseys moved to Washington, D.C. Frances Kelsey became a medical officer at the Food and Drug Administration (FDA), reviewing applications from drug companies that wished to market new medicines.

Kelsey's first application, a seemingly routine request from the respected William S. Merrell Company of Cincinnati, Ohio, arrived on September 8, 1960. Merrell asked permission to sell in the United States a drug already widely used in Europe to help people sleep, relieve anxiety, and ease the nauseating "morning sickness" that often plagued pregnant women. The drug's scientific name was thalidomide. Merrell claimed that thalidomide had shown no major side effects in either animals or the people who took it in Europe, but Kelsey rejected Merrell's application on November 10, saying that the company had not proved the drug's safety. When she rejected Merrill's resubmission in January 1961, Merrell's representative complained to her supervisor, Ralph Smith, but Smith refused to overrule her.

Kelsey's nervousness received support a month later when she read a British medical report stating that thalidomide sometimes apparently caused polyneuritis, a nerve inflammation that could produce lasting damage. Concern about this side effect made her reject Merrell's application a third time at the end of March. Furthermore, remembering her earlier rabbit research, she asked the company to provide evidence that the drug was safe for mothers and fetuses if taken during pregnancy.

Kelsey's worst fears were confirmed when she began to hear disturbing reports about unusual numbers of severely deformed babies born in Europe. The babies' hands and feet were often attached directly to their shoulders and hips like flippers, giving the defect the name of phocomelia, or "seal limbs." Many of the babies had severe internal defects as well. Doctors in Germany and Australia reported that most of the women who gave birth to these babies had taken thalidomide during their first three months of pregnancy. Faced with these reports, thalidomide's German manufacturer stopped making the drug in November, and Merrell, too, withdrew its FDA application. By then, Kelsey had singlehandedly kept the drug off the American market for 14½ months.

On August 7, 1962, President John F. Kennedy awarded Kelsey the Distinguished Federal Civilian Service Medal, praising "her high ability and steadfast confidence in her professional decision." More important in Kelsey's eyes, late in 1962, Congress passed a law barring companies from distributing new drugs for testing purposes, as Merrell had done with thalidomide, without FDA approval.

In that same year, a new branch of the FDA was formed to oversee the distribution of "experimental" knowledge or drugs, and Frances Kelsey was put in charge of it. In 1967, she became director of a newly formed division that monitored the performance of animal and human studies conducted to determine the safety and effectiveness of drugs. The division also tracked the activities of institutional review boards and local committees that help to ensure the rights and welfare of human research subjects in drug trials. She continued this work until 1995, when she became the deputy for science and medicine at the FDA's Office of Compliance. In this position she researches questions on these subjects for the office's director. In 1998 she said she was "still working away."

Further Reading

Hoffman, William, and Jerry Shields. *Doctors on the New Frontier: Breaking Through the Barriers of Modern Medicine.* New York: Macmillan, 1981, 134–156.

"Kelsey, Frances O(ldham)." *Current Biography Yearbook 1965.* New York: H. W. Wilson, 1965, 218–220.

Truman, Margaret. *Women of Courage from Revolutionary Times to the Present.* New York: Morrow, 1976, 219–239.

✳ KING, MARY-CLAIRE
(1946–) *American Geneticist*

Some geneticists merely analyze DNA in test tubes, but Mary-Claire King sees genetics as closely tied to politics. "I've never believed our way of thinking about science is separate from thinking about life," she told interviewer David Noonan in 1990. She has used genetics to study human origins, discover why some people are more susceptible to breast cancer or AIDS than others, and identify the lost children of people murdered by repressive governments. As reporter Thomas Bass has noted, "Any one of her accomplishments could make another scientist's full-time career."

Mary-Claire King was born in Wilmette, Illinois, a suburb of Chicago, on February 27, 1946. Her father, Harvey, was head of personnel for Standard Oil of Indiana. Clarice, her mother, was a housewife. A childhood love of solving puzzles drew Mary-Claire to mathematics, which she studied at Carleton College in Minnesota, graduating cum laude in 1966.

King then went to the University of California (UC) at Berkeley to learn biostatistics, or statistics related to living things. While there she took a class in genetics that appealed to her by presenting aspects of heredity as puzzles. "And furthermore, [research in] it had the possibility of actually being good for . . . people," she told San Jose (California) *Mercury News* reporter Fran Smith in 1991. King changed her study plans accordingly.

King joined other Berkeley students in protesting against the Vietnam War. Disgusted when then-governor Ronald Reagan sent National Guard troops onto the campus in 1969, she moved to Washington, D.C., and began working for consumer advocate Ralph Nader on projects such as determining the effects of pesticides on farmworkers. After about a year, however, Allan C. Wilson, one of King's favorite professors at Berkeley, persuaded her to return and join his molecular biology laboratory.

Wilson was trying to trace human evolution through genetics and molecular biology, and he asked King to compare the genes of humans and chimpanzees. At first she thought she must be doing something wrong because "I couldn't seem to find any differences," but her results proved to be accurate. She proved that more than 99 percent of human genes are identical to those of chimpanzees. This startling research not only became the thesis that earned her a Ph.D. in genetics from Berkeley in 1973 but was featured on the cover of *Science* magazine.

In 1975, King turned to a quite different aspect of genetics: the possibility that women in certain families inherit a susceptibility to breast cancer. Such women develop the disease more often and at a much earlier age than average. Scientists at the time were discovering that all cancer grows out of damaging changes in genes, but usually those changes occur during an individual's lifetime and are caused either by chance or by factors in the environment, such as chemicals or radiation. The damaged genes involved in only a few rare cancers were known to be inherited. King eventually proved that about 5 percent of breast cancers are inherited.

When King began her hunt for the breast cancer gene, geneticists were starting to look for unknown genes among human beings' collection of 100,000 or so by identifying "marker" genes with which the unknown genes were usually inherited. Each marker gene exists in several forms. If an unknown gene is usually inherited along with a certain form of a marker, the chances are high that the unknown gene is physically close to the marker. At first few marker genes were known, but more were found during the 1980s. Finally, in 1990, King localized the breast cancer gene, which she called BRCA1, to halfway down the lower arm of the 17th of the human cell's 23 chromosomes. By then she had become a professor of epidemiology at UC Berkeley's School of Public Health (in 1984) and a professor of genetics in the university's Department of Molecular and Cell Biology (in 1989).

King's laboratory lost the race to identify the breast cancer gene itself; it was found by scientists at the University of Utah in September 1994. However, she has continued to study this and other genes involved in breast cancer (several have now been found) to learn how both the cancerous and the normal forms of the genes function and, perhaps, someday to develop a test that will detect the disease in very early stages. King's work has earned awards such as the Susan G. Komen Foundation Award for Distinguished Achievement in Breast Cancer Research (1992) and the Clowes Award for Basic Research from the American Association for Cancer Research (1994).

King's most unusual genetic project, tied to her lifelong concern for human rights, is helping to reunite families torn apart during the "dirty war" waged in Argentina between 1976 and 1983. During that time, the country's military government kidnapped, tortured, or murdered between 12,000 and 20,000 citizens. Babies born in prison or captured with their mothers were sold or given away, thus becoming lost to their birth families.

In 1977, while the military government was still in control, a group of courageous older women began gathering every Thursday on the Plaza de Mayo in Buenos Aires, opposite the government's headquarters, to protest the loss of their sons and daughters and demand the return of their grandchildren. They called themselves the Abuelas de Plaza de Mayo (Grandmothers of the Plaza of May). When a more liberal government took power in

1983, the group stepped up its campaign to locate the missing children. Even when the children were found, however, the families who had them usually refused to admit that they were adopted or give them up.

Knowing that genetic tests could show, for instance, whether a man was the father of a certain child, two representatives of the grandmothers' group came to the United States and asked for a geneticist to help them prove their relationship to the disputed children. They were sent to Luca Cavalli-Sforza, a renowned Stanford geneticist with whom King had worked, and he in turn referred them to King. King began working with the group in 1984. She now calls Argentina her "second home."

At first King used marker genes to test for relationships in the Argentinian families, but later she adapted a better technique that Allan Wilson developed in 1985. Most human genes are carried on DNA in the nucleus of each cell, but small bodies called mitochondria, which help cells use energy, also contain DNA. Unlike the genes in the nucleus, which come from both parents, mitochondrial DNA is passed on only through the mother and therefore is especially useful in showing the relationship between a child and its female relatives. King says that mitochondrial DNA examination "has proved to be a highly specific, invaluable tool for reuniting the grandmothers with their grandchildren." As a result of King's work, some 50 Argentinian children so far have been reunited with their birth families. The same technique has since been used to identify the remains of people killed in wars or murdered by criminals.

In the late 1990s King and Cavalli-Sforza headed the Human Genome Diversity Project, which plans to document variation in human genes by gathering and studying mitochondrial DNA from some 400 peoples around the world who have lived in the same area for a long time and have been relatively isolated from other groups. This project complements the better-known Human Genome Project, which is working out the sequence of small molecules called bases in all typical human genes. King says the genome diversity project will help people "understand who we are as a species and how we came to be" and will "undercut conventional notions of race and underscore the common bonds between all humans."

In 1995, King moved to Seattle (which she calls "the Athens of genetics") to head a laboratory at the University of Washington. Her laboratory is pursuing a number of projects, including continuation of the human rights work of identifying military murder victims and children separated from their families by war; this work, under the direction of Michele Harvey, now encompasses Bosnia, Rwanda, and Ethiopia as well as Argentina. The lab is also investigating the genetics of inherited deafness and genetic variations that may determine why some people are more easily infected with the AIDS virus after exposure and develop full-blown AIDS more quickly after infection than others. The laboratory's chief focus, however, continues to be the study of BRCA1 and other genes involved in breast and ovarian cancer, including noninherited forms of the disease. "Our goal is to eliminate breast cancer as a cause of death," King says.

Mary-Claire King believes that women bring a special gift to science. "Women tend to tackle questions in science that bridge gaps," she says. "We're more inclined to pull together threads from different areas, to be more integrative in our thinking." She hopes to apply her share of this gift to "try to improve the lives of people. . . . To me, the most interesting questions are those that have potentially a very practical outcome."

Further Reading

Bass, Thomas A. *Reinventing the Future: Conversations with the World's Leading Scientists.* Reading, Mass.: Addison-Wesley, 1994, 219–241.

Bock, Paula. "Mission Possible." *Seattle Times,* May 31, 1998

"King, Mary-Claire." *Current Biography Yearbook 1995.* New York: H. W. Wilson Co., 1995, 308–313.

Noonan, David. "Genes of War." *Discover,* October 1990, 46–52.

✳ KIRCH, MARIA MARGARETHA WINKELMANN

(1670–1720) *German Astronomer*

Maria Kirch, the first woman credited with discovering a comet, not only was denied a formal post as an astronomer because of her gender but was even reprimanded for appearing in public in an observatory. She was born Maria Margaretha Winkelmann in 1670 at Panitsch, near Leipzig, in what is now Germany. Her father, a Lutheran minister, educated his daughter at home. When she showed an interest in astronomy, he sent her to study under Christoph Arnold, a self-taught astronomer nicknamed the "astronomical peasant."

Gottfried Kirch, Germany's foremost astronomer, came to consult the peasant master one day, met Maria, and fell in love. The two married in 1692 and moved to Berlin in 1700. By then Maria had become Gottfried's working partner. They either observed different parts of the sky on the same night or took turns on alternate nights, one watching while the other slept. During one of these solo nights in 1702, Maria spotted a new comet, then considered a major astronomical find. Gottfried took credit for the discovery in the first published account of it, perhaps because he feared ridicule if people learned that the comet had been found by a woman, but in a 1710 revision he admitted that his wife had been the discoverer.

The Kirches also worked together to make calendars sold by the Royal Academy of Sciences in Berlin, and Maria made many of the astronomical calculations the calendars required. (She also published three astrological pamphlets under her own name between 1709 and 1711; at the time, astronomy and astrology overlapped.) After Gottfried died in 1710, Maria asked the academy to let her continue making the calendars, but in spite of the support of the academy's president, renowned mathematician and philosopher Gottfried von Leibniz, its executive counsel, fearing that "what we concede to her could serve as an example in the future," refused.

Kirch joined the private observatory of Baron Frederick von Krosigk in 1712. When the Academy of Sciences appointed her son, Christfried, to his father's old position in 1716, however, she returned to Berlin to act as his "assistant." A year later the council complained that Kirch was "too visible at the observatory when strangers visit" and ordered her to "retire to the background and leave the talking to . . . her son." When she refused to comply, they forced her to leave, even making her give up her house on the observatory grounds. She died of a fever in 1720. Her biographer, Vignole, wrote that "she merited a fate better than the one she received."

Further Reading

Ogilvie, Marilyn Bailey. *Women in Science: Antiquity Through the Nineteenth Century.* Cambridge, Mass.: MIT Press, 1986, 110.

Schiebinger, Londa. *The Mind Has No Sex? Women in the Origins of Modern Science.* Cambridge, Mass.: Harvard University Press, 1989, 84–99.

✳ KLEIN, MELANIE REIZES

(1882–1960) *German/British Psychologist*

Melanie Klein extended the concepts of Freudian psychoanalysis to young children and people with severe mental illness. She was born Melanie Reizes on March 30, 1882, in Vienna, Austria, the youngest of the four children of Moriz Reizes and his wife, Libussa. The family was poor.

Reizes married her cousin, engineer Arthur Klein, in 1903, and had a daughter and two sons, but the marriage was not happy. Around 1912, while the Kleins lived in Budapest, Melanie entered psychoanalysis because of this. She became interested in Sigmund Freud's ideas, and her analyst, Sandor Ferenczi, encouraged her to become an analyst herself.

Freud had doubted that young children could be psychoanalyzed, but Klein disagreed. Her shy five-year-old son, Erich, became her first patient. A paper about Erich's treatment earned her membership in the Hungarian Psychoanalytic Society in 1919. It stressed that exploring the unconscious roots of anxiety was vital in treating children as well as adults.

In 1921, Klein separated from her husband and moved to Berlin. She became a member of the Berlin Psychoanalytic Society in 1922 and began analyzing other children. Some Berlin analysts criticized her because she lacked academic credentials, but her views proved more acceptable to British psychoanalysts. She moved to England in 1926 and joined the British Psycho-Analytic Society a year later.

In contrast to Freud, who thought that the childhood conflicts that sometimes produced mental illness grew out of instinct and focused on the father, Klein felt that the most important conflicts grew out of children's relationships with others, especially their mothers. When children felt that their mothers were denying them, they fantasized hurting the mothers and then feared punishment for this. Klein believed that children—or adults—could overcome such fears, and resulting illness, by realizing that they had the goodness and power to repair imagined damage done to their mothers.

Klein analyzed children as young as three years old. Her techniques, which she described in *The Psychoanalysis of Children* (1960), are still widely used. She gave her young patients toys such as miniature houses, cars, and dolls and encouraged them to use the toys to act out stories about themselves and their families. From symbols and actions in this play she learned what the children were thinking and feeling. She also studied how the children reacted to her as a mother figure.

Freud had concentrated on the relatively mild mental illness called neurosis, but Klein claimed that psychoanalytic techniques could be modified to treat more serious disturbances, including depression and schizophrenia. Her ideas and personality caused great controversy among psychoanalysts. One called her "the most impressive human being I have known," but others complained of her "overweening self-righteousness" and "adamantine dogmatism." Klein died of cancer on September 22, 1960, at the age of 78.

Further Reading

Grosskurth, Phyllis. *Melanie Klein: Her World and Her Work*. Cambridge, Mass.: Harvard University Press, 1995.

Sayers, Janet. *Mothers of Psychoanalysis*. New York: Norton, 1991, 205–257.

Segal, Julia. *Melanie Klein*. Thousand Oaks, Calif.: Sage, 1992.

✳ KOVALEVSKAIA, SOFIA VASILYEVNA ("Sonya")
(1850–1891) *Russian Mathematician*

Sofia Kovalevskaia overcame many barriers to become the first tenured woman professor in modern Europe. She won the prestigious Bordin Prize from the French Academy of Sciences. One of her biographers, Ann Hibner Koblitz, writes that "during her lifetime, Kovalevskaia was regarded as one of the most eminent mathematical analysts in the world."

Sofia, usually called Sonya, was the middle of Vasily and Yelizaveta Korvin-Krukovsky's three daughters (they also had a son). She was born in Moscow on January 15, 1850. Her father was a nobleman and a general in the Russian artillery. When Sonya was six, he retired from the army and moved to an isolated country estate in Palabino, near the Lithuanian border. The family started to put new wallpaper in the house there, but the supply ran out before one room was covered, so they finished the job with printed pages of calculus lectures from the general's student days. "These sheets, spotted over with strange incomprehensible formulae, soon attracted my attention," Sonya wrote in her *Recollections of Childhood*. "I passed whole hours before that mysterious wall, trying to decipher even a single phrase, and to discover the order in which the sheets ought to follow each other."

Wallpaper was just the beginning of Sonya's self-education. When a family friend gave her a physics text, she discovered that she needed to know trigonometry in order to understand it and worked out the basic ideas of that branch of mathematics on her own. The friend's amazed report of this, coupled with the girl's own pleas, persuaded Korvin-Krukovsky to let her obtain private tutoring in St. Petersburg.

That seemed as far as Sonya could hope to go, since Russian universities did not admit women. Some universities elsewhere in Europe did, but unmarried Russian women could not leave the country without their parents' permission. Young women in Sonya's forward-looking set of friends sometimes got around this by making marriages of convenience with men who accompanied them to a university and then left them. Sonya and her sister explored this idea with Vladimir Kovalevsky, a 26-year-old geology student. Kovalevsky agreed—so long as the bride was Sonya. He wrote to his brother that in addition to being "extremely well-educated," she was "lively, sweet, and very pretty." They married in October 1868.

In 1869 the Kovalevskys went to Germany's University of Heidelberg. Sonya was not allowed to enroll there, but she attended lectures. According to Julia Lermontova, a friend who moved in with the Kovalevskys shortly after their arrival, professors who met Kovalevskaia (female form of Kovalevsky) "spoke of her as something extraordinary." Sonya and her new husband, too, appeared to be truly in love. "This was the only time I have known Sonya to be really happy," Lermontova wrote later. Soon, however, more female friends arrived; the Kovalevskys' apartment became overcrowded, and Vladimir Kovalevsky moved out.

After two years at Heidelberg, Kovalevskaia went to Berlin in the hope of studying under Karl T. Weierstrass, the "father of mathematical analysis." Weierstrass tried to get rid of her by giving her problems that he normally assigned only to his most advanced students, but when she solved them, he became one of her staunchest supporters. He tutored her without charge for the next four years and came to see her almost as a daughter.

Weierstrass helped Kovalevskaia gain permission to apply for a doctorate from the University of Göttingen, even though she had not attended that university. She submitted three papers as possible dissertations. The most important showed how much information was needed to solve certain differential equations, which show how a change in one quantity, or variable, is related to a change in one or more other quantities. A second paper predicted the shape of the rings around the planet Saturn, which at the time were thought to be liquid. Kovalevskaia showed that, rather than being ellipses as previous mathematicians had assumed, the rings would be egg shaped. Her third paper concerned the mathematics of ellipses. Göttingen granted her degree, *summa cum laude*, in 1874, making her one of the first women to obtain a degree from a German university.

Difficult as it had been, obtaining a degree proved far easier than obtaining a job. Kovalevskaia finally gave up and returned to Russia late in 1874. There she became reunited with her husband, who now taught paleontology in Moscow. For the first time they truly lived as man and wife, and they had a daughter in 1878. The girl, Sofia, was nicknamed Fufa.

For six years Kovalevskaia abandoned her mathematical career and tried to be a conventional wife and mother, but she later referred to this life as "the soft slime of bourgeois existence" and said that Fufa was the only good thing that came out of it. She and Vladimir Kovalevsky did not get along, and their problems were worsened by his growing mental instability and tendency to make disastrous financial investments. They separated in 1880 and, leaving Fufa in Moscow with Lermontova, Kovalevskaia returned to Berlin and then to Paris. There she was elected to the Mathematical Society and carried out research on the way light travels through crystals. Meanwhile, back in Russia, Kovalevsky killed himself on April 15, 1883.

Weierstrass had asked Gösta Mittag-Leffler, a former student who was now a professor of mathematics at the University of Stockholm, to help Kovalevskaia find work. Mittag-Leffler finally persuaded the Swedish university to hire her as a lecturer in autumn 1883. On her arrival, some Stockholm newspapers hailed her as "a princess of science," but playwright August Strindberg claimed that "a female professor of mathematics is . . . a monstrosity." After a year, apparently agreeing with Mittag-Leffler's view of Kovalevskaia rather than Strindberg's, the university offered her a five-year salaried professorship. In 1885 she began teaching mechanics as well.

Kovalevskaia was delighted to be lecturing, teaching, and doing research. In 1886 she sent for Fufa. The tradition-minded townspeople criticized her, however, and she in turn began to find Swedish society boring and longed for Paris or St. Petersburg. She even became somewhat tired of mathematics. She joined Anna Charlotte Leffler-Edgren, Mittag-Leffler's sister, in writing a play, and on her own she wrote short stories, articles, poetry, novels, and her autobiography.

In 1886 the French Academy of Sciences offered its highest award, the Bordin Prize, to the best paper describing the rotation of a solid body around a fixed point. Kovalevskaia had studied this subject when she wrote about the rings of Saturn, so she decided to enter the contest. To prevent favoritism, all entries were submitted anonymously, with a short phrase in place of the author's name. The judges agreed that the best of the 15 entries was the one signed with the saying, "Say what you know, do what you must, come what may," noting that "the author's method . . . allows him to give a complete solution [of the problem] in the most precise and elegant form." When the authors' identities were revealed, the astounded judges learned they had used the wrong pronoun: The paper was Kovalevskaia's.

The French science academy was so impressed with Kovalevskaia's work that it not only awarded her the Bordin Prize in December 1888 but added another 2,000 francs to it. When she refined the paper in 1889, it won an additional 1,500 kroner from the Swedish Academy of Science and earned her a permanent professorship at the university—the first granted to a woman in Europe in modern times. Her paper was later called "one of the most famous works of mathematical physics in the 19th century."

In spite of these successes, Kovalevskaia was not happy. She had fallen in love with a Russian sociologist and historian, Maxim Kovalevsky (a distant relative of her late husband's family), and their relationship was stormy. They spent the holidays in France at the end of 1890 and may have been planning to marry the following year, but Kovalevskaia caught a chill on the journey back to Stockholm that developed into pneumonia. She died of it on February 10, 1891, just three weeks after her 41st birthday.

Further Reading

Alic, Margaret. *Hypatia's Heritage: A History of Women in Science from Antiquity Through the Nineteenth Century.* Boston: Beacon Press, 1986, 163–173.

Henderson, Harry. *Modern Mathematicians.* New York: Facts On File, 1996, 36–45.

Kennedy, Don. *Little Sparrow: A Portrait of Sofia Kovalevsky.* Athens: Ohio University Press, 1983.

Koblitz, Ann H. *A Convergence of Lives: Sofia Kovalevskaia—Scientist, Writer, Revolutionary.* New Brunswick, N.J.: Rutgers University Press, 1993.

Kovalevsky, S. *Recollections of Childhood.* Translated by Isabel F. Hapgood, with a biography by Anna Carlotta Leffler. New York: Century, 1895.

✳ LADD-FRANKLIN, CHRISTINE
(1847–1930) *American Mathematician and Psychologist*

Christine Ladd-Franklin made important contributions in two very different scientific areas: symbolic logic and the theory of color vision. She was born to Eliphalet and Augusta Ladd in Windsor, Connecticut, on December 1, 1847. She spent her childhood in New York City, where her father was a well-to-do merchant, and then in Windsor, to which he moved his family after he retired in 1853. After Christine's mother died when she was 13, she lived with her grandmother in Portsmouth, New Hampshire.

Ladd studied at Vassar College for two years, majoring in mathematics (she would have preferred physics but could not get access to laboratory equipment), and obtained her B.A. in 1869. She then taught high school science for nine years. In 1878 she asked Johns Hopkins University to admit her as a graduate student in mathematics. The university did not accept women at the time, but Hopkins mathematics professor James J. Sylvester had read her papers in a British mathematical journal and asked that she be allowed to attend as a "special status" student. The university agreed, but in order to avoid setting a precedent, it did not put her name in its official list of students.

Ladd fulfilled all the requirements for a Ph.D. by 1882, but the university refused to grant her a degree. (It finally made up this lack in 1926, when she was 78 years old.) She married Fabian Franklin, a fellow Johns Hopkins mathematician, in August of that year. They had two children, of whom one, Margaret, survived into adulthood.

Ladd-Franklin, as Christine now called herself, made her first contributions in the field of symbolic logic. They concerned syllogisms, three-part statements such as "If all *as* are *bs,* and all *bs* are *cs,* then all *as* are *cs.*" In the early 1880s she reduced all such statements to a single formula and showed how to use it to tell whether a syllogism was valid.

Around 1886, Ladd-Franklin moved from mathematics to psychology, specifically the theory of vision. The connection, for her, lay in the way two eyes combine separate images into one, the study of which requires both mathematics and psychology. Later she concentrated on color vision. She studied with two authorities in the field, G. E. Müller of Göttingen University and Hermann von Helmholtz of the University of Berlin, and combined parts of their opposing theories into her own hypothesis about the way color vision had evolved.

She first presented it at the International Congress of Psychology in 1892. She believed that the most primitive form of vision, which did not include colors, evolved into vision of blue and yellow. The chemical associated with yellow then broke down into products that allowed vision of reds and greens, producing advanced color vision.

Johns Hopkins made Ladd-Franklin a lecturer in psychology and logic in 1904. She continued to teach there until 1909, when Fabian Franklin, now a journalist, moved to New York City. Ladd-Franklin lectured and did research at Columbia University from 1914 until her retirement in 1927. Her ideas, some of which are still accepted, were collected in a book, *Colour and Colour Theories*, in 1929. She died in New York on March 5, 1930, at the age of 82.

Further Reading

Hurvich, Dorothea Jameson. "Ladd-Franklin, Christine." In *Notable American Women, 1607–1950, vol. II: G–O*, edited by Edward T. James, 354–356. Cambridge, Mass.: The Belknap Press of Harvard University Press, 1971.

Ogilvie, Marilyn Bailey. *Women in Science: Antiquity Through the Nineteenth Century*. Cambridge, Mass.: MIT Press, 1986, 116–117.

✳ LEAKEY, MARY DOUGLAS NICOL
(1913–1996) *British Paleontologist and Anthropologist*

Mary Leakey made many of the discoveries of bones of human ancestors for which her better-known husband, Louis S. B. Leakey, became famous. After his death she was celebrated in her own right for such finds as the earliest known fossil footprints of humans walking upright. "It was Mary who really gave that team scientific validity," Gilbert Grosvenor, chairman of the National Geographic Society, once said.

Leakey was born Mary Douglas Nicol on February 6, 1913, in London. Her father, Erskine Nicol, was a landscape painter. One of his favorite places to paint was southwestern France, where beautiful paintings by Stone Age artists had been discovered in caves. Mary loved exploring the caves and decided that she wanted to study early humans.

Nicol met archaeologists Alexander Keiller and Dorothy Liddell in the late 1920s and began assisting Liddell on summer digs, drawing artifacts found at the sites. She also increased her knowledge of archaeology by going to lectures at the London Museum and London University. Another woman archaeologist, Gertrude Caton-Thompson, soon asked Nicol to illustrate one of her books as well.

In 1933, Caton-Thompson invited Nicol to a dinner party she was giving for a visiting scientist named Louis S. B. Leakey. Leakey, born of British parents and raised in Kenya, was starting to become known for his studies of early humans and their ancestors. He asked Nicol to make some drawings for him, and the two fell in love, even though Leakey was 10 years older than Nicol, married, and the father of two children.

Nicol traveled to Africa with Leakey in 1935 and for the first time gazed "spellbound" at his favorite site, Olduvai Gorge in Tanzania, near the Kenyan border, a view that she once said "has . . . come to mean more to me than any other in the world." The two married on December 24, 1936, as soon as Leakey's divorce became final, and were, in Mary's words, "blissfully happy." They later had three sons, Jonathan, Richard, and Philip. Richard, like his parents, would become famous for studies of early humans.

The Leakeys became close professional as well as personal partners. They excavated several Stone Age sites in Kenya and Tanzania during the 1930s, and Mary continued during World War II while Louis worked for British intelligence. After the war, Louis spent part of his time at the Coryndon Museum in Nairobi, of which he became curator in 1946, while Mary went on digging at Olduvai and elsewhere. In 1948 she made the couple's first big find, the skull of an ape called *Proconsul africanus*. The finding of this 16-million-year-old distant human ancestor in East Africa gave weight to the idea that humans had originated in Africa, rather than in Asia as had been thought. It also made the Leakeys world famous.

Mary continued her work at Olduvai during the 1950s and also explored a site in Tanzania where people living during the Late Stone Age, when the Sahara was a fertile valley, had painted thousands of people and animals on rocks, revealing such details as clothing and hairstyles. She copied some 1,600 of these paintings, a task she later called "one of the highlights" of her career. The best of her drawings were published in a book in 1983.

Mary Leakey made another major discovery on July 17, 1959. She and Louis had been excavating together at Olduvai, but on that day Louis was sick and stayed in camp. Walking in the oldest part of the site, Mary spotted a piece of bone in the ground. It proved to be part of an upper jaw, complete with two large, humanlike teeth. She dashed back to camp and burst into Louis's tent, shouting, "I've got him! I've got him!" What she eventually had was about 400 bits of bone, which she painstakingly assembled into an almost complete skull of a 1.75-million-year-old humanlike creature that the Leakeys named *Zinjanthropus*, or "Zinj" for short.

The discovery of *Zinjanthropus* extended the timeline of human evolution back by a million years. Louis Leakey at first believed that Zinj was a "missing link" between humans and apes, but later research showed that it was an australopithecine, a member of a family of humanlike beings that developed alongside the earliest true humans. A few years later the Leakeys found a skull of a new human species as well. They named it *Homo habilis*, or "handy man," because of the many tools found nearby.

Louis and Mary Leakey drifted apart during the 1960s, and their marriage was over in all but name by the time Louis died of a heart attack in 1972. Mary continued working, and in 1978 she made what she felt was her most important discovery: three sets of fossil footprints crossing a patch of hardened volcanic ash at Laetoli, Kenya, about 30 miles south of Olduvai. The footprints looked so fresh that, she said, "they could have been left this morning," but tests showed that they had been made about 3.6 million years ago, much earlier than humans had been thought to be walking upright. Leakey noted that no tools were found in the area,

which suggested that humans had begun to walk upright before they started to make tools. "This new freedom of forelimbs posed a challenge," Leakey wrote in *National Geographic*. "The brain expanded to meet it. And mankind was formed."

Mary Leakey received many awards for her work, including the Hubbard Medal of the National Geographic Society, which she shared with Louis in 1962; the Boston Museum of Science's Bradford Washburn Award; and the Gold Medal of the Society of Women Geographers. Age and failing eyesight forced her to give up fieldwork in the early 1980s. She died in Nairobi on December 9, 1996, at age 83. F. Clark Howell, professor emeritus of anthropology at the University of California at Berkeley, said that she left "an unparalleled legacy of research and integrity."

Further Reading

Leakey, Mary. *Disclosing the Past*. Garden City, N.Y.: Doubleday, 1984.
———. *Olduvai Gorge: My Search for Early Man*. New York: Collins, 1979.
"Leakey, Mary (Douglas)." *1985 Current Biography Yearbook*. New York: H. W. Wilson, 1985, 257–60.
Morell, Virginia. *Ancestral Passions*. New York: Simon & Schuster, 1996.

✳ LEAVITT, HENRIETTA SWAN
(1868–1921) *American Astronomer*

In addition to determining the brightness of thousands of stars, Henrietta Swan Leavitt discovered the first method of measuring large-scale distances in the universe. She was born on July 4, 1868, in Lancaster, Massachusetts, one of George and Henrietta Leavitt's seven children. Her father was a minister. She grew up in Cambridge and later in Cleveland, Ohio.

Leavitt studied for two years at Oberlin College in Ohio, then transferred to Radcliffe in 1888 and graduated in 1892. A class she took in her senior year interested her in astronomy. She began doing volunteer work for the Harvard Observatory in

Henrietta Leavitt's study of a type of star called Cepheid variables at the Harvard College Observatory around 1912 led to development of the first method of measuring large-scale distances in the universe. (Courtesy Harvard College Observatory)

1895 and joined the paid staff in 1902. She was one of a number of women "computers," including WILLIAMINA FLEMING and ANNIE JUMP CANNON, whom Edward Pickering, the head of the observatory, hired to work on the observatory's large projects.

Astronomers had first measured stars' brightness by comparing the stars by eye. As more astronomical work came to be done through photographs, the scale of brightness had to be recalibrated because film registers slightly different wavelengths of light than the eye. Pickering began a large project to do this in 1907 and put Leavitt in charge of it, making her the chief of the photographic photometry department. She first calculated the brightness of 46 stars near the North (Pole) Star, selected to repre-

sent all degrees of brightness, then extended the work to other parts of the sky. In 1913 the International Committee on Photographic Magnitudes adopted Leavitt's "North Polar Sequence" as its brightness standard.

Leavitt's true interest, however, was variable stars, which brighten and dim on a regular schedule. She discovered some 2,400 of these stars, mostly in the two Magellanic Clouds, which were later shown to be small galaxies. Many variables in the Small Magellanic Cloud were a type called Cepheids, and Leavitt showed in 1912 that the longer a Cepheid's period (the time of one cycle of brightening and dimming), the brighter the star was at its brightest. Stars' apparent brightness is affected by their distance from earth, but since all

Cepheids in the cloud were about equally far away, she concluded that their periods were related to their true brightness.

Leavitt would have liked to follow up on her finding, but Pickering did not encourage his women "computers" to do independent or theoretical work. CECILIA PAYNE-GAPOSCHKIN, another of the Harvard women astronomers, wrote that keeping Leavitt confined to photometry "was a harsh decision, which condemned a brilliant scientist to uncongenial work, and probably set back the study of variable stars for several decades."

Other astronomers turned Leavitt's discovery into what astronomer VERA RUBIN calls "the most fundamental method of calculating distances in the universe." If a Cepheid's period was known, its true brightness could be calculated, and if its true brightness was known, its distance from earth could be calculated by comparing the true brightness with the apparent brightness. By using Cepheids as yardsticks, astronomers could determine the distance of any group of stars in which these stars were embedded.

Leavitt never achieved the fame that came to Cannon or Fleming. Some of her fellow women astronomers, however, thought she was the brightest of the Harvard group. She died of cancer on December 12, 1921, at age 52.

Further Reading

Hoffleit, Dorrit. "Leavitt, Henrietta Swan." In *Notable American Women, 1607–1950, vol. II: G–O*, edited by Edward T. James. Cambridge, Mass.: The Belknap Press of Harvard University Press, 1971, 382–383.

Mack, Pamela E. "Straying from Their Orbits: Women in Astronomy in America." In *Women of Science: Righting the Record*, edited by G. Kass-Simon and Patricia Farnes. Bloomington: Indiana University Press, 1990, 102–104.

✳ LEHMANN, INGE
(1888–1993) *Danish Geologist*

Inge Lehmann used the effects of waves sent through the earth by earthquakes to prove that the planet has a solid core. She was born in Copenhagen, Denmark, in 1888. Her father was a professor of psychology at the University of Copenhagen. Lehmann, in turn, studied mathematics and physical science there from 1907 to 1910 and also spent a year at Britain's Cambridge University. She then worked in the insurance industry for eight years before returning to the University of Copenhagen. She earned a M.S. in mathematics in 1920 and one in geodesy in 1928.

Lehmann began her professional life in 1925 at the new Royal Danish Geodetic Institute and became the head of the institute's seismology department in 1928. Indeed, for two decades she was Denmark's only seismologist. Geologists knew that a layer of molten rock lay below the earth's surface, and at the time they thought this layer went all the way to the planet's center. Lehmann, however, noticed that one type of earthquake wave, called P prime, did not act as it would be expected to do if the earth's entire core was molten. She concluded in 1936 that these waves were being reflected off a dense core of solid material that began 869 miles (1,400 kilometers) from the earth's center. Other geologists refused to accept this idea at first, but in time the evidence supporting it grew too great to deny.

Lehmann retired in 1953 and died 40 years later at the amazing age of 105. Among the honors she received were the Gold Medal of the Royal Danish Society of Science (1965), the Bowie Medal of the American Geophysical Union (1971), and the Medal of the Seismological Society of America (1977). In 1997 the American Geophysical Union named a medal after her—the first that this group has named for a woman—to be awarded in recognition of outstanding research on the structure, composition, and dynamics of the earth's core.

Further Reading

"Lehmann, Inge," CWP at physics.UCLA.edu. Available online. URL: http://www.physics.ucla.edu/~cwp.html. Updated in 1996.

Nies, Kevin Allison. *From Sorceress to Scientist.* Tarzana: California Video Institute, 1990, 56–58.

✳ LEVI-MONTALCINI, RITA

(1909–) *Italian/American Medical Researcher*

Drawing on research begun in her bedroom during World War II, Rita Levi-Montalcini discovered a substance that makes nerves grow. It plays a vital part in the development of humans and animals and in future may be a medical treatment. For its discovery Levi-Montalcini and her coworker, Stanley Cohen, shared the Nobel Prize in physiology or medicine in 1986.

Rita Levi-Montalcini was born in Turin, Italy, on April 22, 1909. She has a twin sister, Paola, and an older brother and sister. Her father, Adamo Levi, was an engineer and factory owner. Rita admired him but feared his temper and felt closer to her mother, Adele, whose maiden name was Montalcini. Rita later combined her father's and mother's last names in her own.

Rita felt she was "drifting along in the dark," with no idea of what to do with her life, until she was 20, when a family friend's painful death from cancer made her decide to become a physician. Having received only the minimal education allotted to girls, she had to take tutoring before she could qualify for medical school. She entered the Turin School of Medicine in 1930 and earned her M.D. with honors in 1936. While still a student she became an assistant to one of her professors, Giuseppe Levi (no relation), and she continued in that capacity after graduation. From him she learned how to study spiderlike nerve cells in the nervous systems of embryo chickens.

Fascist leader Benito Mussolini had taken control of Italy in 1925. His regime did not persecute Jews as intensely as that of Nazi Germany, but in 1938 it passed a law that deprived all Jews of academic jobs. Both Levi and Levi-Montalcini thus became unemployed. Levi-Montalcini was discouraged until a friend from medical school reminded her of all the good scientific work that had been done with limited laboratory equipment. "One doesn't lose heart in the face of the first difficulties,"

Building on research begun in her bedroom during World War II, Italian-born Rita Levi-Montalcini worked at Washington University to codiscover a vital natural substance called nerve growth factor. She and coworker Stanley Cohen shared the 1986 Nobel Prize in physiology or medicine for their discovery.
(Courtesy Washington University Archives, St. Louis, Mo.)

he told her. He suggested that she try to continue her chick embryo research at home.

The attempt seemed like "a voyage of adventure" to Levi-Montalcini, so she set up what she called a "private laboratory *a la* Robinson Crusoe" in her bedroom. She made a small heater into an incubator for her eggs and sharpened sewing needles to use as scalpels for cutting up the tiny embryos. She continued even after World War II began and her family had to move to a small house in the hills to escape the Allied bombing of Turin. There her laboratory shrank to a corner of the living room, and the eggs she experimented on later became part of the family's meals.

In her makeshift laboratory Levi-Montalcini set out to duplicate the experiments of a researcher named Viktor Hamburger, who had shown that when a limb was cut off a developing embryo, the nerves starting to grow into that limb died. He thought this happened because the cells were no longer receiving some substance from the limb that they needed in order to mature. Levi-Montalcini, however, found that the cells did mature before they died. She suspected that the unknown substance kept the cells alive and attracted them toward the limb rather than helping them mature. She published the results of her research in a Belgian science journal.

Mussolini fell from power in July 1943, to the relief of many Italians, but German troops took control of the country a month and a half later. Now, for the first time, Jewish families in Italy were in real danger. Using assumed names, Rita and most of her family hid for a year with a friend of Paola's in Florence. They returned to Turin after the Allies freed Italy in the spring of 1945.

In 1946, Levi-Montalcini received a surprise letter from Viktor Hamburger, who had read the report of her findings about his research. He was now a professor at Washington University in St. Louis, and he invited her to come to the United States and work with him for a semester. She agreed, little knowing that the "one-semester" visit that began in 1947 would last 30 years.

Levi-Montalcini's work took a new direction in 1950, when Hamburger told her about research done by a former student, Elmer Bücker. Bücker had grafted tissue from a mouse cancer onto a chick embryo and found that the tumor made nerve fibers from the embryo multiply and grow toward it, just as a grafted limb would have. Levi-Montalcini could not see why cancer tissue should have this effect, so she set out to repeat Bücker's experiments. She found that some mouse cancers produced an amount of nerve growth "so extraordinary that I thought I might be hallucinat-

ing" when she viewed it under the microscope. Nerves grew not only into the tumor but into nearby organs of the embryo. Levi-Montalcini noted that the nerve cells did not make contact with other cells, however, as they would have if stimulated by an extra limb.

Levi-Montalcini decided that she would have a better chance of identifying this "nerve-growth promoting agent" if she studied its effects on nerve tissue in laboratory dishes rather than on whole embryos, which contained many substances that affected growth and development. She therefore spent several months in Rio de Janeiro, Brazil, learning the techniques of tissue culture from a former student of Giuseppe Levi's. At first she had trouble making her experiments work, but she finally found one tumor that made nerves grow out from a chick embryo ganglion, or nerve bundle, "like rays from the sun."

In January 1953 a new coworker, biochemist Stanley Cohen, joined Hamburger's group. He set out to learn the chemical nature of Levi-Montalcini's mystery substance, which those in the lab were beginning to call nerve growth factor (NGF). His skill in chemistry perfectly complemented Levi-Montalcini's in working with embryos and tissues. "You and I [separately] are good," Cohen once told her, "but together we are wonderful." Levi-Montalcini, for her part, later called the six years she worked with Cohen "the most intense and productive years of my life." Among other things, they learned that NGF was a protein, one of a large family of chemicals that carry out most activities in living cells.

Levi-Montalcini had been made a full professor at Washington University in 1958, but Hamburger was unable to gain a similar appointment for Cohen. Deciding that he needed more security, Cohen reluctantly gave up his research with Levi-Montalcini and moved to Vanderbilt University in Tennessee in 1959. Levi-Montalcini heard the news of his departure "like the tolling of a funeral bell."

Levi-Montalcini had become a United States citizen in 1956, but she also kept her Italian citizenship and stayed in close touch with her family. In 1959 she decided that she wanted to spend more time with them, so she arranged with Washington University to establish a research outpost in Rome. This research unit was greatly enlarged in 1969 and became part of a new Laboratory of Cell Biology, run by Italy's National Council of Research. Levi-Montalcini directed the cell biology laboratory for the next 10 years, and in 1977 she moved back to Italy for good. She shares an apartment in Rome with Paola, an artist, whom she calls "part of myself."

Levi-Montalcini received many awards for her work on NGF, including the prestigious Lasker Award for medical research in 1986. The Lasker is often considered a prelude to a Nobel Prize, and so it proved to be for her. In October 1986 she learned that she was to share that year's prize in physiology or medicine with Stanley Cohen.

Levi-Montalcini officially retired in 1979, but she continues to do research. In 1986 she found that NGF can spur the growth of brain cells as well as those from the spinal cord, which suggests that it might someday be used in a treatment for brain-damaging conditions such as Alzheimer's disease and strokes. She has also found that some cells in the immune system both produce and respond to NGF, suggesting a link between this disease-fighting system and the nervous system. "The moment you stop working, you are dead," she once told an interviewer, and Rita Levi-Montalcini clearly is not dead yet.

Further Reading

Dash, Joan. *The Triumph of Discovery: Women Scientists Who Won the Nobel Prize.* Parsippany, N.J.: Silver Burdett, 1991, 99–131.

Levi-Montalcini, Rita. *In Praise of Imperfection.* New York: Basic Books, 1988.

———. *Saga of the Nerve Growth Factor.* River Edge, N.J.: World Scientific Publications, 1997.

Lindop, Laurie. *Dynamic Modern Women: Scientists and Doctors.* New York: Holt, 1997, 63–72.

McGrayne, Sharon Bertsch. *Nobel Prize Women in Science: Their Lives, Struggles, and Momentous Discoveries.* New York: Birch Lane Press, 1993, 201–223.

LEVY, JERRE
(1938–) *American Brain Researcher and Psychologist*

Jerre Levy has helped to show that the two halves, or hemispheres, of the brain process information in different ways. She was born on April 7, 1938, in Birmingham, Alabama, and grew up in the small Albama town of Demopolis. Her father, Jerome, owned a clothing store.

Even more than most children, young Jerre asked her parents constant questions. "When you grow up, you can spend your entire life asking and answering questions," her mother told her. "People who get paid for asking questions are called *scientists*." When she reached high school, however, an aptitude counselor told her that American universities did not allow women to become scientists—except possibly in the field of psychology, and even then only with difficulty.

Levy experienced some of that difficulty first-hand. After receiving an undergraduate degree in psychology from the University of Miami in 1962, she entered the university's graduate program in biological psychology. When she applied for a research assistantship to support her studies during her third year, however, she was informed that such assistantships were now restricted to male students. The chairman of the department explained that it was a waste of money to support female students, since "no university would ever hire a woman." Levy, divorced and the mother of two young children, finally obtained an assistantship in the university's School of Marine Science.

After a year and a half, Levy transferred to the graduate program in biology at the California Institute of Technology (Caltech) and joined the laboratory of Roger Sperry. Sperry was studying people whose corpus callosum, a thick bundle of nerve fibers that normally connects the two hemispheres of the brain, had been cut surgically as a treatment for uncontrollable epilepsy. Sperry showed that each isolated hemisphere had its own mental world that could not be communicated to the other hemisphere. It was therefore possible to study the functions of each side of the split brain without the influence of the other side.

Studies of patients with damage to one side of the brain had already established that the left hemisphere processes most verbal information, whereas the right hemisphere is the specialist in processing faces and spatial information. Based on her studies of split-brain patients, Levy proposed that the two hemispheres differ in their strategy of information processing. For instance, the left hemisphere, she suggested, analyzes specific details of pictures, whereas the right hemisphere combines the details into a whole.

After receiving her Ph.D. from Caltech in 1970, Levy did postdoctoral work at the University of Colorado and Oregon State University. She then went to the University of Pennsylvania, where she was an assistant and then associate professor from 1972 to 1977. She joined the University of Chicago in 1977 and is currently a full professor in that university's psychology department.

Levy has changed her thinking about the brain many times. For example, she found that the conclusion that the left hemisphere is analytical and the right hemisphere holistic—a distinction still widely repeated in the popular press—may be true only of nonverbal pictorial information, in which the right hemisphere specializes, whereas for verbal information, the specialty of the left hemisphere, the reverse is true. Each hemisphere can do higher-order, holistic thinking about the kind of information in which it specializes.

Most of Levy's research has concentrated on the links between brain organization and behavior in normal people, including studies of differences in brain function between men and women and between left- and right-handers. She has also studied the dominant role of the right hemisphere in the perception and expression of emotional information, communication between the two brain hemispheres in children and adults, and the different ways that the left and right hemispheres process printed words.

Clearly, Levy has achieved the life her mother had promised her. "I want to find out how the brain operates," she says. "And to do that, I have to ask all sorts of questions."

Further Reading

Durden-Smith, Jo, and Diane deSimone. "Interview: Jerre Levy." *Omni*, January 1985, 69–70, 98–102.
Goldberg, Joan Rachel. "The Creative Mind: Jerre Levy." *Science Digest*, July 1984, 47, 90, 92.

✳ LEVY, JULIA
(1934–) *Canadian Medical Researcher*

Julia Levy helped to develop a new treatment for cancer that combines drugs and light. Her father was a Dutch banker who worked in Asia; her mother, British. Julia was born on May 15, 1934, in Singapore, an island in the Malay Peninsula that was then a British colony, and spent her early years in different parts of Southeast Asia. Her father sent her, her sister, and her mother to live with an uncle in Canada when World War II began, and he joined them there after the war.

Julia Levy was drawn to medical research from an early age. She studied bacteriology and immunology at the University of British Columbia in Vancouver, earning a B.A. with honors in 1955. She married soon after her graduation and moved with her husband to England, where he, too, studied for a career in medical research. She continued her own studies, earning a Ph.D. in experimental pathology from the University of London in 1958. "That's where I really learned to *do* science," she says.

Levy and her husband returned to Canada after obtaining their degrees, and Levy began teaching at the University of British Columbia, where she is a full professor today. She soon divorced, after which she had to manage raising two children alone as well as teaching and doing research. In the 1970s she married again, to a man who studied the philosophy of science, and had a third child.

During this time, Levy also began research on new treatments for cancer. Her first ones involved a combination of boosting the immune system's ability to fight tumors and using anticancer drugs that are sensitive to light. She continues this work at Quadra Logic Technologies, now QLT PhotoTherapeutics, a Vancouver drug research company that she and four colleagues started in 1981. In 1998 she was the company's president and CEO.

At Quadra Logic, Levy developed an improved version of her cancer treatment. A patient is given a light-sensitive anticancer drug and then a fiber optic tube is threaded into the tumor. Laser light is transmitted through the fiber optic cables, activating the drug only in the area of the tumor. This keeps the drug from poisoning healthy cells. Levy has also explored using light-sensitive drugs as treatments for other illnesses, including age-related vision loss and AIDS. Today she is studying the effects of these drugs on the immune system in the hope of using them to treat arthritis and other diseases caused when immune cells attack body tissues.

Levy was elected to the Royal Society of Canada, the country's top scientific body, in 1981. She was also appointed to the National Advisory Board of Science and Technology in 1987. Levy advises women interested in science, "Go for it! . . . Women can do anything!"

Further Reading

Levy, Julia. "Julia Levy, Professor," Department of Microbiology & Immunology, University of British Columbia, web page. Available online. URL: http://www.microbiology.ubc.ca/jlevy.html. Updated August 22, 1996.

May, Elizabeth. *Claiming the Future: The Inspiring Lives of Twelve Canadian Women Scientists and Scholars.* Markham, Ontario: Pembroke Publishers, 1991, 23–26.

✳ LONSDALE, KATHLEEN YARDLEY
(1903–1971) *British Crystallographer*

Kathleen Lonsdale used X-ray crystallography, in which X-ray beams are shone through the regularly arranged atoms and molecules in crystals, to determine the shapes of key parts of the molecules of carbon-containing compounds. She was born Kathleen Yardley, the youngest of 10 children, in Newbridge, Ireland, on January 28, 1903. Her post-

master father, Henry, was an alcoholic, and her mother left him when Kathleen was five, taking her younger children to Seven Kings, a London suburb.

Yardley studied mathematics and physics at the Bedford College for Women, earning a B.S. in 1922. William H. Bragg then invited her to join his X-ray crystallography laboratory at University College, London. She accompanied him to the Royal Institution the following year. She earned an M.S. in 1924 from University College.

In 1927, Yardley married Thomas Lonsdale, another crystallographer. They had three children, Jane, Nan, and Stephen, between 1929 and 1934. Until 1930 they lived in Leeds, and Kathleen began some of her most important research at Leeds University. It concerned a group of six atoms called a benzene ring, an important part of many organic, or carbon-containing, compounds, including explosives, dyes, and drugs. Lonsdale showed that, contrary to what many organic chemists had believed, the ring was flat and shaped like a hexagon. This groundbreaking crystallography study, published in 1929, became her doctor of science thesis and, says UCLA professor K. N. Trueblood, "had an enormous impact on organic chemistry."

Even before she did her work on the benzene ring, Kathleen Lonsdale and a coworker, William Astbury, began calculating tables of X-ray patterns in common crystals. This painstaking work, which Lonsdale continued at home after her family's return to London in 1930, made her the first woman crystallographer to earn a worldwide reputation. She continued to revise and edit expanded versions of these tables for much of her life, and they are still an essential reference for crystallographers.

Lonsdale rejoined Bragg's laboratory at the Royal Institution in 1934. There she developed the technique of shining multiple X-ray beams through a crystal from different angles and used it to determine the spacing of carbon atoms in natural and artificial diamonds. A rare form of diamond found in meteorites was named "lonsdaleite" in her honor in 1966.

In 1946, after Bragg's death, Lonsdale returned to University College, where she became the institution's first woman professor and established her own crystallography department. She became head of the crystallography department in 1949. In her later years she studied the mineral deposits, or "stones," that can form in the kidney, bladder, and gallbladder. She retired in 1968.

In 1945, Lonsdale became one of the first two women admitted as full members to Britain's top science organization, the Royal Society. She was made a Dame Commander of the British Empire, the equivalent of a knighthood, in 1956, and received the Davy Medal of the Royal Society in 1957. In 1966 she became the first woman president of the International Union of Crystallography and in 1967 the first woman president of the British Association for the Advancement of Science. She died of cancer on April 1, 1971. J. M. Robertson says of her, "Very few have made so many important advances in so many different directions."

Further Reading

Julian, Maureen M. "Women in Crystallography." In *Women of Science: Righting the Record,* edited by G. Kass-Simon and Patricia Farnes, 354–359. Bloomington: University of Indiana Press, 1990.

"Lonsdale, Kathleen Yardley," CWP at physics.UCLA.edu. Available online. URL: http://www.physics.ucla.edu/~cwp.html. Updated on January 13, 1998.

✳ LOVE, SUSAN
(1948–) *American Physician and Medical Researcher*

Susan Love is one of the country's most respected—and most outspoken—authorities on women's health, particularly breast cancer. She was born in Little Silver, New Jersey, on February 9, 1948, but grew up partly in Puerto Rico, to which her father, James Love, a machinery salesman, was transferred when Susan was 13 years old. After another move, she went to high school in Mexico City.

An order of nuns, the Sisters of Notre Dame, ran the school Susan attended in Puerto Rico, and one of the nuns sparked her interest in medicine.

She entered a small women's college run by the order, Notre Dame of Maryland, in 1966. After two years at the college she decided to become a nun herself, but she found the life too restrictive and quit after six months.

Love took premedical training at Fordham University, then applied to medical schools on the East Coast, only to find that most had already filled their tiny quota of women. She was finally admitted to the State University of New York's Downstate Medical College in Brooklyn, from which she graduated near the top of her class in 1974. She decided to become a surgeon. "In surgery, you figure out what's wrong and then you go in and fix it. . . . That's what I like," she told *Boston Magazine*'s Anita Diamant.

When Love began private practice in 1980, she found that most of the cases other surgeons referred to her were breast cancer patients. "I saw I could make a contribution" as a breast cancer surgeon, she told *Advocate* interviewer Tzivia Gover. She became director of the breast clinic at Beth Israel Hospital and then, in 1982, a surgical oncologist (cancer specialist) for the Dana Farber Cancer Institute Breast Evaluation Center. In 1988 she helped to found the Faulkner Breast Center, part of Boston's Faulkner Hospital; this center was the first in the country to have a multidisciplinary, all-woman staff. Love became an assistant professor of surgery at Harvard Medical School as well.

Love began to feel that the standard cancer treatments—surgery, radiation, and drugs, which she refers to as "slash, burn, and poison"—were woefully inadequate. So were the education and psychological support that most women with breast cancer received from their (usually male) doctors. She summarized her opinions and advice in *Dr. Susan Love's Breast Book* (1990), which *Ms.* magazine called "one of the most important books in women's health in the last decade." In 1990 she cofounded the National Breast Cancer Coalition, a lobbying organization that has helped to raise the national budget for breast cancer research from $90 million to $430 million.

Love has challenged several widely held medical opinions. For instance, she has questioned the value of monthly breast self-examination and of mammograms (breast X rays for early detection of cancer) for most women under 50. She also complains that many women with early breast cancer are encouraged to have a mastectomy, or complete removal of the breast, when simple removal of the cancerous tissue and its immediate surroundings (lumpectomy) followed by radiation would give them an equally good chance of survival. More recently she has questioned the widespread use of hormone replacement for women who have reached menopause.

In 1992, Love became the director of the new Revlon/UCLA Breast Center in Los Angeles. The center's aim was to integrate all the specialists involved in each woman's treatment, but this approach proved too difficult to carry out. Love left the Breast Center and retired from surgery in 1996. "I . . . want to do research and . . . the political stuff, and I can't do it all," she says. She is now going to business school to become what she calls "bilingual"—speaking the languages of both business and medicine. She also raises her daughter, Katie, with her longtime partner, Helen Cooksey, and directs the Santa Barbara Breast Cancer Institute.

At the UCLA School of Medicine, where she is an adjunct professor of surgery, Love is researching a new method of breast cancer detection, which involves threading a tiny fiber-optic tube, or endoscope, through the milk ducts in a woman's nipple to look for cancerous tissue. She hopes that the work of other scientists, such as her friend MARY-CLAIRE KING, will reveal ways to prevent or cure breast cancer through gene or hormone therapy.

Whether or not Susan Love proves correct in her criticism of particular medical treatments, she is surely right to encourage women to take a more educated and assertive role in deciding about their health care. As she told Anita Diamant, "My job is . . . to be an educator. I teach a woman what she needs to know to make a valid decision [about her treatment] for herself."

Further Reading

Diamant, Anita. "The Passion of Dr. Love." *Boston Magazine*, October 1988, 163–165, 218–228.

Felner, Julie. "Dr. Susan Love Cuts Through the Hype on Women's Health." *Ms.*, July-August 1997, 37–46.

Stabiner, Karen. *To Dance with the Devil: The New War on Breast Cancer*. New York: Delacorte, 1997.

✳ LOVELACE, AUGUSTA ADA BYRON
(1815–1852) *British Mathematician and Computer Scientist*

Even though they were written 100 years before electronic computers were invented, Ada Lovelace's instructions for Charles Babbage's "analytical engine" have been called the world's first computer programs. She was born Augusta Ada Byron in London on December 10, 1815. The short, stormy marriage between her father, George Gordon, Lord Byron, the famous British poet, and her mother, the former Anne Isabella (Annabella) Milbanke, ended a month after Ada's birth, when Byron departed, never to see his daughter again. Byron's flamboyant lifestyle had put him completely at odds with the quiet but equally strong-willed Annabella, whose love of mathematics made Byron call her the "Princess of Parallelograms."

Ada, tutored extensively at home, shared her mother's fondness for mathematics. At a party in 1833 she met mathematician Charles Babbage, who had invented a machine that he called a difference engine. Navigation, insurance, and other fields were coming to depend on tables of figures that required repeated calculations, but these calculations, done by hand, often contained errors. Babbage's machine solved polynomial equations (then called "difference equations") automatically, making the preparation of tables based on them faster and more accurate.

Babbage had built a small model of his device and obtained a government grant to produce a full-scale version. Unfortunately, the technology of the time could supply neither the power nor the thousands of precisely machined parts that the machine needed, and by the time he met Ada, Babbage had lost the government funding and much of his own money without ever building the machine.

Ada also met a young nobleman, William King, who later became the Earl of Lovelace, and they married in 1835. They later had three children. King encouraged his wife to pursue her intellectual interests, including her friendship with Babbage.

In addition to the difference engine, Babbage had designed a more general-purpose machine that he called the analytical engine. It would have performed any kind of calculation once figures and instructions were programmed into it. A Frenchman, Joseph M. Jacquard, had invented an automatic loom that wove patterned cloth based on instructions fed into it on punched cards, and Babbage thought that his machine, too, might use punched cards. After the failure of the difference engine, however, no one wanted to invest money in something even more complex, so this second machine existed only on paper. Conceptually it is the ancestor of modern computers.

An Italian mathematician, Luigi F. Menebrea, wrote a paper in French in 1842 that described the workings of the analytical engine and the theory behind it. Babbage wanted the paper translated into English, and Ada Lovelace offered to do the job. Her finished work included notes of her own that were three times as long as Menebrea's manuscript, including sample sets of instructions for the machine. Babbage wrote that these notes "entered fully into almost all the very difficult and abstract questions connected with the subject." It was not considered proper for a woman of Lovelace's class to put her name on a public document, so her work, published in a collection of scientific papers in 1843, was signed only with the initials A.A.L. For 30 years no one knew that she was the author.

In her notes to Menebrea's paper, Lovelace offered a warning against overestimating the powers of computing machines that is still timely: "The Analytical Engine has no pretensions whatever to originate anything. . . . The machines . . . must be programmed to think and cannot do so for themselves." On the other hand, she noted, also correctly, that in the process of reducing operations into forms

In the early 1840s, Ada Lovelace, daughter of famed British poet Lord Byron, wrote instructions for Charles Babbage's invention, the analytical engine, that were in essence the world's first computer programs. As this picture shows, Lovelace was also very attractive and enjoyed social life. (Courtesy Science Museum/Science & Society Picture Library)

that could be used by the machine, "the relations and the nature of many subjects . . . are necessarily thrown into new lights, and more profoundly investigated." She wrote to Babbage in 1845, "No one knows what . . . awful energy and power lie yet undeveloped in that wiry little system of mind."

Differences in their working styles (Babbage tended to be sloppy, whereas Lovelace, like her mother, was meticulous and bossy) put a strain on the relationship between Lovelace and Babbage, and the two never worked together on a major project again, although they remained friends.

Meanwhile, Lovelace pursued a variety of interests, including ideas about the functioning of the brain. She hoped to work out "a law or laws for the mutual action of the molecules of the brain . . . a *Calculus of the Nervous System*," an idea that, like her computer programs, was far ahead of its time.

Another interest, unfortunately, was horse racing, for which Lovelace believed that she had developed an infallible mathematical betting system. Lord Lovelace joined his wife in placing bets at first, but he stopped when he lost money. Ada, however, became addicted to gambling and fell deep into debt, having to pawn the Lovelace family jewels twice (her mother redeemed them). She also became addicted to laudanum, or morphine.

Ada Lovelace died of cancer of the uterus on November 27, 1852, when she was only 36 years old, but she was not forgotten. In the late 1970s the U.S. Department of Defense created a computer language for programming missiles, planes, and submarines and named it Ada in her honor.

Further Reading

Alic, Margaret. *Hypatia's Heritage: A History of Women in Science from Antiquity Through the Nineteenth Century.* Boston: Beacon Press, 1986, 157–163.

Nilson, Karen. "Ada Byron Lovelace." In *Celebrating Women in Mathematics and Science*, edited by Miriam P. Cooney, 57–65. Reston, Va.: National Council of Teachers of Mathematics, 1996.

Stein, Dorothy. *Ada: A Life and a Legacy.* Cambridge, Mass.: MIT Press, 1985.

Toole, Betty Alexandra, ed. *Ada, the Enchantress of Numbers.* Mill Valley, Calif.: Strawberry Press, 1992.

M

✳ **MAATHAI, WANGARI MUTA**
(1940–) *Kenyan Ecologist*

Wangari Maathai, the first woman in East and Central Africa to obtain a Ph.D., has used her scientific background to design grassroots programs that preserve the environment. Former U.S. Assistant Secretary of State for African Affairs Chester Crocker has called her "the leading environmentalist on the African continent."

Wangari Muta Maathai was born on April 1, 1940, and raised in Nyeri, Kenya, a rural area that she told writer Aubrey Wallace was "very green, very productive." Her Kikuyu family taught her to respect nature. In 1960 she won an American government scholarship and attended Mount St. Scholastica College in Atchison, Kansas, from which she earned a B.S. in biology in 1964. She received an M.S. from the University of Pittsburgh in 1965 in anatomy and tissue culture, growing cells in laboratory dishes.

Maathai returned to Kenya in 1966. She worked her way up through the University of Nairobi, becoming a senior lecturer, associate professor, and, finally, in 1976, head of the anatomy department. She earned a Ph.D. from the university in 1971. She was the first woman to do each of these

things. She also married a businessperson in 1969, and they had three children.

Maathai's marriage ended in a bitter divorce in the mid-1970s, and she then decided to run for parliament. This required quitting her job at the university. After her political campaign was barred on a technicality, the university refused to take her back, ending her academic career. This move, on top of the divorce, made Maathai painfully aware for the first time of the amount of jealousy her successes had aroused in her male colleagues. "Sometimes we don't quite realize that not everybody's clapping when we're succeeding," she told interviewer Mary Anne French.

Maathai began to focus on the human and environmental degradation she had seen in the countryside. She had become aware that, as she said later, "poverty and need have a very close relationship with a degraded environment. It's a vicious circle." Women and trees, she concluded, were at the heart of the problem. Up to 97 percent of Kenya's forests had been cut down, either to clear land for cash crops or to provide wood for cooking fires. Women therefore had to spend more time looking for firewood, which left less for cooking. They began to feed their children low-nutrient, processed foods that did not require cooking, which often led to malnutrition. Cutting down trees also removed the roots that held the continent's thin topsoil in place, causing much of it to be eroded away by wind and water. This reduced soil fertility and made a further contribution to hunger.

Maathai decided that women and trees might also be a solution. Most of Kenya's farmers were women, and if each planted a "green belt" of trees around her farm, it would make a huge difference. With a little help, anyone could plant and tend a tree, and native trees could provide food, firewood, shade, and beauty as well as reducing soil erosion and air pollution. "Trees are miracles," she has said.

Typically, Maathai started her project with herself. On June 5—World Environment Day—1977, she planted seven trees in a park in Nairobi, and the Green Belt Movement was born. Maathai's new organization gained the backing of the National Council of Women of Kenya, which helped it spread the word in cities and the countryside. "Soon, people from all over the country were asking where they could find seedlings," Maathai reported to *UNESCO Courier.* By 1997, some 80,000 Green Belt Movement members in Kenya, mostly women, had planted 15 million trees, and the movement had spread to over 30 other African countries. Maathai described this work in *The Green Belt Movement* (1985) and *The Green Belt Movement: Sharing the Approach and the Experience* (1988).

One reason for the movement's success, Maathai has explained, is that it is kept firmly under local control. The organization enters an area only when it is invited. Green Belt Movement employees then provide training and equipment to help local women establish a nursery for raising seedling trees. Village women receive free trees from the nursery, plant them, and appoint "rangers," usually children or disabled people, to follow up on the trees' care. The women are paid a small sum for each tree that survives more than three months. Maathai also emphasized in a 1992 speech that the movement does much more than plant trees. It "is about hope. It tells people that they are responsible for their own lives. . . . It raises an awareness that people can take control of their environment."

In the late 1980s, concluding that planting trees was not enough, Maathai began taking a more direct role in politics in the hope of improving Kenyans' social and economic conditions. This put her in conflict with the country's government, which has frequently harassed and arrested her and once clubbed her into unconsciousness. She nonetheless continues her political as well as environmental activities. Awards she has received for those activities include the Woman of the Year Award (1983), the Right Livelihood Award (1984), the Windstar Award for the Environment (1988), the Woman of the World Award (1989), the Goldman Environmental Prize (1991), and the Jane Addams International Women's Leadership Award (1993).

Maathai sometimes misses her scientific career. "I would love to go back into an academic institution," she wrote in *Ms.* magazine in 1991. Nonetheless, she said, "I have . . . felt . . . like I was being useful, so I have no regrets." Above all, she is proud of having shown that, as she says, "One person *can* make the difference."

Further Reading

"Maathai, Wangari." *Current Biography Yearbook 1993.* New York: H. W. Wilson, 1993, 353–357.

Sirch, Willow Ann. *Eco-Women: Protectors of the Earth.* Golden, Colo.: Fulcrum Kids, 1996, 64–71.

Vollers, Maryanne. "Healing the Ravaged Land." *International Wildlife*, January-February 1988, 5–11.

Wallace, Aubrey. *Eco-Heroes.* San Francisco: Mercury House, 1993, 1–21.

✳ McCLINTOCK, BARBARA
(1902–1992) *American Geneticist*

Working in her cornfields while other geneticists investigated molecules, Barbara McClintock was ignored for decades because her discoveries ran as counter to the mainstream as her methods. In the end, though, she proved that, contrary to what almost everyone had thought, genes could move and control other genes. Organisms thus could partly shape their own evolution.

Barbara preferred her own company almost from her birth in Hartford, Connecticut, on June 16, 1902. As a baby, she played happily by herself; as a teenager, she liked to spend time simply "thinking about things." She grew up in Brooklyn, then a somewhat rural suburb of New York City, to which her father, a physician for Standard Oil, moved the family when she was six. Her parents, Thomas and Sara McClintock, encouraged independence in their four children by allowing them to skip school.

Barbara became determined to go to college, even though, as she said later, her mother feared that a college education would make her "a strange person, a person that didn't belong to society. . . . She was even afraid I might become a college professor." Thomas McClintock took Barbara's side, however, and in 1919 she enrolled in the College of Agriculture at Cornell University, which offered free tuition to New York residents.

McClintock took a course in the relatively new science of genetics in her junior year, and by the time she graduated in 1923, she had decided to make genetics her career. As a graduate student in the university's botany department, she studied Indian corn, a type of maize (corn) in which the kernels on each ear have different colors. The color pattern is inherited.

McClintock made her first important discovery while still a graduate student. Geneticists were realizing that inherited traits were determined by information contained in microscopic wormlike bodies called chromosomes. Each cell has a number of pairs of chromosomes, and each pair looks only slightly different from the others. McClintock was the first to work out a way to tell the 10 pairs of maize chromosomes apart.

McClintock earned her M.A. in botany in 1925 and her Ph.D. in 1927, after which Cornell hired her as an instructor. In 1931 she and another woman scientist, Harriet Creighton, carried out an experiment that firmly linked changes in chromosomes to changes in whole organisms, a link that some geneticists had still doubted. This experiment

Barbara McClintock's pioneering studies of corn genetics at Cold Spring Harbor Laboratory in New York in the 1950s and 1960s showed that genes could move and could control other genes, suggesting a mechanism by which living things could affect their own evolution. After being ignored for decades, her work won a Nobel prize in 1983. (Courtesy Cold Spring Habor Laboratories Archives)

has been called "one of the truly great experiments of modern biology."

McClintock was earning a national reputation in genetics, but Cornell refused to promote her because she was a woman. Rather than remain an instructor forever, she resigned shortly after her landmark paper was published. For the next several years she led an academic gypsy life, living on grants and dividing her research time among three universities in different parts of the country. She did her commuting in an old Model A Ford, which she repaired herself whenever it broke down.

In 1936 the University of Missouri at Columbia, one of the institutions at which McClintock had done part-time research, gave her a full-time position as an assistant professor. While there she studied changes in chromosomes and inherited characteristics made by X rays, which damaged genetic material and greatly increased the number of mutations, or random changes, that occurred in it. This university, too, refused to treat her with the respect she felt she deserved, and she resigned in 1941.

McClintock was unsure what to do next until a friend told her about the genetics laboratory at Cold Spring Harbor, on Long Island. Run by the Carnegie Institution of Washington, which steel magnate and philanthropist Andrew Carnegie had founded, it had been the first genetics laboratory in the United States. McClintock moved to Cold Spring Harbor in 1942 and remained there the rest of her life.

The discovery in the 1940s that the complex chemical deoxyribonucleic acid (DNA) was the carrier of most genetic information and the working out of DNA's chemical structure and method of reproduction in 1953 revolutionized genetics, turning attention away from whole organisms or even cells and toward molecules. Geneticists saw genes, now shown to be parts of DNA molecules, as unalterable except by chance or the sort of damage that X rays produced. Francis Crick, the codiscoverer of DNA's structure, expressed what he called the "central dogma" of the new genetics by saying, "Once 'information' has passed into protein [chemicals that carry out cell activities and express characteristics] *it cannot get out again*."

Barbara McClintock meanwhile went her own way, working with her unfashionable corn and "letting the material tell" her what was happening in its genes. Contrary to Crick's central dogma, she found genes that apparently could change both their own position on a chromosome and that of certain other genes, even moving from one chromosome to another. This movement, which she called transposition, appeared to be a controlled rather than random process. Furthermore, if a transposed gene landed next to another gene, it could turn that gene

on (make it active, or capable of expressing the characteristic for which it carried the coded information) if it had been off, or vice versa. Genes that could control their own activity and that of other genes had not been recognized before. McClintock suspected that such genes and their movement played a vital part in organisms' development before birth.

Even more remarkable, some controlling genes appeared able to increase the rate at which mutations occurred in the cell. McClintock theorized that these genes might become active when an organism found itself in a stressful environment. Increasing the mutation rate increased the chances of a mutation that would help the organism's offspring survive. If a gene that increased mutation rate could be turned on by something in the environment, then organisms and their environment could affect their own evolution, something no one had thought possible.

McClintock attempted to explain her findings at genetics meetings in the early 1950s, but her presentations were met with blank stares or even laughter. She offered ample evidence for her claims, but her conclusions were too different from the prevailing view to be accepted. The chilly reception "really knocked" McClintock, as she later told her biographer, Evelyn Fox Keller, and after a while she stopped trying to communicate her research. Most geneticists forgot, or never learned, who she was; one referred to her as "just an old bag who'd been hanging around Cold Spring Harbor for years." She did not let rejection stop her work, however. "If you know you're right, you don't care," she said later.

A certain measure of recognition came to McClintock in the late 1960s. In 1967, the same year in which she officially retired (in fact, her work schedule continued unchanged), she received the Kimber Genetics Award from the National Academy of Sciences. She was awarded the National Medal of Science in 1970. Only in the late 1970s, however, did other geneticists' work begin to support hers in a major way. Researchers found transposable elements, or "jumping genes" as they became popularly known, in fruit flies and other organisms, including humans. The idea that some genes could control others was also proved.

The trickle of honors became a flood in the late 1970s and early 1980s. McClintock won eight awards in 1981 alone, the three most important of which—the MacArthur Laureate Award, the Lasker Award, and Israel's Wolf Prize—came in a single week. Then, in October 1983, when she was 81 years old, she learned that she had won the greatest scientific award of all, a Nobel Prize. She was the first woman to win an unshared Nobel in physiology or medicine.

These honors and their attendant publicity irritated McClintock more than they pleased her. She complained, "At my age I should be allowed to . . . have my fun," which meant doing her research in peace. McClintock continued to have her scientific "fun" among the corn plants almost until her death on September 2, 1992, just a few months after her 90th birthday.

Some people saw Barbara McClintock's solitary life as lonely and perhaps even sad, but she never viewed it that way. As she said shortly before she died, "I've had such a good time. . . . I've had a very, very satisfying and interesting life."

Further Reading

Fedoroff, Nina, and David Botstein, eds. *The Dynamic Genome.* New York: Cold Spring Harbor Laboratory Press, 1992.

Keller, Evelyn Fox. *A Feeling for the Organism.* San Francisco: W. H. Freeman, 1983.

Kittredge, Mary. *Barbara McClintock.* New York: Chelsea House, 1991.

"McClintock, Barbara." *Current Biography Yearbook 1984.* New York: H. W. Wilson, 1984.

McGrayne, Sharon Bertsch. *Nobel Prize Women in Science: Their Lives, Struggles, and Momentous Discoveries.* New York: Birch Lane Press, 1993, 144–174.

✳ McNALLY, KAREN COOK
(1940–) *American Geologist*

Karen McNally has predicted earthquakes by identifying "seismic gaps," areas where expected earth movement has not taken place and sudden large movements are thus more likely. Born in 1940, she felt earthquakes while growing up in Clovis, California, but she was more interested in learning ranch work from her father and music from her mother.

McNally's parents persuaded her to go to nearby Fresno State College, but she sought independence in an early marriage. She studied part-time while raising two daughters, which she calls a "superhuman task." Magazine articles interested her in geology, and in 1966 she divorced her husband and moved, daughters and all, to the University of California at Berkeley to learn more about it. She completed her bachelor's degree in 1971, a master's degree in 1973, and a Ph.D. in geophysics in 1976.

While doing postdoctoral work at the California Institute of Technology (Caltech) in Pasadena, McNally learned about the seismic gap theory, a new approach to earthquake prediction. Normally the immense plates that make up the earth's crust slide past each other smoothly, a bit at a time, causing "microquakes" detectable only with a seismograph. Friction, however, can lock plates together in a certain area for decades or even centuries. Because the plates as a whole continue to move, pressure builds up in that area. When the pressure finally fractures the rock and releases the plates, a large amount of motion usually occurs all at once, causing a major earthquake. Some geologists believed that if seismographs were placed in areas identified as having "seismic gaps"—long preceding periods with little or no earth movement—they might detect fracturing that presaged a big quake.

One seismic gap lay on the western coast of Mexico south of Oaxaca. In 1977 geophysicists from Japan and Texas warned that this area was ripe for a large quake. McNally and geologists from Mexico's National University got seven portable seismographs installed there by November 1. For weeks their recordings showed a buildup of tremors, but then, on November 29, McNally says, "there was absolute silence" for part of the day—followed by a Richter 7.8 quake within 31 miles (50 kilometers) of where her group had predicted it. Their seismographs captured a complete picture of this major earthquake, which McNally compares to finding a live dinosaur.

McNally and others predicted five more Mexican quakes, including a Richter 8.1 quake that devastated Mexico City on September 19, 1985. She has used information from these and other quakes to refine the seismic gap theory. She believes that, as pressure in a gap area builds up, weak spots at the ends give way first, producing small quakes. Cracks then start spreading throughout the area's rock, perhaps producing the phenomena sometimes seen just before earthquakes, such as changes in groundwater levels. Cracking and shaking increase until, finally, the strongest rocks break and a major quake occurs.

McNally remained at Caltech until 1986, eventually rising to the rank of associate professor, and then moved to the University of California at Santa Cruz, where in 1998 she was a professor of geophysics. She has been the director of the university's Institute of Tectonics and its Charles F. Richter Seismology Laboratory.

Further Reading

Boraiko, Allen A. "Earthquake in Mexico." *National Geographic*, May 1986, 655–675.
Overbye, Dennis. "The Earthquake Trapper." *Discover*, July 1981, 49–54.

 ## MAKHUBU, LYDIA PHINDILE
(1937–) *Swazi Medical Researcher and Chemist*

Lydia Makhubu has studied plants used in traditional African medicine and has improved the education and advancement of African women scientists. In 1980 the Voice of America called her "one of the outstanding scientists, men or women, in . . . Botswana, Lesotho, and Swaziland."

Lydia Phindile Makhubu was born on July 1, 1937, at the Usuthu Mission in Swaziland, a country in southeastern Africa. Her father frequently worked in health clinics, so she grew up around doctors and laboratories. She studied mathematics and chemistry at Pius XII College in the nearby country of Lesotho, completing a B.S. in 1963. She then won a Canadian

Lydia Makhubu did research on the chemical nature and medical effects of plants used by traditional healers in her native Swaziland. She is vice-chancellor of the University of Swaziland and the president and cofounder of the Third World Organization of Women in Science.
(Courtesy Lydia Makhubu)

Commonwealth Scholarship and earned a master's degree at the University of Alberta in Edmonton in 1967, followed by a Ph.D. in medicinal chemistry from the University of Toronto in 1973. She was the first Swazi woman to earn a Ph.D.

Makhubu returned home, then began teaching and researching at the University of Swaziland. She became a lecturer in the chemistry department in 1973, a senior lecturer in 1979, and a full professor in 1980. She was dean of the science faculty between 1976 and 1980. Today her teaching efforts center on outreach science education in her own country, for which she formed the Royal Swaziland Society of Science and Technology in 1977 (she is still its president), and on improving educational opportunities for women scientists from developing countries, for which she helped to found the Third World Organization of Women in Science (TWOWS) in 1989. She was the latter group's first chairperson and has been its president since 1993. Because of women's traditional focus on family and society, Makhubu believes, women scientists can "influenc[e the] scientific agenda to take into account social concerns and . . . influenc[e] society to embrace the positive aspects of science and technology."

Most of Makhubu's research has concerned the chemical nature and medical effects of plants used by traditional Swazi healers. She wanted the healers' knowledge preserved and also to have their system "elevated and standardized so that it serves [the people] properly," she told a Voice of America interviewer in 1980. If the effects of the plants were known more precisely, for instance, healers could better determine the proper dosage to use.

Makhubu is an administrator as well as a teacher and researcher. She was made pro-vice-chancellor of the University of Swaziland in 1978 and vice-chancellor in 1988, a position she still holds in 1999. She is the first woman in southern Africa to hold such a high post. In 1989–90 she also became the first woman to head the Association of Commonwealth Universities. She is married to surgeon Daniel Mbatha and has a son and daughter.

Further Reading

Science in Africa. Washington, D.C.: Voice of America, 1982.

Yount, Lisa. *Twentieth-Century Women Scientists.* New York: Facts On File, 1996, 86–93.

✳ MARGULIS, LYNN ALEXANDER
(1938–) *American Microbiologist and Geneticist*

Lynn Margulis has proposed or supported several ideas that, although rejected at first, eventually resulted in major changes in biologists' thinking. A colleague calls her "one of the most outspoken people in biology."

Lynn Alexander was born on March 5, 1938, in Chicago, the oldest of the four daughters of Morris and Leona Alexander. Her father headed a company that made marker stripes for roads and was also a lawyer and politician. Her mother was, she says, a "glamorous housewife." In an autobiographical essay, Lynn described her child self as "passionate, hungry for knowledge, grabby of the leading roles, . . . and nature loving."

Lynn entered the University of Chicago when she was only 15. Inspired by an innovative program that featured works by great scientists instead of textbooks, she decided to become a scientist. She also met Carl Sagan, a physics graduate student, who "shared with me his keen understanding of the vastness of time and space." They married in 1957, just after Lynn earned her B.A., and later had two sons, Dorion and Jeremy. Lynn Sagan earned an M.A. in zoology and genetics at the University of Wisconsin at Madison in 1960 and then studied cells and their evolution at the University of California at Berkeley, completing a Ph.D. in 1965.

Scientists at the time believed that in most living things, all genetic information was carried in a part of the cell called the nucleus; the only exceptions were simple microorganisms that lacked a nucleus. Lynn Sagan, however, learned that some geneticists in the early part of the century had proposed that certain other bodies within the cell, called organelles, might also contain genetic material. These scientists had suggested that the organelles were once free-living bacteria that had come to reside inside other bacteria early in the evolution of living things. Eventually the bacteria formed a mutually beneficial relationship, or symbiosis, that became so close that they could not survive without each other; indeed, they became a single organism. This microorganism was the ancestor of cells with nuclei.

Most other geneticists regarded this "serial endosymbiosis theory" as ridiculous, but Sagan disagreed. From her own research and that of others she gathered a wealth of material that supported it. For instance, in the early 1960s she and others found that chloroplasts, the organelles that make food in green plants, and mitochondria, organelles that help cells use energy, both contain DNA, the chief chemical carrier of genetic information. This DNA was similar to that found in bacteria, just as the endosymbiosis theory predicted. Furthermore, both chloroplasts and mitochondria proved to resemble certain types of free-living microorganisms.

Sagan assembled her ideas into a long paper and began submitting it to scientific journals. Fifteen rejected or lost it before the *Journal of Theoretical Biology* finally printed it in 1966. By then her "turbulent" marriage to Carl Sagan had ended in divorce, and she had just begun teaching and researching at Boston University.

In greatly expanded form, this paper became Lynn Sagan's first book, *Origin of Eukaryotic Cells* (cells with nuclei), published in 1970 in spite of a letter from the National Science Foundation saying that the book's ideas were "totally unacceptable to important molecular biologists." Eleven years later, when it was issued in a revised edition as *Symbiosis in Cell Evolution*, the ideas in it had become widely accepted. William Culberson, professor of botany at Duke University, has said, "The reason that the symbiotic theory is taken seriously [today] is Margulis. She's changed the way we look at the cell." More recently, Margulis has maintained that bacteria called spirochetes were the ancestors of cell organelles that provide movement and even of sensory and nerve cells. She has provided evidence to support this, but it remains more debatable than the case for mitochondria and chloroplasts.

Meanwhile, Lynn married Thomas N. ("Nick") Margulis, a crystallographer, in 1967 and with him had two more children, Zachary and Jennifer. Although she has described this marriage as "healthier and happier" than the one with Sagan, it, too, ended in divorce, in 1980.

After Lynn Margulis became a professor at Boston University in 1977, she continued to espouse unpopular ideas and see them proven right. For instance, she supported a classification scheme first proposed by the late Robert H. Whittaker of Cornell University. Instead of dividing all living things into the traditional two kingdoms of plants and animals, Whittaker listed five kingdoms: animals, plants, fungi, protists (organisms with cell nuclei that do not belong to the first three groups; Margulis prefers the term protoctists), and monera (bacteria and other microorganisms without cell nuclei). This classification is widely used today.

Perhaps the most fiercely debated of Margulis's stands is her support of James E. Lovelock's Gaia theory. Lovelock, a British chemist, proposed beginning in the early 1970s that, as Margulis puts it, "life does not randomly 'adapt' to an inert environment; rather, the nonliving environment of the Earth is actively made, modulated and altered by the . . . sum of the life on the surface of the planet." For instance, processes in the bodies of living things, chiefly microorganisms, keep the planet's surface temperature within the narrow limits that can sustain life. The theory, named after the ancient Greek goddess of the earth, has been interpreted by some to mean that the earth is, in essence, a single living organism.

Lynn Margulis is no more discouraged by others' doubts now than she ever was—and she now has the position and honors to make herself heard. She was elected to the National Academy of Sciences in 1983 and became a Distinguished University Professor at the University of Massachusetts in Amherst in 1988. Her writings, both scientific and popular, about evolution and microbes (some coauthored with her oldest son, Dorion Sagan) have been prolific. Paleontologist Niles Eldredge calls her "one of the most original and creative biologists of our time."

137

Further Reading

McDermott, Jeanne. "Lynn Margulis—Unlike Most Microbiologists." *Coevolution Quarterly*, Spring 1980, 31–38.

Mann, Charles. "Lynn Margulis: Science's Unruly Earth Mother." *Science*, April 19, 1991, 378–381.

"Margulis, Lynn." *Current Biography Yearbook 1992*. New York: H. W. Wilson, 1992, 372–376.

Royte, Elizabeth. "Attack of the Microbiologists." *New York Times Magazine,* January 14, 1996, 21–23.

✳ MARIA THE JEWESS (Mary, Miriam)
(first century A.D.) *Egyptian Chemist*

In the first centuries after Christ, alchemists blended religion, art, and science into a mixture that contained the seeds of modern chemistry. Some early alchemists were women, and the best known of these wrote under the name of Maria (or Mary or Miriam) the Jewess. None of her complete works survives, but fragments and references to her appear in the writings of other alchemists. Historians believe that Maria lived in the first century A.D. in Alexandria, Egypt, then one of the world's chief seats of learning.

The work of Maria's about which the most is known is called the *Maria Practica*. It combined the mystical theories of alchemy with practical descriptions of laboratory devices and processes. Among these were several pieces of equipment that Maria probably invented or at least perfected.

The simplest and best known of Maria's devices is the water bath, still found in many kitchens as a double boiler. It consists of two containers, one suspended inside the other. Water is placed in the outer container and heated. The water, in turn, slowly heats the material in the inner container.

Maria also provided the oldest known description of a still, a device used to separate substances in a liquid through the process of distillation. In distillation, a liquid mixture is heated in a closed container until part of the liquid evaporates into a gas. The gas is then piped into a different container

and cooled until it condenses back into liquid. Maria's was a *tribikos*, or three-armed still.

Maria's most complex device was the *kerotakis*, an apparatus for allowing gases to color or otherwise act on metals. The *kerotakis* was shaped like a globe or a cylinder, covered by a domed top. It was placed over a fire, and sulfur, mercury, or arsenic solution was heated in a pan near its bottom. A piece of metal was put on a plate suspended from the cover. As gas from the heated solution rose past the plate, it reacted with the metal. At the top of the dome, as in the still, the gas cooled back into a liquid. The liquid was not carried off, however, but rather ran back down the side of the *kerotakis* to be evaporated again.

Further Reading

Alic, Margaret. *Hypatia's Heritage: A History of Women in Science from Antiquity Through the Nineteenth Century*. Boston: Beacon Press, 1986, 36–39.

Ogilvie, Marilyn Bailey. *Women in Science: Antiquity Through the Nineteenth Century*. Cambridge, Mass.: MIT Press, 1986, 128–129.

✳ MARRACK, PHILIPPA ("Pippa")
(1945–) *British-American Immunologist*

Philippa Marrack explores how the immune system protects the body against disease-causing organisms and other invaders and why it sometimes attacks the body's own tissues instead. Born in Ewell, England, on June 18, 1945, Pippa, as people call her, first became interested in the immune system while a graduate student at Britain's prestigious Cambridge University. She earned a B.A. from Cambridge in 1967 and a Ph.D. in 1970.

Marrack came to the United States to do her postdoctoral work and has remained ever since (she holds dual British and United States citizenship). While at the University of California at San Diego she met John W. Kappler, and they married in 1974. They have two children, Jim and Kate, and are research partners as well. "Scientifically we don't exist as individuals," Marrack told *Discover* writer Mark Caldwell.

At the National Jewish Center for Immunology and Respiratory Medicine in Denver, Colorado, a laboratory they helped to found in 1979, Marrack and Kappler investigate the unbelievably complex interactions through which the immune system functions. They have developed a theory about why these interactions sometimes go wrong.

The immune system can turn against the body in two ways. In some diseases, such as toxic shock syndrome, bacteria make a poison that causes the system to pour out chemicals that damage the body. In other cases, the immune system turns against particular tissues, causing such diseases as rheumatoid arthritis. Marrack and Kappler believe that both problems are caused by substances they call superantigens.

Antigens are substances on the surface of bacteria, viruses, and other cells that mark them as "foreign" to immune cells. In order to trigger a reaction from the immune system, an antigen molecule must interact with another molecule, called a receptor, on the surface of an immune cell. This normally happens at first with only a few cells, because there are millions of different antigens and receptors and interaction takes place only if antigen and receptor fit together precisely, as a key fits into a lock. Superantigens, however, can lock onto cells even when they fit only part of the receptors. They therefore activate a large number of cells, causing the immune system to overreact or attack the wrong cells.

In addition to working at the National Jewish Center, Philippa Marrack teaches at the University of Colorado Health Science Center. She has been elected to the National Academy of Sciences and has received awards including the Feodor Lynen Medal (1990) and the William B. Coley Award of the Cancer Research Institute (1991).

Further Reading

Caldwell, Mark. "The Immune Challenge." *Discover*, December 1991, 56–61.

Marrack, Philippa, and John W. Kappler. "How the Immune System Recognizes the Body." *Scientific American*, September 1993, 81–89.

✳ MATZINGER, POLLY
(1947–) *American Immunologist*

Polly Matzinger's theories could change the way scientists view the immune system, the body's defense network, and may free organ transplant recipients from lifelong bondage to dangerous drugs. Born on July 21, 1947, to a former nun and a Dutch Resistance fighter, Matzinger as a young woman took jobs ranging from dog trainer to carpenter to Playboy "bunny" because "everything gets boring after a while." One night, while working as a cocktail waitress in Davis, California, she overheard two customers from the nearby University of California (UC) campus discussing their research and asked them questions they couldn't answer. "You should be a scientist," one told her. He eventually persuaded Matzinger to study science at UC Davis.

In the process of earning a Ph.D. from UC San Diego, she became interested in the immune system. In 1989 she joined the National Institute of Allergy and Infectious Diseases (NIAID), part of the National Institutes of Health in Bethesda, Maryland, where she now heads a laboratory.

In the late 1940s scientists came to believe that the key feature of the immune system's defense mechanism was the system's power to distinguish between the body's own cells and material that was "foreign," or didn't belong to the body. In this way it identified, say, a bacterium or a virus. Matzinger felt something was wrong with this picture, but she could find no way to approach the problem until 1989, when Ephraim Fuchs, a colleague in a neighboring laboratory, raised the same questions that had disturbed her. Together they formulated and began testing a new theory of the way the immune system worked.

Rather than reacting to "foreignness," Matzinger and Fuchs believe, the immune system reacts to danger—specifically, to substances released by damaged or dying cells. Normal death does not break cells open, but tissue injury or attack by microorganisms does, making chemicals spill out. Matzinger believes that immune cells called dendritic cells detect these chemicals and, in turn, alert other immune cells, the T cells, which then attack whatever is causing the damage. The attack occurs only when the T cells receive both a sample of the damage-causing factor and a signal from the dendritic cells. Matzinger and Fuchs first described their "danger" theory in 1994.

Like SUZANNE ILDSTAD, Matzinger has tried to find ways to keep the immune system from attacking grafted tissues or organs without using drugs that block the system's overall activity. Matzinger thinks drugs that block signals from the dendritic cells might prevent graft rejection. Unlike present antirejection drugs, these drugs would be needed only until the graft heals. Such drugs have produced promising results in animals.

Further Reading

Larkin, Marylynn. "Polly Matzinger: Immunology's Dangerous Thinker." *Lancet*, July 5, 1997, 38.

Holzman, David. "Controlling the Immune System's Armies." *Technology Review*, August–September 1995, 19–20.

Richardson, Sarah. "The End of the Self." *Discover*, April 1996, 81–87.

✳ MAURY, ANTONIA CAETANA
(1866–1952) *American Astronomer*

Antonia Maury improved a star classification system and studied pairs of stars that orbit each other. She was born on March 21, 1866, in Cold Spring, New York, to parents who both had ties to science. Her father, Mytton Maury, was an amateur naturalist as well as an Episcopal minister. Her mother, Virginia, was the sister of Henry Draper, the first person to photograph stars' spectra, the patterns of rainbow colors and dark lines made by passing the stars' light through a prism.

Antonia Maury was educated at home, mainly by her father, until she went to Vassar College, where MARIA MITCHELL interested her in astronomy. Maury graduated in 1887 with honors in astronomy, physics, and philosophy. By that time her aunt, Henry Draper's wealthy widow, had endowed a large project at the Harvard Observatory to classify stars according to differences in their photographed spectra, and Maury's father asked Edward Pickering, the observatory's director, to employ Antonia on this work. In 1888, Pickering added her to his staff of women "computers."

Pickering and Maury clashed constantly. He wanted her to apply the classification system he and WILLIAMINA FLEMING had worked out, but Maury devised a new system. He demanded that she work quickly, whereas she wanted to dwell on minute details such as differences in the thickness and sharpness of dark lines in the spectra. Maury worked on a catalogue of bright northern stars until the early 1890s and then resigned from the observatory. The catalogue was finally published in 1897 with Maury's name on the title page, the first time an observatory publication had so credited a woman.

For almost 20 years Maury pursued a varied career of lecturing, tutoring, and environmental work. She also sometimes visited the observatory to continue research on her special interest, pairs of stars called spectroscopic binaries. The stars in these pairs were so close together that the eye could not tell them apart, even with the best telescopes. Only the doubling of lines in their spectra revealed that there were two stars. She and Pickering had first identified such pairs in 1889. Maury observed changes in the spectra of one particularly intriguing binary, Beta Lyrae, for years and published a book about them in 1933.

Meanwhile, other astronomers vindicated the approaches that Pickering had derided. Danish astronomer Ejnar Hertzsprung told Pickering in 1905 that in some ways, Maury's star classification system was better than Pickering's. Hertzsprung used the differences in the appearance of spectral lines that Maury had pointed out to confirm that stars of the same color could differ in size and brightness. The diagram of star development that he and Henry Russell constructed on the basis of these differences became a cornerstone of astrophysics.

Maury again joined the Harvard Observatory staff in 1918, remaining there until her retirement in 1935 and continuing to visit yearly thereafter. She got along well with Pickering's successor, Harlow Shapley, who encouraged her research on binaries. The American Astronomical Society awarded her the Annie Jump Cannon Prize in 1943 for her star catalogue and classification system. She died in New York on January 8, 1952.

Further Reading

Hoffleit, Dorrit. "Maury, Antonia Caetana De Paiva Pereira." In *Notable American Women: The Modern Period*, edited by Barbara Sicherman and Carol Hurd Green, 464–466. Cambridge, Mass.: The Belknap Press of Harvard University Press, 1980.

Mack, Pamela E. "Straying from Their Orbits: Women in Astronomy in America." In *Women of Science: Righting the Record*, edited by G. Kass-Simon and Patricia Farnes, 94–97, 105. Bloomington: Indiana University Press, 1990.

✳ MAYER, MARIA GERTRUDE GOEPPERT
(1906–1972) *American Physicist*

Maria Mayer worked out a theory that explains how particles are arranged in the atomic nucleus. It won her a share of the Nobel Prize in physics in 1963. Nonetheless, she was denied a paying academic position for most of her life.

Maria Gertrude Goeppert was born in Kattowitz, then part of Germany (it is now Katowice, Poland), on June 28, 1906. When she was four, her father, a physician, moved his family to Göttingen and became a professor of pediatrics at the famous university there. (Maria liked to brag that "on my father's side, I am the seventh straight generation of university professor.") He fostered Maria's interest in science, while her mother, also named Maria, shared with her a love of music and social life.

Maria began studying mathematics at Göttingen University in 1924. After meeting professors and students in the "young and exciting" field of atomic physics, however, she changed her major in 1927. Physics, like mathematics, involved "puzzle solving," but in physics, she said later, the "puzzles [were] created by nature, not by the mind of man."

Maria's father died in 1927, and her mother began taking in boarders to support the family. One boarder was a lanky American chemistry student named Joseph E. (Joe) Mayer, who looked for a room in the Goeppert house in 1928 after a German friend told him that "the prettiest girl in Göttingen" lived there. Mayer apparently agreed with that evaluation, and Maria Goeppert was equally pleased with him. They married on January 19, 1930. Shortly thereafter, Maria finished her Ph.D. Her thesis is considered a fundamental contribution to quantum mechanics.

The newlywed Mayers moved to the United States. Joe became an assistant professor of chemistry at Johns Hopkins University, but there was no job for Maria because antinepotism rules, common at the time, forbade the hiring of both husband and wife—and it was always the wife who was left out. Maria did important research on dye chemistry during this time, but the only money she received was a few hundred dollars a year for helping a professor with his German correspondence.

Maria became a naturalized U.S. citizen in 1933, and her daughter, Maria Anne (Marianne), was born shortly thereafter. In 1937 she and Joe began work on a textbook on statistical mechanics, which described the behavior of molecules. (It was published in 1940.) Maria gave birth to her second child, Peter, just before Joe moved to Columbia University in 1938. Like Johns Hopkins, Columbia refused to give Maria a job.

As World War II loomed, the Mayers were among the European expatriate scientists who urged the United States to sponsor a research program to develop an atomic bomb. When the program, code-named the Manhattan Project, began, the head of the Columbia chemistry department asked Maria to help search for ways to separate the bomb's potential fuel, the radioactive form of uranium,

Maria Mayer's shell theory explained how particles are arranged in the atomic nucleus and won her a share of a Nobel Prize in physics in 1963, but because she was married to a fellow scientist, antinepotism laws kept her from obtaining a paying academic position for most of her career.
(Courtesy National Academy of Sciences)

vited to join them early in 1946. This time Maria was made an associate professor—she said that Chicago was "the first place where I was not considered a nuisance, but greeted with open arms"—though she still did not receive a salary. She did, however, earn part-time pay as a senior researcher at the nearby Argonne National Laboratory. The lab's head, Robert G. Sachs, had been one of her first graduate students and was glad to hire her.

The group of physicists at the University of Chicago in the late 1940s and 1950s was one of the premier gatherings of scientists in the 20th century. One observer called their weekly seminars "conversation[s] of the angels." One subject they often discussed was the arrangement of particles in the atomic nucleus. Physicists knew that electrons orbited the nucleus in distinct layers called shells, and some had suggested that particles in the nucleus might also be arranged in shells, but little physical or mathematical evidence had been found to support this idea. The most commonly accepted model of the nucleus pictured it as something like a drop of water, in which protons and neutrons moved randomly.

Beginning in 1947, Maria Mayer worked with Edward Teller on a theory of the origin of the chemical elements. In the course of researching this project, Mayer noticed that elements whose nuclei contained certain numbers of protons or neutrons—what came to be called her "magic numbers"—were unusually abundant and stable, almost never undergoing radioactive decay. Teller and others shrugged off this fact, but Mayer "kept thinking why, why, *why* do they exist?" She suspected that they had something to do with nuclear particles being arranged in shells. The numbers might represent filled shells in the nucleus that kept atoms from breaking down radioactively, just as filled electron shells kept elements from reacting chemically. Still, she could not prove her idea.

Mayer frequently talked over her ideas with Enrico Fermi. One day in 1948, as Fermi was leaving her to answer a telephone call, he asked offhandedly, "Is there any indication of spin-orbit coupling?" Mayer suddenly realized that this was the missing

from the more common, nonradioactive form. He even offered to pay her. Her work proved to have little direct effect on the bomb project, but, she said later, "It was the beginning of myself standing on my own two feet as a scientist, not leaning on Joe."

After the war, Enrico Fermi, Edward Teller, and several other of the Mayers's friends from their Göttingen days worked at the University of Chicago's new Institute for Nuclear Studies (later the Enrico Fermi Institute), and the Mayers were in-piece of her puzzle. Spin-orbit coupling means that the direction in which a particle spins helps to determine which orbit or shell it will occupy. Spin-orbit coupling among electrons is weak, but Mayer realized that if it was powerful in the nucleus, requiring much more energy for particles to spin in one direction than in the other, it could explain her magic numbers and prove that nuclear particles are arranged in shells. "I got so excited it wiped everything out," she said later. She worked out the calculations to confirm her idea in 10 minutes.

Maria published a description of her theory in April 1950. A German researcher, Hans D. Jensen, thought of the same idea independently and published his account of it at about the same time. The two met later in 1950 and worked together on a book, *Elementary Theory of Nuclear Shell Structure*, which was published in 1955.

In 1959 the newly formed University of California at San Diego invited both Mayers to join its faculty—and, for the first time, it offered to hire Maria at the same salary and rank (full professor) as Joe. The Mayers were glad to accept. Unfortunately, a few months after their arrival in 1960, Maria suffered a stroke. She continued her research, however.

Maria Mayer's shell theory won the 1963 Nobel Prize in physics. She shared the prize with Jensen and another nuclear physicist, Eugene Wigner. She was only the second woman to win the physics prize. She was pleased, of course, but she said later that "winning the prize wasn't half as exciting as doing the work itself." She continued to refine her theory in the years that followed, meanwhile receiving other awards, including election to the National Academy of Sciences. Mayer died of heart disease on February 20, 1972, at the age of 65.

Further Reading

Dash, Joan. *A Life of One's Own.* New York: Harper & Row, 1973, 231–346.

———. "Mayer, Maria Gertrude Goeppert." In *Notable American Women: The Modern Period,* edited by Barbara Sicherman and Carol Hurd Green, 466–468. Cambridge, Mass.: The Belknap Press of Harvard University Press, 1980.

McGrayne, Sharon Bertsch. *Nobel Prize Women in Science: Their Lives, Struggles, and Momentous Discoveries.* New York: Birch Lane Press, 1993, 175–200.

"Mayer, Maria Goeppert." *Current Biography Yearbook 1964.* New York: H. W. Wilson, 1964, 287–289.

Sachs, Robert. *Maria Goeppert-Mayer, 1906–1972, A Biographical Memoir.* Washington, D.C.: National Academy of Sciences, 1979.

MEAD, MARGARET
(1901–1978) *American Anthropologist*

Margaret Mead, perhaps the best-known anthropologist of her time, brought basic ideas from the study of humankind into mainstream culture. Her writings suggested that people's personalities and expectations about such things as gender roles are shaped more by their culture than by their genes.

Margaret was born on December 16, 1901, in Philadelphia. She was the oldest of five children, of whom four were girls. Her father, Edward Mead, taught economics at the University of Pennsylvania's Wharton School of Business. Her mother, Emily, was a sociologist. Margaret was educated mostly at home by her mother and grandmother, who taught her to observe the people around her (starting with her brother and sisters) and even take notes.

In 1919, Margaret entered DePauw University in Indiana, planning to major in English, but she felt out of place there and transferred to Barnard College, a women's college affiliated with Columbia University. After meeting Franz Boas and RUTH BENEDICT, the leading anthropologists of their day, at Columbia, she changed her major to anthropology. She graduated from Barnard in 1923.

Mead married Luther Cressman, who was then planning to become a minister, and began working for an master's degree in psychology at Columbia, which she earned in 1924. She continued to use her maiden name professionally. For her Ph.D. fieldwork she decided to find out whether teenage girls on the Pacific islands of Samoa felt the anxieties and frustrations that American adolescents did. Beginning in 1925, when she was 23 years old, she spent nine months on the island of Tau, becoming friends with the native women and children and living as they did. The island girls called the diminutive Mead "Malekita" and, as far as she could tell, spoke freely to her about their lives.

After she returned from Samoa in 1926, Mead became assistant curator of ethnology (cultural anthropology) at the American Museum of Natural History in New York. She maintained an office there all her life, becoming associate curator in 1942 and curator in 1956.

Meanwhile, Mead's Samoan research earned her a Ph.D. from Columbia in 1929 and also became the basis of her first book, *Coming of Age in Samoa*, which was published in 1928. Aimed at a popular audience, the book painted a charming picture of an easygoing people who saw nothing wrong with sexual activity before marriage and seemed to suffer

Margaret Mead studied cultures all over the world, from Samoa and New Guinea to the United States. Her research suggested that such things as gender roles are determined more by culture than by biology.
(Courtesy Library of Congress)

few of the anxieties that American teenagers felt. It became a best-seller and made Mead famous.

Mead set out to study the Manus people of the Admiralty Islands in New Guinea, north of Australia, in 1928. This time she did not do her fieldwork alone. On the ship to Samoa three years before she had met a young New Zealand anthropologist, Reo Fortune, and the two had fallen in love. On her way to New Guinea, Mead, now divorced from Cressman, stopped in New Zealand to marry Fortune, and the two went on to the islands together.

Mead and Fortune studied four peoples of New Guinea over the next several years. Their field trips became the basis for scientific papers and Mead's next two popular books, *Growing Up in New Guinea* (1930) and *Sex and Temperament in Three Primitive Societies* (1935). Both books presented the idea that personality and behavior patterns, including those assigned on the basis of gender, were determined largely by culture and that each culture encouraged a certain type of temperament and discouraged others, giving the culture itself a kind of personality. Mead had learned these ideas from Boas and Benedict.

Mead met Gregory Bateson, another anthropologist doing research in New Guinea, in 1932 and again fell in love. She divorced Fortune and then married Bateson in March 1936. They had a daughter, Mary Catherine, in December 1939. Mead and Bateson did further research in New Guinea and also worked together on a study of the Balinese people of Indonesia, *Balinese Character* (1941), which featured many photographs. They were among the first anthropologists to use photography extensively in their work. After 15 years, together, to Mead's grief, Bateson ended their marriage.

Mead partly put aside her research to do government-related work during World War II. She also turned her anthropologist's eye on the culture of the United States and presented the results in another popular book, *And Keep Your Powder Dry: An Anthropologist Looks at America* (1942). The book compared American culture with seven others Mead had studied. According to Roger Revelle of the American Association for the Advancement of Science, Mead "became a kind of modern oracle because of her sensitivity to what was significant in American life."

Mead thereafter constantly expanded the range of her prolific writings and lectures, both academic and popular. In addition to making additional research trips to the Pacific islands, New Guinea, and Bali, during which she noted changes in groups she had visited earlier, she wrote and spoke on everything from family life and education to ecology and nutrition. She once commented, "The anthropologist's one special area of competence is the ability to think about a whole society and everything in it."

Mead received many honorary degrees and other awards for her work, including a gold medal from the Society for Women Geographers in 1942 and election to the National Academy of Sciences in 1974, the latter by one of the highest votes recorded in an academy election. She was president of the American Association for the Advancement of Science in 1974.

Mead officially retired from the Museum of Natural History in 1964, but she continued to work there for many years afterward. "Sooner or later I'm going to die, but I'm not going to retire," she told reporters on her 75th birthday. She died in New York on November 15, 1978, at the age of 76.

In 1983, several years after her death, Mead's reputation suffered a blow when Australian anthropologist Derek Freeman published a book claiming that the conclusions in her famous early book on Samoa had been incorrect. Drawing on his own field research and early documents, Freeman maintained that Samoans suffered as much anxiety as any other people and were rather possessive sexually. He said that Mead's informants had told her false stories about their free sexual life both because they thought that was what she wanted to hear and as a form of gentle teasing, and she had been young and naive enough to believe them.

Most of Mead's admirers say that even if Freeman's allegations are correct, they have little impact on her overall importance, which is based on a lifetime of research and thought. Biographer Jane Howard notes, "Her early fieldwork may have been hurried and imperfect, but her generous view of human nature endures and the energy and volume of her later achievements are staggering."

Further Reading

Bateson, Mary Catherine. *With a Daughter's Eye: A Memoir of Margaret Mead and Gregory Bateson.* New York: William Morrow, 1984.

Freeman, Derek. *Margaret Mead in Samoa: The Making and Unmaking of an Anthropological Myth.* Cambridge, Mass: Harvard University Press, 1983.

Howard, Jane. *Margaret Mead: A Life.* New York: Simon & Schuster, 1984.

Mead, Margaret. *Blackberry Winter: My Earlier Years.* New York: William Morrow, 1972.

———. *Letters from the Field 1925–1975.* New York: Harper & Row, 1977.

✳ MEITNER, LISE
(1878–1968) *German/Swedish Physicist*

Walking through the snowy Swedish countryside, Lise Meitner and her nephew, Otto Frisch, concluded that the nucleus of an atom could be split. This realization not only transformed scientists' understanding of atoms but led to the creation of nuclear power and the atomic bomb.

Lise Meitner was born on November 7, 1878, in Vienna, Austria. Her father, Philipp, was a wealthy lawyer. Lise, the third of the Meitners' eight children, learned a love of music from her mother, Hedwig. From childhood on, Lise also displayed what she later called a "marked bent" for physics and mathematics. Inspired by reading about MARIE CURIE, she decided that she, too, wanted to become a physicist and study radioactivity.

Standard education for girls of the time did not prepare them for a university, but Lise took extra tutoring and entered the University of Vienna in 1901. She erned a doctorate in physics in 1905, the first physics doctorate that the university had ever granted to a woman.

Wanting to study under Max Planck, the founder of quantum physics, Meitner went to the University of Berlin in 1907. There she persuaded

Otto Hahn, a chemist about her own age who was also studying radioactivity, to hire her as an assistant. The only problem was that Emil Fischer, the head of the institute in which Hahn worked, refused to allow a woman in its classrooms or laboratories. Hahn and Meitner had to work in a basement room that had been a carpentry workshop. The years they spent there, however, were happy and productive. When things were going well, Meitner recalled later, "we sang together in two-part harmony, mostly songs by Brahms." The pair's working conditions improved in 1912, when they moved to the new Kaiser Wilhelm Institutes in Dahlem, a Berlin suburb.

World War I interrupted their work—Hahn remained at the university to do war research, while Meitner served as an X-ray technician in a field hospital—but they continued it when they could. In 1918, soon after the war ended, they announced their discovery of a new element, the second heaviest then known. They named this radioactive element proto-actinium, "before actinium" in Latin, because it slowly broke down into another element called actinium. The name was later shortened to protactinium.

The discovery of protactinium made Hahn and Meitner famous. Meitner won the Leibniz Medal from the Berlin Academy of Science and the Leiben Prize from the Austrian Academy of Science. She was made head of a new department of radioactivity physics at the Kaiser Wilhelm Institutes in 1918 and became Germany's first woman full physics professor (at the University of Berlin) in 1926. Swiss physicist Albert Einstein called her "the German Marie Curie." She and Hahn no longer worked together as often as before, but they remained good friends. Meitner's chief research subject in the 1920s was the behavior of beta particles, negatively charged particles given off during the breakdown of radioactive atoms. Meitner believed, correctly, that these particles were electrons from the nucleus.

Meitner wrote later that in those years "we were young, happy, and carefree—perhaps politically too carefree." When the National Socialist (Nazi) party took over the German government in

1933, she and her fellow scientists began to sense that their carefree days were over. Those who were Jewish lost their jobs or suffered other forms of persecution. Meitner, although of Jewish background, was safe at first because she was an Austrian citizen and also, she said later, "too valuable to annoy." Her safety ended, however, in March 1938, when Germany seized control of Austria, making all Austrians German citizens and therefore subject to German laws.

Meitner and her friends knew that she must leave the country immediately, but Adolf Hitler's government no longer granted travel visas to scientists. They decided that the best way for her to escape was to pretend to take a vacation to Holland, which did not require a visa. The train was stopped at the German border, however, and a Nazi military patrol confiscated her passport, an Austrian one that had expired 10 years before. "I got so frightened, my heart almost stopped beating," Meitner wrote later. "For ten minutes I sat there and waited, minutes that seemed like so many hours." Fortunately, the patrol then returned her passport and allowed the train to proceed.

Meitner went on to Sweden and began working at the Nobel Institute of Theoretical Physics in Stockholm, but anxiety and homesickness made research difficult. "I feel like a wind-up doll that automatically does certain things, gives a friendly smile, and has no real life in itself," she wrote to Hahn in the fall of 1938. When Italian nuclear physicist Enrico Fermi and his wife, Laura, visited Meitner toward the end of the year, Laura saw her as "a worried, tired woman with the tense expression that all refugees have."

In Germany, meanwhile, Otto Hahn and a new partner, Fritz Strassmann, like a number of other European nuclear physicists, were bombarding heavy elements with subatomic particles called neutrons in the hope of creating artificial elements that were heavier than uranium, the heaviest natural element. (Physicists had learned that an atom under the right conditions could capture a neutron and emit a beta particle, thus becoming an atom of the next heaviest element.) To their amazement, when

Driven away from her research in Germany by the anti-Jewish Nazi government, Lise Meitner nonetheless provided the insightful interpretation in 1938 that experiments performed by her former scientific partner, Otto Hahn, had split the atomic nucleus. The codiscovery by Meitner and her nephew, Otto Frisch, of nuclear fission led to the development of nuclear energy and the atomic bomb. (Courtesy Herzfeld Collection, Emilio Segrè Visual Archives, American Institute of Physics)

Hahn and Strassmann exposed uranium to neutrons, they got what appeared to be barium, a much lighter element. Hahn described this puzzle to Meitner in a letter in December 1938 and asked if she could explain it.

147

When she received Hahn's letter, Meitner was spending Christmas vacation in the Swedish village of Kungälv with her nephew, Otto Frisch, another physicist. The two discussed the letter as they walked in the snow, and it suddenly occurred to them that Hahn's results could be explained if, rather than simply adding or subtracting a particle or two from the uranium nucleus, he had split it almost in half. Doing so would produce barium and krypton, a gaseous element that was hard to detect.

Physicists had thought splitting atomic nuclei was not possible because very powerful forces held the nucleus together. Most physicists thought the nucleus was like a drop of water, held together by the equivalent of surface tension. The electric charge of a heavy nucleus partly offsets this force, however, and Meitner and Frisch concluded that under some conditions, as Frisch wrote later, the nucleus might become "a very wobbly drop—like a large thin-walled balloon filled with water." A neutron might then split it.

Scrawling calculations in the snow, Meitner and Frisch figured out that, according to the theories of Albert Einstein, splitting a uranium nucleus should release 200 million electron volts, 20 million times more than an equivalent amount of TNT. This energy would not be obvious in a sample of uranium as small as those Hahn had used, but it could be detected with the right instruments. Frisch hurried back to his laboratory to repeat Hahn's experiments and look for the energy. He found it, and he and Meitner began drafting a paper about their discovery. Borrowing the term biologists use to describe the process by which a cell splits in half to reproduce, Frisch called the atomic splitting "fission." Meitner and Frisch's announcement that the atom could be split rocked the world of physics in 1939.

Six years later it rocked the wider world as well. Living in semiretirement in neutral Sweden, Meitner knew nothing of the development of the atomic bomb until August 6, 1945, when headlines announced that the United States had dropped such a bomb on the Japanese city of Hiroshima. She called the news "a terrible surprise, like a bolt of lightning out of the blue." In an interview shortly afterward, she said, "You must not blame us scientists for the uses to which war technicians have put our discoveries . . . My hope is that the atomic bomb will make humanity realize that we must, once and for all, finish with war."

Otto Hahn received a Nobel Prize in 1944 for his part in the discovery of nuclear fission. For unknown reasons, Meitner was not so honored. She did receive other awards, however, including Germany's Max Planck Medal (1949) and the Enrico Fermi Award from the U.S. Atomic Energy Commission in 1966 (she shared this prize with Hahn and Fritz Strassmann). Meitner was the first woman to receive the latter prize.

Lise Meitner continued to live and do research in Sweden, even after she officially retired in 1947. In 1960 she moved to England to be near Otto Frisch, then a professor at Cambridge University. She died on October 27, 1968, a few days before her 90th birthday. She once wrote that she had decided when she was young that her life "need not be easy provided only that it was not empty." She certainly succeeded in that aim.

Scientists eventually did learn how to create artificial elements heavier than uranium. In 1982, when element 109 was created, its inventors named it meitnerium in honor of Lise Meitner. The leader of the research team called Meitner "the most significant woman scientist of this century."

Further Reading

Hermann, Armin. *The New Physics: The Route into the Atomic Age.* Bonn-Bad Godesberg: Inter Nationes, 1979.

McGrayne, Sharon Bertsch. *Nobel Prize Women in Science: Their Lives, Struggles, and Momentous Discoveries.* New York: Birch Lane Press, 1993, 37–63.

Rife, Patricia. *Lise Meitner and the Dawn of the Nuclear Age.* Cambridge, Mass.: Birkhauser, 1998.

Sime, Ruth. *Lise Meitner: A Life in Physics.* Berkeley: University of California Press, 1996.

Wilson, Jane, ed. *All in Our Time: The Reminiscences of Twelve Nuclear Pioneers.* Chicago: Bulletin of the Atomic Scientists, 1974.

MERIAN, MARIA SIBYLLA
(1647–1717) *German/Dutch*
Zoologist

Maria Sibylla Merian united science and art to produce some of the first detailed drawings of insect life cycles. She was born on April 2, 1647, in Frankfurt, Germany, the daughter of Swiss artist and engraver Matthäus Merian and his second wife, Johanna. Merian died when Maria was three, but her stepfather, painter Jacob Marell, trained her in his studio. From the start, her favorite artistic subject was insects. At age 13 she was putting descriptions and drawings of the life cycle of silkworms in her journal. She wrote, "I collected all the caterpillars that I could find, in order to observe their metamorphosis [change of form] . . . I withdrew from human society and engaged exclusively in these investigations . . . I learned . . . art . . . so that I could draw . . . them as they were in nature."

In 1665, Maria Merian married a fellow apprentice, Johann Graff, and they moved to Nuremberg. They had two daughters, Johanna and Dorothea. During her married years Maria Graff taught painting and embroidery and sold paints and cloth on which she had painted flowers. She also continued to study caterpillars and in 1679 issued a book, *Wonderful Metamorphosis and Special Nourishment of Caterpillars,* that contained 50 meticulous drawings of the life cycles of caterpillars and the plants they fed on. She was one of the first scientific illustrators to make her drawings from living rather than preserved specimens. She also published several books of flower designs for artists and embroiderers.

Graff moved back to Frankfurt in 1682 to care for her widowed mother. She issued a second volume of caterpillar drawings a year later. Around 1685 she joined a religious sect called the Labadists and moved with her mother and daughters to the group's settlement in Walta Castle in Friesland. She separated from her husband and resumed her maiden name.

In 1691, after her mother died, Maria Merian and her daughters went to Amsterdam, where she once again began selling paints and painted cloth. When she saw collections of insects and other animals from the Dutch colony of Surinam, on the northern coast of South America, she "resolved . . . to undertake a great and expensive trip to Surinam so that I could continue my observations." Such a trip was difficult, even dangerous, and Merian was now 52 years old. Nonetheless, she and Dorothea went to Surinam in July 1699 and remained there for two years.

The colony's Indian natives and African slaves told Merian about the local plants and insects and brought her samples. She drew these and other small animals, such as lizards and snakes, and even a few larger ones, including a crocodile. Illness forced her to return to Amsterdam in September 1701, but by then she had a large portfolio. She published 60 of her drawings in her masterwork, *Metamorphosis Insectorum Surinamensium (Metamorphosis of the Insects of Surinam),* in 1705. The book's text included her observations, native lore, and even recipes related to the pictured plants and animals.

Merian's beautiful books remained popular long after her death in 1717. The Russian czar Peter the Great was so impressed with them that he made a collection of her original plates and other works, including her diary. Biologists named six plants, two beetles, and nine butterflies after her.

Further Reading

Davis, Natalie Zeman. *Women on the Margins: Three Seventeenth Century Lives.* Cambridge, Mass.: Harvard University Press, 1995.

Merian, Maria Sibylla. *Butterflies, Beetles, and Other Insects: The Leningrad Book of Notes and Studies.* New York: McGraw-Hill, 1976.

Schiebinger, Londa. *The Mind Has No Sex? Women in the Origins of Modern Science.* Cambridge, Mass.: Harvard University Press, 1989, 68–79.

✳ MEXIA, YNES ENRIQUETTA JULIETTA
(1870–1938)   *American Botanist*

Ynes Mexia braved sheer cliffs, river rapids, and disease-carrying insects to gather thousands of plants and other specimens, many new to science, from the most inaccessible parts of Mexico and South America. She was born on May 24, 1870, in Washington, D.C., where her father, Enrique Mexia, was representing the Mexican government. Her parents were separated during much of her childhood. She and her half siblings lived with their mother, the former Sarah Wilmer, in Texas and later with their father in Mexico.

After two short, unhappy marriages (to Herman de Laue, a German-Spanish merchant who died in 1904, and D. Augustin Reygados), Mexia moved to San Francisco, where she did social work. She became a United States citizen in 1924. (Until then, like her father, she had been a Mexican citizen.) Hikes with the Sierra Club stirred her interest in nature, and in 1921 she enrolled at the University of California at Berkeley as a special student. After a class on flowering plants introduced her to botany, she decided to become a collector of plant specimens.

Mexia's first journey, made with Stanford botanist Roxanna Ferris to western Mexico in the fall of 1925, was cut short when she fell down a cliff, but

Ynes Mexia called herself "an adventuress" and loved traveling through the most inaccessible parts of Mexico and South America, where she gathered thousands of plant specimens, some of types new to science. She is seen here at a ranch in Patagonia, Argentina, in 1936.
(Courtesy University and Jepson Herbaria, University of California, Berkeley)

150

she nonetheless brought back 500 plants, several of which were unknown to science. One, *Mimosa mexiae*, became the first of a number that were named after her. She found that, even though she was now 55 years old, she thrived on a collector's rough, adventurous life.

Mexia made seven more collecting trips during the next 12 years. In addition to Mexico, she visited Brazil, Peru, Ecuador, Chile, and Argentina, covering terrain ranging from Amazon rain forests to the high Andes. Each journey netted thousands of perfectly preserved specimens. She discovered many new species and even one new genus.

In addition to making solo trips, Mexia sometimes accompanied other scientists, who benefited from her knowledge of Spanish and of Latin American cultures and environments. T. Harper Goodspeed of the University of California, who traveled with her in the Andes, said that "the advice and information she gave us concerning primitive life in the Andes and how to become adjusted to it was invaluable." He added that she was "the true explorer type and happiest when independent and far from civilization. She always made light of the privations and dangers which, at sixty-five years of age and alone except for native helpers, she endured for long periods." Mexia died of lung cancer on July 12, 1938.

Further Reading

Bonta, Marcia Myers. *Women in the Field: America's Pioneering Women Naturalists.* College Station, Tex.: Texas A&M University Press, 1991, 103–114.

Ewan, Joseph. "Mexia, Ynes Enriquetta Julietta." In *Notable American Women, 1607–1950, vol. II: G–O,* edited by Edward T. James, 533–534. Cambridge, Mass.: The Belknap Press of Harvard University Press, 1971.

✳ MITCHELL, MARIA
(1818–1889) *American Astronomer*

Maria Mitchell won a gold medal for discovering a comet and was the first American woman to become internationally known as an astronomer. She was born on August 1, 1818, in Nantucket, Massachu-

setts, the third of 10 children. Her father, William Mitchell, was an avid amateur astronomer and shared his interest with her. Her mother, Lydia, encouraged her to read.

Mitchell's formal schooling, some of it in a school run by her father, ended when she was 16. In 1836 she became the librarian of the Nantucket Atheneum, or subscription library, a job she kept for 20 years. She read the library's books in the daytime and continued stargazing with her father in the evenings. Their observatory was now on top of the Pacific Bank building, to which the family had moved when her father became the bank's principal officer. There she and her father made measurements for the United States Coast Survey that helped in determination of time, latitude, and longitude.

The 29-year-old Mitchell was scanning the heavens alone on October 1, 1847, when she spotted a blurry object in a part of the sky where none had appeared before. She concluded that it was a comet and ran downstairs to tell her father about it. Recognizing that it was a new one, he informed his friend, William Cranch Bond, the head of the Harvard Observatory. A new comet was considered a major astronomical discovery, and in 1831 the king of Denmark had offered a gold medal to the next person to find one through a telescope. Mitchell received the gold medal a year after she had spotted the comet, and the comet was named after her.

Mitchell's discovery—and the unusual fact that it was made by a woman—made her famous. In 1848 she became the first woman elected to the American Academy of Arts and Sciences. She was also elected to the newly established American Association for the Advancement of Science in 1850. Indeed, she was the only woman member for almost a hundred years. The director of the Smithsonian Institution sent her a $100 prize.

Beginning in 1849, Mitchell's fame brought her a new part-time job, computing information about the movements of Venus (considered a suitable subject to assign to a woman) for the *American Ephemeris and Nautical Almanac,* a national publication that provided tables of data about the

Maria Mitchell once said, "I believe in women even more than I do in astronomy." Winner of a gold medal in 1848 for discovering a comet, Mitchell founded the Vassar College astronomy department (she was the world's first woman professor of astronomy) and inspired generations of students. She is shown here in the college observatory around 1877, seated at left with student Mary W. Whitney.

(Vail Brothers photo, Special Collections, Vassar College Libraries, Poughkeepsie, N.Y.)

movements of the heavenly bodies for the use of sailors and others. On a trip to Europe in 1857, Mitchell's reputation also helped her gain entrance to observatories and meet such noted scientists as Sir John Herschel (CAROLINE HERSCHEL's nephew) and MARY SOMERVILLE.

After Mitchell's mother died in 1861, she and her father moved to Lynn, Massachusetts, where one of her married sisters lived. Four years later her life changed dramatically when she received an offer from a representative of wealthy brewer and philanthropist Matthew Vassar to become a professor of astronomy and director of the observatory at the women's college that Vassar was founding in Poughkeepsie, New York. Mitchell greeted her first students when the Vassar Female College opened on September 20, 1865, and continued to teach there for 23 years. She was the world's first woman professor of astronomy.

Mitchell did some original research and made many astronomical observations at Vassar, including taking daily photographs of sunspots and other changes on the surface of the sun and studying Jupiter, Saturn, and their moons. She felt, however, that she had to choose between research and teaching, and she believed she had more to give to teaching. Her classes emphasized mathematical training and direct experience rather than lectures or memorization, and she encouraged her students to ask questions. She refused to give grades, saying, "You cannot mark a human mind because there is no intellectual unit." Several of her students, including ANTONIA MAURY and ELLEN SWALLOW RICHARDS, became well-known scientists. (Richards traded astronomy for chemistry.)

Mitchell also forwarded the education of women by helping to found the Association for the Advancement of Women in 1873. She was the group's president in 1875 and 1876 and headed its committee on science from 1876 until her death. "I believe in women even more than I do in astronomy," she once said.

Mitchell retired from Vassar on Christmas Day, 1888, and returned to Lynn, where some of her family still lived. She died there on June 28, 1889.

During her lifetime she was awarded three honorary degrees, and after her death a group dedicated to preserving her memory and carrying on her work, the Maria Mitchell Association, was formed on Nantucket. A crater on the moon has also been named after her.

Maria Mitchell once wrote: "The best that can be said of my life . . . is that it has been industrious, and the best that can be said of me is that I have not pretended to be what I was not." Most who knew her would have said this estimate was much too modest.

Further Reading

Kohlstedt, Sally Gregory. "Maria Mitchell and the Advancement of Women in Science." In *Uneasy Careers and Intimate Lives: Women in Science 1789–1979,* edited by Pnina G. Abir-Am and Dorinda Outram, 129–146.

Mitchell, Maria. *Life, Letters, and Journals.* Boston: Lee and Shepard, 1896; reissued by Reprint Service, 1991.

Ogilvie, Marilyn Bailey. *Women in Science: Antiquity Through the Nineteenth Century.* Cambridge, Mass.: MIT Press, 1986, 133–139.

Wright, Helen. "Mitchell, Maria." In *Notable American Women, 1607–1950, vol. II: G–O,* edited by Edward T. James, 554–556. Cambridge, Mass.: The Belknap Press of Harvard University Press, 1971.

✳ MORAWETZ, CATHLEEN SYNGE
(1923–) *American Mathematician*

Cathleen Morawetz is an expert on waves, an area of applied mathematics that affects everything from airplane design to medical imaging, and is one of the few women truly prominent in mathematics today. She was born in Toronto, Ontario, Canada, on May 5, 1923. Her father was applied mathematician J. L. Synge. Her mother, Elizabeth Allen Synge, had also studied mathematics at Trinity College, Dublin, but was persuaded not to pursue a career in it. Both parents were Irish.

Cathleen Synge was not good at arithmetic as a child and began studying mathematics only because a high school teacher urged her to do so in order to win a scholarship to the University of Toronto. At the university she studied physics and chemistry as well as mathematics. Cecilia Krieger, a woman mathematician who taught at the university and was also a family friend, encoutaged Synge to pursue mathematics as a career. During her senior year, Synge met engineering student Herbert Morawetz, the son of a Jewish manufacturer who had fled Czechoslovakia after the Germans took over the country. The two became engaged soon after Cathleen graduated in 1945 and married while she was studying for her master's degree in applied mathematics at the Massachusetts Institute of Technology (MIT), which she completed in 1946. They later had three daughters and a son.

As a result of a chance meeting with her father, another famous mathematician, Richard Courant, offered Cathleen Morawetz a job soldering computer connections in his lab at New York University (NYU). When she arrived there in the spring of 1946, however, she found that Courant's assistant had already hired a man to do the work. Not wanting to leave her stranded, Courant then asked her to edit a book he and another mathematician had written, *Supersonic Flow and Shock Waves.* "I learned the subject that way," Morawetz said in 1979. The application of partial differential equations to the behavior of waves became her specialty, and what was later the Courant Institute of Mathematical Sciences became her home. She earned a Ph.D. from NYU in 1951, doing her thesis on differential equations of imploding shock waves in fluids. She had become a naturalized citizen of the United States the previous year.

Morawetz's studies of waves have been used to improve the design of airplane wings, especially those of planes that fly at about the speed of sound. At these speeds, shock waves change the air flow over the wings, increasing drag and slowing the plane down. Understanding the wave patterns of the air flow lets engineers design the wings in a way that keeps most shock waves from forming. The mathematics of waves is also important in X-ray diffraction studies of crystals and in CAT scans, ultrasound, and other medical imaging technology.

Cathleen Morawetz's honors include the Krieger-Nelson Award of the Canadian Mathematical Society (1997), the Lester R. Ford Award of the Mathematical Association of America (1980), and election to the National Academy of Sciences and the American Academy of Arts and Sciences. She was named Outstanding Woman Scientist by the Association for Women in Science in 1993 and was also recognized by the National Organization of Women for combining a successful career and a family. On receiving the latter honor, she joked, "Maybe I became a mathematician because I was so crummy at housework." In 1995 she became the second woman president of the American Mathematical Society.

Morawetz was a full professor at NYU by 1979 and was director of the Courant Institute from 1984 to 1988—the first woman in the United States to head a mathematical institute. Morawetz was NYU's Samuel F. B. Morse Professor of Arts and Sciences until 1993, when she retired and became a professor emerita. She has also been a trustee of Princeton University and the Sloan Foundation and a director of NCR, a large computer company. Administration "suits me," she says. "I like the relationship with human beings." She believes that her strong point in administration, as in mathematics, is common sense.

Further Reading

Albers, J., Gerald L. Alexanderson, and Constance Reid. *More Mathematical People: Contemporary Conversations.* Boston: Harcourt Brace Jovanovich, 1990, 220–238.

Kolata, Gina Bari. "Cathleen Morawetz: The Mathematics of Waves." *Science*, October 12, 1979, 206–207.

Tanne, Janice Hopkins. "Riding the Waves." *New York*, December 21–28, 1992, 103–106.

✳ MORGAN, ANN HAVEN
(1882–1966) *American Zoologist and Ecologist*

One reporter described Ann Haven Morgan in 1945 as "a gray-haired lady knee-deep in muck and

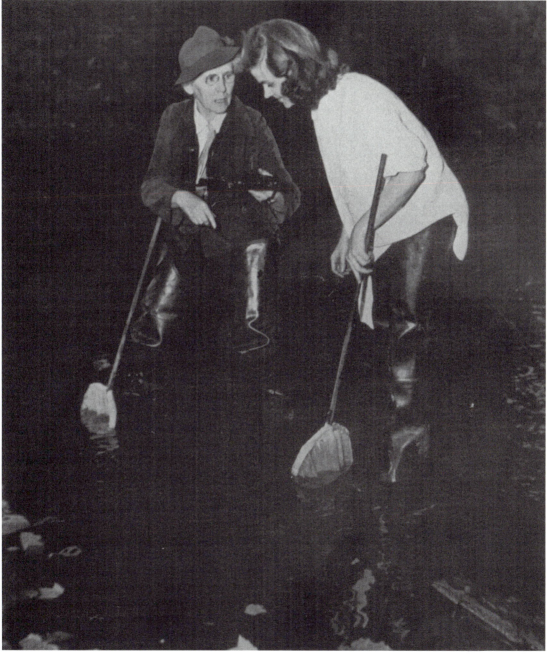

Ann Haven Morgan (left) seen here with a Mount Holyoke student, enjoyed getting "knee-deep in muck and water" to study the ecology of pond life. Her interest in insects earned her such nicknames as "Mayfly Morgan" and "The Water Bug Lady." (Courtesy Mount Holyoke College Archives and Special Collections)

water ferociously pursing nasty little herbivora and carnivora with a net." These tiny living things did not seem nasty to Morgan, however. She provided new understanding of the relationships among them and urged people to preserve them.

Morgan was born in Waterford, Connecticut, on May 6, 1882, the oldest of Stanley and Julia Morgan's three children. She entered Wellesley College in 1902 and transferred to Cornell University two years later, completing her B.A. in 1906. She then became an assistant and instructor at Mount Holyoke, a women's college in Massachusetts. She returned to Cornell for her Ph.D, which she earned in 1912. Her thesis was on mayflies, causing her biology students at Cornell to nickname her "Mayfly Morgan."

Morgan then went back to Mount Holyoke, where she taught during the academic year for the rest of her career. She became an associate professor in 1914, head of the zoology department in 1916, and a full professor in 1918. During the summers she taught and researched at several institutions, including the Marine Biological Laboratory at Woods Hole, Massachusetts.

Although insects remained a specialty, Morgan was also interested in fish, amphibians, plants, and everything else that lived in and around ponds. She summarized her observations of pond ecology in *Field Book of Ponds and Streams: An Introduction to the Life of Fresh Water* (1930), her best-known book, which was used by both amateur and professional naturalists. She also wrote *Field Book of Animals in Winter* (1939), a study of hibernation and other adaptations that help animals survive in the cold. She did much of the research for this book at a pond on Mount Tom in Massachusetts, hiking up through the snow from the trolley line and chopping holes in the pond's frozen surface to set traps for the water bugs she was studying. The trolley car crews called her the Water Bug Lady.

Morgan retired in 1947 and devoted herself thereafter to conservation. She stressed the relationships among living things, including humans, and their effects on behavior in *Kinships of Ani-*

mals and Man, a textbook she wrote for college zoology courses in 1955. "Now that the wilderness is almost gone," she wrote in this book, "we are beginning to be lonesome for it. We shall keep a refuge in our minds if we conserve the remnants." Morgan died of cancer on June 5, 1966, at the age of 84.

Further Reading

Blaisdell, Muriel. "Morgan, Ann Haven." In *Notable American Women: The Modern Period*, edited by Barbara Sicherman and Carol Hurd Green, 497–498. Cambridge, Mass.: The Belknap Press of Harvard University Press, 1980.

Bonta, Marcia Myers. *Women in the Field: America's Pioneering Women Naturalists*. College Station Tex.: Texas A&M University Press, 1991, 245–249.

✳ MOSS, CYNTHIA
(1940–) *American Zoologist*

Cynthia Moss's study of wild African elephants, lasting over 25 years, is comparable to JANE GOODALL's long-term study of chimpanzees. Other scientists have called Moss's work "invaluable" and "irreplaceable."

Cynthia was born in Ossining, New York, on July 24, 1940, the younger of the two daughters of newspaper publisher Julian Moss and his wife, Lillian. As a child she loved the outdoors. She went to Smith College, earning a B.A. in philosophy in 1962, and then became a news researcher and reporter for *Newsweek*. In 1967, after receiving "beautiful" letters from a friend who had moved to Africa, she took a leave of absence to see the continent for herself. When she arrived, she says, "I had this overwhelming sense that I'd come home."

Moss's trip included a visit to the camp of British elephant researcher Iain Douglas-Hamilton in Tanzania, where she says she "became completely hooked on elephants." She worked with Douglas-Hamilton off and on until 1970, when his project ended. She then supported herself by writing for *Life* and *Time* and helping other scientists while looking for funding and a site for her own elephant study. The ideal site proved to be Amboseli National Park in Kenya, home to one of the last undisturbed elephant herds in Africa.

What has come to be known as the Amboseli Elephant Research Project began in 1972. Most of its funding has come from Washington, D.C.'s African Wildlife Foundation (AWF). Moss, the project's director, has studied more than 1,600 elephants, which she identifies by differences in their ears. She told *Current Biography* that observing generations of the animals is "like reading a very good . . . family saga. You get so involved you don't want to put it down." By studying a single population over a long period, she has revealed much about elephant behavior and provided information that helps conservationists protect the animals. For instance, she has found that, as she told interviewer Marguerite Holloway, "Elephants have a really complex problem-solving intelligence, like a primate might have."

Douglas-Hamilton had discovered that the leader of an elephant family group is the oldest female—the matriarch. The group, whose members eat, rest, and play together, usually consists of several related females, or cows, and their calves. Adult males stay in separate, looser groups and associate with the family groups only during mating.

Moss has found that the family group is only the smallest unit of a many-tiered society. Several such groups make up a larger unit, the bond group. When elephants from different family groups but the same bond group meet, they stage an elaborate greeting ceremony. "I have no doubt even in my most scientifically rigorous moments that the elephants are experiencing joy when they find each other again," Moss has written. Bond groups, in turn, unite in still larger groups called clans, which share the same territory but do not have greeting ceremonies. The biggest subgroup in elephant society is the subpopulation, of which Amboseli has two.

Elephant communication is also complex. Moss and her coworkers have documented 25 different vocalizations, some of which, as KATHARINE PAYNE discovered, involve infrasound—sound too low for

human ears to hear, which carries well over long distances. These sounds help different groups stay in contact.

Joyce Poole, formerly of the Kenya Wildlife Service, joined Moss's project in 1976 and has made important contributions to it. For instance, Poole has found that African male elephants often enter a hyperaggressive state called musth, which had previously been reported only in Asian elephants. Moss and Poole have concluded that musth helps males compete for females in heat.

Moss has found that elephant females can change their reproductive patterns in response to the environment. Females normally become sexually mature when they are about 11 years old, but if conditions are harsh, their bodies may delay puberty until age 15 or later. Similarly, a cow usually has a calf about once every four years, but during a food shortage, the interval may be lengthened to seven years or more.

In the late 1980s, after learning that poaching for ivory and loss of habitat had halved Africa's elephant population during a single decade, Moss turned her focus to conservation. She and Poole went to Washington in 1988 to warn the AWF of the growing threat to the animals. Thanks to the efforts of AWF and other conservation groups, the Convention on International Trade in Endangered Species declared the African elephant an endangered species in October 1989 and banned the sale of ivory in January 1990. Since then, demand for ivory and loss of elephants to poaching have both dropped dramatically. The species has partly recovered, though Moss warns that it is still threatened.

Cynthia Moss has received several awards for her groundbreaking studies, including the Smith College medal for alumnae achievement (1985) and a conservation award from the Friends of the National Zoo and the Audubon Society. However, she feels that her greatest reward is continuing to share the lives of the elephant families she knows so well in "their good times and bad times through the seasons and the years."

Further Reading

Holloway, Marguerite. "On the Trail of Wild Elephants." *Scientific American*, December 1994, 48–50.

"Moss, Cynthia." *Current Biography Yearbook 1993*. New York: H. W. Wilson, 1993, 413–418.

Moss, Cynthia. *Elephant Memories: Thirteen Years in the Life of an Elephant Family*. New York: Morrow, 1988.

———— and Martyn Colbeck. *Echo of the Elephants: The Story of an Elephant Family*. New York: Morrow, 1992.

Pringle, Lawrence, and Cynthia Moss. *Elephant Women*. New York: Atheneum, 1997.

NEWTON TURNER, HELEN ALMA

(1908–1995) *Australian Geneticist and
Mathematician*

Helen Alma Newton Turner has used her knowledge of statistics and genetics to put sheep breeding
on a scientific basis. She was born in Sydney on May
15, 1908, the oldest of three children. Her family
moved frequently, which perhaps began her lifelong
love of travel. She studied chemistry, mathematics,
and architecture at the University of Sydney and
graduated with honors in architecture in 1930.

Newton Turner's real career began in 1931,
when she became secretary to Ian Clunies Ross, first
chairman of Australia's Council for Scientific and
Industrial Research (CSIR). Clunies Ross was then
head of the McMaster Laboratory in the government's Division of Animal Health, and Newton
Turner's work for him interested her in statistics
related to animal breeding. She returned to the
University of Sydney to take statistics courses.
Clunies Ross employed her in the laboratory as a
statistician and helped her obtain additional training in Britain and the United States.

After World War II, Newton Turner began to
specialize in the genetics of sheep breeding. Clunies
Ross established a separate section dealing with this

topic within CSIR's new Division of Animal Genetics in 1956, and Newton Turner became its head.
In addition to overseeing ongoing breeding experiments, she began new ones aimed at determining
the inheritance of different characteristics of wool.
She introduced the discipline of population genetics
to Australia and used it to make major improvements in the quality and quantity of wool. She also
co-wrote a textbook on the theoretical aspects of
quantitative genetics as applied to sheep breeding.

Newton Turner traveled all over the world to
lecture and to study and improve breeding programs, especially in developing nations. She urged
breeders to make exact measurements and keep
careful records. She has received honors including
the Order of the British Empire (1977), the Order
of Australia (1987), the Farber Memorial Medal for
distinguished services to agriculture, and two honorary doctorates. In 1973 she was elected one of the
two women Foundation Fellows of the Australian
Academy of Technological Sciences, and in 1990
she was elected a fellow of the Australasian Association of Animal Breeding and Genetics.

Newton Turner continued to work after her
retirement in1976, for instance writing a history of
sheep breeding and genetics. As the University of
Sydney noted in granting her an honorary doctor's

degree, "The scope of [her] work is immense . . . The amount of work is prodigious . . . the quality . . . is outstanding." She died on November 26, 1995.

Further Reading

Allen, Nessy. "Australian Women in Science: Two Unorthodox Careers." In *Women's Studies International Forum,* 551–562. New York: Pergamon Press, 1992.

✳ NICE, MARGARET MORSE
(1883–1974) *American Zoologist*

Austrian zoologist Konrad Lorenz, usually credited with cofounding ethology, the study of the behavior of animals in nature, once said that this honor really belonged to bird researcher Margaret Morse Nice. She was born Margaret Morse on December 6, 1883, in Amherst, Massachusetts, the fourth of the seven children of Anson Daniel and Margaret Morse. Her father was a professor of history at Amherst College. By the time she was nine, Margaret was taking notes on the behavior of birds.

Morse went to college at Mount Holyoke in Massachusetts, from which she earned a bachelor's degree in 1906. She then became a "dutiful daughter-at-home" until lectures by a professor from Clark University in Worcester, Massachusetts, revived her interest in studying nature professionally. She went to Clark in 1907, studied there for two years, and finally was awarded a master's degree in ornithology (bird study) in 1915. While at Clark, Morse met and fell in love with physiologist Leonard Blaine Nice. They married in 1909, and Margaret Nice gave up plans for further academic study. They had five daughters, Constance, Marjorie, Barbara, Eleanor, and Janet. Observing them, Margaret wrote several papers on language development and related subjects in child psychology.

In 1919, when the Nices were living in Norman, Oklahoma, Margaret decided to return to her childhood "vision of studying nature and trying to protect the wild things of the earth." Her first project, in which she enlisted her husband and daughters (she later praised Constance's "unquenchable zeal

for climbing . . . trees") was a study of mourning doves. This work kept the dove hunting season from being extended by showing that the birds continued nesting through September and even into October.

Nice's most important research focused on the song sparrows near her home in Columbus, Ohio, where the family moved in 1928. Previous scientists had not tried to distinguish one bird from another, but Nice banded her sparrows so she could identify particular birds. Her careful and lengthy observations allowed her to outline the life history of the species at a level of detail never achieved before. Renowned ornithologist Ernst Mayr said that Nice "almost single-handedly initiated a new era in American ornithology. . . . She early recognized the importance of a study of bird *individuals . . .* [as] the only method to get reliable life history data."

Nice's work became a book, *Population Study of the Song Sparrow,* published in 1937. (A second volume appeared in 1943.) The book won the Brewster Medal in 1942. By then Nice was already greatly respected in birding circles, having been made a member of the American Ornithological Union in 1931, only the fifth woman to be so honored, and a fellow of the union in 1937. Earlier days of being denigrated as "just a housewife" had long passed. Nice later received two honorary degrees as well, and a Mexican subspecies of song sparrow was named after her.

In 1936 the Nices left Ohio for Chicago, where opportunities for bird observation were limited. Margaret turned some earlier experiences into a book called *The Watcher at the Nest* (1939), but mostly she devoted herself to "rais[ing] . . . friends for wildlife" and educating the public about the need for conservation. She died on June 26, 1974, at age 90.

Further Reading

Bonta, Marcia Myers. *Women in the Field: America's Pioneering Women Naturalists.* College Station, Tex.: Texas A&M University Press, 1991, 222–231.

Nice, Margaret M. *Research Is a Passion with Me.* Toronto: Consolidated Amethyst Communications, 1979.

Trautman, Milton B. "Nice, Margaret Morse." In *Notable American Women: The Modern Period,* edited by Barbara Sicherman and Carol Hurd Green, 506–507. Cambridge, Mass.: The Belknap Press of Harvard University Press, 1980.

☀ NOETHER, EMMY (Amalie)
(1882–1935)   *German Mathematician*

Emmy Noether helped to explain Einstein's theory of relativity and the behavior of particles inside the atom and developed a new form of algebra that united many fields. Mathematician Norbert Wiener wrote shortly before Noether's untimely death that she was "one of the ten or twelve leading mathematicians of the present generation in the entire world."

Amalie Noether, always known as Emmy, was born on March 23, 1882, in Erlangen, Germany. Her father, Max, taught mathematics at Erlangen University, and her brother, Fritz, also became a mathematician. Around age 18, Emmy decided to do so as well, even though women were barred by law from enrolling at most German universities, including Erlangen. (Its academic senate had concluded in 1898 that the presence of women "would overthrow all academic order.") For two years she attended lectures given by Erlangen professors who were family friends, then audited other classes for a semester at Göttingen University. When Erlangen opened its doors to women in 1904, she returned home and enrolled there.

At Erlangen, Noether studied mostly with her father and a friend of his, Paul Gordan. Gordan specialized in invariants, or constants, and Noether did her thesis (which she later called "a jungle of formulas") on this subject. She was awarded her doctorate, with highest honors, in December 1907. For eight years afterward she helped her father (even sometimes giving his lectures after his health failed) without pay or title, since as a woman she could not join a university faculty. Meanwhile, she published papers about invariants that began her international reputation.

Emmy Noether's mathematical genius helped to explain the workings of relativity and quantum physics and showed underlying similarities in seemingly different fields of algebra. Driven out of her native Germany by the Nazi government's anti-Semitism, she established herself anew at Bryn Mawr College.
(Courtesy Bryn Mawr College Archives)

Noether's work attracted the attention of David Hilbert and Felix Klein, two renowned mathematicians at Göttingen, and she accepted an invitation to join them there in 1916. Her expertise in invariants helped them work out the mathematics behind Albert Einstein's general theory of relativity. Mathematician Hermann Weyl, a friend of Noether's, later said that "For two of the most significant sides of the theory of relativity, she gave . . . the genuine and universal mathematical formulation."

161

Hilbert and Klein wanted Noether to have a faculty position, but other professors objected. One asked, "What will our soldiers [then fighting in World War I] think when they return to the university and find that they are expected to learn at the feet of a woman?" Hilbert snapped back, "I do not see that the sex of the candidate is an argument against her admission. . . . The [academic] senate is not a public bathhouse."

The minister of education finally permitted Noether to lecture as Hilbert's assistant, but she was not given a title or paid a salary. Only in 1919, after women's legal and social position had been somewhat liberalized, was she made a *Privatdozent*, the lowest faculty rank. She could then lecture under her own name, but she still was not paid. In 1922 she was made an "unofficial extraordinary professor." Eventually she was given a tiny stipend, but she never became a regular professor at Göttingen.

Professor or not, Noether made important advances. In 1918, for instance, she formulated Noether's Theorem, which showed that the conservation laws of physics are identical with the laws of symmetry and therefore are independent of time and place. This theorem proved extremely important in the new field of quantum physics, which describes the behavior of subatomic particles.

Mathematicians were equally impressed with Noether's work in another new field, abstract algebra—a field that, indeed, she helped to found. Instead of focusing on problems and formulas, Noether's algebra dealt with concepts or ideals. She showed that the same basic rules underlay many fields of mathematics. "She saw connections between things that people hadn't realized were connected before," says algebraist Martha K. Smith. In 1932 Noether received the Teubner Memorial Prize.

When the National Socialists (Nazis) took control of Germany in 1933, Noether became a target because she was an independent Jewish woman with pacifist and leftist political sympathies. She lost her job in April 1933, one of the first six Göttingen professors the Nazis fired. She just calmly moved her small classes into her apartment. Hermann Weyl later said, "Her courage, her frankness, . . . her conciliatory spirit were, in the midst of all the hatred and meanness, despair, and sorrow . . . , a moral solace." Still, Noether's friends convinced her that she must leave Germany while she still could. After much searching, they found her a post at Bryn Mawr, a respected women's college in Philadelphia, and she went there in fall 1933.

On April 10, 1935, Emmy Noether underwent what should have been a routine operation. Four days later, probably because of an infection, she developed a high fever and lost consciousness. She died on April 14, 1935, at age 53. In a letter sent to the *New York Times* soon after her death, Albert Einstein wrote that Noether was "the most significant creative mathematical genius thus far produced since the higher education of women began."

Further Reading

Brewer, James W., and Martha K. Smith. *Emmy Noether: A Tribute to Her Life and Work.* New York: Marcel Dekker, 1981.

Dick, Auguste (tr. H. I. Blocher). *Emmy Noether 1882–1935.* Boston: Birkhäuser Boston, 1981.

Henderson, Harry. *Modern Mathematicians.* New York: Facts On File, 1996, 47–57.

McGrayne, Sharon Bertsch. *Nobel Prize Women in Science: Their Lives, Struggles, and Momentous Discoveries.* New York: Birch Lane Press, 1993, 64–89.

✳ NOGUCHI, CONSTANCE TOM
(1948–) *American Medical Researcher*

Constance Tom Noguchi's research has improved the understanding and treatment of sickle cell disease, a serious inherited blood disorder that usually strikes people of African descent. She was born in Kuangchou (Canton), China, on December 8, 1948. Her father, James Tom, a Chinese-American engineer, had married a Chinese woman, Irene Cheung, while working in China. They had three daughters before returning to the United States (when Connie was seven months old) and added a fourth later.

Connie Tom's childhood on the edge of San Francisco's large Chinese community blended Chinese and American elements. Some of her father's many books stirred her interest in science, as did a high school class in which students designed, researched, and carried out their own experiments.

She attended the University of California at Berkeley, planning to become a physician, but she changed her major to physics. In her senior year she married a medical student, Phil Noguchi, and they later had two sons. She graduated in 1970.

Connie Noguchi continued her studies at George Washington University in Washington, D.C., and earned a Ph.D. in theoretical nuclear physics in 1975. She then joined the National Institutes of Health (NIH), the group of large government research institutes in Bethesda, Maryland, where she has been ever since. (She currently works in the laboratory of chemical biology in the National Institute of Diabetes, Digestive, and Kidney Diseases.) Her work has won awards including the Public Health Special Recognition Award (1993) and the NIH EEO Recognition Award (1995).

Most of Noguchi's research has concerned sickle-cell disease, which is caused by a single defective gene. People who inherit the gene from both parents make an abnormal form of hemoglobin, the red pigment that carries oxygen in the blood. This substance causes red blood cells, normally disk shaped, to curve like a sickle. The curved cells sometimes clog small blood vessels, depriving tissues of oxygen and causing pain and illness.

Noguchi and her coworkers have studied hydroxyurea, a drug that increases the quantity of an alternate form of hemoglobin that normally exists in the blood in only tiny amounts. This form is not damaged by the defective gene, so increasing it increases the number of healthy red cells. "It's like doing gene therapy without having to add new genes," Noguchi says. Noguchi has investigated the possibility of combining hydroxyurea with other drugs, such as a hormone that produces new red cells, so that it can be used in smaller amounts and thus cause fewer side effects.

Constance Tom Noguchi's work at the National Institutes of Health has led to increased understanding of and improved treatment for sickle-cell disease, a painful inherited blood disease that usually strikes people of African descent. (Courtesy Constance Tom Noguchi)

Today, Noguchi is studying the way genes interact to produce hemoglobin and other red blood cell chemicals in both normal people and those with sickle-cell disease. She hopes that this basic research will lead to new treatments for the illness, perhaps even repair of the gene that causes it.

Further Reading

Asian-American Biographies. Paramus, N.J.: Globe Fearon, 1994.

Yount, Lisa. *Asian-American Scientists.* New York: Facts On File, 1998, 76–83.

✳ **NOVELLO, ANTONIA COELLO**
(1944–) *American Physician*

Antonia Novello was the first woman and the first Hispanic to become U.S. surgeon general. She was born in Fajardo, Puerto Rico, on August 23, 1944. Her father, Antonio Coello, died when she was eight years old. She and her brother were raised by their mother, Ana Delia Flores, a junior high school principal, and stepfather, Ramon Rosario, an electrician.

Tonita, as she was called as a child, was sick much of the time because of a birth defect. (It was finally corrected by surgery when she was 18.) Admiration for the doctors who cared for her, as well as determination to prevent other children from suffering as she had, encouraged her to become a physician. She earned her bachelor's degree in 1965 and her M.D. in 1970 from the University of Puerto Rico.

In 1970, Coello married flight surgeon Joseph Novello, and both continued their studies at the University of Michigan Medical Center in Ann Arbor. Antonia was named Intern of the Year by the center's department of pediatrics in 1971, the first woman to be so honored. From 1976 to 1978 she had a private pediatric practice in Virginia, but she quit because she found dealing with seriously ill children too painful. "When the pediatrician cries as much as the parents [of the children] do, . . . it's time to get out," she told *People* magazine.

In 1978, Novello joined the U.S. Public Health Service and the National Institutes of Health (NIH), the large conglomerate of federal research institutes in Bethesda, Maryland. She also trained in health services administration at the Johns Hopkins School of Public Health in Baltimore, earning a master's degree in 1982. She worked with Congress, for instance, in helping to draft the National Organ Transplant Act of 1984. In 1986 she became deputy director of the National Institute of Child Health and Human Development, one of the institutes at NIH, and a professor of pediatrics at the Georgetown University School of Medicine.

Nominated by President George Bush, Novello became the country's fourteenth surgeon general on March 9, 1990. She said her motto would be "Good science and good sense." During her term in office she emphasized the health concerns of children and young people, women, and Hispanics, "speak[ing] up for the people who are not able to speak for themselves." She criticized companies that marketed cigarettes and alcohol to youths.

Novello stepped down from the surgeon general's job in 1993. Since then she has been a special representative for UNICEF and a professor at Johns Hopkins University Medical School.

Further Reading

Howes, Kelly King. "Antonia Novello." In *Latinas! Women of Achievement,* edited by Diane Telgen and Jim Kamp, 273–278. Detroit: Visible Ink Press, 1996.
Krucoff, Carol. "Antonia Novello: A Dream Come True." *Saturday Evening Post,* May/June 1991, 38–41, 92.

✳ **NUTTALL, ZELIA MARIA MAGDALENA**
(1857–1933) *Mexican Archaeologist*

Zelia Nuttall, the only woman archaeologist of her time to study Mexico's pre-Columbian history, rediscovered two valuable native picture histories. She was born in San Francisco on September 6, 1857, to Robert Nuttall, a physician, and Magdalena Nuttall. Zelia spent much of her childhood traveling in Europe with her family and had little formal education.

After the Nuttalls returned to San Francisco, Zelia met Alphonse Louis Pinart, a Frenchman studying ethnology, or human cultures, and they married in 1880. She traveled with him to research projects, and they had a daughter, Nadine, in 1882. The marriage was unhappy, however, and the couple separated in 1884 and divorced in 1888.

Zelia Nuttall first visited Mexico in 1884, armed with an interest in the country's ancient history stirred by her half-Mexican mother and training in anthropology acquired from Pinart. Her paper on terra cotta figurines from Teotihuacán, published in 1886, attracted the attention of pioneer anthropologist Frederic W. Putnam, who made her an honorary special assistant in Mexican archaeology at Harvard's Peabody Museum. Putnam also helped her be elected as a fellow of the American Association for the Advancement of Science in 1887.

Nuttall lived and researched in Germany from 1886 to 1899, after which she returned to the United States and then, in 1902, to Mexico. She was field director of the University of California's archaeological research in Mexico in 1904 and helped famed anthropologist Franz Boas establish the International School of American Archaeology and Ethnology. She was also a founding member of the American Anthropological Association.

One of Nuttall's chief contributions to Mexican archaeology was her rediscovery of two native codices, or picture books, brought to Europe by the Spanish and subsequently buried in obscure libraries. Nuttall reintroduced them to the scholarly world in 1902 and 1903 and proved that they and others like them were historical documents. One is still known as the *Codex Nuttall.*

Nuttall also researched the life of British explorer Sir Francis Drake. Her 1914 book, *New Light on Drake*, is still considered a major historical work. She died of cancer on April 12, 1933, at the age of 75.

Further Reading

Parmenter, Ross. "Glimpses of a Friendship: Zelia Nuttall and Franz Boas." In *Pioneers of American Anthropology,* edited by June Helm. Seattle: University of Washington Press, 1966.

———. "Nuttall, Zelia Maria Magdalena." In *Notable American Women, 1607–1950, vol. II: G–O*, edited by Edward T. James, 640–642. Cambridge, Mass.: The Belknap Press of Harvard University Press, 1971.

✳ OCAMPO-FRIEDMANN, ROSELI
(1937–)   *American Botanist*

Roseli Ocampo-Friedmann and her husband, Imre Friedmann, have found living microorganisms inside Antarctic rocks and under the permanently frozen ground of the Far North. She was born Roseli Ocampo in Manila, the Philippines, on November 23, 1937, to Eliseo A. and Generosa Ocampo.

Ocampo earned a B.S. in botany from the University of the Philippines in 1958. Then, in 1963, she came to Hebrew University in Jerusalem to do graduate work and met Hungarian-born Imre Friedmann, who two years earlier had discovered that microscopic algae and cyanobacteria (sometimes called blue-green algae) could live under the surface of rocks in inhospitable deserts. Ocampo grew and studied some of these micrtoorganisms in the laboratory as her master's degree project and discovered that she was outstandingly successful at getting them to thrive in test tubes. She had what Friedmann calls a "blue-green thumb."

Ocampo earned her master's degree in 1966, returned to the Philippines, and worked for a while for the National Institute of Science and Technology in Manila. In 1968 she joined Friedmann at Florida State University in Tallahassee, where she completed her Ph.D. in 1973. She married Friedmann in 1974.

Now a scientist couple working together, Roseli and Imre Friedmann traveled to deserts all over the world, looking for algae and other microorganisms. Roseli Ocampo-Friedmann, as she now called herself, added new organisms each year to her growing collection of living cultures. In the mid-1970s, Friedmann found microorganisms inside rocks from Antarctica, and, after many weeks of work, Ocampo-Friedmann succeeded in culturing them in the laboratory.

As the Friedmanns continued their Antarctic research, Imre went to Antarctica and Roseli remained in Tallahassee to make cultures from the rock samples he sent. After two years, however, they realized that chances of contamination and damage would be reduced if she came along to start cultures on the spot. Roseli therefore made five trips with Imre to the southern continent. Since then the two have extended their research to Siberia, where they have studied bacteria in the permanently frozen ground, or permafrost, that underlies the Arctic tundra. The Friedmanns' research attracted media attention in the late 1970s and again in 1996 because scientists believe that the microorganisms the couple has

Roseli Ocampo-Friedmann's "blue-green thumb" has helped her culture the unusual microorganisms that she and her husband, Imre Friedmann, have found inside rocks in such inhospitable climates as Antarctica and the Siberian tundra. She is seen collecting new specimens here. These organisms may be similar to ones that once lived on Mars.
(Courtesy E. Imre Friedman)

studied inside frozen rocks might be similar to those that could once have existed on Mars.

Today Roseli Ocampo-Friedmann continues to use her "blue-green thumb" in research with her husband at Florida State University in Tallahassee. Since 1987 she has also been a full professor at Florida A&M University, where she teaches general biology and microbiology. She received a resolution of commendation from the state government of Florida in 1978 and the U.S. Congressional Antarctic Service Medal from the National Science Foundation in 1981. Her collection of cultures of microorganisms from extreme environments all over the world now numbers close to a thousand different types.

Further Reading

Hively, Will. "Looking for Life in All the Wrong Places." *Discover*, May 1997, 77–85.
Land, Barbara. *The New Explorers: Women in Antarctica.* New York: Dodd, Mead, 1981, 189–200.

OHTA, TOMOKO
(1933–) *Japanese Geneticist*

Tomoko Ohta has helped to develop the relatively new scientific branch of population genetics, which studies the mechanisms of evolutionary change at the molecular level. She was born in Aichi Prefecture, near Nagoya, Japan, on September 7, 1933.

One of the first women to attend the University of Tokyo, Ohta studied horticulture (the science of growing garden plants) and obtained a bachelor's degree in agriculture in 1956. Lack of money delayed her graduate studies, but she finally earned a Ph.D. in population genetics from North Carolina State University in 1967. Her thesis presented a probability-based model of how a particular genetic feature can survive in a population.

After gaining her doctorate, Ohta returned to Japan and joined the National Institute of Genetics in Mishima. There she worked for population geneticist Motoo Kimura, helping him find evidence to support his theory of how particular body chemicals evolved. Kimura and Ohta believe that most evolution at the molecular level is caused by random processes rather than Darwinian natural selection. This "neutral mutation-random drift" theory is still controversial, but it is valuable because it provides testable predictions about the rate of molecular evolution. Ohta has developed her own theory, the "nearly neutral" hypothesis, to explain some aspects of molecular evolution by the interaction of random and selective forces.

Ohta headed the first laboratory of the department of population genetics at the National Institute of Genetics from 1977 to 1984 and was a professor at the institute from 1984 until 1997, when she retired to become a professor emerita and adjunct professor. She was a vice director of the institute in 1990–91. In 1981 she became the first winner of the Saruhashi Prize, a prize for women scientists established by KATSUKO SARUHASHI. She has also won the Japan Academy Prize (1985) and the Weldon Memorial Prize from Britain's Oxford University (1986), and she was made an honorary foreign member of the American Academy of Arts and Sciences in 1984.

Further Reading

Koppel, Toomas. "Our Thinking Is Difficult to Change." *Science*, April 16, 1993, 402.

Myers, Fred. "Women Scientists: It's Lonely at the Top." *Science*, October 23, 1992, 566.

P

(1907–) *American Botanist and Ecologist*

Ruth Patrick made pioneering studies on the effects of pollution on freshwater ecology and invented a sensitive tool for evaluating water pollution. She was born on November 26, 1907, in Topeka, Kansas, but grew up in Kansas City, Missouri. Her father, Frank Patrick, was a lawyer, but his hobby was studying diatoms, one-celled algae (plantlike living things) that are the base of the food chain in fresh water. When Ruth was good, he let her look through his microscope.

Patrick attended Coker College in South Carolina, graduating in 1929. During a summer at Cold Spring Harbor Laboratory in New York she met fellow biology student Charles Hodge IV. They married in 1931, but Patrick continued to use her maiden name professionally. They had one son. (Since 1995, Patrick has been married to Lewis H. Van Dusen, Jr.) Patrick earned a master's degree in 1931 and a Ph.D. in botany in 1934, both from the University of Virginia.

Patrick has spent most of her professional life at the Academy of Natural Sciences in Philadelphia, which she joined part-time in 1937 and full-time in 1945. She was the chairperson of its board of trus-

tees from 1973 to 1976 and is now its honorary chairperson. In 1947 she established a department of limnology (freshwater ecology) at the academy, now called the Environmental Research Division, and directed it until 1973; she is still its curator. She has also been an adjunct professor at the University of Pennsylvania since 1970.

Patrick's first favorite study subject, like her father's, was diatoms. With Charles Reimer she produced a monumental two-part work on the subject, *Diatoms of the United States,* published in 1966. She then expanded her research to include general ecology and biodiversity in rivers. She is considered the cofounder the discipline of limnology.

Patrick was concerned with pollution's effect on ecology long before RACHEL CARSON made the issue fashionable. Patrick's research showed that diatoms are sensitive indicators of pollution in freshwater, and she invented the diatometer, which determines the presence and kind of water pollution by measuring numbers of different species of diatoms. Patrick was also a pioneer in pointing out that scientists needed to study ecological communities, not just single species, to determine the effects of pollution.

Unlike Carson, Patrick has had a relatively cordial relationship with industry, for which she has often worked as a consultant. She has even been a

Ruth Patrick of the Academy of Natural Sciences of Philadelphia is credited with cofounding the discipline of limnology, or freshwater ecology. She also invented a device that detects pollution in freshwater and has written a massive book on rivers.
(Courtesy the Academy of Natural Sciences of Philadelphia)

director of Pennsylvania Power and Light Company and of du Pont—the first woman and the first environmentalist ever on the board of the latter. "We have to develop an atmosphere where the industrialist trusts the scientist and the scientist trusts the industrialist," she has said.

Patrick was elected to the National Academy of Sciences in 1970 and was president of the American Society of Naturalists from 1975 to 1977. She is also a member of the American Academy of Arts and Sciences. In 1975, Patrick won the John and Alice Tyler Ecology Award, the highest-paying award in science (it outpays even the Nobel Prize), and has used the money to prepare the multivolume *Rivers of the United States*, published

beginning in 1994. Her recent awards include the Benjamin Franklin Award from the American Philosophical Society (1993) and the American Society of Limnology and Oceanography's Lifetime Achievement Award and the National Medal of Science, both received in 1996. She continues to study the diverse life in rivers and to develop ways to monitor its health.

Further Reading

Holden, Constance. "Ruth Patrick: Hard Work Brings Its Own (and Tyler) Award." *Science*, June 6, 1975, 997–999.

Vare, Ethlie Ann, and Greg Ptacek. *Mothers of Invention.* New York: Morrow, 1988, 179–180.

✳ PATTERSON, FRANCINE ("Penny")
(1947–) *American Psychologistt*

By teaching American Sign Language to Koko and Michael, captive-born lowland gorillas, Francine Patterson says that she, like other scientists who have done similar work with chimpanzees, has "helped to dismantle an intellectual barrier long thought to separate humans from the great apes: the ability to use language."

Penny Patterson has taught American Sign Language to Koko, a zoo-born lowland gorilla, demonstrating that apes, like humans, can use language. Here she holds a kitten that became Koko's "pet."
(Photo Ronald H. Cohn, courtesy Gorilla Foundation)

Francine, or Penny as she is always called, was born in Chicago in 1947, one of four boys and three girls. Her father, C. H. Patterson, was a professor of educational psychology at the University of Illinois, so it was not surprising that she, too, attended that university and majored in psychology. She earned her B.A. in 1970.

While doing graduate work at Stanford University, Patterson attended a lecture by Allen and Beatrix Gardner, who had taught American Sign Language (Ameslan or ASL) to a chimpanzee named Washoe. Apes cannot make most sounds in human languages, but they can learn the gestures that make up ASL, which is used by the hearing impaired. Washoe learned a number of Ameslan "words" and constructed meaningful sentences with them. Patterson decided to teach ASL to a gorilla as her doctoral project.

In 1972, with the permission of the San Francisco Zoo, Patterson began teaching ASL to Koko, a year-old female gorilla that had been born at the zoo. "As . . . Koko began to use words that revealed her personality, I . . . recognize[d] sensitiveness, strategies, humor, the stubbornness with which I could identify," Patterson wrote. "The realization that I was dealing with an intelligent and sensitive intellectual . . . sealed my commitment to Koko's future."

Ongoing conflicts with zoo officials led Patterson and her partner, Ronald Cohn, to establish a nonprofit organization called the Gorilla Foundation in 1976 and launch a public appeal for donations to buy Koko from the zoo so that their work could continue. With the help of individuals and the National Geographic Society, they acquired not only Koko but a second gorilla, a male they named Michael. He, too, has learned ASL.

In 1979, after Patterson completed her Ph.D. in developmental psychology at Stanford, she and Cohn moved Koko and Michael to the nearby community of Woodside, where they still live. They added a third gorilla, a male named Ndume, to the group in 1991. Ndume, on loan from the Cincinnati Zoo, is a potential mate for Koko but is not part of the ASL project. The Gorilla Foundation, mean-

while, expanded to support not only Patterson's ongoing work but "improved care and welfare of captive gorillas . . . [and] efforts to . . . preserve gorillas in their natural habitat."

Patterson's awards include the Rolex Award for Enterprise (1978), the PAWS Award for Outstanding Professional Service (1986), and the Kilby International Award (1997). She is presently an adjunct professor of psychology at the University of Santa Clara as well as the president and research director of the Gorilla Foundation. She says that her 26 years of research "shed light on human origins" and "have yielded . . . remarkable access to the gorilla mind."

Further Reading

Hahn, Emily. *Eve and the Apes.* New York: Weidenfeld and Nicolson, 1988, 84–102.

Patterson, F., and W. Gordon. *The Case for Personhood of Gorillas.* In *The Great Ape Project*, edited by Paoloa Cavalieri and Peter Singer. London: Fourth Estate, 1993.

Patterson, Francine G., and Eugene Linden. *The Education of Koko.* New York: Holt Rinehart Winston, 1981.

✳ PAYNE, KATHARINE BOYNTON ("Katy") (1937–) *American Zoologist*

Katharine Payne has helped to develop the field of bioacoustics, which studies the sounds that animals use to communicate, and has made key discoveries about sounds made by whales and elephants. Katy, as she is usually known, was born Katharine Boynton in Ithaca, New York, in 1937. Her father was a professor at Cornell University. While attending Cornell, where she majored in music, Katy met Roger Payne, a biology graduate student, and they married in 1960. During the next few years she and their growing family, which came to include four children, accompanied him on field studies of humpback whales and right whales.

After hearing recordings of vocalizations that humpbacks made under water, Roger Payne realized in 1966 that the sounds formed long, complex, repeating patterns; in short, they were songs, like bird songs. All the male whales in any given area of the ocean sing the same song at a particular time, but, as Katy Payne discovered, the song of each population gradually changes with time, and all the singing whales keep abreast of the changes. Katy spent more than a decade documenting and analyzing this fascinating example of cultural evolution—the passing on of learned traits—in whales. She found an intriguing set of similarities between the gradual changes in whale songs and those in human languages.

Payne became a research associate at Cornell University in 1984. In that same year, while observing elephants at the Metro Washington Park Zoo in Portland, Oregon, she noticed a throbbing in the air near the elephants' cages and suspected that it might be caused by powerful infrasonic vocalizations—sounds pitched too low for human ears to hear. Payne, working with William Langbauer and Elizabeth Marshall Thomas, used recording equipment that could pick up deep sounds to confirm her guess. No one had ever suspected that land animals could use infrasound to communicate, but low-frequency sound travels through air exceptionally well, and Payne thought that elephants' use of infrasound might give them a long-distance communication system.

Payne and various associates have been following up this notion ever since. They have not only demonstrated elephants' use of infrasound but built up an understanding of how the animals use these unusual calls to help coordinate their widespread and highly complex societies. For instance, in Amboseli National Park in Kenya in 1985 and 1986, Payne and Joyce Poole, working with the same elephants CYNTHIA MOSS has studied, recorded an extensive vocabulary of elephant calls and found them rich in infrasound. The existence of these calls helps to explain how widely separated elephant groups can move in parallel over long time periods as they feed and how male elephants find females during the brief periods when the latter are in breeding condition. In 1998, working with several meteorologists, Payne was trying to determine the effect of the atmosphere on infrasound communications used by elephants, lions, and certain other

animals. In addition to her scientific work, Payne writes, she is an "active conservationist with a strong concern for the health and survival of wild animals and wild places."

Further Reading

Payne, Katharine. *Elephants Calling*. New York: Crown, 1992.
———. *Silent Thunder: In the Presence of Elephants*. New York: Simon and Schuster, 1998.
Sirch, Willow Ann. *Eco-Women: Protectors of the Earth*. Golden, Colo: Fulcrum Kids, 1996, 46–53.

✳ PAYNE-GAPOSCHKIN, CECILIA HELENA
(1900–1979)   *American Astronomer*

Cecilia Payne-Gaposchkin did important studies of very bright stars and of variable stars, whose brightness changes over time. She was born Cecilia Helena Payne in Wendover, England, in 1900. Her father, Edward Payne, was a lawyer, and her mother, the former Emma Pertz, a painter.

While Payne was at Newnham College, part of Cambridge University, lectures by famed astrophysicist Arthur Eddington interested her in that field. Unable to find work as an astronomer in Britain after her graduation in 1922, Payne went to the Harvard Observatory in Cambridge, Massachusetts. She remained there for the rest of her career, becoming a United States citizen in 1931. She earned a Ph.D. from Radcliffe in 1925 with a thesis that related stars' temperature to their type and the composition of their atmospheres, which Yerkes Observatory astronomer Otto Struve called "the most brilliant Ph.D. thesis ever written in astronomy." Payne had to spend most of her time at the observatory tediously measuring the brightness and distance of stars in photographs, but she still managed to study her favorite subject, stars with high luminosity or intrinsic brightness.

While attending an astronomical meeting at Germany's Göttingen University in 1933, Payne met Sergei Gaposchkin, a Russian astronomer then working in Berlin. She helped him find a job at Harvard, and they married early the following year. Cecilia thereafter used the name Payne-Gaposchkin. The couple had three children. Cecilia remained more highly regarded as an astronomer and—rare for a woman scientist—even better paid than her husband, but Harvard was nonetheless slow to grant her official recognition. She was given the title of "astronomer" in 1938 but was made a tenured professor only in 1956, near the end of her career.

Payne-Gaposchkin and her husband published an immense catalogue of variable stars in 1938. She also determined which chemical elements were most common in different kinds of stars. She was elected to the American Philosophical Society in 1936, and in 1943 she became one of the first women elected to the American Academy of Arts and Sciences. She also was part of the council that ran the Harvard Observatory in the mid-1940s. She won a medal from the Radcliffe Alumnae Association in 1949 and the achievement award of the American Association of University Women (AAUW) in 1957. Payne-Gaposchkin died in 1979.

Further Reading

Kidwell, Peggy A. "Cecilia Payne-Gaposchkin: Astronomy in the Family." In *Uneasy Careers and Intimate Lives: Women in Science 1789–1979*, edited by Pnina G. Abir–Am and Dorinda Outram, 216–238. New Brunswick, N.J.: Rutgers University Press, 1987.

Mack, Pamela E. "Straying from Their Orbits: Women in Astronomy in America." In *Women of Science: Righting the Record*, edited by G. Kass-Simon and Patricia Farnes, 105–107.

Payne-Gaposchkin, Cecilia. *Cecilia Payne-Gaposchkin: An Autobiography and Other Recollections.* New York: Cambridge University Press, 1984.

✳ PEREY, MARGUERITE CATHERINE
(1909–1975) *French Chemist and Physicist*

Marguerite Perey discovered francium, the 87th element in the periodic table. She was born in

Villenoble, France, in 1909, and educated in Paris. In 1929, when she was just 20 years old, she began working at the Radium Institute in Paris, first as a personal assistant to MARIE CURIE, the institute's founder, and then as a radiochemist. In 1939, while studying the breakdown of radioactive actinium, Perey discovered a new radioactive element, the last natural element to be isolated. It has a half-life of only 21 minutes. Just as Curie had done with polonium, Perey named the new element after her native country. Francium is the heaviest element in the alkali metal group.

Perey earned a doctor of science degree from the Sorbonne in 1946. Between 1946 and 1949 she was the chief of research at the National Center for Scientific Research, a part of the Radium Institute. She then moved to Strasbourg University in Alsace (northeastern France). She became professor of nuclear chemistry there in 1949 and director of the Laboratory of Nuclear Chemistry in the university's Nuclear Research Center, a laboratory she had helped to found, in 1958.

Perey won many awards, including the Legion of Honor and the Grand Prix de la Ville de Paris in 1960 and the Lavoisier Prize of the Academy of Sciences and the Silver Medal of the Chemical Society of France in 1964. In 1962 she became the first woman elected to the prestigious French Academy of Sciences, and she received special lauréat awards from that group in 1950 and 1960. She was made a commander of the National Order of Merit in 1974. Perey died in 1975 at the age of 65 after a 15-year battle with cancer, probably caused by her exposure to radioactivity.

Further Reading

Nakada, Daniel. "Perey, Marguerite Catherine," CWP at physics.UCLA.edu. Available online. URL: http://www.physics.ucla.edu/~cwp.html. Posted 1996.

Uglow, Jennifer S. *The International Dictionary of Women's Biography.* New York: Continuum, 1982, 368–369.

PERT, CANDACE BEEBE
(1946–) *American Medical Researcher*

Candace Pert discovered molecules in the brain that attach to natural chemicals that resemble opiates (narcotics). She has also done pioneering research on chemical links between the brain and the rest of the body and on a drug that may be a valuable treatment for AIDS and other diseases.

Pert was born Candace Dorinda Beebe on June 26, 1946, in New York City and grew up in Wantagh, Long Island. Her parents were Robert and Mildred Beebe. Robert Beebe held a variety of jobs, from selling ads to arranging band music, and Mildred was a court clerk.

Beebe majored in English at nearby Hofstra University, but while there she met an Estonian psychology student, Agu Pert, who interested her in science. She and Pert married in 1966, before she finished her bachelor's degree, and soon had the first of their three children. Candace finished her degree at Bryn Mawr, where Agu went to do further graduate work, and this time she took classes in chemistry and psychology.

Candace Pert began doing doctoral research at Johns Hopkins Medical School under Solomon Snyder, an expert on brain chemistry, in 1970. He suggested that she look for the opiate receptor, a substance whose existence was strongly suspected but had not been proven. Like many other chemicals that act on the body and brain, opiates become active only when they attach to receptor molecules on the surfaces of cells. Each chemical or group of chemicals has its own receptor, which appears only on the kinds of cells that chemical affects. At the time Pert started her research, receptors for only a few body chemicals had been identified.

In September 1972, after many attempts, Pert succeeded in "tagging" opiate receptors in animal brain tissue with radioactive material. These were the first receptors located in the brain and the first that bound to a substance that did not exist naturally in the body. Publication of Pert's results in early 1973 not only earned her Ph.D. (in 1974) but made her famous.

In late 1975 two researchers in Scotland identified the first of the endorphins, the group of opiate-like natural brain chemicals to which Pert's receptors normally attach. Pert, meanwhile, adapted her technique to map receptors for opiates and other chemicals in different parts of the brain. She and Michael Kuhar of Johns Hopkins found opiate receptors in brain areas involved in perception of both pain and pleasure.

In 1975, Candace and Agu Pert joined the National

Candace Pert became famous while still a graduate student for discovering receptor molecules that attach to natural brain substance resembling opiates such as morphine. Since then, she has developed a possible treatment for AIDS and has shown that cells in the brain and the immune system often respond to the same molecules, providing a link between the body and the mind.
(Courtesy Candace B. Pert)

Institute of Mental Health (NIMH), one of the government-sponsored National Institutes of Health in Bethesda, Maryland. Candace soon was heading her own laboratory. She won the Arthur S. Fleming Award for outstanding government service in 1978. She was angry, however, to be left out of a much larger award, the Albert and Mary Lasker Award for Biomedical Research, which Snyder and the two Scottish researchers shared in that same year. Opinions differ about whether she was denied the award because she was still a graduate student when she did her opiate receptor research or because she was a woman.

In 1983, Pert became chief of a new section on brain biochemistry within the clinical neuroscience branch of NIMH, the only woman section chief in the institute at the time. She studied peptides, small molecules similar to proteins, many of which carry messages from one part of the body to another. Beginning in the early 1980s, she and others found that many message-carrying peptides have receptors both in the brain and on cells of the immune system, which defends the body against disease.

Pert's research on peptides and receptors took a new turn in 1984 when she found that one kind of receptor on immune system cells called CD-4 cells also appeared in the brain. Other scientists showed that HIV, the virus that causes AIDS, enters CD-4 cells by way of this receptor. Pert believed that AIDS might be prevented or halted by a drug that blocked the receptors, and she began working with another NIH researcher, Michael Ruff, on this idea. Candace and Agu Pert had divorced in 1982, and in 1986 she married Ruff. That same year the two began publishing accounts of their research on a substance they called Peptide T, which was similar to the part of the virus that binds to the CD-4 receptor.

Pert (who has continued to use the name under which she did her earlier research) and Ruff felt that NIH was not supporting the Peptide T research fully enough, so at the end of 1987 they left NIH and started their own company to pursue it. Although subsequent work with the drug ran into difficulties, recent research has given a boost to the couple's belief that it may combat some effects of AIDS, especially wasting and brain damage, and work against other kinds of diseases as well by blocking a second receptor called a chemokine receptor. Tests of Peptide T continue.

Pert has also focused during the 1990s on the links between brain and body, especially between the brain and the immune system, that her peptide and receptor research revealed. (She calls peptides "the molecules of emotion.") She and other researchers who believe that these links allow physical and mental health to influence each other have formed a new field called psychoneuroimmunology. Pert, who won the Kilby Award in 1993, and Ruff continue their "search for truth" as research professors at Georgetown University Medical Center in Washington, D.C.

Further Reading

Goldberg, Jeff. *Anatomy of a Scientific Discovery.* New York: Bantam, 1988.

Pert, Candace B. *Molecules of Emotion: Why You Feel the Way You Feel.* New York: Scribners, 1997.

Yount, Lisa. *Contemporary Women Scientists.* New York: Facts On File, 1994, 94–106.

QUIMBY, EDITH HINKLEY
(1891–1982)   *American Physicist and Medical Researcher*

Edith Quimby made the use of radiation in medicine safer and more effective and helped to develop a new scientific specialty called radiation physics or nuclear medicine. She was born Edith Hinkley on July 10, 1891, in Rockford, Illinois, one of the three children of Arthur S. Hinkley and his wife, Harriet. Arthur Hinkley worked as an architect and a farmer. The family moved frequently during Edith's childhood.

Hinkley majored in mathematics and physics at Whitman College in Walla Walla, Washington, and graduated with a B.S. in 1912. She then taught high school science before winning a fellowship to the University of California in 1914. She married fellow UC physics student Shirley L. Quimby in 1915 and obtained her master's degree in physics in 1916.

The Quimbys moved to New York City in 1919, after which Edith worked with Gioacchino Failla, chief physicist at the Memorial Hospital for Cancer and Allied Diseases. Failla's assistant at first, Quimby later became his full collaborator, promoted from assistant to associate physicist in 1932.

High-energy radiation had been used for some years to treat cancer and certain other diseases, but such treatments could be dangerous to both patients and health care workers. Quimby measured the amount of radiation given off by different quantities of radioactive materials and the amount that penetrated the bodies of laboratory animals, greatly improving methods of determining doses of radiation that were both safe and effective. She also invented safer ways to handle and dispose of radioactive materials. In her later career she researched the use of artificial radioactive materials, such as radioactive sodium, in cancer treatment and medical diagnosis and research.

Quimby became an assistant professor of radiology at Cornell University Medical College in 1941. Then, in 1942, both Failla and Quimby joined the faculty of Columbia University's College of Physicians and Surgeons, where Quimby taught courses in radiation physics. An associate professor at first, she became a full professor in 1954.

Quimby received a number of awards for her work, including the Janeway Medal from the American Radium Society (1940), the Gold Medal of the Radiological Society of North America (1941), and the Gold Medal of the American College of Radiology (1963). She was one of the founding members of the American Association of Physicists in Medicine and was president of the

American Radium Society in 1954. Quimby retired in 1960, becoming an emeritus professor, and died on October 11, 1982, at age 91.

Further Reading

"Quimby, Edith." *Current Biography Yearbook 1949.* New York: H. W. Wilson, 1949, 492–493.

Veglahn, Nancy. *Women Scientists.* New York: Facts On File, 1991, 48–56.

Yost, Edna. *Women of Modern Science.* New York: Dodd, Mead, 1960.

 QUINN, HELEN RHODA ARNOLD
(1943–) American Physicist

Helen Quinn is helping to refine physicists' understanding of how particles and forces work within the atom. She was born Helen Arnold in Melbourne, Australia, on May 19, 1943. Raised with three brothers, she told writer Charles C. Mann that she "learned very young how to make myself heard."

Quinn's father took a job in Belmont, California, when Quinn was in her second year at the University of Melbourne, and she decided to move to the United States with him. She began attending nearby Stanford University, from which she earned a bachelor's degree in physics in 1963, a master's degree in 1964, and a Ph.D. in 1967. She married Daniel Quinn in 1966, has two children, and has become a U.S. citizen. She worked at Harvard during much of the 1970s but returned to Stanford in 1978 and has worked there ever since at the university's atom-smasher research facility, the Stanford Linear Accelerator Center (SLAC).

Quinn's work often focuses on experimental implications and tests of theories about the subatomic world. At Harvard, working with Joel Primack and Thomas Applequist, she made some of the first studies of the implications and predictive power of the theory now known as the Standard Model of Fundamental Particles and Interactions. Then, with Howard Georgi and Steven Weinberg, she worked out circumstances under which electromagnetism, the strong force, and the weak force, the three forces that hold atoms together, become identical at very high energies. This research was "the highlight of my Harvard years," Quinn says.

At Stanford, Quinn and Roberto Peccei arrived at an explanation of the fact that a basic symmetry of the laws of physics called CP (the combination of C, or particle-antiparticle symmetry, and P, or parity [mirror image]) symmetry, holds true for strong interactions but not for weak interactions. To achieve a theory in which this is naturally true, Peccei and Quinn had to propose another near symmetry of the universe. This symmetry, as yet unverified, is called Peccei-Quinn symmetry. Their theory predicts the existence of extremely lightweight particles called axions that almost never interact with other particles. Physicists are currently trying to detect axions.

In addition to doing research, Quinn has been SLAC's education and public outreach manager since 1988. She is also president of the Contemporary Physics Education Project, a nonprofit group that writes material for high school and college classes. Quinn is a fellow of the American Physical Society and was elected to the American Academy of Arts and Sciences in 1998.

Further Reading

Mann, Charles C. "Wanted: Wayward Particles." *Discover,* December 1991, 50–55.

Quinn, Helen R., and Martha Keyes. "Helen R. Quinn," CWP at physics.UCLA.edu. Available online. URL: http://www.physics.ucla.edu/~cwp.html. Updated on May 22, 1997.

R

✳ RAJALAKSHMI, R.
(1926–) *Indian Biochemist*

R. Rajalakshmi combined biochemistry, psychology, and common sense to create programs that prevent and treat malnutrition in her native India. She was born in 1926 in Quilon, part of the state of Kerala, and grew up in Madras, where her father, G. S. Ramaswami Iyer, was a postal audit officer. The many books he brought home stirred her interest in science.

From the start, Lakshmi refused to fit others' expectations. At age five she added *raja*, which means "royal," to her given name, and has used this as her chief name ever since. She also went to college, which few Indian women did. She earned a degree in mathematics from Wadia College in Poona in 1945. She married a Wadia classmate, C. V. Ramakrishnan, in 1951, and they had a son and daughter. She also obtained a teaching certificate from Lady Willingdon Training College in 1949, a master's degree in philosophy from Banaras Hindu University in 1953, and a Ph.D. in psychology from McGill University in Montreal, Canada, in 1958.

In 1955, Ramakrishnan became head of the biochemistry department at the University of Baroda. Rajalakshmi often helped him and his stu-dents, but she was not given a position or a salary. Only in 1964, after the couple almost left Baroda for another institution that offered paying positions to both, did the university finally hire her. She was part of the university's foods and nutrition department until 1967. She then joined her husband in the department of biochemistry, where she became a full professor in 1976.

Rajalakshmi found that most Indian nutrition courses and aid programs were based on American or European textbooks. They recommended foods such as beef, eggs, and milk, which were expensive or unavailable in India. She designed replacement programs that provided complete nutrition through familiar plant foods that poor Indians could purchase and prepare easily. She says that this sensible approach was "quite original and almost unique at the time." She and Ramakrishnan also showed that some nutrition standards of the earlier programs had been wrong. They proved that people could survive with less protein than had been thought, for instance.

Rajalakshmi headed Baroda's biochemistry department from 1984 to 1986, when she and Ramakrishnan retired. Since then her interests have included yoga and visiting her children in the United States. In the 1990s she and her husband moved to the United States. She says she is proud that in both her career and her personal life, "I have generally not compromised on principles and have stood up for what I consider right."

Further Reading

Rajalakshmi, R. "Autobiography of an Unknown Woman." In *Women Scientists: The Road to Liberation*, edited by Derek Richter, 185–210. London: Macmillan, 1982.

Yount, Lisa. *Twentieth-Century Women Scientists*. New York: Facts On File, 1996, 74–85.

✳ RICHARDS, ELLEN HENRIETTA SWALLOW

(1842–1911) *American Chemist*

Ellen Swallow Richards, the first woman graduate of the Massachusetts Institute of Technology (MIT), was one of the first scientists to use chemistry to check the purity of air, water, and food. She taught housewives how to use science to improve their families' health and was one of the founders of ecology, which studies interactions in the environment of living things.

Ellen Henrietta Swallow was born on December 3, 1842, in Dunstable, Massachusetts, the only child of Peter and Fannie Swallow. Her father was a schoolteacher, farmer, and storekeeper, and her mother also taught school. She wrote later that she was "born with a desire to go to college," but she had to endure years of what she called "Purgatory" before she saved enough money to enroll in 1868 at Vassar College in Poughkeepsie, New York. Her only complaint about Vassar was that, because of the common belief that women were too frail for arduous academic work, "they won't let us study enough." She was inspired by the astronomy classes of MARIA MITCHELL and the chemistry classes of Charles Farrar, and Farrar's insistence that chemistry be used to solve practical problems made her decide to major in that subject. She earned her B.A. in 1870.

Swallow decided to continue her education at the new Institute of Technology in Boston, which later became MIT. The college had never had a woman student, but officials told Swallow in December 1870 that she would be admitted as a special student in chemistry at no charge. She thought the college was recognizing her financial need, but she learned later that she had received free tuition so that the president "could say I was not a student, should any of the trustees or students make a fuss about my presence. Had I realized upon what basis I was taken," she added, "I would not have gone." Nonetheless, she was pleased to become "the first woman to be accepted at any 'scientific' school." She earned a B.S. in chemistry from MIT in 1873, as well as a master's degree from Vassar. She went on to complete the requirements for a doctorate, but MIT would not give her the degree because, she wrote, "the heads of the department did not wish a woman to receive the [university's] first D.S. in chemistry."

Swallow's friends on MIT's chemistry faculty included William R. Nichols, whom she assisted in an examination of the state's water supply for the Massachusetts State Board of Health that began in 1872. Biographer Robert Clarke says that Swallow's work on this survey made her "a preeminent international water scientist even before her graduation." She struck up an even closer relationship with Robert Hallowell Richards, the young head of the metallurgical and mining engineering laboratory, and they married in June 1875. Ellen Richards used her chemistry skills to help her husband, and he in turn encouraged her to continue her scientific career. For her analysis of metals in ores she was made the first woman member of the American Institute of Mining and Metallurgical Engineers in 1879.

In 1876 a chemistry laboratory for women opened at MIT, with John Ordway as its head and Richards as his unpaid assistant. She was made a paid instructor in chemistry two years later. When the lab closed in 1883 because women students were then allowed to use the same facilities as men, Richards feared she would no longer "have anything to do or anywhere to work," but the university opened the country's first institute in sanitary chemistry soon after, and she again became an assistant to William Nichols, who headed it. Her title became instructor in sanitary chemistry.

The laboratory's chief job was analyzing air, water, and food. Scientists were realizing the link between illness and pollution of these vital elements, and governments were starting to demand chemical analysis of them as a safeguard to public health. Richards wrote: "The day is not far distant when a city will be held as responsible for the purity of the air in its school-houses, the cleanliness of the water in its reservoirs, and the reliability of the food sold in its markets as it now is for the condition of its streets and bridges." With A. G. Woodman, she summarized her teachings on this subject in *Air, Water, and Food for Colleges*, published in 1900.

Richards supervised the laboratory during a new survey of Massachusetts water directed by Nichols's successor, Thomas M. Drown, between 1887 and 1889. She and her students showed that chlorine in fresh water had to come either from seawater or from human pollution and that the amount from seawater changed in a predictable way with changes in distance from the ocean. They made a "normal chlorine map" that showed how much chlorine a sample of clean water from anywhere in the state ought to contain. If a sample held more chlorine than this, the extra chlorine had to come from pollution. Richards thus established the world's first water purity tables and the first state water quality standards. She taught that "water rightly read is the interpreter of its own history," containing traces of every substance it has encountered.

During this same period the state Board of Health asked the MIT laboratory to analyze samples of groceries. Richards and her students found that many foods were adulterated, or mixed with nonfood substances such as sawdust. Some of these were hazardous to health. On her own time, Richards also was a consultant to industry, analyzing everything from water to wallpaper and soap to saucepans. For instance, she studied oils used in factories to find out which ones were likely to produce spontaneous combustion. She virtually eliminated this fire hazard by recommending the use of mineral oils instead of animal oils.

From about 1890 on, Richards concentrated on the practical education of homemakers. She believed that many medical and social problems could be solved or avoided if housewives learned how to make food, water, and air clean and healthful. She redesigned her own home as a demonstration laboratory. In 1890 she and others also opened the New England Kitchen, which sold nutritious, inexpensive meals and let people watch the meals being prepared. The poor families who bought the meals did not always like the kitchen's "Yankee" cuisine (one old woman grumbled, "I don't want to eat what's good for me; I'd ruther eat what I'd ruther"), but the idea of the demonstration kitchen was widely copied, for instance at Jane Addams's famous Hull House.

Richards and others who shared her interest developed the idea of scientifically based household management into a new discipline called home economics. In 1908 they formed the American Home Economics Association, dedicated to "the improvement of living conditions in the home, the institutional household and the community." They chose Richards as the association's first president, an office she kept until 1910. She wrote many books, articles, and lectures on the subject.

Richards's understanding of the way interactions between the living and nonliving environment shape the life of living things led her to call in 1892 for "the christening of a new science" that she termed "oekology," from the Greek word for "household." Ernst Haeckel and some other European biologists proposed a similar idea at about the same time. The modern discipline of ecology echoes the latter scientists' focus on plants and animals, but Richards was more interested in the environment of human beings. The claim that Richards "founded ecology" is somewhat exaggerated, but both the environmental and the consumer education movements descend in part from her work.

Ellen Richards died on March 30, 1911, of heart disease at the age of 68. Many prizes, funds, and buildings were named for her, including the Ellen H. Richards Fund for research in sanitary chemistry at MIT and Pennsylvania College's Ellen H. Richards Institute for research to improve standards of living. Her best memorial, however, was the improved health in American homes and cities that resulted from her reforms.

Further Reading

Clarke, Robert. *Ellen Swallow: The Woman Who Founded Ecology*. Chicago: Follett, 1973.

Hunt, Caroline L. *The Life of Ellen H. Richards*. Boston: Whitcomb & Barrows, 1912.

James, Janet Wilson. "Richards, Ellen Henrietta Swallow." In *Notable American Women, 1607–1950, vol. III: P–Z*, edited by Edward T. James, 143–146. Cambridge, Mass.: The Belknap Press of Harvard University Press, 1971.

Stern, Madeleine B. *We the Women: Career First of Nineteenth-Century America*. Artemis: 1974, 118–144.

Trescott, Martha Moore. "Women in the Intellectual Development of Engineering: A Study in Persistence and Systems Thought." In *Women of Science: Righting the Record*, edited by G. Kass-Simon and Patricia Farnes, 150–156. Bloomington: Indiana University Press, 1990.

✳ ROBINSON, JULIA BOWMAN
(1919–1985)   *American Mathematician*

Julia Bowman Robinson made advances in logic and number theory and helped to find the answer to what an eminent mathematician called one of the greatest unsolved problems in mathematics. She was born in St. Louis, Missouri, on December 8, 1919, the second daughter of Ralph Bowers and Helen Hall Bowman. Her father owned a machine tool and equipment company. She grew up in Arizona and San Diego, California, with her sisters, father, and stepmother (her mother died when Julia was two).

At the University of California at Berkeley, Bowman for the first time found others who shared her interest in mathematics. One was a young professor, Raphael M. Robinson, with whom she took long walks. They married in late 1941. By then Julia had obtained a bachelor's (1940) and a master's degree (1941). She would have liked to raise a family, but

a childhood illness had seriously damaged her heart, and she learned that pregnancy might kill her. Her husband reminded her that "there was still mathematics," and she resumed her studies, obtaining a Ph.D. in 1948.

As a consultant for the Rand Corporation in 1949–50, Robinson proved that in a "zero sum game"—a game in which there are two players, one of whom must win and one lose—a situation in which each player follows a strategy that is the average of the values of the previous two moves would converge toward a solution of the game (that is, one of the players would win). Mathematician David Gale told Robinson he thought her theorem was the most important one in elementary game theory.

Robinson's chief achievement, however, concerned the 10th in a list of unsolved mathematical

University of California at Berkeley mathematician Julia Robinson helped to solve a problem described by an eminent mathematician as one of greatest unsolved problems in mathematics.
(Courtesy American Mathematical Society)

problems made by German mathematician David Hilbert around 1900. The problem was to find out whether one could determine whether a diophantine equation had a solution that could be expressed in integers (whole numbers). In 1961, working with Martin Davis and Hilary Putnam, Robinson proposed that this problem could be approached by studying exponentiation (numbers increasing by a power) and polynomials (equations that use both multipliers and powers).

Early in 1970, Robinson learned that a young Russian, Yuri Matijasevich, had used her work to solve the problem. As she had suspected, the solution was negative: One cannot determine whether a diophantine equation has an integer solution. Far from being angry that Matijasevich had arrived at the solution before her, she wrote to him: "It is beautiful, it is wonderful. If you really are 22 [he was], I am especially pleased to think that when I first made the conjecture [that the answer to the problem was no], you were a baby and I just had to wait for you to grow up!"

Robinson was awarded many honors for her part in solving Hilbert's problem. In 1975 she became the first woman mathematician elected to the National Academy of Sciences, and Berkeley made her a full professor even though her health kept her from taking a full teaching load. She was also elected a member of the American Academy of Arts and Sciences. She received a MacArthur "genius" fellowship in 1982, and in 1983–1984 she was the American Mathematical Society's first woman president. Her heart was repaired in 1961, but she died of leukemia on July 30, 1985.

Robinson once wrote: "Rather than being remembered as the first woman this or that, I would prefer to be remembered, as a mathematician should, simply for the theorems I have proved and the problems I have solved." She is sure to be remembered in both ways.

Further Reading

Henderson, Harry. *Modern Mathematicians.* New York: Facts On File, 1996, 102–111.

Koppy, Joan Fisher. "Julia Bowman Robinson." In *Celebrating Women in Mathematics and Science*, edited by Miriam P. Cooney, 159–170. Reston, Va.: National Council of Teachers of Mathematics, 1996.

Reid, Constance. "Julia Robinson." In *More Mathematical People*, edited by Donald J. Albers, Gerald L. Alexanderson, and Constance Reid, 262–280. Boston: Harcourt Brace Jovanovich, 1990.

❋ RUBIN, VERA COOPER
(1928–) *American Astronomer*

Vera Rubin has made several discoveries that produced major changes in astronomers' view of the structure of the universe. She was born Vera Cooper in Philadelphia on July 23, 1928, one of Philip and Rose Cooper's two daughters. Her father was an electrical engineer. From childhood on, she has said, "I just couldn't look at the sky without wondering how anyone could do anything but study the stars."

Cooper studied astronomy at Vassar College in New York, graduating in 1948. There she met Robert Rubin, a young physicist studying at Cornell. They married just after her graduation, and she followed him to Cornell for her master's degree work even though its astronomy department was small.

For her thesis project, Rubin studied the motion of galaxies. She found that galaxies at about the same apparent distance from earth were moving faster in some parts of the sky than in others, a result that no astronomical theories could explain. Rubin's work earned her degree in 1951, but when she presented it at a meeting of the American Astronomical Society, she says she was all but politely hooted off the stage. She and others, including SANDRA FABER, have since confirmed it.

Soon afterward, the Rubins moved to Washington, D.C. Vera stayed home at first to take care of her young son (she later had a daughter and two more sons), but she missed astronomy so much that she burst into tears each time she read an issue of the *Astrophysical Journal.* Her husband urged her to begin studying for her doctorate at nearby Georgetown University.

Rubin's project this time used mathematics to determine the distribution of galaxies in the local part of the universe. Its result was just as unsettling as her earlier conclusion. Galaxies were supposed to be distributed evenly in space, but Rubin found that this was not so. More recently, astronomers such as MARGARET GELLER have confirmed by observation that the universe has a "lumpy" structure, in which clusters of galaxies are separated by nearly empty voids. The reason for this still is not known.

Rubin received her Ph.D. from Georgetown in 1954 and remained on its faculty for 11 years, meanwhile raising her family. In 1965 she joined the Department of Terrestrial Magnetism (DTM), part of the Carnegie Institution of Washington, where she still works. Despite its name, the DTM sponsors projects of many types, including astronomical ones.

Around 1970, Rubin and another DTM astronomer, Kent Ford, measured how fast stars in different parts of Andromeda, the nearest full-size

Astronomer Vera Rubin's research at the Carnegie Institution of Washington's Department of Terrestrial Magnetism has helped to show that the universe is "lumpy" and consists mostly of matter that no one can see or, so far, identify. She is shown here with a machine that helps her detect small changes in galaxies' light. These changes tell her how fast different parts of the galaxies are rotating.
(Courtesy Vera C. Rubin and Carnegie Institution of Washington)

galaxy to ours, were rotating around the galaxy's center. They assumed that most of the galaxy's mass was near its center, as most of its light was. If this was so, gravity should cause stars near the center of the galaxy to move faster than those near the edge. Rubin and Ford found, however, that stars near the edges of the galaxy were moving as fast, sometimes faster, than those near the center.

Rubin and Ford showed in the mid-1970s that other galaxies follow this same pattern. Indeed, some stars in the outer parts of galaxies move so fast that they ought to escape the galaxies' gravity and fly off into space, yet that does not happen. This suggests that the galaxies contain a large amount of mass that no one can see. Rubin and others have since confirmed that 90 percent of the universe is made up of what has come to be called "dark

matter." No one knows what this material is.

Rubin's startling and important discoveries have won her election to the National Academy of Sciences and, in 1993, the National Medal of Science, the U.S. government's highest science award. In 1996 she also was awarded the Gold Medal of London's Royal Astronomical Society. Rubin was the first woman to receive this medal since CAROLINE HERSCHEL.

Further Reading

Bartusiak, Marcia. "The Woman Who Spins the Stars." *Discover*, October 1990, 88–94.

Rubin, Vera. *Bright Galaxies, Dark Matters*. New York: Springer-Verlag, 1996.

Yount, Lisa. *Contemporary Women Scientists*. New York: Facts On File, 1994, 83–93.

S

☀ SABIN, FLORENCE RENA
(1871–1953)   *American Medical Researcher*

Florence Sabin succeeded in three different careers: teaching, research, and—after her retirement, in her seventies—public health reform. She was born in Central City, Colorado, on November 9, 1871. Her mother, the former Serena Miner, had been a teacher. Florence spent her first years in small mining towns where her father, George K. Sabin, worked as an engineer, but the family moved to Denver in 1875. Three years later Serena Sabin died, and Florence and her older sister, Mary, went to live with relatives in Chicago and, later, Vermont. Florence went to Smith College, from which she graduated with a B.S. in mathematics and zoology in 1893.

After teaching and saving her money for three years, Sabin enrolled in Johns Hopkins Medical School, one of the few good medical schools that admitted women, and earned her M.D. in 1900. She wanted to do research, and Franklin Paine Mall, the head of Hopkins's anatomy department, became her mentor. While still a medical student she prepared a three-dimensional model of a baby's mid- and lower brain more accurate than any made before. Her 1901 laboratory manual based on this model, *An Atlas of the Medulla and Midbrain,* became a standard textbook.

In 1902, Sabin became Mall's assistant, the first woman member of the Hopkins medical faculty. She was made an associate professor of anatomy in 1907. She became a full professor in 1917, the first woman to achieve that rank at Johns Hopkins, but this title was a consolation prize for not making her head of the anatomy department on Mall's death, a position that Mall's wife believed that he himself would have wanted her to have. Mall's wife said that "only the lingering prejudice against women . . . prevented Sabin's well-merited advancement."

Sabin's most important research at Johns Hopkins concerned the lymphatic system, a network of vessels that carries a milky fluid called lymph. Lymph contains chemicals and cells that belong to the immune system. Anatomists had thought that the lymphatic system developed before birth from spaces in the tissues, separately from the circulatory system, but Sabin showed that lymph vessels budded from veins. She summarized her findings in a 1913 book, *The Method and Growth of the Lymphatic System.*

During her years at Hopkins, Sabin also used a technique for staining living cells that she had learned in Germany to investigate the origin of

Florence Sabin's research at Johns Hopkins Medical School and the Rockefeller Institute showed how the blood and immune systems develop before birth and revealed new facts about the bacteria that cause tuberculosis and their effects on the body. After her retirement from science and teaching she had a third career as a public health reformer in Colorado. This photo was taken around 1919.
(Courtesy Sophia Smith Collection, Smith College)

blood cells and blood vessels. She once stayed up all night watching the blood system develop in a chick embryo, ending with the embryo's heart making its first beat. She called it "the most exciting experience of my life."

Sabin was as well known for her teaching as for her research. She taught that "it is more important for the student to be able to find out something for himself than to memorize what someone else has said." She saw research as a way to improve teaching. "No one can be a really great educator unless he himself is an investigator," she said.

Simon Flexner, scientific director of the prestigious Rockefeller Institute (later Rockefeller University) in New York City, invited Sabin to join the institute in 1925 and set up a new department of cellular studies. He called her "the greatest living woman scientist and one of the foremost scientists of all time." She accepted, becoming the first woman to receive a full membership in the institute. There she did research on cells of the immune system and on the immune response to the microbe that caused tuberculosis. She also learned which chemicals in the microbe damaged the body.

Sabin retired from the Rockefeller Institute in 1938, at age 68, and went to live with her sister in Denver. Her third career began in 1944, when John Vivian, then governor of Colorado, invited her to head the subcommittee on health of the state's Post-War Planning Committee. Vivian may have chosen Sabin because he believed a report that described her as a "nice little old lady with her hair in a bun . . . who has spent her entire life in a laboratory, doesn't know anything about medicine on the outside, and won't give any trouble," but if so, he received a surprise. Later, Governor W. Lee Knous more accurately called her "Florence the atom bomb."

Sabin in fact had always been interested in public health. Far from rubber-stamping Colorado's existing health laws, she launched into a thorough investigation that took her all over the state. She found that both the laws and their enforcement were woefully inadequate. The "little doctor," as she came to be known, then drafted a legislative program for public health reform, assembled piles of evidence to show the need for it, and hounded legislators and officials until they passed most of it in 1947. She made similar reforms in Denver when the city's mayor made her head of the Interim Board of Health and Hospitals in 1947 and, later, of the Department of Health and Welfare and of the permanent Board of Health and Hospitals.

Florence Sabin was one of the best known and most honored women scientists of her time. In 1924 she became the first woman president of the American Association of Anatomists, and a year later she received the even greater honor of becoming the first woman elected to the prestigious National Academy of Sciences. In the 1930s she received a host of honorary degrees and other awards from various colleges, including the National Achievement Award (1932) and the M. Carey Thomas Prize (1935). Finally, in 1951, she won the Albert and Mary Lasker Award for medical research, one of the highest awards in American science. Sabin stopped her public activities at the end of 1951 and spent the last years of her life caring for her ailing sister. Sabin died of a heart attack on October 3, 1953, just short of her 82nd birthday.

Further Reading

Bluemel, Elinor. *Florence Sabin: Colorado Woman of the Century.* Boulder: University of Colorado Press, 1959.

Brieger, Gert E. "Sabin, Florence Rena." In *Notable American Women: The Modern Period*, edited by Barbara Sicherman and Carol Hurd Green, 614–616. Cambridge, Mass.: The Belknap Press of Harvard University Press, 1980.

Kronstadt, Janet. *Florence Sabin.* Broomall, Pa.: Chelsea House, 1990.

McMaster, Philip D., and Michael Heidelberger. "Florence Rena Sabin." *Biographical Memoirs of the National Academy of Sciences* 34 (1960), 271–319.

✳ SARUHASHI, KATSUKO
(1920–) *Japanese Geologist and Chemist*

Katsuko Saruhashi studied carbon dioxide levels in seawater long before people began to suspect that this gas might increase temperatures on earth. She also tracked the spread of radioactive debris from atomic bomb tests.

Saruhashi was born in Tokyo, Japan, on March 22, 1920. While she was a student at Toho University, from which she graduated in 1943, she met government meteorologist Yasuo Miyake, who became her friend and mentor. After World War II

ended, he hired her as a research assistant in his new Geochemical Research Laboratory, part of the Japanese Transport Ministry's Meteorological Research Institute.

Around 1950, Miyake suggested that Saruhashi measure the concentration of carbon dioxide (CO_2) in seawater. "Now everyone is concerned about carbon dioxide, but at the time nobody was," Saruhashi says. Indeed, she had to design most of her own techniques for measuring the gas. Her project earned her a doctor of science degree from the University of Tokyo in 1957, the first doctorate in chemistry that the university gave to a woman.

Katsuko Saruhashi studied carbon dioxide in seawater long before people became concerned about the role of this gas in global warming. She also measured the spread of fallout from atomic bomb tests in the 1950s. She established a prize to honor outstanding Japanese women scientists and is currently executive director of the Geochemistry Research Association. She is seen here in her office in 1995.
(Courtesy Katsuko Saruhashi)

In the early 1950s the United States, the Soviet Union, and several other nations tested nuclear bombs at remote sites, filling the air with radioactive debris. Concern about such fallout led the Japanese government to ask Miyake's laboratory in 1954 to measure the amount of radioactive material reaching Japan in rain and the amount found in seawater off the country's coast. Miyake put Saruhashi in charge of this project, which she says was the first of its kind. She found that fallout from an American bomb test on the Pacific island of Bikini reached Japan in seawater a year and a half after the test. She later measured fallout in other parts of the world as well. Evidence gathered by Saruhashi and others helped protesters persuade the United States and the Soviet Union to give up above-ground tests of nuclear weapons in 1963.

Saruhashi also continued her measurements of carbon dioxide in seawater, finding that water in the Pacific releases about twice as much CO_2 into the atmosphere as it absorbs from the air. (There is about 60 times more CO_2 dissolved in seawater than in air.) This result suggests that the ocean is unlikely to weaken possible global warming by absorbing excess CO_2.

Saruhashi was made director of the Geochemical Research Laboratory in 1979. She retired from this post a year later. In 1990, after Miyake's death, she became executive director of the Geochemistry Research Association in Tokyo, which Miyake founded in 1972. She still held this post in 1998. Honors she has received include election to the Science Council of Japan in 1980 (she was its first woman member). She won the Miyake Prize for geochemistry in 1985 and the Tanaka Prize from the Society of Sea Water Sciences in 1993.

When Saruhashi retired from the directorship of the Geochemical Laboratory, her coworkers gave a gift of 5,000,000 yen (about $50,000). She used the money as an initial fund to establish the Saruhashi Prize, given each year since 1981 to a Japanese woman making important contributions to the natural sciences. Its first recipient was population geneticist TOMOKO OHTA. Saruhashi says the prize "highlight[s] the capabilities of women scientists. . . . Each winner

has been not only a successful researcher but . . . a wonderful human being as well."

Further Reading

Normile, Dennis. "A Prize of One's Own." *Science*, April 16, 1993, 424.
Yount, Lisa. *Twentieth-Century Women Scientists.* New York: Facts On File, 1996, 50–58.

✳ SCOTT, CHARLOTTE ANGAS
(1858–1931) *American Mathematician*

Charlotte Scott taught mathematics to generations of Bryn Mawr students and made important contributions to algebraic geometry. She was born in Lincoln, England, on June 8, 1858, to the Reverend Caleb Scott and his wife, Eliza Ann. Her father was the principal of a small college as well as a Congregationalist minister.

Scott enrolled in Girton College, a women's college of Cambridge University, in 1876. She completed her studies with honors in 1880, scoring eighth highest in the difficult tripos examination, though her score was not officially announced because she was a woman. She taught mathematics at Girton for several years afterward, meanwhile continuing her own studies at the University of London. She earned a bachelor of science in 1882 and a doctorate in 1885.

In the year Scott obtained her doctorate, M. Carey Thomas, the first head of Bryn Mawr College in Pennsylvania, invited her to head the college's mathematics department. Scott accepted, becoming the only woman on Bryn Mawr's six-person faculty. She taught there for 40 years, earning the department a worldwide reputation and attracting such mathematical stars as ANNA PELL WHEELER and EMMY NOETHER.

Scott also made important contributions as a theoretical mathematician. In an early text, *An Introductory Account of Certain Modern Ideas in Plane Analytical Geometry* (1894), she treated point and line coordinates together to show the principles they had in common. She later helped to develop the new field of algebraic geometry by showing the "geometrical reality" beneath singularities and intersections of plane algebraic curves. She proved that complicated singularities could be broken down into clusters of simpler ones. Her peers ranked her 14th among the world's top 93 mathematicians.

Scott helped to found the American Mathematical Society in 1894, serving on its council (the only woman member) from 1894 to 1897 and as its first woman vice president in 1906. She retired from Bryn Mawr in 1925 and returned to England. She died at Cambridge on November 8, 1931.

Further Reading

Green, Judy, and Jeanne Laduke. "Contributors to American Mathematics: An Overview and Selection." In *Women of Science: Righting the Record*, edited by G. Kass-Simon and Patricia Farnes, 125–127. Bloomington: Indiana University Press, 1990.

Lehr, Marguerite. "Scott, Charlotte Angas." In *Notable American Women, 1607–1950, vol. III: P–Z*, edited by Edward T. James, 249–250. Cambridge, Mass.: The Belknap Press of Harvard University Press, 1971.

✳ SEIBERT, FLORENCE BARBARA

(1897–1991) *American Microbiologist and Biochemist*

Florence Seibert showed how even "pure" water could cause illness. She also purified the substance used in the skin test by which doctors screened people for tuberculosis, greatly increasing the test's accuracy. She was born on October 6, 1897, in Eaton, Pennsylvania, to George and Barbara Seibert, the middle of their three children. Her father owned a rug business.

A childhood attack of infantile paralysis, or polio, left Florence with a severe limp. When she enrolled at Goucher College in Baltimore, her father stayed there for a week, thinking he might need to take her home again, but Florence thrived. "I learned . . . that I was not an invalid but was able to stand on my own two feet with a chance to make a

contribution to the world," she wrote in her autobiography, *Pebbles on the Hill of a Scientist.*

Seibert studied mathematics, biology, and chemistry at Goucher, graduating in 1918. After working briefly for a paper mill, she went on to study biochemistry at Yale. As her doctoral project, she investigated the puzzling fact that injection of certain supposedly harmless substances sometimes caused fevers in humans or animals. At first she deepened the mystery when she found that even injections of distilled water, which should have been perfectly pure, could cause fever. This could pose a serious health problem, since medicines were often dissolved in distilled water before being injected.

Seibert learned that, even though the heat of distillation killed bacteria in the water, poisons made by the microbes remained in the steam and sometimes dripped back into the water. These substances caused the fevers. A trap that kept steam droplets from reentering the water solved the problem. Seibert won the Ricketts Prize in 1924 and the John Elliott Memorial Award from the American Association of Blood Banks in 1962 for this early work.

After earning her Ph.D. in 1923, Seibert transferred to the University of Chicago, where she worked in the Ricketts Laboratory, eventually becoming an assistant professor in biochemistry. She joined the laboratory of Esmond Long, working part-time with him and part-time at the Sprague Memorial Institute, and moved with him in 1932 to the Henry Phipps Institute in Philadelphia, part of the University of Pennsylvania.

Most of Seibert's research during her years with Long was devoted to purifying tuberculin, a substance made by tuberculosis bacteria that was used in a skin test to screen people for that then-common disease. "Old tuberculin," as the crude bacterial preparation was called, contained many impurities, and the amount of actual tuberculin in it varied from batch to batch. The skin test could be dependable only if tuberculin was purified, and Florence Seibert devoted 35 years to this painstaking task. Two new techniques for separating compounds in a mixture that she learned about in Sweden, high-speed centrifugation and electrophoresis, eventually allowed her to perfect a purified protein derivative (PPD) of tuberculin that became the standard for the United States in 1941 and for the world in 1952.

In 1938, Seibert became the first woman to receive the Trudeau Medal of the National Tuberculosis Association. Other awards included the First Achievement Award of the American Association of University Women (1943) and the Garvan Medal of the American Chemical Society. Seibert became a full professor at the University of Pennsylvania in 1955 and retired three years later to St. Petersburg, Florida, with her younger sister, Mabel. She continued research in her home on microorganisms associated with cancers in mice and rats.

Seibert was inducted into the National Women's Hall of Fame in 1990, when she was 92 years old. She died the following year.

Further Reading

O'Hern, Elizabeth Moot. *Profiles of Pioneer Women Scientists.* Washington, D.C.: Acropolis Books, 1985, 57–67.

Seibert, Florence B. *Pebbles on the Hill of a Scientist.* St. Petersburg, Fla.: Petersburg Printing Co., 1968.

Yost, Edna. *American Women of Science.* New York: Lippincott, 1955, 177–195.

✳ SIMPSON, JOANNE MALKUS
(1923–) *American Meteorologist*

Joanne Simpson, the first woman to earn a Ph.D. in meteorology, has chased hurricanes in planes; studied ways to increase rain and calm storms; and worked out valuable models of clouds, storms, and heat balance in the tropics. She was born Joanne Malkus on March 23, 1923, in Boston to a newspaper editor father and a reporter mother. In a 1973 speech she described her childhood as "intellectual but unhappy," making her determined to "get somewhere and be somebody."

Joanne learned meteorology at the University of Chicago as part of a special training program during World War II. She taught the subject to military recruits while continuing her own education, earning a B.A. in 1943 and an M.S. in 1945. Unlike other women who learned meteorology during the war, she refused to leave this "men's field" when the conflict ended. In 1949 she became the first woman to gain a doctorate in meteorology (from the University of Chicago). While working on her Ph.D., she also was an instructor at the Illinois Institute of Technology, married, and was the mother of a young child. She divorced soon afterward.

Joanne remained at the Illinois Institute of Technology until 1951, eventually becoming an assistant professor. She then worked at the Woods Hole Oceanographic Institution until 1960. There her main research subjects were winds, especially those involved in fierce tropical storms such as hurricanes, and the way that the movement of heat in the tropical atmosphere contributes to such storms. She married again and had three more children, though in time this marriage also failed. In 1960 she became a full professor at the University of California at Los Angeles (UCLA).

Joanne became the director of the National Oceanic and Atmospheric Administration's experimental meteorology laboratory in Coral Gables, Florida, in 1964 and remained there until 1974. She has said she forged this laboratory "out of nothing . . . on a shoestring." She married fellow meteorologist Robert Simpson in 1965 and hoped to do research with him on the project, but government nepotism rules blocked that plan.

In the late 1960s and early 1970s Simpson did research on cumulus clouds, the large, thick clouds that produce rain. She created the first mathematical, one-dimensional computer model of such clouds and tested it by observation. She also experimented with cloud seeding, a technique for increasing rainfall, and continued her study of hurricanes, often personally flying research planes into their centers.

Simpson became the Corcoran Professor of Environmental Sciences at the University of Virginia in 1974 and kept that post until 1979. During that time she also worked with her husband in a private company, Simpson Weather Associates. She used extensive new data to refine her hypothesis about heat flow in the tropical ocean and atmosphere.

Since 1979, Simpson has worked for the Goddard Space Flight Center in Greenbelt, Maryland, first as head of the center's Severe Storms Branch and then, beginning in 1988, as the chief scientist of its Meteorology and Earth Science Directorate. She was also project scientist for the Tropical Rainfall Measuring Mission from 1986 until the mission was launched in 1997. She has continued her studies of tropical storms and extended her cloud modeling to show how clouds merge into systems that produce over 90 percent of tropical rainfall.

Simpson has won a number of awards during her career. They include the Meisinger Award of the American Meteorological Society (1962), a gold medal from the Department of Commerce (1972), NASA's Exceptional Scientific Achievement Medal (1982), the first Nordberg Award for Earth Sciences (1994), and a NASA Outstanding Leadership medal. She was president of the American Meteorological Society in 1989.

Further Reading

Noble, Iris. *Contemporary Women Scientists.* New York: Julian Messner, 1979, 31–48.

Simpson, Joanne. "Meteorologist: Joanne Simpson." In *Women and Success: The Anatomy of Achievement,* edited by Ruth B. Kundsin, 62–67. New York: William Morrow, 1974.

✳ SITHOLE-NIANG, IDAH
(1957–) *Zimbabwean Biochemist and Geneticist*

Idah Sithole-Niang is developing ways to use genetic engineering to improve food crops in her native Zimbabwe. She was born in that southeast African country on October 2, 1957. She won scholarships to study at the University of London, where she learned biochemistry and earned a B.S. in 1982, and at Michigan State University in Lansing, where she earned a Ph.D. in 1988.

In Michigan, Sithole did genetic studies of both viruses and plants. After she became a lecturer in biochemistry at the University of Zimbabwe in 1992, she combined these two subjects, focusing on viruses that infect plants. The type of virus she has studied the most, the potyvirus, affects cowpeas, a legume that is one of Zimbabwe's chief food crops. She has identified and worked out the structure of genes that code for the chemicals that make up the potyvirus, and she hopes to insert some of these genes into cowpeas and thereby make them resistant to the virus.

In another set of experiments, Sithole has studied a gene that could be introduced into cowpeas to make them resistant to a common family of herbicides called atrazines. Maize (corn) is naturally resistant to these herbicides, which are sprayed on cornfields to control weeds. If cowpeas were also resistant to atrazine, they could be grown in fields with maize, both enriching the soil and providing a cheap source of food.

Sithole is married to Cheikh I. Niang, and they have one son. She has received a number of fellowships and awards, including the U.S. Agency for International Development Fellowship (1983–88) and a Rockefeller Foundation Biotechnology Career Fellowship (1992–95). In the late 1990s, Sithole-Niang, as she began calling herself in 1996, has broadened her interests to include policy issues such as the safety of genetically engineered organisms. She is a member of the Interim Biosafety Board and has been updating biosafety guidelines and regulations for Zimbabwe.

Further Reading

Sithole, Idah. "Women and Science in Zimbabwe: Some Issues that Still Persist." In *Science in Africa: Women Leading from Strength,* 27–36, 173. Washington, D.C.: American Association for the Advancement of Science, 1993.

✳ SLYE, MAUD CAROLINE
(1869–1954) *American Geneticist and Cancer Researcher*

By breeding thousands of mice, Maud Slye showed that some cancers can be inherited. She was born to James and Florence Slye in Minneapolis on February

8, 1869, the middle of their three children. Her father was a lawyer. Maud grew up in Iowa, but her mother moved the family back to Minnesota when her father died, just after Maud finished high school.

Slye worked as a stenographer in St. Paul for almost 10 years before saving enough money to continue her education. She entered the University of Chicago in 1895 but had to leave for health reasons after three years. She finished her bachelor's degree at Brown University in 1899.

Slye taught at a teacher's college in Rhode Island most of the time until 1908, when Charles Otis Whitman, a professor she had met earlier, invited her to return to the University of Chicago as a graduate assistant. She became interested in the genetics of cancer after observing that all the members of a herd of cows that developed a type of eye tumor came from the same ranch and therefore probably were related. She investigated this subject in laboratory mice, some strains of which had high rates of cancer.

During her lifetime of research, Slye bred some 150,000 mice. She took exceptional care of her animals, even skimping on her own meals to feed them when funding was scarce. Her laboratory was called a "mouse utopia." Her funding improved after 1911, when she joined the University of Chicago's Sprague Memorial Institute. In 1919 she became director of the university's Cancer Laboratory, and in 1926 she became an associate professor of pathology.

Cancer genetics has proved far more complicated than the picture Slye painted; she thought that only one or, at most, two genes were involved in the disease. Still, her work was important because it showed clearly that a tendency to develop cancer could be inherited, which many researchers of her time had doubted. She won several honors for it, including gold medals from the American Medical Association (1914) and the American Radiological Society (1922). She also won the University of Chicago's Ricketts Prize in 1915. Slye retired in 1944 and died on September 17, 1954, of heart disease.

Further Reading
McCoy, J. J. *The Cancer Lady: Maud Slye and Her Heredity Studies.* Nashville: T. Nelson, 1977.
Parascandola, John. "Slye, Maud Caroline." In *Notable American Women: The Modern Period*, edited by Barbara Sicherman and Carol Hurd Green, 651–652. Cambridge, Mass.: The Belknap Press of Harvard University Press, 1980.

✳ SOMERVILLE, MARY FAIRFAX
(1780–1872) *British Mathematician*

In spite of determined attempts to block her education, Mary Somerville learned enough mathematics and science to explain complicated theories to a popular audience. She was born to Sir William and Margaret Fairfax on December 26, 1780, in Jedburgh, Scotland, but grew up in the seaside village of Burntisland. Her father, a vice admiral in the British navy, was often away from home. The large Fairfax family had little money.

As a child, Mary was free to roam the shores and fields around her home except for one "utterly wretched" year in a girls' boarding school, where she felt equally confined by torturous clothing and boring memorization. She led an active social life in her teen years, even becoming known as the "Rose of Jedburgh" because of her beauty. Yearning for something more was stirred one day when, as she recounted in her memoirs, she spotted a mathematical puzzle in a fashion magazine that contained "strange-looking lines mixed with letters, chiefly *X*s and *Y*s." A friend explained, "It's a kind of arithmetic; they call it Algebra." Another chance remark led her to geometry. She had to ask her brother's tutor to buy her books on these subjects because it was not considered proper for a young woman to enter a bookstore.

After Mary obtained her books, her parents tried to stop her from studying them because, like many people of their time, they feared that too much intellectual effort could harm a woman's physical and mental health. ("We shall have Mary in a straightjacket one of these days," her father worried.)

Like SOPHIE GERMAIN's parents, they tried to stop their daughter from studying at night by taking away her supply of candles. Mary, however, had memorized the formulas she wanted to work on and simply lay in the dark, solving problems in her head.

In 1804, Mary married Samuel Greig, a distant cousin who was a captain in the Russian navy. They had two sons. Greig died three years after the marriage, and Mary and the boys returned to Burntisland. Her family still considered her "eccentric and foolish," but as a widow she had more money and independence than before and could pursue learning more openly.

Mary married another cousin, William Somerville, in 1812. Unlike Greig, Somerville, an army surgeon, supported his wife's educational ambitions. After he became head of the Army Medical Department in 1816 and they moved to London, he introduced her to leading scientists of the day. They had three daughters, one of whom died young.

Mary Somerville did a few experiments in physics and wrote scientific papers during this period. One paper, which her husband presented to the prestigious Royal Society (since women could not attend its meetings) in 1826, associated magnetism with ultraviolet light from the sun. Though later shown to be incorrect, Somerville's papers were well received. Still, she concluded that she lacked originality as a scientist, a condition she unfortunately believed was true of all women. "I have perseverance and intelligence but no genius," she wrote. "That spark from heaven is not granted to the [female] sex."

In 1827, Lord Henry Brougham, head of an educational group called the Society for the Diffusion of Useful Knowledge, asked Mary Somerville to write a translation and explanation of Pierre Laplace's *Mécanique céleste* (*Celestial Mechanics*), an influential but difficult work that summarized what was known about the mathematics of gravity. Published in 1831 as *The Mechanisms of the Heavens*, the book that resulted was a great success. Laplace himself said that Somerville was the only woman, and one of the few people of either gender, who understood his work. The book's lengthy preface, written by Somerville and republished on its own in 1832,

explained the mechanical principles that governed the solar system and the mathematics behind Laplace's ideas. This included differential and integral calculus, for which she provided original proofs and diagrams. The book remained a college text for nearly 100 years.

In 1834, Somerville published a second book, *On the Connexion of the Physical Sciences*, a summary of current scientific ideas that showed the relationships among seemingly different fields. "In all [physical sciences] there exists such a bond of union, that proficiency cannot be attained in any one without knowledge of others," she wrote in the book's preface. The book went through 10 revised editions. A remark in one, suggesting that unusual features in the orbit of the planet Uranus might be caused by an as-yet-unknown planet that lay beyond, led John Couch Adams to calculate the planet's orbit, which resulted in the discovery of Neptune.

Somerville's third book, *Physical Geography*, was published in 1848. It described new ideas in geology, including the belief that the earth was extremely old. It became the most popular of her books, though some critics denounced Somerville as "godless" for agreeing with scientists who said that the earth was much older than the age calculated from the Bible.

Somerville wrote one more book, *Molecular and Microscopic Science*, which discussed advances in chemistry, physics, and biology. It was published in 1869, when she was 89 years old. The science in this book was outdated, however, and reviews were "kindly rather than laudative."

Somerville's books made her the best-known woman scientist of the 19th century. A bust of her was placed in the great hall of the British Royal Society in 1831, and she and CAROLINE HERSCHEL were both made honorary members of the Royal Astronomical Society—the first women to achieve this status—in 1835. In that same year, Somerville received a lifetime pension from the king. The British Royal Geographical Society and the Italian Geographic Society both gave her gold medals.

The Somervilles had moved to Italy in the 1840s in the hope of improving William Somerville's health, and Mary stayed there after his death in 1865. She was still working on mathematics problems on the day she died, at Naples in 1872, at the age of 92. In 1879 a women's college at Oxford University was named for her.

Further Reading

Osen, Lynn M. *Women in Mathematics.* Cambridge, Mass.: MIT Press, 1974, 95–116.

Ogilvie, Marilyn Bailey. *Women in Science: Antiquity Through the Nineteenth Century.* Cambridge, Mass.: MIT Press, 1986, 161–166.

Patterson, Elizabeth C. *Mary Somerville and the Cultivation of Science, 1815–1848.* Norwell, Mass.: Kluwer Academic Publications, 1983.

Somerville, Mary. *Personal Reflections, from Early Life to Old Age, of Mary Somerville.* New York: AMS Press, 1975.

✳ STEVENS, NETTIE MARIA
(1861–1912) *American Geneticist*

Nettie Stevens was one of two scientists who discovered what determines whether a living thing will be male or female. She was born in Cavendish, Vermont, to Ephraim and Julia Stevens on July 7, 1861. Her father was a carpenter. After earning a credential from Westfield Normal School in 1883, she spent the first part of her adult life as a teacher and librarian. Eventually, however, she decided on a career in research. She enrolled at Stanford University, in California, in 1896, earning a bachelor's degree in 1899 and a master's degree in physiology a year later.

While doing doctoral research at Bryn Mawr, Stevens met genetics pioneer Thomas Hunt Morgan and became interested in this subject herself. Morgan helped her win a fellowship to study overseas. She earned her doctorate in 1903 and then joined the faculty of Bryn Mawr, rising to the rank of associate professor and becoming beloved as a teacher. She told one student, "How could you think your questions would bother me? They never will, so long as I keep my enthusiasm for biology; and that, I hope, will be as long as I live."

Nettie Stevens, seen here pursuing research at the Stazione Zoologica in Naples, Italy, codiscovered in 1905 the genetic factor that determines whether a living thing will be male or female.
(Courtesy Bryn Mawr College Archives)

Geneticists were just beginning to associate the "factors" that controlled inheritance of traits, first described by Austrian monk Gregor Mendel in 1866, with threadlike bodies called chromosomes in the nucleus, or central body, of cells. In her most important research, Stevens observed that although all unfertilized eggs of the common mealworm contained the same 10 chromosomes, that was not true of this insect's sperm. One chromosome in some sperm cells, which she called X, resembled one seen in the egg. In other sperm cells, this chromosome was replaced by another, smaller one, which she termed Y. She speculated that if an egg was fertilized by a sperm carrying an X chromosome, the resulting offspring would be female. If the egg was fertilized by a sperm carrying a Y, the offspring would be male.

Stevens's discovery confirmed the link between chromosomes and inheritance as well as showing how gender is determined. She also proved that inheritance of gender followed the rules that Mendel had worked out. She published her results in 1905. So did Edmund B. Wilson, a better-known male scientist, who had made the same finding independently. The two are properly given equal credit for the discovery, although some books have ignored or downplayed Stevens's contribution.

Stevens later found similar chromosome differences in other insects, and other scientists confirmed her conclusions as well. She also made the important discovery that chromosomes exist in pairs. Edmund Wilson wrote that she was "not only the best of the women investigators, but one whose work will hold its own with that of any of the men of the same degree of advancement." Unfortunately, Stevens died of breast cancer on May 4, 1912, at the age of 51, limiting her late-blooming career to only 12 years.

Further Reading

Ogilvie, Marilyn Bailey, and Clifford J. Choquette. "Nettie Maria Stevens (1861–1912)." *Proceedings of the American Philosophical Society*, 125: 4 (August 1981), 292–311.

Ris, Hans. "Stevens, Nettie Maria." In *Notable American Women, 1607–1950, vol. III: P–Z*, edited by Edward T. James, 372–373. Cambridge, Mass.: The Belknap Press of Harvard University Press, 1971.

Veglahn, Nancy J. *Women Scientists*. New York: Facts On File, 1991, 15–25.

❋ STEWART, ALICE
(1906–   )   *British Medical Researcher*

Finding that X-raying pregnant women often led to leukemia in their children, Alice Stewart was the first scientist to show that low-level radiation could harm human health. Stewart was born into the large family of two physician parents in England, on October 4, 1906. (Being one of many children, she told interviewer Gail Vines, meant that she "learn[ed] not to mind about battles.") She earned a master's degree in 1930 and an M.D. in 1934 from Cambridge University.

Aided by the demand for women workers created by World War II, Stewart, then married and the mother of two children, joined the Nuffield Department of Clinical Medicine at Cambridge's rival university, Oxford. What she calls her "semi-ingenuity in thinking up things" helped her devise ways to protect the health of workers in several war-related industries. As a result, she became the youngest woman ever to be made a fellow of the Royal College of Physicians.

Soon after the war ended, Stewart found herself the head of Oxford's new department of social medicine (public health)—just as the university cut off most of the department's funding. "If I'd been a man, I would never have stood it," she told Vines, "but being a woman I didn't have all that number of choices." Looking for a high-profile project that might restore support, she decided to find out why unusually large numbers of young children were dying of leukemia. She asked medical officers all over England to interview mothers of children with cancer and of healthy children of the same age. The interviews showed that the mothers of sick children were twice as likely to have been X-rayed during pregnancy as the mothers of healthy ones. "That set the jackpot going and . . . has kept me in the business of low-level radiation ever since."

When Stewart issued her first report in 1956, she says, "I was unpopular . . . because . . . X-rays were a favourite toy of the medical profession." She extended her work into what became the Oxford Survey of Childhood Cancers, which eventually listed 22,400 childhood cancer deaths from all over Britain between 1953 and 1979. When the larger sample confirmed her first findings, she told *Ms.* interviewer Amy Raphael, "my research practically brought prenatal X rays to a halt."

Stewart retired from Oxford around 1976 and moved to the University of Birmingham, where she is still a senior research fellow. In the mid-1980s she and collaborator George Kneale, supported by a $2 million grant from the Three Mile Island Public Health Fund, investigated the effects of radiation on American nuclear plant workers. They found, among other things, that the chances of developing cancer from low-level exposure increase greatly once workers pass the age of 50. Some authorities have questioned Stewart's findings, but in 1986 she won the Right Livelihood Award, sometimes called the "alternative Nobel Prize," and the *New York Times* once called her "the Energy Department's most influential and feared scientific critic." Stewart told Gail Vines that her secret weapon is that "I know that I am going to be right." To Amy Raphael she added, "My epitaph would have to be . . . 'She stuck with the job.'"

Further Reading

Raphael, Amy. "Alice Stewart, Rebel Scientist." *Ms.*, July–August 1996, 31–33.

Vines, Gail. "Alice Stewart." In *Beyond the Glass Ceiling: Forty Women Whose Ideas Shape the Modern World*, edited by Sian Griffiths. Manchester: Manchester University Press, 1996, 231–236.

 STEWART, SARAH
(1906–1976) *American Microbiologist and Cancer Researcher*

Sarah Stewart was one of the first to show that viruses could cause cancer in mammals. She was born to George and Maria Andrade Stewart on August 16, 1906, in Tecalitlan, Mexico, where her father, an engineer, owned several mines. An uprising when Sarah was five years old forced her family to flee to the United States, and they eventually settled in New Mexico.

Stewart graduated from New Mexico State University in 1927 with bachelor's degrees in home economics and general science. She obtained a master's degree in bacteriology from the University of Massachusetts at Amherst in 1930, then worked as an assistant bacteriologist at the Colorado Experimental Station for three years. She studied for a Ph.D. at the University of Colorado School of Medicine and later at the University of Chicago, earning her degree from the latter in 1939.

In 1936, Stewart joined the Microbiology Laboratory at the National Institutes of Health (NIH), the group of large, government-sponsored research institutes in Bethesda, Maryland. From then until 1944 she did research on bacteria that can survive without air and on ways to protect people against diseases they cause, such as botulism. Meanwhile, she grew interested in viruses and the possibility that they might cause cancer.

The Microbiology Laboratory did not care about cancer, so Stewart transferred to the National Cancer Institute in NIH in 1947. Researchers there, however, regarded her belief that viruses could cause cancer in mammals (they were known to do so in birds) as "eccentric" at best. She thought they were ignoring her because she was not a medical doctor, so she went back to school at Georgetown University and, at age 39, earned an M.D. (the first one Georgetown had given to a woman). All this did was lose her her job at the Cancer Institute, although the institute's director found her a laboratory in the Public Health Service hospital in Baltimore.

In 1953, New York researcher Ludwik Gross found a virus that appeared to produce cancer in mice. While attempting to verify Gross's discovery, Stewart found a second virus that seemed to cause a mouse leukemia. In 1956 she asked BERNICE EDDY, a friend and fellow NIH researcher, to help her grow this virus in mouse cells in laboratory dishes. Stewart and Eddy found that their virus caused cancer in every kind of animal into which they injected it. They named it the SE polyoma virus: SE for "Stewart and Eddy," and polyoma meaning "many tumors."

Most other researchers were skeptical when Stewart and Eddy first announced their findings in 1957, but their work persuaded others to start looking into cancer-causing viruses. "The whole place just exploded after Sarah found polyoma," Alan Rabson of the National Cancer Institute told writer Edward Shorter. "It was a major, major discovery." These scientists confirmed the women's results, and Stewart's ideas became accepted. President Lyndon Johnson gave her the Federal Women's Award in 1965.

Stewart continued to work with cancer-causing viruses for the rest of her career. She and others showed that viruses could produce cancer in birds, mice, cats, and hamsters. She also isolated viruses from several human cancers, though she could not prove that the viruses caused the disease. She died—of cancer, ironically—on November 27, 1976. Bernice Eddy said of her, "She was a forceful individual who did not let anything stand in [her] way if she could help it."

Further Reading

O'Hern, Elizabeth Moot. *Profiles of Pioneer Women Scientists.* Washington, D.C.: Acropolis Books, 1985, 161–169.

Shorter, Edward. *The Health Century.* New York: Doubleday, 1987, 196–198, 201–204.

T

 TAUSSIG, HELEN
(1898–1986) *American Physician*

Helen Taussig designed an operation that saved thousands of "blue babies," children born with a certain kind of heart defect. She also helped to keep an epidemic of birth defects in Europe caused by a drug called thalidomide from repeating itself in the United States. She was born in Cambridge, Massachusetts, on May 24, 1898, to Frank Taussig, a Harvard economics professor, and his wife, Edith, also a teacher. Helen was the youngest of their four children. Her mother died when she was 11 years old.

Helen began college at Radcliffe, then transferred to the University of California at Berkeley after two years to gain a "broader experience." She graduated from there in 1921. She had decided to become a doctor and wanted to take her medical training at Harvard, but its medical school did not admit women. She got permission to take a few courses there, and she took others at Boston University. Alexander Begg, her anatomy professor at Boston, was one of the few who encouraged her. One day he thrust a beef heart into her hand, saying, "Here, it wouldn't hurt you to become interested in

a major organ of the body." Thus began Taussig's study of the heart.

Taussig followed Begg's advice to go to Johns Hopkins Medical School, from which she earned her M.D. in 1927. She specialized in pediatric cardiology, or heart diseases of children. In 1930, Edwards Park, the school's chairman of pediatrics, put her in charge of his new pediatric cardiology clinic. She was devoted to her patients, whom she called her "little crossword puzzles" because of their often mysterious ailments. Most doctors identified heart defects by sounds heard through a stethoscope, but Taussig, left somewhat deaf by a childhood illness, used her eyes instead. She examined children with a fluoroscope, which produced real-time X-ray images, and also observed the movements of their chests as they breathed.

Taussig became especially interested in heart problems caused by birth defects. One set of four defects that occurred together was called tetralogy of Fallot, after the French physician who had first described it. The two most important defects were a narrowing of the pulmonary artery, which takes blood from the heart's right ventricle to the lungs to receive oxygen, and a hole in the wall of muscle that separates the right half of the heart from the left. Taussig was the first to realize that these defects kept most blood from reaching the lungs, thus slowly starving the children of oxygen. The oxygen shortage made their skin look bluish, earning them the nickname of "blue babies." They rarely lived past childhood.

Another common defect, the ductus arteriosus, was a short vessel that connected the aorta, the main vessel that carries blood into the body, to the pulmonary artery. The ductus normally exists in a fetus but seals off at birth. If this does not happen, pressure from the aorta pushes too much blood into the lungs, damaging their delicate tissue. Some hapless children had both a tetralogy of Fallot and an open ductus arteriosus. Neither defect could be repaired directly because heart surgery was still very primitive.

In 1939, Boston surgeon Robert Gross devised an operation for closing an open ductus arteriosus. This usually restored the health of children in whom the ductus was the only defect, but Taussig noticed that if children also had tetralogy of Fallot, the operation made them worse. It occurred to her that the ductus arteriosus actually helped children with tetralogy of Fallot by allowing more blood to reach their lungs. Their lungs were not harmed because so little blood came to them from the pulmonary artery. Why not, then, make an artificial ductus in these children?

Gross was not interested in Taussig's idea, but Alfred Blalock, chief of surgery at Johns Hopkins, was more willing to take a chance on it when she described it to him in 1943. Experimenting on dogs, he perfected an operation in which he joined the subclavian artery, which carries blood to the arms in humans, to the pulmonary artery.

Blalock first tried the surgery on a human baby, Eileen Saxon, on November 29, 1944. "It was like a miracle," the child's mother told an interviewer. Soon afterward, Taussig herself witnessed the "miracle" during an operation on what she described as a "small, utterly miserable, six-year-old boy. . . . When the clamps were released [after Blalock had joined the blood vessels] the anesthesiologist said suddenly, 'He's a lovely color now!' I walked around to the head of the table and saw his normal,

Helen Taussig of Johns Hopkins devised an operation that restored the health of "blue babies," born with a group of defects that affected their heart and circulation, by bringing needed oxygen to their lungs. She also helped to prevent an epidemic of birth defects in Europe, caused when pregnant women took the drug thalidomide, from spreading to the United States. This portrait of Taussig was taken in 1966.
(Courtesy the Alan Mason Chesney Medical Archives of the Johns Hopkins Medical Institutions)

pink lips. From that moment the child was healthy, happy, and active."

Blalock and other surgeons went on to perform this miracle on some 12,000 other children. Furthermore, one noted surgeon says, the Blalock-Taussig "blue baby" operation showed that extremely sick children could survive surgery and thus "prompted surgeons to venture where they had not dared to venture previously. The result is much of present-day cardiac surgery." The operation continued to be used until surgery advanced enough for the heart defects themselves to be repaired.

Taussig, meanwhile, went on treating her young "crossword puzzles" and training doctors in pediatric cardiology, the specialty she had helped to develop. She became a professor of pediatrics, Johns Hopkins's first woman full professor, in 1959.

In January 1962 a young West German doctor who had come to study under Taussig told her that in some parts of Europe there had been a sudden increase in the number of children born with a severe birth defect called phocomelia, or "seal limbs." These children's hands and feet were attached directly to their trunks, giving a flipperlike appearance. They often had internal defects as well. A German physician had published his belief that phocomelia might result when pregnant women took a popular drug called thalidomide, or Contergan, often prescribed to control their morning nausea.

Taussig immediately flew to Europe to study the problem. When she returned, she presented her findings to FRANCES KELSEY of the federal Food and Drug Administration (FDA), who had already blocked a drug company's request to sell thalidomide in the United States. Taussig's report confirmed Kelsey's doubts. By this time the American company had withdrawn its FDA application, but thousands of samples of thalidomide had been distributed to physicians for "test" purposes. Taussig's urgent warnings kept most of these doctors from giving the drug to their patients and thus helped to prevent most cases of phocomelia in America. Kelsey and Taussig also successfully campaigned for new FDA rules requiring testing of drugs on pregnant animals.

Helen Taussig retired from Johns Hopkins in 1963, but she continued to work at the cardiology clinic and do research. In 1965 she became the first woman president of the American Heart Association. President Lyndon Johnson gave her the Medal of Freedom, the highest award the United States can give a civilian. A 1977 article called Taussig "probably the best-known woman physician in the world." She moved to Pennsylvania in the late 1970s and was killed there in a car accident on May 21, 1986.

Further Reading

Baldwin, Joyce. *To Heal the Heart of a Child: Helen Taussig, M.D.* New York: Walker, 1992.

Lindop, Laurie. *Dynamic Modern Women: Scientists and Doctors.* New York: Holt, 1997, 83–94.

Nuland, Sherwin B. *Doctors: The Biography of Medicine.* New York: Random House, 1989, 430–455.

Yount, Lisa. *Contemporary Women Scientists.* New York: Facts On File, 1994, 1–12.

✳ TROTULA OF SALERNO
(11th century; died 1097?) *Italian Physician*

Trotula wrote a text on the diseases of women that was used for centuries. She probably belonged to the aristocratic di Ruggiero family and lived during the 11th century in Salerno, a town near Naples in southern Italy. Salerno's medical school was considered the best in Europe at the time and was the only one that admitted Muslims, Jews, and women. Indeed, its "women of Salerno," a group of women physicians, were famous.

Trotula is thought to have taught at the medical school as well as treating patients. She was married to another physician, Joannes Platearius, and had two sons, Johannes and Matthias, who were also physicians and writers. The four wrote a medical encyclopedia called *Practica Brevis*.

Trotula's chief surviving book is the *Passionibus Mulierum Curandorum (Diseases of Women)*, sometimes called Trotula Major. It includes material on normal birth and the care of newborns. (A second book, Trotula Minor, deals with cosmetics and skin diseases.) In the preface to her major work, Trotula explained how she had come to practice medicine. "Women on account of modesty . . . dare not reveal the difficulties of their sicknesses to a male doctor.

Wherefore I, pitying their misfortunes . . . , began to study carefully the sicknesses which most frequently trouble the female sex." She probably wrote her book at least partly to tell male doctors facts about women's bodies that their patients might not want or be able to communicate.

Trotula's book quoted the best ancient medical authorities, such as Galen and Hippocrates, and also presented some ideas that were ahead of its time. For instance, Trotula wrote that "conception is hindered as often by a defect of the man as of the woman," a radical notion in a day when infertility was almost always blamed on the woman. Trotula showed understanding of her patients' psychological as well as physical needs. Victorian historians were surprised at her outspokenness about sexual matters, but feminist scholars say that such an attitude would have been expected in a woman doctor.

Trotula's medical advice was more sensible and less based on magic than that of most of her contemporaries. She told doctors to diagnose illness by observing such things as urine, pulse, and color of the face. She urged cleanliness, a healthy diet, and freedom from stress as treatments for many conditions. If more was needed, she recommended mild treatments, usually herbs and oils, rather than harsh medications, bleeding, or surgery. She said to approach patients with gentleness and optimism. It was little wonder that midwives and physicians relied on her text for so long.

Further Reading

Alic, Margaret. *Hypatia's Heritage: A History of Women in Science from Antiquity Through the Nineteenth Century.* Boston: Beacon Press, 1986, 50–55.

Brooke, Elisabeth. *Women Healers: Portraits of Herbalists, Physicians, and Midwives.* Rochester, Vt.: Healing Arts Press, 1995, 28–39.

Trotula. *The Diseases of Women,* translated by Elizabeth Mason-Hohl. Los Angeles: Ward Ritchie, 1940.

VAN DOVER, CINDY LEE

(1954–) *American Marine Biologist*

Cindy Lee Van Dover is the first scientist and first woman certified as a submersible pilot. Her discovery that certain deep-sea shrimp are sensitive to light has led to new speculations about hot-water vents on the ocean floor and the strange communities that live around them. She was born on May 16, 1954, in Red Bank, New Jersey, to James K. and Virginia Van Dover.

In 1977, the same year Cindy Van Dover earned a B.S. in environmental science from Rutgers University, scientists' picture of the deep sea changed drastically. They had believed that very few organisms lived there because, as far as was known, all life ultimately depended on creatures that could make food from the sun's energy through the process of photosynthesis, and sunlight did not penetrate the water below about 900 feet (300 meters). Then, however, oceanographers in tiny craft called submersibles, exploring spots on the seafloor where the earth's continental plates were spreading apart, found vents through which fountains of water spewed, black with mineral deposits and heated to 650°F. by the magma below. These vents were surrounded by bizarre life forms that included white

mats of bacteria, eyeless shrimp, and eight-foot-tall, red-tipped tube worms.

Van Dover saw her first hydrothermal vent community—so beautiful that it had been nicknamed the Rose Garden—in a dive in the submersible *Alvin*, owned by the Woods Hole Oceanographic Institution, in 1985, the same year she earned a master's degree in ecology from the University of California at Los Angeles. The following year, studying for a doctorate in a combined program from the Massachusetts Institute of Technology and Woods Hole, she began looking at a species of shrimp found only around the vents. In videotapes of living vent communities, she noticed two bright lines on the shrimps' backs not visible on her preserved specimens. She dissected this area and found that the lines were flaps of tissue connected to large nerves. This suggested that the tissue was a sense organ. Van Dover then had what seemed at first an outlandish idea: Could it be a type of eye?

Other scientists to whom Van Dover sent samples of the tissue said that features of its structure and chemistry supported her idea that it might sense light. No light around the vents had been reported, but, Van Dover thought, the vent water was so hot that some of its heat energy might shade into dim red light, just as a heater coil glows red. She asked a

Cindy Van Dover, the first woman and first scientist certified as a submersible pilot, discovered that shrimp living around hot-water vents in the black depths of the sea can detect light given off by the vents. She is shown here entering a small submersible for another trip to the seafloor.
(Photo, T. Shirley, courtesy Cindy Van Dover)

geologist taking a sensitive camera down on *Alvin* to turn off the sub's lights—which had not been done before—and see whether the camera spotted any light near the vents. He did so in June 1988 and sent back the startling message: "VENTS GLOW."

After receiving her doctorate in 1989, Van Dover spent nine months learning how to pilot *Alvin* herself. She was the first scientist and the first woman whom the navy certified as a submersible pilot-commander. She piloted *Alvin* on 48 dives between 1990 and 1992.

Van Dover returned to scientific work in 1993 and is now pursuing another seemingly outlandish idea. As far as is known, all vent creatures depend on the bacteria there, which can make food from sulfur compounds in the water by a process completely different from photosynthesis. Some microorganisms, however, can carry on photosynthesis in light as dim as the vent light Van Dover helped to discover, and she is trying to find vent microbes that can photosynthesize. If she succeeds, she will have uncovered the first example of natural photosynthesis that does not require sunlight. Some scientists have speculated that life on earth originated around undersea vents, and Van Dover's idea suggests that photosynthesis may have begun there, too.

Van Dover has remained affiliated with Woods Hole throughout her career. She has also been a visiting scholar at Duke University in North Carolina (1994–95), an associate professor at the University of Alaska at Fairbanks (1995–98), and science director of the West Coast National Undersea Research Center. In 1998 she became an assistant professor at the College of William and Mary in Virginia. *Ms.* magazine chose her as its Woman of the Year in 1988, and she has also won several scientific awards, including the Vetlesen Award from Woods Hole (1990) and the NOAA/MAB Research Award (1996).

Today, in addition to studying vent light and its possible contribution to photosynthesis, Van Dover is researching other aspects of the ecology of vent communities and the effects of deep-sea waste disposal on underwater life. In 1999 she plans to lead a scientific team on an exploration of vents beneath the Indian Ocean. She also works to increase support for exploring the deep sea. "We actually know more about the surface of Mars and Venus . . . than we know about the topography of our own seafloor," she has said, yet the health of the communities of creatures that live there "may be critical to the balance of the world's oceans" and to life on land as well.

Further Reading

Kunzig, Robert. "Between Home and the Abyss." *Discover*, December 1993, 67–75.

Van Dover, Cindy Lee. "Depths of Ignorance." *Discover*, September 1993, 37–39.

———. *Deep-Ocean Journeys.* Reading, Mass.: Addison-Wesley, 1996.

Zimmer, Carl. "The Light at the Bottom of the Sea." *Discover*, November 1996, 63–73.

✳ VRBA, ELISABETH
(1942–) *South African/American Paleontologist*

Charles Darwin's theory of evolution claimed that species appeared or died out gradually because of random changes that gave some members of a species a competitive advantage over others. Elisabeth Vrba, however, believes that evolution sometimes makes sudden jumps and that climate change drives most of them, including the ones that led to modern humans.

Elisabeth was born on May 27, 1942, in Hamburg, Germany. Her father, a law professor, died when she was two years old, and her mother moved to Namibia, in southern Africa. Elisabeth majored in zoology and statistics at the University of Cape Town, South Africa, graduating with honors. She moved to Pretoria in 1967, married civil engineer George Vrba, and began teaching high school.

Vrba began working for the Transvaal Museum in 1968, at first as an unpaid assistant. About 10 years later she became the museum's deputy director and was put in charge of its collection of fossil hominids, the ancestors of humans. Based on her studies of both these fossils and fossil antelopes, she has devised a theory she calls the turnover pulse hypothesis.

Vrba noticed that many changes occurred in both hominid and antelope species about 5 million years ago, and she suspects that these changes grew out of a shift in climate demonstrated by fossil and geologic evidence. Much of the world became drier and colder at that time, and large parts of Africa's formerly solid blanket of forests were replaced by grassland. Species of forest-living antelopes and apes either clung to the remaining forestlands or died out and were replaced by new species that could adapt to grassland. The forest apes eventually became chimpanzees, gorillas, and (in Asia) orangutans, whereas the grassland ape was *Australopithecus afarensis*, the first hominid. Vrba believes that two similar climate changes, one between 2.8 and 2.5 million years ago and the other about 900,000 years ago, led respectively to the appearance of the human genus *(Homo)* and the spread of the human ancestor *Homo erectus* out of Africa.

In the turnover pulse hypothesis, Vrba has generalized these ideas to propose that changes in climate are the chief cause of rapid changes in species and perhaps of evolution itself. She is not the first to suggest that the pace of evolution sometimes speeds up nor to suggest that changes in the environment, especially climate, produce widespread changes in species. She is, however, one of the

strongest believers in a link between these two ideas. "Making a new species requires a physical event to force nature off the pedestal of equilibrium," she told *Discover* writer Ellen Shell.

Not everyone agrees with Vrba's hypothesis. Two 1996 studies of fossils from Lake Turkana in East Africa, where rocks can be dated very precisely, say that rather than showing the sharp peak between 2.8 and 2.5 million years ago that Vrba claims, changes in mammal species spread fairly smoothly over a much longer period, between 3 million and 2 million years. A study of North American mammal fossils also contradicts Vrba's results.

Vrba, with her husband and daughter, moved to the United States in 1986. She joined the faculty of Yale University, where she is now a tenured professor. The controversy her ideas stir does not bother her, she told Ellen Shell: "I'm interested in pushing out the frontiers of science, not sailing my boat through tranquil seas."

Further Reading

Monastersky, Richard. "Out of Arid Africa." *Science News*, August 3, 1996, 74–75.

Shell, Ellen Ruppel. "Waves of Creation." *Discover*, May 1993, 55–61.

Vrba, Elisabeth S. "The Pulse that Produced Us." *Natural History*, May 1993, 47–51.

WEXLER, NANCY SABIN

(1945–) *American Psychologist and
Medical Researcherr*

Nancy Wexler has turned a family tragedy into a
new understanding of a deadly inherited disease.
She was born on July 19, 1945, in Washington,
D.C., to Milton Wexler, a psychoanalyst, and his
wife, Leonore.

In August 1968, when Nancy was 22 years old
and her parents had been divorced for four years,
her father told her and her older sister, Alice, that
he had just learned that their mother was suffering
from an inherited brain disorder called Huntington's disease (formerly Huntington's chorea).
He explained that the disease, which usually does
not reveal itself until middle age, produces a slow
slide into insanity accompanied by uncontrollable
twisting or writhing movements. There is no cure
or treatment. Because the disease is caused by a
single dominant gene, Nancy and Alice each had a
50–50 chance of developing it as well.

The news was devastating, but Milton Wexler
said later that Nancy "went from being dismal to
. . . wanting to be a knight in shining armor going
out to fight the devils." Of a similar mind, Milton
contacted the Committee to Combat Hunt-

ington's Chorea, an organization led by Marjorie
Guthrie, who had been married to famed folk singer
Woody Guthrie, the disease's best-known victim.
Milton opened a chapter of the group in Los Ange-
les, and Nancy set up another in Michigan, where
she was studying psychology at the University of
Michigan at Ann Arbor. She did her thesis research
on the psychological effects of belonging to a family
suffering from a hereditary disease, earning her
Ph.D. in 1974.

Guthrie's organization was devoted mainly to
improving care, but the Wexlers were more interested in research. In 1974, Milton Wexler, with
Nancy's help, founded a new organization for this
purpose, the Hereditary Disease Foundation.
Nancy became the foundation's president in 1983.

The group agreed that identifying the gene that
causes Huntington's was probably the best approach to a treatment or cure. At minimum, doing
so would create a test that showed who would get
the disease before signs of it developed, which
would help people at risk plan their future. In
October 1979 a researcher from the Massachusetts
Institute of Technology named David Housman
told the foundation about a new technique that
narrowed down the location of unknown genes by
using known marker genes called restriction

fragment length polymorphisms (RFLPs). The more often a certain form of a RFLP was inherited with a certain form of an unknown gene in a given family, the more likely the unknown gene was to be near the RFLP on the same chromosome.

The only problem was that, at that time, only one human RFLP was known. Finding a RFLP that happened to be near the Huntington's gene might take decades. Still, the Hereditary Disease Foundation gave Housman a grant to try his idea, and Nancy Wexler arranged additional funding through the Congressional Committee for the Control of Huntington's Disease and Its Consequences, of which she had been made executive director in 1976.

To determine inheritance patterns, the researchers needed a large family in which some members had Huntington's disease. Luckily Nancy Wexler, investigating another aspect of the disease, had learned of such a family in Venezuela and visited it earlier in 1979. In 1981 she and an international research team made the first of what became yearly trips to collect skin and blood samples from this family for testing. The Venezuelans cooperated when they learned that Wexler's own family had the disease and she, too, had given samples. In return for the family's help, Wexler's team gave them medical and social aid (the family is very poor), and Wexler personally provided what a Venezuelan team member called "immeasurable love."

At first the RFLP project had unusually good luck. James Gusella of Massachusetts General Hospital, who was put in charge of the testing, found a RFLP inherited with the Huntington's gene in 1983. It was only the 12th RFLP he had tried. In addition to giving a great boost to the gene hunt, this identification made possible a test that would tell with about 96 percent accuracy whether someone would develop Huntington's disease.

To improve the chances of locating the Huntington's gene, the Hereditary Disease Foundation, beginning in 1984, persuaded six laboratories in the United States and Britain to share their results and credit. John Minna, a scientist in the group, told Wexler's sister, Alice, "The person that made all of

the HD [Huntington's Disease] thing work . . . was Nancy. . . . It was her acting as . . . glue and go-between, doing whatever was necessary, that was the real key." The group finally found the Huntington's gene in 1993 and is now learning how it does its deadly work.

Nancy Wexler has helped to guide research that discovered the gene that causes Huntington's disease, a devastating brain disorder that killed Wexler's mother, and has personally tracked the disease through generations of a large family in Venezuela. In return for the Venezuelans' cooperation in the research, Wexler has given sick family members such as this child what a coworker called "immeasurable love." (Courtesy Peter Ginter and the Hereditary Disease Foundation)

Nancy Wexler's other personal contribution has been tracing the ancestry of the Venezuelan family. Their family tree now spans 10 generations, including some 14,000 members, and covers both walls of a corridor outside Wexler's office at the Columbia University Medical Center, whose faculty she joined in 1985. (She became a full professor in 1992.) Wexler won the Albert Lasker Public Service Award in 1993 for her contributions to the search for the Huntington's gene and for "increasing awareness of all genetic disease."

Today, Wexler focuses on the implications of testing for inherited diseases. In 1989 she was made head of a committee that oversees research on the ethical, social, and legal questions raised by the Human Genome Project, which aims to work out the "code" of the complete collection of human genes. Information from this project eventually will make testing possible for any inherited disease or genetic weakness. Such testing could yield medical benefits, but test results could also be used to deny people medical insurance or employment. Wexler is trying to find ways to keep such tragedies from happening, just as she has worked to create hope out of the tragedy that struck her own life.

Further Reading

Murray, Mary. "Nancy Wexler." *New York Times Magazine*, February 13, 1994.

Wexler, Alice. *Mapping Fate: A Memoir of Family, Risk, and Genetic Research.* New York: Random House/Times Books, 1995.

"Wexler, Nancy S." *Current Biography Yearbook 1994.* New York: H. W. Wilson, 1994, 607–611.

Yount, Lisa. *Genetics and Genetic Engineering.* New York: Facts On File, 1997, 98–117.

✳ WHEELER, ANNA JOHNSON PELL
(1883–1966) *American Mathematician*

Anna Johnson Pell Wheeler was an expert in linear algebra as well as an outstanding teacher and administrator. She was born Anna Johnson, the third child of Swedish immigrants Andrew and Amelia Johnson, on May 5, 1883, in Hawarden, Iowa. She grew up in Akron, where her father was a furniture dealer and undertaker.

Anna Johnson earned her B.A. from the University of South Dakota in 1903. There a professor, Alexander Pell, encouraged her to do graduate study in mathematics. She earned master's degrees from the University of Iowa in 1904 and Radcliffe College in 1905. She then won a Wellesley fellowship to study at the renowned University of Göttingen, Germany, in 1906–07. Pell joined her in Göttingen in 1907, and they were married there.

Anna Pell earned a Ph.D. from the University of Chicago in 1910. From 1911 to 1918 she taught at Mount Holyoke in South Hadley, Massachusetts, after which she moved to Bryn Mawr. In 1925, four years after Alexander Pell's death, Anna became a full professor and head of Bryn Mawr's mathematics department, succeeding CHARLOTTE ANGAS SCOTT. She married classics scholar Arthur Leslie Wheeler in that same year and moved to Princeton to be with him, teaching part-time at Bryn Mawr until his death in 1932 and then returning to full-time.

In addition to her fame as a teacher and administrator, Wheeler was well known as a research mathematician. Her specialty was linear algebra of infinitely many variables, a branch of what is now called functional analysis, and applications to differential and integral equations. In 1927 the American Mathematical Society invited her to give its Colloquium Lectures; she was the only woman so honored until 1980. She served on the society's council and board of trustees.

Anna Wheeler retired in 1948 and died on March 26, 1966, just before her 83rd birthday. According to science historians Judy Green and Jeanne Laduke, Wheeler "received more recognition from the mathematical community before World War II than perhaps any other American woman."

Further Reading

Grinstein, Louise S. "Wheeler, Anna Johnson Pell." In *Notable American Women: The Modern Period*, edited by

Barbara Sicherman and Carol Hurd Green, 725–726. Cambridge, Mass.: The Belknap Press of Harvard University Press, 1980.

———. and Paul J. Campbell. "Anna Johnson Pell Wheeler: Her Life and Work." *Historia Mathematica* 9 (1982): 43–44.

Ogilvie, Marilyn Bailey. *Women in Science: Antiquity Through the Nineteenth Century.* Cambridge, Mass.: MIT Press, 1986, 173–174.

✳ WILLIAMS, ANNA WESSELS
(1863–1954) *American Microbiologist*

Anna Williams made advances in identification and treatment of infectious diseases that saved thousands of lives, though men were often given credit for her work. She was born on March 17, 1863, in Hackensack, New Jersey, to William and Jane Williams, the second child of six. Her father was a teacher and school official. Anna wrote that she first became interested in science when she looked through a teacher's "wonderful microscope."

Williams earned a certificate from the New Jersey State Normal School in 1883 and began teaching school. In 1887, however, her sister almost died while giving birth to a dead baby. Wanting to prevent similar tragedies, Williams decided to become a physician. She earned an M.D. from the Women's Medical College of the New York Infirmary in 1891 and remained at the school as an instructor in pathology for several years.

In 1894, Williams joined the new New York City Department of Health Laboratory, the country's first city-run laboratory for diagnosis of disease. Its chief job was identifying disease-causing microbes in tissue, blood, food, or drink. A volunteer at first, Williams was hired in 1895 as an assistant bacteriologist. A biography of the laboratory's director, W. H. Park, said that Williams "became more indispensable . . . with each year of service."

The laboratory also carried out research on infectious diseases, and Williams made her greatest contributions in this area. Scientists had found a way to make an antitoxin that counteracted the toxin, or poison, produced by the bacteria that caused a serious disease called diphtheria, which killed thousands of children yearly. Making the antitoxin required toxin, however, and finding a strain of bacteria that produced large amounts of toxin dependably was hard. In 1894, Williams identified such a strain, which became known as the Park-Williams Strain—or just the Park 8 Strain, although Park had not even been in the laboratory when Williams found it. It became the standard strain used for diphtheria toxin production.

Williams's second important discovery involved rabies. At the time, the only test for this fatal disease took two weeks. In 1904, while examining infected brain tissue under a microscope, Williams noticed certain cells that did not appear in normal brains. An Italian physician, Adelchi Negri, made the same discovery a short time later. The cells became known as Negri bodies rather than Williams bodies because Negri published his description before Williams did. They became the basis of a much faster test for rabies. Williams improved on Negri's version of the test, producing one that gave results in half an hour rather than several hours. Her form became standard.

Williams studied many other infectious diseases, including scarlet fever, typhoid fever, pneumonia, and influenza, and coauthored several books about disease-causing microorganisms with Park. She became assistant director of the New York laboratory in 1906. In 1932 she became chairperson of the Laboratory Section of the American Public Health Association, the first woman to hold such a post. She retired in 1934 and moved to New Jersey, where she lived until her death on November 20, 1954.

Further Reading

O'Hern, Elizabeth Moot. *Profiles of Pioneer Women Scientists.* Washington, D.C.: Acropolis Books, 1985, 32–45.

Robinton, Elizabeth D. "Williams, Anna Wessels." In *Notable American Women: The Modern Period*, edited by Barbara Sicherman and Carol Hurd Green, 737–739. Cambridge, Mass.: The Belknap Press of Harvard University Press, 1980.

※ **WONG-STAAL, FLOSSIE (Yee-ching Wong)**
(1946–) *American Geneticist and Medical Researcher*

Flossie Wong-Staal has been a leader in research on AIDS since the disease and the virus that causes it were first identified. She was born Yee-ching Wong in Kuangchou, or Canton, China, on August 27, 1946. Her father, Sueh-fung Wong, was a cloth exporter-importer. In 1952, not long after Communists took over the Chinese government, the Wong family moved to Hong Kong. Yee-ching became Flossie after the American nuns at her school asked students' parents to select English names for them, and her father chose the one given to a typhoon (tropical storm) that had just swept through the city.

Flossie's teachers assigned her to study science, and she found she liked it. When she went to college at the University of California at Los Angeles

Working in the laboratory of Robert Gallo at the National Institutes of Health, Flossie Wong-Staal helped to identify the first virus shown to cause cancer in humans and the virus that causes AIDS. She now heads a center for AIDS research at the University of California at San Diego.
(Courtesy Flossie Wong-Staal)

(UCLA), she specialized in molecular biology, the study of the structure and function of the chemicals in living things. This relatively new field was filled with excitement as scientists deciphered the genetic code. She graduated in 1969.

In 1971, while working for her Ph.D. at UCLA, Wong married medical student Steven Staal. They later had two daughters, Stephanie and Caroline. Wong-Staal, as she called herself after her marriage, earned her degree in 1972, winning the Woman Graduate of the Year award.

Both Staal and Wong-Staal found jobs at the National Institutes of Health (NIH), the group of government-sponsored research institutes in Bethesda, Maryland, in 1973. Wong-Staal worked in the laboratory of Robert Gallo at the National Cancer Institute. At the time, Gallo was one of the few researchers investigating the possibility that viruses could cause cancer in humans. Wong-Staal found genes in human cells similar to ones in viruses that caused cancer in monkeys and apes. Gallo has written that she "evolve[d] into one of the major players in my group. Because of her insight and leadership qualities, she gradually assumed a supervisory role."

In 1981, Gallo's group identified the first virus proven to cause a human cancer, a rare form of leukemia. They named it human T-cell leukemia virus (HTLV); T cells are one type of immune system cell in the blood. They later found a second, similar virus, which they called HTLV-2.

Meanwhile, other scientists were studying a strange illness that had appeared mostly among homosexual men in large cities. They eventually called it acquired immunodeficiency syndrome, or AIDS, because it devastated its victims' immune systems. Gallo and Wong-Staal were struck by the fact that the as-yet-unknown agent that caused AIDS chiefly attacked T cells and was transmitted through sexual contact, transfer of blood, or from mother to unborn child—just like their HTLVs.

While checking out the possibility that one of their viruses caused the disease, Gallo's group found a previously unknown virus similar to theirs. They named it HTLV-3. Scientists in France's Pasteur

Institute isolated what proved to be the same virus at the same time, late 1983. The two labs have shared credit for discovering the virus, which came to be called the human immunodeficiency virus, or HIV.

Gallo's lab then turned to a full-time study of HIV. In 1984, Flossie Wong-Staal became the first to clone (copy) the virus's genes. She also worked out the chemical sequence of each gene and determined its function. Most of the genes controlled the speed of the virus's growth. Wong-Staal's work helped to explain why most people infected with HIV remain seemingly healthy for years before developing AIDS.

In 1990, Wong-Staal, by then divorced from Steven Staal, left Gallo's lab and moved with her younger daughter to the University of California at San Diego. There she heads a center devoted to AIDS research. One approach to treatment she has investigated inserts a gene coding for a chemical called a ribozyme into immune system cells. The ribozyme snips HIV's genetic material into several pieces, preventing it from reproducing.

One sign of Wong-Staal's fame is the number of times that researchers cite her work in their own papers. The more important a piece of research is, the more often it is cited. A 1990 survey conducted by the Institute of Scientific Information in Philadelphia showed that Wong-Staal's papers were cited more than those of any other woman scientist during the 1980s.

Further Reading

Baskin, Yvonne. "Intimate Enemies." *Discover*, December 1991, 16–17.

Gallo, Robert. *Virus Hunting*. New York: New Republic/Basic Books, 1991.

Yount, Lisa. *Asian-American Scientists*. New York: Facts On File, 1998, 67–75.

✳ WRIGHT, JANE COOKE
(1919–) *American Cancer Researcher*

Jane Cooke Wright, descended from a family of African-American physicians and researchers, made important contributions to the development of che-motherapy (drug treatment) for cancer. She was born in New York City on November 30, 1919, to Louis Tompkins Wright and Corinne Cooke Wright. Her father was then a surgeon at Harlem Hospital, the first African-American doctor on the staff of any New York City hospital.

Wright went to Smith College, graduating in 1942. She earned her M.D. with honors from New York Medical College in 1945. She married David D. Jones, a lawyer, in 1947 and had two daughters. Wright once said that she could not think of a better way of life than combining a medical career with raising a family.

Louis Wright established the Cancer Research Foundation at Harlem Hospital in 1948, and a year later he invited Jane to join him there. She took part in several of the center's pioneering studies in cancer chemotherapy. When he died in 1952, she took over his position as head of the foundation. In 1955 she joined the faculty of New York University, where in time she became associate professor of research surgery. She returned to New York Medical College in 1967 and became professor of surgery, associate dean, and director of the college's new cancer research laboratory.

Some cancer patients and some tumors are more sensitive to any given anticancer drug than others, so it is hard to determine in advance the best drug and dosage to give. Working with JEWEL PLUMMER COBB, Wright tried to develop a system in which cells from a patient's tumor was grown in a laboratory dish, a process called tissue culture, and different drugs were tried on the culture before being given to the patient. The two also used tissue culture to test new drugs. Their system did not succeed in the long run, but some of their methods are still used, and they learned important information about the way different kinds of drugs affect cancer cells.

Awards Wright received include a Spirit of Achievement Award from the Albert Einstein School of Medicine and a 1975 award from the American Association for Cancer Research. She retired in 1987. Summing up her attitude toward her research, she told reporter Fern Eckman, "There's lots of fun in exploring the unknown. There's no greater thrill than having an experiment turn out . . . [so] that you make a positive contribution."

Further Reading

Haber, Louis. *Women Pioneers of Science.* New York: Harcourt Brace Jovanovich, 1979, 117–127.

Jackson, George F. *Black Women Makers of History.* Oakland, Calif. GRT Book Printing, 1975, 182–184.

Yount, Lisa. *Black Scientists.* New York: Facts On File, 1991, 67–79.

✳ WRINCH, DOROTHY MAUD

(1894–1976) *British/American Mathematician and Chemist*

Bridging barriers between scientific disciplines, Dorothy Wrinch helped to found molecular biology with her mathematics-based theory about the structure of protein molecules. She was born on September 12, 1894, in Rosario, Argentina, to engineer Edward Wrinch and his wife, Ada. One account says that when Dorothy's father first took her to school in Rosario, he told her teachers, "This child is to be a mathematician." Her parents returned to England while she was still a child, and she grew up in London.

Wrinch attended Girton, a women's college in Cambridge University, from 1913 to 1918, earning a B.A. and an M.A. She studied both mathematics and philosophy. After graduation, she taught mathematics at the University of London. She earned an M.S. in 1920 and a D.S. in 1922.

In 1922, Wrinch married John Nicholson, a mathematical physicist at Oxford, and they had a daughter, Pamela, in 1928. Unusual for the time, Wrinch continued to work under her maiden name. She obtained an M.A. from Oxford in 1924 and began tutoring full time at Lady Margaret Hall, one of the university's colleges for women. In 1927 she was appointed a lecturer for three years, the first woman granted a university lectureship in mathematics at Oxford. She used a group of her papers in mathematical physics and applied mathematics as the basis for a second D.S. degree, the first that

Oxford had given to a woman, in 1929. Wrinch separated from Nicholson, an alcoholic, in 1930, and they divorced in 1938.

Wrinch contributed to many fields during her life, including several branches of pure and applied mathematics, sociology, and, finally, biology and chemistry. She did her most important work, development of the first precise theory of the structure of proteins, in the late 1930s. At that time, scientists thought that understanding the structure of proteins would reveal "the secret of life" because proteins were believed to carry inherited information. Attempts to understand protein structure led to establishment of molecular biology, the study of the structure and function of chemicals in living things, which now dominates much of biological laboratory research.

Wrinch proposed that proteins were made up of six-sided units called cyclols, which interlocked to form two-dimensional sheets. This theory—and Wrinch's sometimes strident insistence on it—aroused great controversy, with Nobel Prize–winning scientists taking both sides. It could explain much of what was known about the behavior of proteins, but, despite Wrinch's claims to the contrary, little direct evidence supported it.

Wrinch was a visiting scholar at Johns Hopkins University from 1939 to 1941 and hoped to remain to the United States, but the contention about her theory made finding a permanent position hard. Otto Glaser, a biologist at Amherst College in Massachusetts, helped her in this aim, and they married in 1941. Wrinch became a U.S. citizen in 1943 and began teaching full-time at Smith College in 1944.

Wrinch's later achievements included the book *Fourier Transforms and Structure Factors* (1946), which described the mathematics of X-ray crystallography. She spent most of her time, however, trying to prove her cyclol theory. Research in the early 1950s confirmed that cyclols existed in nature, but they did not prove to be the key to protein structure that Wrinch had hoped. By that time, furthermore, attention had shifted to nucleic acids when they rather than proteins

213

At Oxford University in the 1930s, Dorothy Wrinch devised the first precise theory of the structure of proteins, vital biological molecules that at the time were thought to carry inherited information. Beginning in the 1940s, she continued her research and teaching at Smith College, where she is seen here explaining her ideas to a special studies class.
(Courtesy Sophia Smith Collection, Smith College)

were shown to be the carriers of inherited information. Wrinch retired from Smith in 1971 and died in February 1976, at age 82.

Further Reading

Abir-Am, Pnina G. "Synergy or Clash: Disciplinary and Marital Strategies in the Career of Mathematical Biologist Dorothy Wrinch." In *Uneasy Careers and Intimate Lives: Women in Science 1789-1979*, edited by Pnina G. Abir-Am and Dorinda Outram, 239–280. New Brunswick, N.J.: Rutgers Univerity Press, 1987.

Julian, Maureen M. "Women in Crystallography." In *Women of Science: Righting the Record*, edited by G. Kass-Simon and Patricia Farnes, 364–368. Bloomington: Indiana University Press, 1990.

✳ WU, CHIEN-SHIUNG
(1912–) *American Physicist*

"This small, modest woman was powerful enough to do what armies can never accomplish," a reporter from the *New York Post* wrote of Chien-shiung Wu in 1957. "She helped destroy a law of nature." In a difficult, painstaking experiment, Wu proved that what had been considered a basic law of physics did not always hold true.

Chien-shiung Wu was born in Liu-ho, a town near Shanghai, China, on May 29, 1912. Her father, Wu Zong-yee (Chinese place their family names first), was a school principal. Unlike most top of the world," as she put it, for anyone interested in the interior of atoms.

Wu earned her doctorate in 1940. In 1942 she married Luke Yuan, a fellow physicist whom she had met at Berkeley. They had a son, Vincent, in 1945. Her research specialty became beta decay, in which a neutron in the nucleus of a radioactive atom spontaneously breaks apart, releasing a fast-moving electron (a beta particle) and a second particle called a neutrino, which has no mass or charge. A proton is left behind, automatically converting the atom into an atom of a different element.

After teaching physics at Smith College for a year, Wu (who continued to use her maiden name professionally) moved to Columbia University in March 1944 and joined the Manhattan Project, the research project that led to the creation of the atomic bomb. Her work consisted chiefly of looking for ways to produce more of the radioactive form of uranium. She also improved the design of Geiger counters, which detect radiation.

Wu remained at Columbia after the war, rising to the rank of associate professor in 1952, and continued her studies of beta decay. She became a U.S. citizen in 1954. She was known as a fair but exacting teacher (she once said, "In physics . . . you must have total commitment. It is not just a job. It is a way of life") and a meticulous experimentalist. Indeed, a fellow scientist said of her, "She has virtually never made a mistake in her experiments." This latter reputation brought two other Chinese-born physicists, Chen Ning Yang and Tsung Dao Lee, to her late in 1956, asking for help in finding out whether a groundbreaking idea they had was correct.

Some materials in nature are either "right handed" or "left handed"; in other words, they are mirror images of each other. For instance, particles in the atomic nucleus can spin either clockwise or counterclockwise. Since 1925, physicists had believed that physical reactions would be the same (have parity, or equality) whether the particles involved in them were right handed or left handed. This was called the law of conservation of parity. When one form of radioactive decay appeared to

Chien-shiung Wu's painstaking experiment helped two fellow Chinese-born American researchers disprove what had been thought to be a fundamental law of physics.
(Courtesy Emilio Segrè Visual Archives, American Institute of Physics)

Chinese of his day, he believed that girls should receive the same education as boys.

When Chien-shiung studied physics in high school, she says "I soon knew it was what I wanted to go on with." She continued her education at the National Central University in Nanjing, from which she graduated in 1936. She decided to do her graduate work in the United States and enrolled in the University of California at Berkeley, then "the violate the parity law, most physicists thought that an error must have occurred, but Yang and Lee made the shocking suggestion in mid-1956 that the parity law might not hold true in weak nuclear interactions, which include radioactive decay.

Wu decided to test Yang and Lee's idea with an experiment that used radioactive cobalt, or cobalt-60. A strong electromagnetic field could make the cobalt atoms line up, just as iron filings do near a magnet, and spin along the same axis. Wu could then count the number of beta particles thrown from their nuclei in different directions as the atoms decayed. If the parity law held true for weak interactions, the number of particles thrown off in the direction of the nuclei's spin would be the same as the number thrown the opposite way. If the law did not hold, the numbers would differ.

There was only one problem: At normal temperatures, the cobalt atoms would move around too much to line up under the magnet. The experiment therefore had to be done at almost absolute zero (-459.67°F or -273.15°C), the temperature at which all atomic motion due to heat stops. Wu took her work to the National Bureau of Standards in Washington, D.C., the only laboratory in the country where material could be cooled to such a low temperature. During the testing, as she repeated the experiment many times, Wu often got only four hours of sleep a night. "It was . . . a nightmare," she said later. "I wouldn't want to go through [it] again."

At the end of the nightmare, however, the results were clear: Far more beta particles flew off in the direction opposite the nuclei's spin than in the direction that matched the spin. The law of parity therefore did not apply to weak interactions. This finding, which Wu announced on January 16, 1957, caused a great sensation. Lee and Yang won a Nobel Prize in 1957 for their theory. Wu was not so honored, but in 1958 she became a full professor at Columbia and was elected to the National Academy of Sciences.

Wu remained at Columbia for the rest of her career, where she was, as Emilio Segrè, one of her former professors at Berkeley, put it, the "reigning queen of nuclear physics." She continued to make important discoveries and tests of others' theories and to win awards for her work, including the Comstock Award of the National Academy of Sciences and the National Medal of Science, the country's highest science award. She retired in 1981.

Soon after her parity experiment, Wu told a group of students, "It is the courage to doubt what has long been established, the incessant search for its verification and proof, that pushed the wheel of science forward." Wu has made major contributions to pushing that wheel.

Further Reading

Lindop, Laurie. *Dynamic Modern Women: Scientists and Doctors.* New York: Holt, 1997, 95–105.

McGrayne, Sharon Bertsch. *Nobel Prize Women in Science: Their Lives, Struggles, and Momentous Discoveries.* New York: Birch Lane Press, 1993, 255–279.

"Wu, Chien-shiung." *Current Biography Yearbook 1959.* New York: H. W. Wilson, 1959, 491–492.

Yount, Lisa. *Contemporary Women Scientists.* New York: Facts On File, 1994, 38–47.

Y

 YALOW, ROSALYN SUSSMAN
(1921–) *American Physicist and Medical Researcher*

Rosalyn Yalow and her research partner, Solomon Berson, invented a technique called radioimmunoassay that measures substances in body fluids so accurately that reporters have said it could detect a lump of sugar dropped into Lake Erie. For this advance Yalow won a Nobel Prize in 1977.

Yalow was born Rosalyn Sussman on July 19, 1921, in the South Bronx area of New York City. Her parents, Simon and Clara Sussman, had grown up in the city's immigrant community. Simon Sussman owned a small paper and twine business, which earned just enough money for his family to live on. "If you wanted something, you worked for it," Yalow recalled.

Even as a child, Rosalyn was aggressive and determined. A family story told how a stern first-grade teacher hit her older brother, Alexander, on the knuckles with a ruler to discipline him, sending him home in tears. When Rosalyn reached the same grade, the teacher hit her, too—and Rosalyn hit her back. Sent to the principal's office, she explained that she had been waiting for years to avenge her brother. "That's the attitude that made

it possible for me to go into physics," she told writer Sharon McGrayne.

By the time Rosalyn was eight, she had decided that she was going to be a "big deal" scientist—"I liked knowing things," she told McGrayne—and marry and have a family to boot. She went to Hunter College, which charged no tuition to New York City residents. There her attention turned to physics because, as she says, "In the late thirties . . . nuclear physics was the most exciting field in the world." She graduated with high honors in January 1941.

As a Jewish woman with little money, Sussman had three strikes against her in trying to get into a graduate school or medical school. At first she thought her only hope was to work as a secretary at Columbia University Medical School, which would allow her to take classes there for free. Impending war drained universities of men and created new openings for women, however, and Sussman obtained a teaching assistantship in physics at the University of Illinois in Champaign-Urbana. On her first day of classes there in fall 1941 she met another Jewish New Yorker, a rabbi's son from Syracuse named Aaron Yalow. They married on June 6, 1943, and later had two children. From the start, Yalow supported his wife's career.

Working at the Bronx Veterans Administration Hospital, Rosalyn Yalow and her research partner, Solomon Berson, developed the radioimmunoassay, a technique that uses radioisotopes to measure extremely small amounts of biological substances in fluids. In 1977, after Berson's death, Yalow won a share of the Nobel Prize in physiology or medicine for this research.
(Courtesy Rosalyn S. Yalow)

Once the Yalows finished their Ph.D.s in 1945—Rosalyn was only the second woman to earn a physics doctorate from Illinois—they returned to New York. Rosalyn became an engineer at the Federal Telecommunications Laboratory, the first woman to hold this position, and then, when the laboratory moved away a year later, began teaching at Hunter. Hunter had no research facilities, however, and she wanted to do research. Aaron suggested that she look into the new field of medical physics. It focused mostly on radioisotopes, radioactive forms of elements that were usually made in the atom-smasher machines invented during the war.

Rosalyn Yalow consulted EDITH QUIMBY, a pioneer researcher in medical physics at Columbia, and Quimby in turn introduced Yalow to her boss, Gioacchino Failla. On Failla's recommendation, the Bronx Veterans Administration (VA) Hospital hired Yalow in December 1947. Her laboratory, one of the first radioisotope laboratories in the United States, was a former janitor's closet, and she had to design and build most of her own equipment. Until 1950 she continued to teach at Hunter as well, inspiring and mentoring such students as MILDRED DRESSELHAUS.

In the fall of 1950, Yalow found her ideal professional partner in a young physician named Solomon A. Berson. Their collaboration lasted 22 years. One coworker told Sharon McGrayne that Yalow and Berson had "a kind of eerie extrasensory perception. Each knew what the other was thinking. . . . Each had complete trust and confidence in the other."

The VA thought of radioisotopes mainly as a cheaper substitute for radium in the treatment of cancer, but Yalow and Berson learned that these substances could also be attached to molecules and used to track chemicals through reactions in the body or in test tubes. In one of their first studies, published in 1956, they used radioisotope tagging to show that the immune systems of diabetics, who must take daily injections of the hormone insulin to make up for their body's lack of it, formed substances called antibodies in response to the insulin they took, which came from cows or pigs and thus was slightly different from human insulin.

This finding was startling enough—researchers had believed that insulin molecules were too small to produce such a response—but more important, Berson and Yalow realized that they could turn their discovery on its head to create a very sensitive way of measuring insulin or almost any other biological substance in body fluids. They injected the substance they wanted to test for into laboratory animals, making the animals produce antibodies to it. They then mixed a known amount of these antibodies with a known amount of the radioactively tagged substance and a sample of the fluid to be tested.

Antibodies attach to molecules of the substance that caused their formation. The nonradioactive substance in the sample attached to some of the antibodies, keeping the radioactive substance from doing so. After a certain amount of time, Yalow and Berson measured the radioactive material not attached to the antibodies. The more substance had been in the sample, the more radioactive material would be left over. This test, the radioimmunoassay, can detect as little as a billionth of a gram of material. In 1978, *Current Biography Yearbook* called it "one of the most important postwar applications of basic research to clinical medicine."

Berson and Yalow first described radioimmunoassay in 1959. They spent the 1960s perfecting the test and persuading researchers to use it. Scientists applied their technique to make a host of discoveries about the way hormones and other substances function in health and disease. Radioimmunoassay has also revealed illegal drugs, helped doctors work out the best dose of medicines, and screened donated blood for viruses.

Yalow and Berson worked together only part-time after 1968, when Berson became a professor at Mount Sinai School of Medicine and Yalow became acting chief of the hospital's radioisotope service. Still, they remained close until Berson died suddenly of a heart attack in 1972, at age 54. His death devastated Yalow both personally and professionally. She found she had to prove her worth all over again as a solo researcher, and she did so by making discoveries about a variety of hormones.

Yalow accumulated many honors for her work, including the American Medical Association's Scientific Achievement Award and election to the National Academy of Sciences in 1975. In 1976 she became the first woman to win the Albert Lasker Basic Medical Research Award, often considered a prelude to a Nobel Prize in physiology or medicine. A year later she finally won the "Big One"—the Nobel Prize itself. It was the first time that the surviving member of a partnership was honored for work done by both. (She shared the prize with two other researchers who had made discoveries about hormones in the brain.) Yalow was the second woman (after GERTY CORI) to win a Nobel in physiology or medicine and the first American-born woman to win any science Nobel Prize. In 1988 she also won the National Medal of Science, the highest science award in the United States.

Yalow retired in 1991, but in 1998 she was still coming in to her office at the Veterans Administration Hospital and doing some research, although her health had begun to fail. During the 1990s she gave many lectures on such subjects as nuclear power, which she feels is unjustly feared; the need for better science education in the United States; and the need for more women scientists. "The world cannot afford the loss of the talents of half its people," she said in her Nobel Prize acceptance speech.

Further Reading

Dash, Joan. *The Triumph of Discovery: Women Scientists Who Won the Nobel Prize.* New York: Julian Messner, 1991, 35–65.

McGrayne, Sharon Bertsch. *Nobel Prize Women in Science: Their Lives, Struggles, and Momentous Discoveries.* New York: Birch Lane Press, 1993, 333–355.

Straus, Eugene. *Rosalyn Yalow, Nobel Laureate: Her Life and Work in Medicine.* New York: Plenum Press, 1998.

Veglahn, Nancy. *Women Scientists.* New York: Facts On File, 1991, 106–116.

"Yalow, Rosalyn S(ussman)." *Current Biography Yearbook 1978.* New York: H. W. Wilson, 1978, 458–460.

✳ YENER, KUTLU ASLIHAN
(1946–) *Turkish/American Archaeologist*

Aslihan Yener's discovery of mines and metal-refining sites have changed researchers' understanding of metalworking and trade in the ancient Middle East. She has also developed a new method of determining the chemical composition of artifacts. She was born on July 21, 1946, in Istanbul, Turkey, but her parents, businessman Reha Turkkan and his wife, Eire Guntekin, brought her to the United States when she was just six months old. She and her younger sister grew up in New Rochelle, New York, where, she says, she "almost lived at the Natural History Museum."

Yener studied chemistry at Adelphi University in Garden City, New York, but after a few years she "got the travel bug" and went to Turkey. She transferred to Robert College (later Bosphorus University) in Istanbul in 1966 and changed her major to archaeology. After graduating in 1969, she studied at Columbia University from 1972 to 1980 and earned a Ph.D.

Yener first did chemical analyses of lead and silver in objects from the ancient Middle East to determine which mines they came from. This helped her form a picture of trade in the area. She then turned to tin, an important metal because it was both relatively rare and essential for making bronze. Bronze, an alloy of copper and tin, was used to make most metal objects between about 3000 and 1100 B.C., a period now called the Bronze Age.

In 1987, while Yener was an associate professor in history at Bosphorus University (a post she held from 1980 to 1988) as well as working for the Turkish Geological Research and Survey Directorate, she found the remains of a Bronze Age tin mine in the Taurus Mountains, which in ancient times were part of an area called Anatolia. Lead and silver mines had been found there before, but ancient writings had claimed that tin was imported from

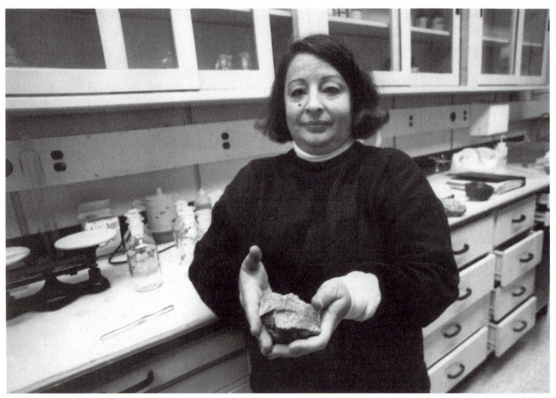

Kutlu Aslihan Yener of the University of Chicago's Oriental Institute discovered a tin mine and a refining center in Turkey's Taurus Mountains that were active during the Bronze Age, between 3,000 and 5,000 years ago. She is shown holding a piece of a pottery crucible from the refining site in which tin ore was heated to extract the metal. Recently she has developed a technique to analyze the chemical composition of different parts of ancient artifacts.
(Courtesy University of Chicago)

much farther east. Yener's 1989 discovery of a city where tin ore had been refined, at a site called Goltepe near her mine, provided confirming evidence that Anatolia had been an important source of tin. Her findings have changed archaeologists' understanding of trade in this period, when complex civilizations and international trade were starting to appear.

Yener has worked for the Oriental Institute of the University of Chicago since 1994 and is now an associate professor there. In early 1998 she announced a new technique for analyzing the chemical composition of ancient objects. It uses Argonne Laboratories' Advanced Photon Source, a device that passes high-energy X rays through objects and acts as a "chemical microscope." The technique can determine the composition of different parts of the same object, revealing how objects were made and mended. "This is the most important scientific development in archaeology since the discovery of radiocarbon dating," the most widely used method of estimating the ages of ancient artifacts, Yener claimed in a press release.

Further Reading

Bass, Thomas. "Land of Bronze." *Discover*, December 1991, 63–66.

Yount, Lisa. *Twentieth-Century Women Scientists*. New York: Facts On File, 1996, 107–115.

Z

 ZHAO YUFEN
(1948–)   *Chinese Biochemist*

Zhao Yufen has made discoveries about the importance of the element phosphorus in biochemistry, including a possible role in the origin of life. She was born in Qi County of Hunan Province, China, in 1948, but her family moved to the island of Taiwan when she was still a baby, and she grew up there. She studied chemistry as an undergraduate at Tsinghua University in Taiwan, then earned a doctorate in organic chemistry in 1975 from the State University of New York at Stony Brook. She worked as an industrial chemist in the United States before moving back to mainland China with her family in 1979. She then became a teacher and researcher in organic chemistry at the Chemistry Research Institute of the Chinese Academy of Sciences.

Zhao's special interest is the role of phosphorus in organic (carbon-containing) and biological compounds. She told an international scientific meeting in 1988 that phosphorus "boasts the function of regulating and controlling the activities of biological elements, much like the central control room of an airport." She has developed a method for creating new phosphorus-containing organic compounds, including one substance that shows promise as an anticancer drug. Some of her studies have also indicated a possible role for phosphorus in the origin of life.

In 1991, Zhao Yufen joined Tsinghua University in Beijing, on mainland China, and established there a laboratory devoted to phosphorus. She received a second-class technical progress award from the Chinese Academy of Sciences in 1988 and later was made a general member of that prestigious body, the youngest person ever to receive this honor. In 1998 she was a professor of the department of chemistry, dean of the National Education Committee's open laboratory of bioorganic phosphorus chemistry, and vice dean of the school of life science and engineering at Tsinghua University.

Further Reading

Huang Wei. "In What Once Is Man's World." *Beijing Review*, March 9-15, 1992, 29–30.

RECOMMENDED SOURCES ON WOMEN SCIENTISTS AND MATHEMATICIANS

Abir-Am, Pnina G., and Dorinda Outram, eds. *Uneasy Careers and Intimate Lives: Women in Science 1789–1979.* New Brunswick, N.J.: Rutgers University Press, 1987.

Abram, Ruth J. *Send Us a Lady Physician: Women Doctors in America, 1835–1920.* New York: W. W. Norton, 1985.

Agnes Scott College. "Biographies of Women Mathematicians." Available online. URL: http://www.agnesscott.edulriddle/women/ women.htp

Ainley, Marianne Gosztonyi, ed. *Despite the Odds: Essays on Canadian Women and Science.* Montreal: Véhicule Press, 1990.

Alic, Margaret. *Hypatia's Heritage: A History of Women in Science from Antiquity Through the Nineteenth Century.* Boston: Beacon Press, 1986.

Ambrosser, Susan, ed. *No Universal Constants: Journeys of Women in Science and Engineering.* Philadelphia: Temple University Press, 1990.

American Association for the Advancement of Science. *Science in Africa: Women Leading from Strength.* Washington, D.C.: American Association for the Advancement of Science, 1993.

American Women in Science series. Bethesda, Md.: Equity Institute, 1987.

Arnold, Lois Barber. *Four Lives in Science: Women's Education in the Nineteenth Century.* New York: Schocken Books, 1984.

Bailey, Brooke. *The Remarkable Lives of 100 Women Healers and Scientists.* Holbrook, Mass.: Bob Adams, 1994.

Bailey, Martha J. *American Women in Science: A Biographic Dictionary.* Santa Barbara, Calif.: ABC-Clio, 1994.

Benjamin, Marina, ed. *Science and Sensibility: Gender and Scientific Inquiry, 1780–1945.* Cambridge, Mass.: Blackwell, 1991.

Bleier, Ruth, ed. *Feminist Approaches to Science.* New York: Pergamon Press, 1986.

———. *Science and Gender.* New York: Pergamon Press, 1984.

Bonta, Marcia Myers. *Women in the Field: America's Pioneering Women Naturalists.* College Station, Tex.: Texas A&M University Press, 1991.

Brooke, Elisabeth. *Women Healers: Portraits of Herbalists, Physicians, and Midwives.* Rochester, Vt.: Healing Arts Press, 1995.

Camp, Carole A. *American Astronomers: Searchers and Wonderers.* Springfield, N.J.: Enslow, 1996.

Chaff, Sandra L., et al., eds. *Women in Medicine: A Bibliography of the Literature on Women Physicians.* Metuchen, N.J.: Scarecrow Press, 1977.

Chang, Hsiao-lin. *Vital Force on the Development of the Chinese Nation: Women Scientists and Technicians in China.* China: China Intercontinental Press, 1995.

Chipman, Susan F., et al., eds. *Women and Mathematics: Balancing the Equation.* Mahwah, N.J.: Lawrence Erlbaum Associates, 1985.

Clewell, Beatriz C., and Bernice Anderson. *Women of Color in Mathematics, Science & Engineering: A Review of the Literature.* Washington, D.C.: Center for Women Policy Studies, 1991.

Cole, Jonathan R. *Fair Science.* New York: Columbia University Press, 1987 (reprint of 1979 ed.).

Cooney, Miriam P., ed. *Celebrating Women in Mathematics and Science.* Reston, Va.: National Council of Teachers of Mathematics, 1996.

CWP [Contributions of Women to Physics] at physics.UCLA.edu. Available online. URL: http://www.physics.ucla.edu/~cwp.html.

Dash, Joan. *The Triumph of Discovery: Women Scientists Who Won the Nobel Prize.* Parsippany, N.J.: Silver Burdett, 1990.

Discover. "Special Issue: A Celebration of Women in Science." December 1991.

Emberlin, Diane. *Contributions of Women in Science.* Minneapolis: Dillon Press, 1977.

Epstein, Vivian Sheldon. *History of Women in Science for Young People.* Denver, Colo.: VSE Publisher, 1994.

Etzkowitz, Henry, et al. "The Paradox of Critical Mass for Women in Science." *Science,* October 7, 1994, 51–54.

Facklam, Margery. *Wild Animals, Gentle Women.* New York: Harcourt Brace Jovanovich, 1978.

Fausto-Sterling, Anne, and Lydia L. English. *Women and Minorities in Science: Course Materials Guide.* Providence, R.I.: Brown University, 1990.

Forbes, Malcolm. *Women Who Made a Difference.* New York: Simon & Schuster, 1990.

Fort, Deborah C., ed. *A Hand Up: Women Mentoring Women in Science.* Washington, D.C.: Association for Women in Science, 1993.

Gacs, Uta, et al., eds. *Women Anthropologists: A Biographical Dictionary.* New York: Greenwood Press, 1988.

Glazer, Penina Migdal, and Miriam Slater. *Unequal Colleagues: The Entrance of Women into the Professions, 1890–1940.* New Brunswick, N.J.: Rutgers University Press, 1987.

Gleasner, Diana C. *Breakthrough: Women in Science.* New York: Walker, 1983.

Gornick, Vivian. *Women in Science: One Hundred Journeys into the Territory.* New York: Simon & Schuster, 1990.

———. *Women in Science: Portraits from a World in Transition.* New York: Simon & Schuster, 1983.

Griffiths, Sian, ed. *Beyond the Glass Ceiling: Forty Women Whose Ideas Shape the Modern World.* Manchester, England: Manchester University Press, 1996.

Grinstein, Louise S., Rose K. Rose, and Miriam H. Rafailovich, eds. *Women in Chemistry and Physics: A Biobibliographic Sourcebook.* Westport, Conn.: Greenwood Press, 1993.

———. and Paul J. Campbell, eds., *Women of Mathematics: A Biobibliographic Sourcebook.* Westport, Conn.: Greenwood Press, 1987.

Haas, Violet B., and Perrucci, Carolyn C., eds. *Women in Scientific and Engineering Professions.* Dearborn: University of Michigan Press, 1984.

Haber, Louis. *Women Pioneers of Science.* New York: Harcourt Brace Jovanovich, 1979.

Herzenberg, Caroline L. *Women Scientists from Antiquity to the Present.* West Cornwall, Conn.: Locust Hill Press, 1986.

Holloway, Marguerite. "A Lab of Her Own." *Scientific American,* November 1993, 94–103.

Hurd-Mead, Kate Campbell. *A History of Women in Medicine, from the Earliest Times to the Beginning of the Nineteenth Century.* Boston: Milford House, 1973 (reprint of 1938 ed.).

James, Edward T., ed. *Notable American Women 1607–1950: A Biographical Dictionary.* Three Volumes. Cambridge, Mass.: The Belknap Press of Harvard University Press, 1971.

Kahle, Jane B., ed. *Women in Science: A Report from the Field.* Bristol, Pa.: Taylor and Francis, 1985.

Kass-Simon, G., and Patricia Farnes, eds. *Women of Science: Righting the Record.* Bloomington: Indiana University Press, 1990.

Keller, Evelyn Fox. *Reflections on Gender and Science.* New Haven, Conn.: Yale University Press, 1985.

Kelly, Farley, ed. *On the Edge of Discovery.* Melbourne, Australia: Text Pub. Co., 1993.

Kennedy, Rebecca, and Michelle Cadoree, eds. "Women in the Sciences." *LC Science Tracer Bullet 90–6.* Washington, D.C.: Library of Congress, 1990.

Kevles, Bettyann. *Watching the Wild Apes: The Primate Studies of Goodall, Fossey, and Galdikas.* New York: Dutton, 1976.

Koshleva, I. *Women in Science.* Tr. Frances Longman. Moscow: Progress Publishers, 1983.

Kreinberg, Nancy. *I'm Madly in Love with Electricity and Other Comments About Their Work by Women in*

Science and Engineering. Berkeley, Calif.: Lawrence Hall of Science/University of California, 1977.

Krishnaraj, Maithreyi. *Women and Science: Selected Essays*. Bombay: Himalaya Publishing House, 1991.

Kundsin, Ruth B., ed. *Successful Women in the Sciences*. New York: New York Academy of Sciences, 1973.

———. *Women and Success: The Anatomy of Achievement*. New York: William Morrow, 1973.

LaBastille, Anne. *Women and Wilderness*. San Francisco: Sierra Club Books, 1980.

Land, Barbara. *The New Explorers: Women in Antarctica*. New York: Dodd, Mead, 1981.

Lankford, John, and Rickey L. Slavings. "Gender and Science: Women in American Astronomy, 1859–1940." *Physics Today*, March 1990, 58–65.

Levin, Beatrice. *Women and Medicine*. Lincoln, Neb.: Media Publishers, 1988.

Lindop, Laurie. *Dynamic Modern Women: Scientists and Doctors*. New York: Holt, 1997.

Lotze, Barbara. *Making Contributions: An Historical Overview of Women's Role in Physics*. College Park, Md.: American Association of Physics, 1984.

McGrayne, Sharon Bertsch. *Nobel Prize Women in Science: Their Lives, Struggles, and Momentous Discoveries*. New York: Birch Lane Press, 1993.

McHenry, Robert, ed. *Famous American Women: A Biographical Dictionary from Colonial Times to the Present*. New York: Dover Publications, 1980.

McLean Media. *Telling Our Stories: Women in Science* CD-ROM. Information available online. see URL: http://www.storyline.com

Marks, Geoffrey, and William K. Beatty. *Women in White*. New York: Charles Scribner's Sons, 1972.

Marlow, Joan. *The Great Women*. New York: Galahad Books, 1979.

May, Elizabeth. *Claiming the Future: The Inspiring Lives of Twelve Canadian Women Scientists and Scholars*. Markham, Ontario: Pembroke Publishers, 1991.

Merchant, Carolyn. *The Death of Nature: Women, Ecology, and the Scientific Revolution*. New York: Harper & Row, 1989.

Montgomery, Sy. *Walking with the Great Apes*. Boston: Houghton Mifflin, 1991.

Morantz, Regina Markell, Cynthia Stodola Pomerleau, and Carol Hansen Fenichel, eds. *In Her Own Words: Oral Histories of Women Physicians*. Westport, Conn.: Greenwood Press, 1982.

Morse, Mary. Women Changing Science: *Voices from a Field in Transition*. New York: Plenum Press, 1995.

Nies, Kevin Allison. *From Sorceress to Scientist*. Tarzana: The California Video Institute, 1990.

Noble, Iris. *Contemporary Women Scientists of America*. New York: Julian Messner, 1979.

O'Connell, Agnes N., and Nancy Felipe Russo. *Models of Achievement: Reflections of Eminent Women in Psychology*. New York: Columbia University Press, 1983.

Ogilvie, Marilyn Bailey. *Women in Science: Antiquity Through the Nineteenth Century*. Cambridge, Mass.: MIT Press, 1986.

——— and Kerry Lynne Meek. *Women and Science: An Annotated Bibliography*. New York: Garland, 1996.

O'Hern, Elizabeth Moot. *Profiles of Pioneer Women Scientists*. Washington, D.C.: Acropolis Books, 1985.

O'Neill, Lois Decker, ed. *The Women's Book of World Records and Achievements*. Garden City, N.Y.: Doubleday, 1979.

Opfell, Olga S. *The Lady Laureates: Women Who Have Won the Nobel Prize*. Metuchen, N.J.: Scarecrow Press, 1986.

Osen, Lynn M. *Women in Mathematics*. Cambridge, Mass.: MIT Press, 1974.

Parker, Lesley H., et al., eds. *Gender, Science, and Mathematics: Shortening the Shadow*. Norwell, Mass.: Kluwer Academic Publishers, 1995.

Perl, Teri H. *Women and Numbers: Lives of Women Mathematicians*. San Carlos, Calif.: Wide World Publishing/Tetra, 1993.

Phillips, Patricia. *The Scientific Lady: A Social History of Women's Scientific Interests, 1520–1918*. New York: St. Martin's, 1990.

Raven, Susan, and Alison Weir. *Women of Achievement: Thirty-five Centuries of History*. New York: Harmony Books, 1981.

Read, Phyllis J., and Bernard L. Whitleib. *The Book of Women's Firsts*. New York: Random House, 1992.

Reed, Elizabeth Wagner. *American Women in Science Before the Civil War*. Minneapolis: University of Minnesota Press, 1992.

Richter, Derek, ed. *Women Scientists: The Road to Liberation*. London: Macmillan, 1982.

Rosser, Sue V. *Biology and Feminism: A Dynamic Interaction*. New York: Twayne, 1992.

———. *Female-Friendly Science*. New York: Pergamon Press, 1995.

Rossiter, Margaret W. *Women Scientists in America: Before Affirmative Action, 1940–1972*. Baltimore: Johns Hopkins University Press, 1995.

————. *Women Scientists in America: Struggles and Strategies to 1940.* Baltimore: Johns Hopkins University Press, 1982.

Rubin, Vera. "Women's Work." *Science 86,* July-August 1986, 58–65.

Sayers, Janet. *Mothers of Psychoanalysis.* New York: W. W. Norton, 1991.

Scarborough, Elizabeth, and Laurel Furumoto. Untold Lives: *The First Generation of Women Psychologists.* New York: Columbia University Press, 1987.

Schiebinger, Londa. *The Mind Has No Sex? Women in the Origins of Modern Science.* Cambridge, Mass.: Harvard University Press, 1989

Schulman, Audrey. "More Women of the Week." Available online. URL: http://www.edu.org/Womens Equity/WOW

Science. March 13, 1992 special issue.

Science. April 16, 1993 special issue.

Science. March 11, 1994 special issue.

Shearer, Benjamin F., and Barbara S. Shearer, eds. *Notable Women in the Life Sciences: A Biographical Dictionary.* Westport, Conn.: Greenwood, 1996.

Shepard, Linda J. Lifting the Veil: *The Feminine Face of Science.* Boston: Shambhala, 1993.

Shiels, Barbara. *Winners: Women and the Nobel Prize.* Minneapolis, Minn.: Dillon Press, 1985.

Sicherman, Barbara, and Carol Hurd Green, eds. *Notable American Women: The Modern Period.* Cambridge, Mass.: The Belknap Press of Harvard University Press, 1980.

Siegel, Patricia Joan, and Kay Thomas Finley. *Women in the Scientific Search: An American Biobibliography.* Metuchen, N.J.: Scarecrow Press, 1985.

Sirch, Willow Ann. *Eco-Women: Protectors of the Earth.* Golden, Colo.: Fulcrum Publishing, 1996.

Stille, Darlene. *Extraordinary Women Scientists.* Danbury, Conn.: Children's Press, 1995.

Stoddard, Hope. *Famous American Women.* New York: Thomas Y. Crowell, 1970.

"Superstars of Science: Black Researchers Are Making Trailblazing Discoveries in Some of the Country's Most Prestigious Labs." *Ebony,* June 1991, 42–46.

Uglow, Jennifer S., ed. *The International Dictionary of Women's Biography.* New York: Continuum Publishing, 1982.

Vare, Ethlie Ann, and Greg Ptacek. *Mothers of Invention.* New York: William Morrow, 1988.

Veglahn, Nancy J. *Women Scientists.* New York: Facts On File, 1991.

Warren, Rebecca Lowe, and Mary H. Thompson. *The Scientist Within You: Experiments and Biographies of Distinguished Women in Science.* Eugene, Ore: ACI, 1995.

Women in the Sciences: A Source Guide. New York: Gordon Press, 1991.

Yost, Edna. *American Women of Science.* Philadelphia: Frederick A. Stokes, 1943.

————. *Women of Modern Science.* New York: Dodd, Mead, 1959.

Yount, Lisa. *Contemporary Women Scientists.* New York: Facts On File, 1994.

————. *Twentieth-Century Women Scientists.* New York: Facts On File, 1996.

Zahm, John Augustine (published under pseud. H. J. Mozans). *Woman in Science.* Cambridge, Mass.: MIT Press, 1974 (reprint of 1913 ed.).

Zuckerman, Harriet, Jonathan R. Cole, and John T. Bruer, eds. *The Outer Circle: Women in the Scientific Community.* New York: W. W. Norton, 1991.

ENTRIES BY FIELD

Anthropology

Benedict, Ruth Fulton 18
Hrdy, Sarah Blaffer 95
Leakey, Mary Douglas Nicol 117
Mead, Margaret 143

Archaeology

Hawes, Harriet Ann Boyd 85
Nuttall, Zelia Maria Magdalena 164
Yener, Kutlu Aslihan 219

Astronomy

Bell Burnell, Susan Jocelyn 16
Burbidge, Eleanor Margaret
   Peachey 26
Cannon, Annie Jump 29
Faber, Sandra Moore 63
Fleming, Williamina Paton
   Stevens 65
Geller, Margaret Joan 76
Herschel, Caroline Lucretia 87
Hypatia 99
Kirch, Maria Margaretha
   Winkelmann 112
Leavitt, Henrietta Swan 118
Maury, Antonia Caetana 140
Mitchell, Maria 151
Payne-Gaposchkin, Cecilia
   Helena 173
Rubin, Vera Cooper 183

Biochemistry

Cori, Gerty Theresa Radnitz 40
Rajalakshmi, R. 179
Seibert, Florence Barbara 190
Sithole-Niang, Idah 192
Zhao Yufen 222

Botany

Brandegee, Mary Katharine
   Layne 24
Eastwood, Alice 53
Edlund, Sylvia 56
Fawcett, Stella Grace Maisie 64
Hildegarde of Bingen 88
Mexia, Ynes Enriquetta Julietta
   150
Patrick, Ruth 169

Brain Research

Bechtereva, Natalia Petrovna 15
Frith, Uta Auernhammer 72
Levy, Jerre 123

Cancer Research

Cobb, Jewel Plummer 38
Slye, Maud Caroline 192
Stewart, Sarah 197
Wright, Jane Cooke 212

Chemistry

Carr, Emma Perry 31
Cleopatra the Alchemist 37
Cremer, Erika 42
Curie, Marie 43
Elion, Gertrude Belle 57
Franklin, Rosalind Elsie 69
Joliot-Curie, Irène 104
Makhubu, Lydia Phindile 135
Maria the Jewess 138
Perey, Marguerite Catherine 174
Richards, Ellen Henrietta
   Swallow 180
Saruhashi, Katsuko 188
Wrinch, Dorothy Maud 213

Computer Science

Hopper, Grace Brewster Murray
   92
Lovelace, Augusta Ada Byron 127

Crystallography

Franklin, Rosalind Elsie 68
Hodgkin, Dorothy Crowfoot 89
Lonsdale, Kathleen Yardley 125

Ecology

Carson, Rachel Louise 33
Colborn, Theodora 39
Duplaix, Nicole 49
Jorge Pádua, Maria Tereza 106
Maathai, Wangari Muta 130
Morgan, Ann Haven 154
Patrick, Ruth 169

Engineering

Ancker-Johnson, Betsy 4
Ayrton, Hertha 10
Dresselhaus, Mildred Spiewak 48
Flügge-Lotz, Irmgard 67
Gilbreth, Lillian Evelyn Moller
    79

Genetics

King, Mary-Claire 109
McClintock, Barbara 131
Margulis, Lynn Alexander 136
Newton Turner, Helen Alma 158
Ohta, Tomoko 167
Sithole-Niang, Idah 192
Slye, Maud Caroline 192
Stevens, Nettie Maria 195
Wong-Staal, Flossie 211

Geology

Ajakaiye, Deborah Enilo 2
Bascom, Florence 13
Gardner, Julia Anna 75
Lehmann, Inge 120
McNally, Karen Cook 134
Saruhashi, Katsuko 188

Immunology

Ildstad, Suzanne 100
Marrack, Philippa 138
Matzinger, Polly 139

Marine Biology

Bennett, Isobel 19
Carson, Rachel Louise 33
Clark, Eugenie 36
Earle, Sylvia Alice 51
Van Dover, Cindy Lee 203

Mathematics

Agnesi, Maria Gaetana 1
Châtelet, Emilie du 35
Daubechies, Ingrid 46
Flügge-Lotz, Irmgard 66
Geiringer, Hilda 76
Germain, Marie Sophie 78
Hypatia 99
Kovalevskaia, Sofia
    Vasilyevna 113
Ladd-Franklin, Christine 116
Lovelace, Augusta Ada Byron 127
Morawetz, Cathleen Synge 153
Newton Turner, Helen Alma 159
Noether, Emmy 161
Robinson, Julia Bowman 182
Scott, Charlotte Angas 189

Somerville, Mary Fairfax 193
Wheeler, Anna Johnson Pell 209
Wrinch, Dorothy Maud 213

Medical Research

Anderson, Elda Emma 6
Elion, Gertrude Belle 57
Levi-Montalcini, Rita 121
Levy, Julia 123
Love, Susan 126
Makhubu, Lydia Phindile 135
Noguchi, Constance Tom 162
Pert, Candace Beebe 175
Quimby, Edith Hinkley 177
Sabin, Florence Rena 186
Stewart, Alice 196
Wexler, Nancy Sabin 207
Wong-Staal, Flossie 211
Yalow, Rosalyn Sussman 217

Medicine

Agnodice 2
Anderson, Elizabeth Garrett 7
Apgar, Virginia 9
Blackwell, Elizabeth 20
Hamilton, Alice 83
Hildegarde of Bingen 88
Jacoba Felicie 103
Jemison, Mae Carol 103
Kelsey, Frances Oldham 108
Love, Susan 126
Novello, Antonia Coello 164
Taussig, Helen 199
Trotula of Salerno 201

Meteorology

Simpson, Joanne Malkus 191

Microbiology

Alexander, Hattie Elizabeth 3
Dick, Gladys Rowena Henry 47
Eddy, Bernice 54
Evans, Alice Catherine 60
Hazen, Elizabeth Lee 86
Margulis, Lynn Alexander 136
Ocampo-Friedmann, Roseli 166
Seibert, Florence Barbara 190
Stewart, Sarah 197
Williams, Anna Wessels 210

Paleontology

Anning, Mary 8
Edinger, Johanna Gabrielle
    Ottelie 55
Gardner, Julia Anna 75
Leakey, Mary Douglas Nicol 117

Vrba, Elisabeth 205

Physics

Ancker-Johnson, Betsy 4
Andam, Aba A. Bentil 5
Anderson, Elda Emma 6
Ayrton, Hertha 10
Bassi, Laura Maria Catarina 14
Blodgett, Katharine Burr 22
Brooks, Harriet 25
Châtelet, Emilie du 35
Curie, Marie 43
Dresselhaus, Mildred Spiewak 48
Franklin, Melissa Eve Bronwen
    69
Hypatia 99
Jackson, Shirley Ann 102
Joliot-Curie, Irène 104
Mayer, Maria Gertrude
    Goeppert 141
Meitner, Lise 146
Perey, Marguerite Catherine 174
Quimby, Edith Hinkley 177
Quinn, Helen Rhoda Arnold 178
Wu, Chien-shiung 214
Yalow, Rosalyn Sussman 217

Physiology

Hyde, Ida Henrietta 97

Psychology

Boden, Margaret 23
Frith, Uta Auernhammer 72
Gilbreth, Lillian Evelyn Moller
    79
Horney, Karen Danielsen 94
Klein, Melanie Reizes 112
Ladd-Franklin, Christine 116
Levy, Jerre 123
Patterson, Francine 171
Wexler, Nancy Sabin 207

Zoology

Bailey, Florence Augusta
    Merriam 12
Colborn, Theodora 39
Duplaix, Nicole 49
Fossey, Dian 67
Galdikas, Biruté M. F. 73
Goodall, Jane 80
Hyman, Libbie Henrietta 98
Merian, Maria Sibylla 149
Morgan, Ann Haven 154
Moss, Cynthia 156
Newton Turner, Helen 159
Nice, Margaret Morse 160
Payne, Katharine 172

ENTRIES BY COUNTRY OF BIRTH

Argentina

Wrinch, Dorothy Maud   213

Australia

Bennett, Isobel   19
Fawcett, Stella Grace Maisie   64
Newton Turner, Helen Alma   159
Quinn, Helen Rhoda Arnold   178

Austria

Cori, Gerty Theresa Radnitz   40
Meitner, Lise   146

Belgium

Daubechies, Ingrid   46

Brazil

Jorge-Pádua, Maria Tereza   106

Britain

Anderson, Elizabeth Garrett   7
Anning, Mary   8
Ayrton, Hertha   10
Bell Burnell, Susan Jocelyn   16
Blackwell, Elizabeth   20
Boden, Margaret   23
Burbidge, Eleanor Margaret
   Peachey   26
Fleming, Williamina Paton
   Stevens   65
Franklin, Rosalind Elsie   69

Goodall, Jane   80
Leakey, Mary Douglas Nicol   117
Lovelace, Augusta Ada Byron   127
Marrack, Philippa   138
Payne-Gaposchkin, Cecilia
   Helena   173
Scott, Charlotte Angas   189
Somerville, Mary Fairfax   193
Stewart, Alice   196

Canada

Brooks, Harriet   25
Edlund, Sylvia   56
Franklin, Melissa Eve Bronwen
   69
Kelsey, Frances Oldham   108
Morawetz, Cathleen Synge   153

China

Noguchi, Constance Tom   162
Wong-Staal, Flossie   211
Wu, Chien-shiung   214
Zhao Yufen   222

Denmark

Lehmann, Inge   120

Egypt

Cleopatra the Alchemist   37
Hodgkin, Dorothy Crowfoot   89
Hypatia   99
Maria the Jewess   138

France

Châtelet, Emilie du   35
Duplaix, Nicole   49
Germain, Marie Sophie   78
Jacoba Felicie   103
Joliot-Curie, Irène   104
Perey, Marguerite Catherine   174

Germany

Cremer, Erika   42
Edinger, Johanna Gabrielle
   Ottelie   55
Flügge-Lotz, Irmgard   67
Frith, Uta Auernhammer   72
Galdikas, Biruté M. F.   73
Geiringer, Hilda   76
Herschel, Caroline Lucretia   87
Hildegarde of Bingen   88
Horney, Karen Danielsen   94
Kirch, Maria Margaretha
   Winkelmann   112
Klein, Melanie Reizes   112
Mayer, Maria Gertrude
   Goeppert   141
Merian, Maria Sibylla   149
Noether, Emmy   161
Vrba, Elisabeth   205

Ghana

Andam, Aba A. Bentil   5

Greece

Agnodice   2

India

Rajalakshmi, R. 179

Ireland

Lonsdale, Kathleen Yardley 125

Italy

Agnesi, Maria Gaetana 1
Bassi, Laura Maria Catarina 14
Levi-Montalcini, Rita 121
Trotula of Salerno 201

Japan

Ohta, Tomoko 167
Saruhashi, Katsuko 188

Kenya

Maathai, Wangari Muta 130

Mexico

Stewart, Sarah 197

Nigeria

Ajakaiye, Deborah Enilo 2

Philippines

Ocampo-Friedmann, Roseli 166

Poland

Curie, Marie 43

Russia

Bechtereva, Natalia Petrovna 15
Kovalevskaia, Sofia Vasilyevna 113

Singapore

Levy, Julia 124

Swaziland

Makhubu, Lydia Phindile 135

Turkey

Yener, Kutlu Aslihan 219

United States

Alexander, Hattie Elizabeth 3
Ancker-Johnson, Betsy 4
Anderson, Elda Emma 6
Apgar, Virginia 9
Bailey, Florence Augusta
    Merriam 12
Bascom, Florence 13
Benedict, Ruth Fulton 18
Blodgett, Katharine Burr 22
Brandegee, Mary Katherine
    Layne 24
Cannon, Annie Jump 29
Carr, Emma Perry 31
Carson, Rachel Louise 33
Clark, Eugenie 35
Cobb, Jewel Plummer 38
Colborn, Theodora 38
Dick, Gladys Rowena Henry 47
Dresselhaus, Mildred Spiewak 48
Earle, Sylvia Alice 51
Eastwood, Alice 53
Eddy, Bernice 54
Elion, Gertrude Belle 57
Evans, Alice Catherine 60
Faber, Sandra Moore 63
Fossey, Dian 67
Gardner, Julia Anna 75
Geller, Margaret Joan 76
Gilbreth, Lillian Evelyn Moller 79
Hamilton, Alice 83
Hawes, Harriet Ann Boyd 85
Hazen, Elizabeth 86
Hopper, Grace Brewster Murray
    92
Hrdy, Sarah Blaffer 95
Hyde, Ida Henrietta 97
Hyman, Libbie Henrietta 98
Ildstad, Suzanne 100

Jackson, Shirley Ann 102
Jemison, Mae Carol 103
King, Mary-Claire 109
Ladd-Franklin, Christine 116
Leavitt, Henrietta Swan 118
Levy, Jerre 123
Love, Susan 126
McClintock, Barbara 131
McNally, Karen Cook 134
Margulis, Lynn Alexander 136
Matzinger, Polly 139
Maury, Antonia Caetana 140
Mead, Margaret 143
Mexia, Ynes Enriquetta Julietta
    150
Mitchell, Maria 151
Morgan, Ann Haven 154
Moss, Cynthia 156
Nice, Margaret Morse 160
Novello, Antonia Coello 164
Nuttall, Zelia Maria Magdalena
    164
Patrick, Ruth 169
Patterson, Francine 171
Payne, Katharine Boynton 173
Pert, Candace Beebe 175
Quimby, Edith Hinkley 177
Richards, Ellen Henrietta
    Swallow 180
Robinson, Julia Bowman 182
Rubin, Vera Cooper 183
Sabin, Florence Rena 186
Seibert, Florence Barbara 191
Simpson, Joanne Malkus 191
Slye, Maud Caroline 192
Stevens, Nettie Maria 195
Taussig, Helen 199
Van Dover, Cindy Lee 203
Wexler, Nancy Sabin 207
Wheeler, Anna Johnson Pell 209
Williams, Anna Wessels 210
Wright, Jane Cooke 212
Yalow, Rosalyn Sussman 217

Zimbabwe

Sithole-Niang, Idah 192

ENTRIES BY COUNTRY OF MAJOR SCIENTIFIC ACTIVITY

Australia
Bennett, Isobel 19
Fawcett, Stella Grace Maisie 64
Newton Turner, Helen Alma 159

Austria
Cremer, Erika 41

Belgium
Daubechies, Ingrid 45

Brazil
Jorge-Pádua, Maria Tereza 106

Britain
Anderson, Elizabeth Garrett 7
Anning, Mary 8
Ayrton, Hertha 10
Bell Burnell, Susan Jocelyn 16
Blackwell, Elizabeth 20
Boden, Margaret 23
Burbidge, Eleanor Margaret
    Peachey 26
Franklin, Rosalind Elsie 69
Frith, Uta Auernhammer 72
Herschel, Caroline Lucretia 87
Hodgkin, Dorothy Crowfoot 89
Klein, Melanie Reizes 112
Lonsdale, Kathleen Yardley 125
Lovelace, Augusta Ada Byron 127
Somerville, Mary Fairfax 193
Stewart, Alice 196

Wrinch, Dorothy Maud 213

Canada
Brooks, Harriet 25
Edlund, Sylvia 56
Galdikas, Biruté M. F. 73
Levy, Julia 125

China
Zhao Yufen 222

Denmark
Lehmann, Inge 120

Egypt
Cleopatra the Alchemist 36
Hypatia 99
Maria the Jewess 138

France
Châtelet, Emilie du 35
Curie, Marie 43
Germain, Marie Sophie 78
Jacoba Felicie 103
Joliot-Curie, Irène 104
Perey, Marguerite Catherine 174

Germany
Edinger, Johanna Gabrielle
    Ottelie 55
Flügge-Lotz, Irmgard 67

Geiringer, Hilda 78
Hildegarde of Bingen 88
Horney, Karen Danielsen 94
Kirch, Maria Margaretha
    Winkelmann 112
Klein, Melanie Reizes 112
Meitner, Lise 146
Noether, Emmy 161

Ghana
Andam, Aba A. Bentil 5

Greece
Agnodice 2
Hawes, Harriet Ann Boyd 85

India
Rajalakshmi, R. 178

Indonesia
Galdikas, Biruté M. F. 73

Italy
Agnesi, Maria Gaetana 1
Bassi, Laura Maria Catarina 14
Levi-Montalcini, Rita 121
Trotula of Salerno 201

Japan
Ohta, Tomoko 167
Saruhashi, Katsuko 188

Kenya

Leakey, Mary Douglas Nicol   117
Maathai, Wangari Muta   130
Moss, Cynthia   156

Mexico

Mexia, Ynes Enriquetta Julietta   150
Nuttall, Zelia Maria Magdalena   164

Netherlands

Merian, Maria Sibylla   149

Nigeria

Ajakaiye, Deborah Enilo   2

Russia

Bechtereva, Natalia Petrovna   15

Rwanda

Fossey, Dian   67

South Africa

Vrba, Elisabeth   205

Suriname

Duplaix, Nicole   49
Merian, Maria Sibylla   149

Swaziland

Makhubu, Lydia Phindile   135

Sweden

Kovalevskaia, Sofia Vasilyevna   113
Meitner, Lise   146

Tanzania

Goodall, Jane   80
Leakey, Mary Douglas Nicol   117

Turkey

Yener, Kutlu Aslihan   219

United States

Alexander, Hattie Elizabeth   3
Ancker-Johnson, Betsy   4
Anderson, Elda Emma   6
Apgar, Virginia   9

Bailey, Florence Augusta Merriam   12
Bascom, Florence   13
Benedict, Ruth Fulton   18
Blackwell, Elizabeth   20
Blodgett, Katharine Burr   22
Brandegee, Mary Katherine Layne   24
Burbidge, Eleanor Margaret Peachey   26
Cannon, Annie Jump   29
Carr, Emma Perry   31
Carson, Rachel Louise   33
Clark, Eugenie   35
Cobb, Jewel Plummer   38
Colborn, Theodora   39
Cori, Gerty Theresa Radnitz   40
Daubechies, Ingrid   46
Dick, Gladys Rowena Henry   47
Dresselhaus, Mildred Spiewak   48
Duplaix, Nicole   49
Earle, Sylvia Alice   51
Eastwood, Alice   53
Eddy, Bernice   54
Edinger, Johanna Gabrielle Ottelie   55
Elion, Gertrude Belle   57
Evans, Alice Catherine   60
Faber, Sandra Moore   63
Fleming, Williamina Paton Stevens   65
Flügge-Lotz, Irmgard   67
Fossey, Dian   67
Franklin, Melissa Eve Bronwen   69
Gardner, Julia Anna   75
Geiringer, Hilda   76
Geller, Margaret Joan   76
Gilbreth, Lillian Evelyn Moller   79
Hamilton, Alice   83
Hawes, Harriet Ann Boyd   85
Hazen, Elizabeth Lee   86
Hopper, Grace Brewster Murray   92
Horney, Karen Danielsen   94
Hrdy, Sarah Blaffer   95
Hyde, Ida Henrietta   97
Hyman, Libbie Henrietta   98
Ildstad, Suzanne   100
Jackson, Shirley Ann   102
Jemison, Mae Carol   103
Kelsey, Frances Oldham   108
King, Mary-Claire   109
Ladd-Franklin, Christine   116
Leavitt, Henrietta Swan   118
Levi-Montalcini, Rita   121

Levy, Jerre   123
Love, Susan   126
McClintock, Barbara   131
McNally, Karen Cook   134
Margulis, Lynn Alexander   136
Marrack, Philippa   138
Matzinger, Polly   139
Maury, Antonia Caetana   140
Mayer, Maria Gertrude Goeppert   141
Mead, Margaret   143
Mexia, Ynes Enriquetta Julietta   150
Mitchell, Maria   151
Morawetz, Cathleen Synge   153
Morgan, Ann Haven   154
Nice, Margaret Morse   160
Noguchi, Constance Tom   162
Novello, Antonia Coello   164
Nuttall, Zelia Maria Magdalena   164
Ocampo-Friedmann, Roseli   166
Patrick, Ruth   169
Patterson, Francine   171
Payne, Katharine Boynton   172
Payne-Gaposchkin, Cecilia Helena   173
Pert, Candace Beebe   175
Quimby, Edith Hinkley   177
Quinn, Helen Rhoda Arnold   178
Richards, Ellen Henrietta Swallow   180
Robinson, Julia Bowman   182
Rubin, Vera Cooper   183
Sabin, Florence Rena   186
Scott, Charlotte Angas   189
Seibert, Florence Barbara   190
Simpson, Joanne Malkus   191
Slye, Maud Caroline   192
Stevens, Nettie Maria   195
Stewart, Sarah   197
Taussig, Helen   199
Van Dover, Cindy Lee   203
Vrba, Elisabeth   205
Wexler, Nancy Sabin   207
Wheeler, Anna Johnson Pell   209
Williams, Anna Wessels   210
Wong-Staal, Flossie   211
Wright, Jane Cooke   212
Wrinch, Dorothy Maud   213
Wu, Chien-shiung   214
Yalow, Rosalyn Sussman   217
Yener, Kutlu Aslihan   219

Zimbabwe

Sithole-Niang, Idah   192

ENTRIES BY YEAR OF BIRTH

Fourth Century B.C.–
Third Century A.D.

Agnodice 2
Maria the Jewess 138

300–1599

Cleopatra the Alchemist 37
Hildegarde of Bingen 88
Hypatia 99
Jacoba Felicie 103
Trotula of Salerno 201

1600–1699

Kirch, Maria Margaretha
    Winkelmann 112
Merian, Maria Sibylla 149

1700–1799

Agnesi, Maria Gaetana 1
Anning, Mary 8
Bassi, Laura Maria Catarina 14
Châtelet, Emilie du 35
Germain, Marie Sophie 78
Herschel, Caroline Lucretia 87
Somerville, Mary Fairfax 193

1800–1849

Anderson, Elizabeth Garrett 7
Blackwell, Elizabeth 20
Brandegee, Mary Katharine
    Layne 24
Ladd-Franklin, Christine 116

Lovelace, Augusta Ada Byron 127
Mitchell, Maria 151
Richards, Ellen Henrietta
    Swallow 180

1850–1899

Anderson, Elda Emma 6
Ayrton, Hertha 10
Bailey, Florence Augusta
    Merriam 12
Bascom, Florence 13
Benedict, Ruth Fulton 18
Blodgett, Katharine Burr 22
Brooks, Harriet 25
Cannon, Annie Jump 29
Carr, Emma Perry 31
Cori, Gerty Theresa Radnitz 40
Curie, Marie 43
Dick, Gladys Rowena Henry 47
Eastwood, Alice 53
Edinger, Johanna Gabrielle
    Ottelie 55
Evans, Alice Catherine 60
Fleming, Williamina Paton
    Stevens 65
Gardner, Julia Anna 76
Geiringer, Hilda 76
Gilbreth, Lillian Evelyn Moller
    79
Hamilton, Alice 83
Hawes, Harriet Ann Boyd 85
Hazen, Elizabeth Lee 86
Horney, Karen Danielsen 94
Hyde, Ida Henrietta 97
Hyman, Libbie Henrietta 98

Joliot-Curie, Irène 104
Klein, Melanie Reizes 112
Kovalevskaia, Sofia Vasilyevna 113
Leavitt, Henrietta Swan 118
Lehmann, Inge 120
Maury, Antonia Caetana 140
Meitner, Lise 146
Mexia, Ynes Enriquetta Julietta
    150
Morgan, Ann Haven 154
Nice, Margaret Morse 159
Noether, Emmy 161
Nuttall, Zelia Maria Magdalena
    164
Quimby, Edith Hinkley 177
Sabin, Florence Rena 186
Scott, Charlotte Angas 189
Seibert, Florence Barbara 190
Slye, Maud Caroline 192
Stevens, Nettie Maria 195
Taussig, Helen 199
Wheeler, Anna Johnson Pell 209
Williams, Anna Wessels 210
Wrinch, Dorothy Maud 213

1900–1909

Apgar, Virginia 9
Alexander, Hattie Elizabeth 3
Bennett, Isobel 19
Carson, Rachel Louise 33
Cremer, Erika 42
Eddy, Bernice 54
Fawcett, Stella Grace Maisie 64
Flügge-Lotz, Irmgard 67

Hopper, Grace Brewster Murray 92
Levi-Montalcini, Rita 121
Lonsdale, Kathleen Yardley 125
McClintock, Barbara 131
Mayer, Maria Gertrude Goeppert 141
Mead, Margaret 143
Newton Turner, Helen Alma 159
Patrick, Ruth 169
Payne-Gaposchkin, Cecilia Helena 172
Perey, Marguerite Catherine 174
Stewart, Alice 196
Stewart, Sarah 197

1910–1919

Bechtereva, Natalia Petrovna 15
Burbidge, Eleanor Margaret Peachey 26
Elion, Gertrude Belle 57
Hodgkin, Dorothy Crowfoot 89
Kelsey, Frances Oldham 108
Leakey, Mary Douglas Nicol 117
Robinson, Julia Bowman 182
Wright, Jane Cooke 212
Wu, Chien-shiung 214

1920–1929

Ancker-Johnson, Betsy 4
Clark, Eugenie 36
Cobb, Jewel Plummer 38

Colborn, Theodora 39
Franklin, Rosalind Elsie 69
Morawetz, Cathleen Synge 154
Rajalakshmi, R. 179
Rubin, Vera Cooper 183
Saruhashi, Katsuko 188
Simpson, Joanne Malkus 191
Yalow, Rosalyn Sussman 217

1930–1939

Boden, Margaret 23
Dresselhaus, Mildred Spiewak 48
Earle, Sylvia Alice 51
Fossey, Dian 67
Goodall, Jane 80
Levy, Jerre 123
Levy, Julia 124
Makhubu, Lydia Phindile 135
Margulis, Lynn Alexander 136
Ocampo-Friedmann, Roseli 166
Ohta, Tomoko 167
Payne, Katharine Boynton 173

1940–1949

Ajakaiye, Deborah Enilo 2
Bell Burnell, Susan Jocelyn 16
Duplaix, Nicole 49
Edlund, Sylvia 56
Faber, Sandra Moore 63
Frith, Uta Auernhammer 72
Galdikas, Biruté M. F. 73
Geller, Margaret Joan 76

Hrdy, Sarah Blaffer 95
Jackson, Shirley Ann 102
Jorge Pádua, Maria Tereza 106
King, Mary-Claire 109
Love, Susan 122
Maathai, Wangari Muta 130
McNally, Karen Cook 134
Marrack, Philippa 138
Matzinger, Polly 139
Moss, Cynthia 156
Noguchi, Constance Tom 162
Novello, Antonia Coello 164
Patterson, Francine 171
Pert, Candace Beebe 175
Quinn, Helen Rhoda Arnold 178
Vrba, Elisabeth 205
Wexler, Nancy Sabin 207
Wong-Staal, Flossie 211
Yener, Kutlu Aslihan 219
Zhao Yufen 222

1950–1960

Andam, Aba A. Bentil 5
Daubechies, Ingrid 46
Franklin, Melissa Eve Bronwen 69
Ildstad, Suzanne 100
Jemison, Mae Carol 103
Sithole-Niang, Idah 192
Van Dover, Cindy Lee 203

CHRONOLOGY

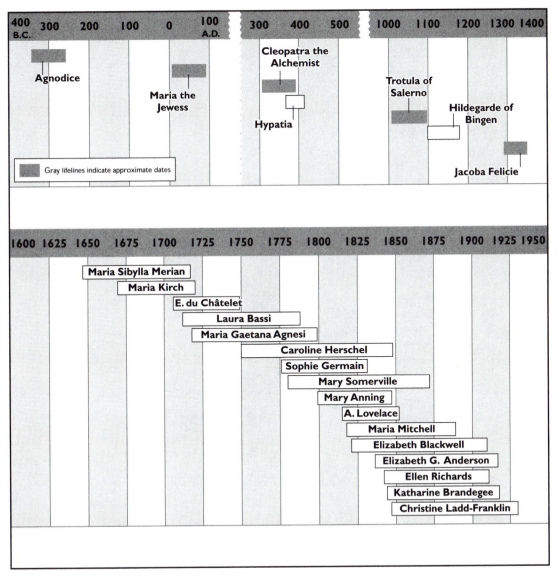

| 400 B.C. | 300 | 200 | 100 | 0 | 100 A.D. | | 300 | 400 | 500 | | 1000 | 1100 | 1200 | 1300 | 1400 |

Agnodice

Maria the Jewess

Cleopatra the Alchemist

Hypatia

Trotula of Salerno

Hildegarde of Bingen

Jacoba Felicie

Gray lifelines indicate approximate dates

| 1600 | 1625 | 1650 | 1675 | 1700 | 1725 | 1750 | 1775 | 1800 | 1825 | 1850 | 1875 | 1900 | 1925 | 1950 |

Maria Sibylla Merian

Maria Kirch

E. du Châtelet

Laura Bassi

Maria Gaetana Agnesi

Caroline Herschel

Sophie Germain

Mary Somerville

Mary Anning

A. Lovelace

Maria Mitchell

Elizabeth Blackwell

Elizabeth G. Anderson

Ellen Richards

Katharine Brandegee

Christine Ladd-Franklin

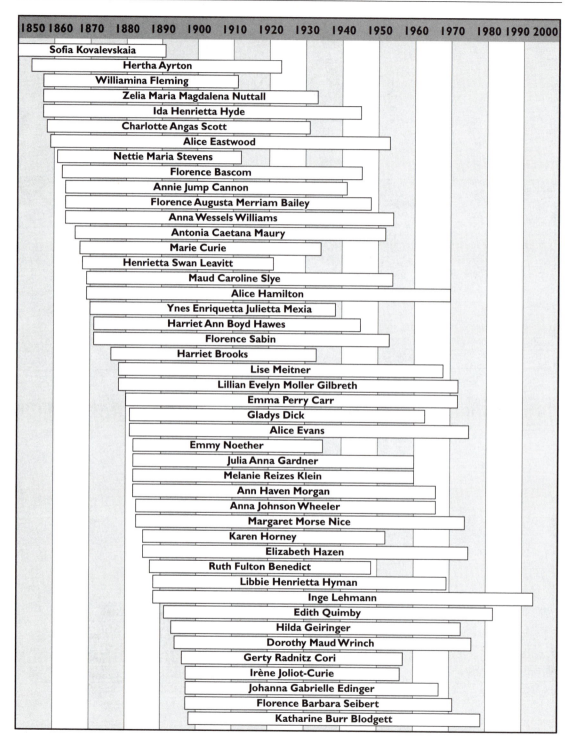

	1850	1860	1870	1880	1890	1900	1910	1920	1930	1940	1950	1960	1970	1980	1990	2000

Sofia Kovalevskaia
Hertha Ayrton
Williamina Fleming
Zelia Maria Magdalena Nuttall
Ida Henrietta Hyde
Charlotte Angas Scott
Alice Eastwood
Nettie Maria Stevens
Florence Bascom
Annie Jump Cannon
Florence Augusta Merriam Bailey
Anna Wessels Williams
Antonia Caetana Maury
Marie Curie
Henrietta Swan Leavitt
Maud Caroline Slye
Alice Hamilton
Ynes Enriquetta Julietta Mexia
Harriet Ann Boyd Hawes
Florence Sabin
Harriet Brooks
Lise Meitner
Lillian Evelyn Moller Gilbreth
Emma Perry Carr
Gladys Dick
Alice Evans
Emmy Noether
Julia Anna Gardner
Melanie Reizes Klein
Ann Haven Morgan
Anna Johnson Wheeler
Margaret Morse Nice
Karen Horney
Elizabeth Hazen
Ruth Fulton Benedict
Libbie Henrietta Hyman
Inge Lehmann
Edith Quimby
Hilda Geiringer
Dorothy Maud Wrinch
Gerty Radnitz Cori
Irène Joliot-Curie
Johanna Gabrielle Edinger
Florence Barbara Seibert
Katharine Burr Blodgett

1850	1860	1870	1880	1890	1900	1910	1920	1930	1940	1950	1960	1970	1980	1990	2000

Helen Taussig

Elda Emma Anderson

Cecilia Payne-Gaposchkin

Erika Cremer

Hattie Elizabeth Alexander

Margaret Mead

Stella Grace Maisie Fawcett

Barbara McClintock

Kathleen Yardley Lonsdale

Irmgard Flügge-Lotz

Bernice Eddy

Maria Goeppert Mayer

Sarah Stewart

Grace Hopper

Alice Stewart

Rachel Carson

Ruth Patrick

Helen Alma Newton Turner

Virginia Apgar

Marguerite Catherine Perey

Isobel Bennett

Rita Levi-Montalcini

Dorothy Hodgkin

Chien-shiung Wu

Mary Nicol Leakey

Frances Kelsey

Natalia Petrovna Bechtereva

Gertrude Belle Elion

Julia Bowman Robinson

Margaret Burbidge

Jane Cooke Wright

Rosalind Franklin

Katsuko Saruhashi

Rosalyn Yalow

Eugenie Clark

Cathleen Synge Morawetz

Joanne Simpson

Jewel Plummer Cobb

R. Rajalakshmi

Betsy Ancker-Johnson

Theodora Colborn

Vera Cooper Rubin

Mildred Spiewak Dresselhaus

Dian Fossey

Tomoko Ohta

1850	1860	1870	1880	1890	1900	1910	1920	1930	1940	1950	1960	1970	1980	1990	2000

Jane Goodall

Julia Levy

Sylvia Earle

Lydia Makhubu

Roseli Ocampo-Friedmann

Katharine Payne

Jerre Levy

Lynn Margulis

Deborah Enilo Ajakaiye

Wangari Muta Maathai

Karen Cook McNally

Cynthia Moss

Uta Auernhammer Frith

Nicole Duplaix

Elisabeth Vrba

Susan Jocelyn Bell Burnell

Maria Tereza Jorge Pádua

Helen Rhoda Quinn

Sandra Moore Faber

Antonia Coello Novello

Sylvia Edlund

Philippa Marrack

Nancy Wexler

Biruté Galdikas

Sarah Blaffer Hrdy

Shirley Ann Jackson

Mary-Claire King

Candace Pert

Flossie Wong-Staal

Kutlu Aslihan Yener

Margaret Joan Geller

Polly Matzinger

Francine Patterson

Susan Love

Constance Tom Noguchi

Zhao Yufen

Suzanne Ildstad

Ingrid Daubechies

Cindy Lee Van Dover

Melissa Eve Bronwen Franklin

Mae Jemison

Idah Sithole-Niang

Aba A. Bentil Andam

INDEX

Boldface numbers indicate entries.
Italic numbers indicate illustrations.

A

Abuelas de Plaza de Mayo 110–111
Academia Europa 72
Academy of Medical Sciences
   (Russia) 15
Academy of Natural Sciences
   (Philadelphia) 169–170
Academy of Science (Sweden) 115
Academy of Sciences (France) 1,
   78–79, 105, 113, 115, 174
actinium 26, 146, 174
acyclovir 59
Ada (computer language) 129
Adams, John Couch 194
Addams, Jane 83, 85, 131, 181
Adelphi University 220
Adhadu Bello University 2–3
Aerodynamische Versuchsanstalt 67
Africa
   human origins in 117
   medicine, traditional 135–136
   women scientists in viii, x, 130,
      135
African Wildlife Foundation 157
Agnesi, Maria Gaetana x, **1–2**
Agnodice vii, x, 2, 103
AIDS 59, 100–101, 109, 111,
   125, 175–176, 211–212
Aiken, Howard 92
aircraft design 47, 67, 153–154
Air, Water, and Food for Colleges
   (Richards) 181

Ajakaiye, Deborah Enilo **2–3**
Alaska, University of 205
Albany Medical College 86
Alberta, University of 135
Albert and Mary Lasker Award *see*
   Lasker Award
Albert Einstein School of Medicine
   212
alchemy 37–38, 138
Alexander, Franz 95
Alexander, Hattie Elizabeth **3–4**
algebra 1, 99, 161–162, 189–190,
   193, 209
Alleghany University of the Health
   Sciences 101
allopurinol 59
Almania, Jacqueline Felicie de *see*
   Jacoba Felicie
Alvin 203, 205
Amboseli Elephant Research
   Project 157, 173
American Academy of Arts and
   Sciences 47, 64, 102, 151, 154,
   168, 170, 174, 178, 183
American Anthropological
   Association 19, 165
American Association for the
   Advancement of Science viii, 2,
   28, 49, 52, 77, 145, 151, 165
American Association of
   Anatomists 188
American Association for Artificial
   Intelligence 23

American Association of Blood
   Banks 190
American Association for Cancer
   Research 110, 212
American Association of
   Engineering Societies 5
American Association of Physicists
   in Medicine 177
American Association of University
   Women 174, 191
American Astronomical Society
   28, 31, 64, 141, 183
American Board of Health Physics 6
American Chemical Society 22,
   32, 191
American College of Radiology 177
American Exploration Society 85
American Folklore, Journal of 18
American Geophysical Union 120
American Heart Association 201
American Home Economics
   Association 181
American Institute of Aeronautics
   and Astronautics 67
American Institute of Chemists 86
American Institute of Mining and
   Metallurgical Engineers 180
American Institute for
   Psychoanalysis 95
American Mathematical Society
   47, 154, 183, 190, 209
American Medical Association
   193, 210

American Meteorological Society 192

American Museum of Natural History 98, 144–145

American Ornithological Union 12–13, 160

American Pediatric Society 3

American Philosophical Society 170, 174

American Physical Society 5, 49, 69, 102, 178

American Physiological Society 97

American Public Health Association 210

American Radiological Society 193

American Radium Society 177–178

American School of Classical Studies 85

American Sign Language 171–172

American Society of Anesthesiologists 10

American Society of Limnology and Oceanography 170

American Society of Microbiology 60–61

American Society of Naturalists 170

Amherst College 213

Among the Birds in the Grand Canyon Country (Bailey) 13

analytical engine 127–128

Anatolia 220–221

Ancker-Johnson, Betsy viii, 4–5

Andam, Aba A. Bentil **5–6**

Anderson, Elda Emma **6**

Anderson, Elizabeth Garrett x, **7–8**, 21

Anderson, Louisa 7

And Keep Your Powder Dry (Mead) 145

Andromeda galaxy 184–185

anesthesiology 9

Annie Jump Cannon Prize 31, 141

Anning, Mary **8–9**

Antarctica 19, 166–167

antibiotics 3, 57, 60, 85, 90–91, 106

antibodies 218–219

antigens 139

antimetabolites 57–58

antinepotism rules ix, 27, 41, 108, 141–142, 191

antisemitism 56, 76, 95, 121–122, 147, 161–162

antitoxin 47, 210

apes 73, 74, 81, 96, 117–118, 171–172, 206, 211 *see also* chimpanzees, gorillas, orangutans

Apgar, Virginia **9–10**

Apgar Score System 9

Apothecaries, Society of 7

Applequist, Thomas 178

Applied Motion Study (Gilbreth) 80

Arctic 56, 166

Argentina, identification of children in 110–111

Argonne National Laboratories 5, 142, 221

Arnold, Christoph 112

Arouet, François Marie *see* Voltaire

arthritis, rheumatoid 58, 90, 101, 125, 131

Arthur S. Fleming Award 176

artifacts, chemical composition of 219–221

Artificial Intelligence and Natural Man (Boden) 23

Association for the Advancement of Psychoanalysis 95

Association for the Advancement of Women 153

Association of Commonwealth Nations 136

Association for Women in Science 154

Astbury, William 125

astrolabe 99

astrology 112

astronaut program (U.S.) 103–104

Astronomical Canon (Hypatia) 99

Atlas of the Medulla and Midbrain, An (Sabin) 186

atomic
    bomb 6, 141–142, 146–148, 215 *see also* Manhattan Project
    bomb tests 188–189
    fission 42, 106, 146–148
    nucleus 188–189

Atomic Energy Commission (France) 106

Atomic Energy Commission (U.S.) 148

AT&T Bell Laboratories 47, 76, 102

Audubon Society 157

Australasian Association of Animal Breeding and Genetics 159

Australian Academy of Technological Sciences 159

Australian National University 65

Australia and New Zeland Association for the Advancement of Science 19

Australian plains, overgrazing in 64–65

Australia, Order of 19

Australian Academy of Science 146

autism 72

autoimmune diseases 58, 101, 125, 138–139

automobile industry 4–5

Avery, Oswald 3

axions 178

Ayrton fan 10–11

Ayrton, Hertha **10–11**

Ayrton, W. E. 10–11

azathioprine 59

AZT 59

B

Babbage, Charles 127–128

baboon tissue transplant to humans 100–101

bacteria 3, 47, 57, 60–61, 91, 139, 187, 190, 197, 210
    as ancestors of nucleated cells 136–138
    in extreme environment 166, 203, 205

Bailey, Florence Augusta Merriam **12–13**, *13*

Bailey, Vernon 12–13

Bali, Mead research in 145

Balinese Character (Mead) 145

Barnard College 26, 143

Baroda, University of 179

Baron-Cohen, Simon 72

Bascom, Florence **13–14**, *14*

Bassi, Laura Maria Catarina ix, x, **14–15**, *15*
Bateson, Gregory 145
Bauer, John 59
Bechtereva, Natalia Petrovna **15–16**
Becquerel, Henri 43–45
Bedford College for Women 125
Begg, Alexander 199
Bell Burnell, Susan Jocelyn **16–18**
Benaras Hindu University 179
Benedict, Ruth Fulton **18–19**, 143, 145
Benjamin Franklin Award 170
Bennett, Isobel **19–20**
benzene ring 125
Berkeley, University of California at 4, 24–25, 69, 77, 79, 109–110, 118, 134, 136, 150, 163, 182–183, 199, 215–216
Berlin Academy of Science 146
Berlin Psychoanalytic Clinic and Institute 94
Berlin Psychoanalytic Society 113
Berlin, University of 42, 76, 94, 116, 146
Bernal, J. D. 71, 90–91
Bernard Gold Medal 105
Berson, Solomon 217–219
beta particles 146–147, 215–216
Beth Israel Hospital 126
B²FH theory 26–27
Big Bang 63–64, 77
bioacoustics 172–173
birds 12–13, 34, 39, 160, 197–198
Birds of New Mexico (Bailey) 12
Birds Through an Opera Glass (Bailey) 12
Birds of Village and Field (Bailey) *12*
Birkbeck College 71
Birmingham, University of 2, 5, 23, 196–197
birth
    defects 9–10, 39, 108–109, 164, 196, 199–201
    development before 39, 108–109, 121–123, 133, 186–187
Black-man of Zinacantan, The (Hrdy) 96

Blackwell, Elizabeth vi, 7 10, 20–22
Blackwell, Emily 21
Blalock, Alfred 200
Blalock-Taussig operation 200
Blodgett, Katharine Burr **22–23**
"blue babies" 199–200
Board of Health and Hospitals (Denver) 187
Boas, Franz 18–19, 143, 145, 165
Boden, Margaret **23**
Boeing 4–5
Bok Prize 64
Bologna, University of 1, 15
Bologna Academy of Science 15
Bond, William Cranch 31, 151
bone marrow transplants 100–101
Bordin Prize 113, 115
Bosphorus University 220
Boston Museum of Science 118
Boston University 137, 199
Botanical Congress, Eighth International 54
Bowie Medal 120
Bradford Washburn Award 118
Bragg, William Henry 90, 125
brain
    atlas of 186
    disorders 72
    electric signals in 15–16, 97
    fossil 55–56
    function 15–16, 72, 123–124, 129
    hemispheres 123–124
    immune system links 123, 175–176
    information processing 16, 23, 72, 123–124
    opiate receptors in 175–176
Brandegee, Mary Katharine Layne *24,* **24–25,** 53
Brandegee, Townshend Stith 25
Brazil, nature protection in 106–107
BRCA1 110–111
Breteuil, Gabrielle-Emilie le Tonnelier de *see* Châtelet, Emilie du
Brewster Medal 12, 160
British Academy 23

British Association for Advancement of Science 126
British Columbia, University of 124
British Psycho-analytic Society 113
British Psychological Society 72
Bronx Veterans Administration Hospital 218–219
Bronx Zoo 49–50
Bronze Age 85, 220–221
Brooks, Harriet **25–26**
Brougham, Henry 194
Brown, Rachel 86
Brown University 80, 193
Brucella 60
brucellosis 60–61
Bryn Mawr 13–14, 22, 75, 76, 97, 161–162, 175, 189–190, 195, 209
Bücker, Elmer 122
buckyballs 48–49
Burbidge, Eleanor Margaret Peachey ix, **26–28**, *27*
Burbidge, Geoffrey 26–28
Burroughs Wellcome 57, 59
Byron, George Gordon, Lord 127–128

C

calculus 1, 113, 194
calendar making 112
California, University of *see* specific campuses
California Academy of Sciences 24–25, 52, 53–54
California Institute of Technology (Caltech) 123, 134–135
Calne, Roy 58–59
Cambridge University 10, 16, 22, 23, 26, 48, 68, 70, 71, 77, 81, 90, 120, 138, 148, 173, 189, 196, 213
Cameron Prize 47
Canadian Mathematical Society 154
cancer 40, 122, 218, 222 *see also* leukemia
    breast 109–111, 126–127
    drugs to fight 38, 57–58, 124–125, 212
    genetics 110–111, 192–193, 211
    other causes 5, 196–197

viruses as cause 54–55, 191, 197–198, 211
Cancer Research Foundation 38, 212
Cancer Research Institute 139
Cannon, Annie Jump **29–31**, *30*, 65, 119, 120
Cape Coast, University of 5
Cape Haze Marine Laboratory 37
Cape Town, University of 205
carbohydrates 40–42
carbon-containing compounds *see* organic chemistry
carbon dioxide 188–189
Carborundum Co. 5
Carleton College 109
Carl Ferdinand Medical School 40
Carnegie Institution of Washington 133, 184–185
Carr, Emma Perry **31–33**, *32*
Carson, Rachel Louise vi, **33–35**, *33*, 39, 169
Case Western Reserve University 56
Caton-Thompson, Gertrude 117
Causae et Curae (Hildegarde of Bingen) 89
Cavalli-Sforza, Luca 111
Cavendish Laboratory 22, 26
CD-4 cells 176
cells
    blood 163, 187
    cancer 38, 57–58, 212
    evolution of 136–137
    growth 121–123
    immune system 100–101, 139–140, 176
    nerve 15–16, 97, 121–123, 176, 210
    organelles 136–137
    receptors on 139, 175–176
Cepheid variables 119–120
Chadwick, James 105
Chain, Ernst 90–91
Châtelet, Emilie du **35–36**
Chemical Pioneer Award 86
Chemical Society of France 174
chemistry, organic *see* organic chemistry
Chemistry Research Institute 222

Chicago Institute of Psychoanalysis 95
Chicago, University of 22, 27, 31, 47, 48, 56, 98, 108, 124, 136, 142, 190, 191, 193, 197, 209, 220, 221
Child, Charles Manning 98
chimpanzees 73, 74, 80–82, 110, 156, 171–172, 206
Chinese Academy of Sciences 222
Chladni, Ernest 78
chlorine in water 181
chloroplasts 137
cholesterol 90
Christian Church, attitudes toward women scientists vii, x, 37, 99
chromatography
    gas 42–43
    liquid *58*
chromosomes 110, 132–133, 195–196, 208
Chrysanthemum and the Sword, The (Benedict) 19
Chrysopoeia (Cleopatra the Alchemist) 37–38
CIGNA 104
Cincinnati, University of 54
Civil War 21
Clark, Eugenie viii, **36–37**, *37*
Clark University 160
classification
    of invertebrates 98
    of living things 137
    of stars 29–31, 65–66, 140–141
Cleopatra the Alchemist **37–38**
climate change, role in evolution 205–206
clouds 191–192
Clowes Award 110
Clunies Ross, Ian 159
Coal Utilization Research Association 70
cobalt 60 216
Cobb, Jewel Plummer 38, **38–39**, 212
COBOL 92–94
Codex Nuttall 165
Cohen, Stanley 121–123

Cohn, Ronald 172
Coker College 169
Colborn, Theodora **39**
Cold Spring Harbor Laboratory 132–133, 169
Colorado, University of 124, 139, 197
Colour and Colour Theories (Ladd-Franklin) 117
Columbia-Presbyterian Medical Center 3, 9
Columbia University 3, 9, 10, 18–19, 26, 86, 116, 141, 143–144, 177, 209, 215, 217, 218, 220
comets, discovery of 87–88, 112, 151–152
Coming of Age in Samoa (Mead) 144–145
Committee to Combat Huntington's Chorea 207
compiler 92–93
computers 5, 23, 46, 48, 92–94, *93*, 127–129, 191
Comstock Award 216
Congressional Committee for the Control of Huntington's Disease 208
Connecticut College 38
Conservation Foundation 39
conservation of parity, law of 215–216
Conservation Service Award 51
Contemporary Physics Education Project 178
Convention on International Trade in Endangered Species 157
Copenhagen, University of 120
Cori, Carl 40–42
Cori, Gerty Theresa Radnitz *40*, **40–42**, 219
Cori cycle 41–42
cori ester 41
corn *see* maize
Cornell University 48, 60, 68, 97, 104, 132, 137, 156, 172–173, 177, 183
Council for Scientific and Industrial Research 159

Counsel to Parent on the Moral Education of Their Children (Blackwell) 21
Courant, Richard 154
Courant Institute of Mathematical Sciences 154
Cradle Society 47
Creative Mind, The (Boden) 23
Creighton, Harriet 132
Cremer, Erika **42–43**
Crete, archaeology of 85
Crete: The Forerunner of Greece (Hawes) 85
Crick, Francis 69,71, 133
crystallography, X-ray 69–71, 76, 82, 91, 125–126, 154, 213
cultures
    effect on individual beliefs 143–145
    "personality" of 18–19, 145
Curie, Irène *see* Joliot-Curie, Irène
Curie, Marie Sklodowska ix, xi, 25–26, *43*, **43–45**, 104–105, 146, 174
Curie, Pierre ix, x, 43–45, 104
cyclol theory 213
Cyril 99

D

dairies 60–61
Dakin, William J. 19
Dana Farber Cancer Institute 126
dark matter 63, 184–185
Dartmouth College 104
Daubechies, Ingrid **46–47**
Davis, Martin 183
Davis, University of California at 67, 97, 139
Davy Medal 126
DDT 34–35
Deep Ocean Engineering 52
Deep Ocean Exploration and Research 52
Deep Ocean Technology 52
Deep Rover 52
De Pauw University 143
Deutsch Versuchsanstalt für Luftfahrt 67

development before birth *see* birth, development before
diabetes 91, 100–101, 218
diamonds 125
diatometer 169
diatoms 169
Diatoms of the United States (Patrick) 169
Dick, George Frederick 47
Dick, Gladys Rowena Henry 47
difference engine 127–128
differential equations 114, 127, 154, 209
diphtheria 210
disabled, home design for 80
Discontinuous Automatic Control (Flügge-Lotz) 67
Discontinuous and Optional Control (Flügge-Lotz) 67
distillation 38, 138, 190
Distinguished Federal Civilian Service Medal 109
Distinguished Service Medal 94
DNA 3, 57, 69–71, 109, 111, 133, 137
    mitochondrial 111, 137
    structure 69–71
Douglas-Hamilton, Iain 156–157
Douglass College 39
Drake, Francis 165
Draper, Henry 31, 65, 140
Draper Medal 31
Dresselhaus, Gene 48–49
Dresselhaus, Mildred Spiewak x, *48*, **48–49**, 218
Drown, Thomas M. 181
Dr. Susan Love's Breast Book (Love) 126
drugs
    anticancer 38, 57–58, 124–125, 212, 222
    development 57, 59, 86
    safety 108–109, 201
ductus arteriosus 200
Duke University 51, 137, 205
Duplaix, Nicole **49–50**
du Pont Co. 170
Durham, University of 5
dyslexia 72

E

Earle, Sylvia Alice **51–52**
Earth
    core 120
    crust 134, 203
    Gaia theory 137
earthquakes
    Mexico 134–135
    prediction 134–135
    San Francisco (1906) 25, 53–54
    waves 120
Eastwood, Alice 25, *53*, **53–54**
Eckert, J. Prosper 92, 94
Ecole Polytechnique 78
ecology 33, 35, 145, 180–181
    freshwater 155–156, 169–170
    ocean 19, 205
    plains 64–65
Eddington, Arthur 173
Eddy, Bernice **54–55**, 197–198
Edge of the Sea, The (Carson) 34
Edinburgh, University of 47
Edinger, Johanna Gabrielle Ottelie **55–56**
Edlund, Sylvia **56–57**
Ehrlich, Paul 96
Einstein, Albert 146, 148, 161, 162, 212
electric arc 10–11
Elementary Theory of Nuclear Shell Structure (Mayer) 143
elements
    artificial 147–148
    changing 26, 147
    creation 26–27, 142, 147–148
    in stars 26–27, 30, 174
elephants 156–158, 172–173
Elion, Gertrude Belle **57–60**, *58*
Elizabeth Garrett Anderson Hospital 7
Ellen H. Richards Fund 182
Ellen Richards Prize 31
ellipses 114
E. Mead Johnson Award 3
emotions, brain changes in 16, 124, 176
Endeavour (space shuttle) 104
endorphins 175

energy cycle in body 40–42, 91
Engineering and Science Hall of
    Fame 59, 94
ENIAC 92
Enrico Fermi Award 148
Environmental Protection Agency 35
environment, preservation of 33,
    35, 39, 106–107, 130–131, 140,
    156, 160, 173
    rain forest 75, 80, 82, 107, 157
    undersea 52, 205
enzymes 41–42, 90
Erlangen University 161
erosion 64–65, 131
Estherville Junior College 6
European Center for Nuclear
    Research 102
Evans, Alice Catherine **60–62**, *61*
evolution 56, 95–97, 131–133,
    136–138, 167–168, 205–206
Evolution of the Horse Brain, The
    (Edinger) 56
Explorers' Club 52

F

Faber-Jackson relation 63
Faber, Sandra Moore **63–64**, 183
Fabricant, Dan 77
facilitating cells 100–101
Failla, Gioacchino 177, 218
Fallot, tetralogy of 199–200
fallout, radioactive *see*
    radioactivity—from bomb tests
Farber Medal 159
Farrar, Charles 180
Faulkner Hospital 126
Fawcett, Stella Grace Maisie **64–65**
Federal Women's Award 198
females, strategies of 95–97
Feodor Lynen Medal 139
Ferenczi, Sandor 112
Fermat's Last Theorem 78
Fermi, Enrico 142–143, 147–148
Fermi National Accelerator
    Laboratory 69, 102
Festuca eastwoodae 53
Field Book of Animals in Winter
    (Morgan) 156

Field Book of Ponds and Streams
    (Morgan) 156
Finbury Technical College 10
Fischer, Emil 146
fission, atomic 42, 106, 146–148
Fleming, Alexander 91
Fleming, Williamina Paton Stevens
    29–31, **65–67**, *66*, 119, 120, 140
flexible surfaces, mathematics of 76
Flexner, Simon 187
Florida A & M University 167
Florida State University 51,
    166–167
Flowmatic 92
Flügge, Wilhelm 67
Flügge-Lotz, Irmgard **67**
food
    crops 192
    purity 180–181
Food and Drug Administration
    108–109, 201
Fordham University 126
Ford, Kent 184–185
Fortune, Reo 145
Fort Wayne College of Medicine 83
Fossey, Dian **67–69**, 73
Fossilen Gehirne, Die (Edinger) 56
fossils 8, 56, 75, 117–118,
    205–206
Fourier, Jean-Baptiste 46
*Fourier Transforms and Structural
    Factors* (Wrinch) 213
Fowler, William 26
francium 174
Frankfurt, University of 56
Franklin Institute of Philadelphia 17
Franklin, Melissa Eve Bronwen **69**
Franklin, Rosalind Elsie **69–71**
Freeman, Derek 145
Free University of Brussels 46
Freiburg, University of 94
French Revolution 78
Fresno State College 134
Freud, Sigmund 94–95, 112–113
Friedmann, Imre 166–167
Friends of the National Zoo 157
Frisch, Otto 146–148
Frith, Uta Auernhammer **72**
Fuchs, Ephraium 139–140

Fuller, Buckminster 49
fullerenes 49
Fullerton, California State
    University at 38–39
FUNATURA 107
functional analysis 209
fungi 86, 91, 137

G

Gaia theory 137
galaxies 27, 63–64
    distribution in universe 63–64,
        76–77, 184
    formation 63–64
    mapping 76–77
    motion 64, 183–185
Galdikas, Biruté M. F. **73–75**, *74*
Gale, David 182
Gallo, Robert 211–212
game theory 182
gamma rays 16, 17, 104
Gaposchkin, Sergei 174
Gardner, Allen and Beatrix 172
Gardner, Julia Anna **75–76**
Garrett, Newson 7
Garvan Medal 22, 32, 191
Gauss, Karl Friedrich 78
Geiringer, Hilda **76**
Geller, Margaret Joan 64, **76–78**
gender
    genetic determination of
        195–196
    roles in culture 143, 145
General Electric Corp. 22
General Mills 5
General Motors 5
genes
    control of other genes 131–133
    marker 110–111, 207–209
    movement of 131–133
genetic diseases 40, 42, 110–111,
    162–163, 192–193, 207–209
genetic engineering 192
genetics 3, 69, 76, 109–111,
    131–133, 163, 192
    of AIDS virus 212
    of cancer 110–111, 192–193,
        211

of gender 195–196
of Huntington's disease
207–209
population 159, 167–168
Geneva Medical College 20
Geochemical Research Laboratory
188–189
Geochemistry Research Association
188–189
Geological Society of America 14, 75
Geological Survey of Canada 56
geophysics 2–3
Georgetown University 164, 176,
183–184, 197
George Washington University 163
Georgi, Howard 178
geovisualization 3
Germain, Marie Sophie **78–79**, 194
Getty, Jeff 100–101
Ghana, radon in 5–6
Gilbreth, Frank Bunker 79–80
Gilbreth, Lillian Moller ix, **79–80**
Gilbreth Inc. 80
Gill, Laura 26
Girton College 10, 189, 213
Glasgow, University of 16
glass, "invisible" 22
glucose 41
glucose-1-phosphate 41
glycogen 41–42
Goddard Space Flight Center 192
Goldman Environmental Prize 131
Goldman Foundation 52
Goltepe 221
Gombe 81–82
Goodall, Jane 68, 73, **80–82**, 156
Goodspeed, T. Harper 151
Gordan, Paul 161
Gorilla Foundation 172
gorillas 73, 74, 81, *171*, 171–172,
206
mountain 67–69
Gorillas in the Mist (Fossey) 68
Göttingen, University of 94, 114,
116, 141, 161–162, 173, 209
Goucher College 3, 190
Gournia 85
gout 59
Grand Prix de la Ville de Paris 174

Great Attractor 64
Great Wall 76–77
Green Belt Movement 131
Green Belt Movement, The
(Maathai) 131
Greenwich Observatory *see* Royal
Greenwich Observatory
Gross, Ludwik 197
Gross, Robert 200
Growing up in New Guinea (Mead)
145
Gulf War 52
Gusella, James 208
Guthrie, Marjorie 207
Guthrie, Woody 207

H

habitat
rain forest 75, 82, 107, 157, 172
undersea 51, 52, 205
Haeckel, Ernst 181
Hahn, Otto 42, 106, 146–148
Hamburger, Viktor 122
Hamilton, Alice **83–85**
*Handbook of Birds of the Western
United States* (Bailey) 12
Harlem Hospital 38, 212
Harvard Museum of Comparative
Zoology 56
Harvard Observatory 29–31,
65–66, 96, 118–120, 140–141,
151, 173–174
Harvard-Smithsonian Center for
Astrophysics 77
Harvard University 23, 29, 64, 66,
69, 76, 77, 84–85, 97, 126, 165,
178, 199
Harvey, Michelle 111
Hawes, Charles Henry 85
Hawes, Harriet Ann Boyd **85–86**
Hawkes, Graham 52
Hazen, Elizabeth Lee **86–87**
health physics 6
heart
defects 199–200
surgery 200–201
Hebrew University 166

Heidelburg, University of 56, 97,
114
Heidelburger, Michael 3
Heineman Prize 64
Helmholtz, Hermann von 116
hemispheres, brain 123–124
hemoglobin 163
Hemophilus influenzae 3
Henri Wilde Prize 105
Henry Draper Star Catalogue 31, 65
Henry Phipps Institute 190
herbarium 24–25, 53–54
Hereditary Disease Foundation
207–208
Herschel, Caroline Lucretia x,
87–88, 153, 185, 194
Herschel, John 88, 153
Herschel, William x, 87–88
Herschel Medal 17
Hertzsprung, Ejnar 140
Hewish, Antony 16–17
hibernation 156
Hilbert, David 161–162, 183
Hildegarde of Bingen x, **88–89**
Hilleman, Maurice 55
Hitchings, George 57, 59
HIV 176, 211–212
Hodgkin, Dorothy Crowfoot **89–92**
Hofstra University 175
home, design of 80, 181
home economics 181
hominids *see* humans, ancestry of
Homo habilis 118
Hoover Medal 80
Hopper, Grace Brewster Murray
92–94, *93*
hormones 39, 42, 90–91, 127,
163, 218–219
Horney, Karen Danielsen **94–95**
Housman, David 207–208
Houssay, Bernardo O. 42
Hoyle, Fred 17, 26–27
Hrdy, Sarah Blaffer **95–97**
HTLVs 211
Hubbard Medal 80, 118
Hubble Space Telescope 28, 63–64
Huchra, John 77
Huckins, Olga Owens 34
Hughes Medal 11

Hull House 83–84, 181
Human Element in Sex, The (Blackwell) 21
Human Genome Diversity Project 111
Human Genome Project 111, 209
humans, ancestry of 73, 81, 109–111, 117–118, 172, 205–206
Hungarian Psychoanalytic Society 113
Hunter College 36, 48, 57, 217–218
Hunter College Hall of Fame Award 49
Huntington's disease 207–209
hurricanes 191
Hyde, Ida Henrietta **97–98**
hydrocarbons 32
hydrometer 99
hydroxyurea 163
Hyman, Libbie Henrietta **98**
Hypatia, vii, x, **99**

I

ichthyosaur 8
Identification of Pathogenic Fungi Simplified (Hazen) 86
Ildstad, Suzanne **100–101**, 140
Illinois Institute of Technology 191
Illinois, University of 38, 69, 97, 172, 217–218
Illinois worker health survey 84
immune system 3, 100–101, 124, 138–140, 211–212, 218
  attacking body 125, 138–139
  attacking organ transplants 58–59, 100–101, 139–140
  development of 186–187
  nervous system, links to 123, 175–176
Index to the Catalogue of 860 Stars Observed by Flamsteed (Herschel) 88
Index to Every Observation of Every Star in the British Catalogue (Herschel) 88
India, nutrition programs in 179

industrial
  engineering 79–80
  medicine 83–85
Industrial Poisons in the United States (Hamilton) 84
Industrial Toxicology (Hamilton) 85
infanticide 96
infrasound 157, 173
inherited diseases *see* genetic diseases
Innsbruck, University of 42–43
insects 34–35, 149, 155–156, 195–196
Institute of Electrical and Electronic Engineers 5
Institute of Electrical Engineers 11
Institute of Medicine 101
Institute of Scientific Information 212
Institutions de Physique (du Châtelet) 36
Instituzione Analitiche, Le (Agnesi) 1
insulin 89, 91, 218
International Committee on Photographic Magnitudes 119
International Congress of Psychology 117
International Critical Tables 32
International School of American Archaeology and Ethnology 165
International Union of Crystallography 126
Introductory Account of Certain Modern Ideas in Plane Analytical Geometry, An (Scott) 189
invariants 161
Inventors' Hall of Fame 59
invertebrates, classification of 98
Iowa, University of 209
Is My Baby All Right? (Apgar) 9
Istanbul University 76
Italian Geographic Society 194
Italy, attitude to women scientists x, 15, 201
ivory trade 157

J

Jackson, Robert 63
Jackson, Shirley Ann **102–103**
Jacoba Felicie vi, viii, **103**

Jane Addams International Women's Leadership Award 131
Jane Goodall Institute 82
Janeway Medal 177
Jansky Award 17
Japan
  attitude to women scientists viii
  culture of 18
Japan Academy Prize 168
Jemison Group 104
Jemison, Mae Carol **103–104**
Jensen, Hans D. 143
John Burroughs Medal 34
John Elliott Memorial Award 190
John M. Olguin Marine Environment Award 52
John Paul Getty Prize 107
John R. McCormick Memorial Institute for Infectious Diseases 47
Johns Hopkins Medical School x, 3, 9, 47, 164, 175, 186–187, 199–201
Johns Hopkins University 13, 34, 75, 83, 116–117, 141, 164, 213
Joliot-Curie, Frédéric 104–106
Joliot-Curie, Irène xi, 44, **104–106**
Jones, Marcus 25
Jorge Pádua, Maria Tereza **106–107**, *107*

K

Kaiser Wilhelm Institutes 146
Kansas, University of 97
Kappler, John W. x, 138–139
Karen Horney Foundation 95
Karl Taylor Compton Award 102
Kavousi 85
Keck Telescopes 63–64
Keiller, Alexander 117
Kelsey, Frances Oldham **108–109**, 201
Kelsey, Fremont Ellis 108
kerotakis 138
Kilby Award 52, 104, 172, 176
Kimber Genetics Award 133
Kimura, Motoo 168
King, Mary-Claire **109–111**, 127

King's College (London) 70–71
Kinships of Animals and Man (Morgan) 156
Kirch, Christfried 112
Kirch, Gottfried 112
Kirch, Maria Margaretha Winkelmann **112**
Klein, Felix 161–162
Klein, Melanie Reizes **112–113**
Klug, Aaron 71
Kneale, George 197
Kosair Crippled Children's Hospital 68
Kovalevskaia, Sofia Vasilyevna **113–115**
Krieger, Cecilia 154
Krieger-Nelson Award 154
Krosigk, Baron Frederick von 112
Kuhar, Michael 175
Kyoto Prize 80

L

Laboratory of Cell Biology 123
Ladd-Franklin, Christine 116–117
Lady Margaret Hall (college) 213
Lady Willingdon Training College 178
Lady with a Spear (Clark) 36
Laetoli, fossil footprints at 118
Lagrange, Joseph 78
Langbauer, William 173
Langevin, Paul 45
Langmuir, Irving 22
language use by apes 171–172
Langurs of Abu, The (Hrdy) 96
Laplace, Pierre 194
Lapparent, Valerie de 77
Lasker Award 123, 133, 176, 188, 209, 219
Laue, Max von 70, 90
Lavoisier Prize 174
Lawrence Berkeley Laboratory 69
Laws of Life (Blackwell) 21
lead in workplaces 84
League of Nations 85
Leakey, Louis 68, 73–74, 81, **117–118**

Leakey, Mary Douglas Nicol 117–118
Leakey, Richard 117
Leavitt, Henrietta Swan 65, **118–120**, *119*
Lee, Tsung Dao 215–216
Leeds University 125
Leffler-Edgren, Anna Charlotte 115
Legion of Honor (France) 174
Legion of Merit (U.S.) 94
Lehmann, Inge viii, **120**
Lehmann Medal 120
Leiben Prize 146
Leibniz, Gottfried von 1, 36, 112, 146
Leibniz Medal 146
Lemelson/MIT Lifetime Achievement Award 59
Leslie, Alan 72
Lester R. Ford Award 154
leukemia 55, 58, 59, 101, 196, 197, 211
Levi, Giuseppe 121
Levi-Montalcini, Rita vii, viii, 121, **121–123**
Levi, Paola 121–123
Levy, Jerre **123–124**
Levy, Julia **124–125**
Lick Observatory 63
Liddell, Dorothy 117
light
    drugs activated by 124–125
    in undersea vents 203–205
limnology 169–170
Linnaean Society 98
Linnaeus, Carl 54
liver 41–42
logic, symbolic 116
London School of Medicine for Women 8
London, University of 70–71, 72, 117, 124, 189, 192, 213
Long, Esmond 190
Lonsdale, Kathleen Yardley **125–126**
lonsdaleite 125
Lorenz, Konrad 160

Los Angeles, University of California at 73–74, 91, 125, 127, 191, 203, 211
Lovelace, Augusta Ada Byron **127–129**, 128
Lovelock, James E. 137
Love, Susan **126–127**
Luis Empain Prize 46
lymphatic system 186

M

Maathai, Wangari Muta **130–131**
Macarthur Awards 47, 76, 134, 183
McClintock, Barbara vii, **131–134**, 132
McGill University 25, 26, 108, 179
McNally, Karen Cook **134–135**
Mae Jemison Academy 104
Magellanic Clouds 119
maize 131–134, 192
Makhubu, Lydia Phindile 135, **135–136**
Mall, Franklin Paine x, 186
Management in the Home (Gilbreth) 80
management, scientific 79–80
Manhattan Project 6, 141, 215
Manhattanville College 49
Margulis, Lynn Alexander **136–138**
Maria the Jewess 38, **138**
Maria Mitchell Association 153
Maria Practica (Maria the Jewess) **138**
Marine Biological Laboratory 34, 156 *see also* Woods Hole Oceanographic Institute
Marine Technology Society 52
Marks, Phoebe Sarah *see* Ayrton, Hertha
Marquet Prize 105
Marrack, Philippa x, **138–139**
Mars, possible life on 167
Maryland, University of 34, 37
Massachusetts General Hospital 208
Massachusetts Institute of Technology (MIT) x, 48–49, 102, 154, 180–182, 203, 207

Massachusetts State Board of Health 180–181
Massachusetts, University of 137, 197
Mathematical Association of America 154
mathematical physics 78, 115, 213
Mathematical Society 114
Matijasevich, Yuri 183
Matzinger, Polly **139–140**
Mauchly, John 92, 94
Maury, Antonia 29, 65, 66, **140–141**, 153
Max Planck Medal 148
Maya culture 96
Mayer, Joseph E. 141–143
Mayer, Maria Goeppert ix, **141–143**, 142
Mayo Medical School 100
Mayr, Ernst 160
M. Carey Thomas Prize 188
M.D., first woman
    in Britain 7–8, 21
    in United States 20
Mead, Margaret 18, **143–146**, 144
Mechanisms of the Heavens, The (Somerville) 194
Medal of Freedom 201
medical physics 177, 218
Medical Research Council 72
Meisinger Award 192
meitnerium 148
Meitner, Lise vii, viii, 42, 106, **146–148**, *147*
melanin 38
Melbourne, University of 64–65, 178
Memorial Hospital for Cancer and Allied Diseases 177
Memorial Institute of Infectious Diseases 83
Mendel, Gregor 195–196
Menebrea, Luigi F. 128
meningitis 3
6-mercaptopurine 57–59
Merian, Maria Sybilla **149**
Merrell, William S., Co. 108–109
Merriam, C. Hart 12
metalworking, ancient 219–221

Metamorphosis Insectorum Surinamensium (Merian) 149
Meteorological Research Institute 188
Method and Growth of the Lymphatic System, The (Sabin) 186
Mexia, Ynes Enriquetta Julietta *150*, **150–151**
Mexico
    plants of 150–151
    pre-Columbian history 164–165
Miami, University of 123
Michelson Medal 17
Michigan State University 192
Michigan, University of 83, 164, 207
Mickle Prize 47
microelectrode 97
microwaves 4–5, 16
Middle Ages, scientific women in vii, x, 89
Middle East, ancient 219–221
milk, bacteria in 60–61
Milwaukee-Downer College 6
Mimosa mexiae 151
Minnesota, University of 100
Mises, Richard von 76
Missouri, University of 132–133
Mitchell, Maria 140, **151–153**, 152, 180
mitochondria 111, 136
Mittag-Leffler, Gösta 114–115
Miyake Prize 189
Miyake, Yasuo x, 188–189
Molecular and Microscopic Science (Somerville) 194
molecules, structure of 31–32, 69–71, 89–91, 125–126
monkeys, behavior 96
Morawetz, Cathleen Synge **153–154**
Morgan, Ann Haven **154–156**, 155
Morgan, Thomas Hunt 195
Morton, John 72
Moss, Cynthia **156–158**, 173
Motor Vehicle Manufacturers' Association 5
mountain building 13–14

Mount Holyoke x, 9, 31–32, 155–156, 160, 209
Mount Saint Scholastica College 130
Mount Wilson Observatory 26–27
Mueller Medal 19
Müller, G. E. 116
Munich, University of 56
Municipal School of Industrial Physics and Chemistry 44
Murray, Joseph 59
muscles 41, 97
Museum of Alexandria 99
Mussolini, Benito 121–122
musth 157
mutations 3, 110, 133, 168

N

Nairobi, University of 130
National Academy of Engineering (U.S.) 5, 49
National Academy of Sciences (U.S.) 31, 47, 64, 98, 133, 137, 139, 143, 145, 154, 170, 183, 185, 188, 216, 219
National Advisory Board of Science and Technology (Canada) 125
National Aeronautics and Space Administration (U.S.) 51, 104, 192
National Book Award (U.S.) 34
National Breast Cancer Coalition (U.S.) 126
National Bureau of Standards (U.S.) 216
National Cancer Institute (U.S.) 197, 211
National Central University (China) 215
National Council of Research (Italy) 123
National Council of Women of Kenya 131
National Education Committee (China) 222
National Foundation-March of Dimes (U.S.) 9–10
National Geographic Society (U.S.) 52, 80, 81, 117, 118, 172

National Institute of Allergy and Infectious Diseases (U.S.) 139
National Institute of Child Health and Human Development (U.S.) 164
National Institute of Diabetes, Digestive and Kidney Disorders (U.S.) 163
National Institute of Genetics (Japan) 168
National Institute of Mental Health (U.S.) 176
National Institute of Science and Technology (Philippines) 166
National Institute of Social Science (U.S.) 80
National Institutes of Health (U.S.) 54–55, 100, 139, 163, 164, 176, 197, 211
National Jewish Center for Immunology and Respiratory Medicine (U.S.) 139
National Medal of Science (U.S.) 49, 59, 133, 170, 184, 216, 219
National Medal of Technology (U.S.) 94
National Oceanic and Atmospheric Administration (U.S.) 52, 191, 205
National Organization of Women (U.S.) 154
National Radio Astronomy Observatory (Britain) 17
National Research Council (U.S.) 32
National Resources Council (U.S.) 52
National Science Foundation (U.S.) 137, 167
National Tuberculosis Association (U.S.) 191
National University (Mexico) 134
National Women's Hall of Fame (U.S.) 59, 191
Naval Ordnance Development Award 94
Nazis 56, 67, 76, 95, 121–122, 146–147, 161–162
Nebraska, University of 47
nebulae 88
Negri, Adelchi 210

Negri bodies 210
Neptune 194
nerve cells 15–16, 97, 121–123, 210
nerve growth factor 121–123
neurosis 95, 113
Neurosis and Human Growth (Horney) 95
Neurotic Personality of Our Time (Horney) 95
neutrons 105–106, 142, 147, 215
neutron star 17
Newark School of Engineering 80
newborns, test for health of 9
Newcomb-Cleveland Award 77
New Guinea, Mead research in 145
New Hospital for Women 7–8
New Jersey Commission on Science and Technology 102
New Jersey Governor's Award in Science 102
New Jersey State Normal School 210
New Light on Drake (Nuttall) 165
New Mexico State University 197
Newnham College 70, 173
New School for Social Research 18, 95
Newton, Isaac 1, 15, 35–36
Newton Turner, Helen Alma **159–160**
New Ways in Psychoanalysis (Horney) 95
New York Cancer Society 55
New York City Department of Health 210
New York Infirmary for Women and Children 10, 21, 210
New York Medical College 212
New York Psychoanalytic Institute 95
New York State Department of Health 86
New York State Institute for the Study of Malignant Diseases 40
New York University 36, 38, 57, 154, 212
Nice, Margaret Morse **160–161**
Nichols, William R. 180–181
Nigeria, geophysics of 2–3
Nigerian Academy of Science 3

Nightingale, Florence 91
NIH EEO Recognition Award 163
NOAA/MAB Research Award 205
Nobel Institute of Theoretical Physics 147
Nobel Prize ix, 17, 22, 25, 40–42, 43, 45, 47, 57–59, 71, 80, 89, 91, 104–106, 119, 121, 132, 134, 141–143, 148, 170, 197, 213, 216, 217–219
Noether, Emmy 161, **161–162**, 189
Noether, Max 161
Noether's Theorem 162
Noguchi, Constance Tom 162–163, 163
Nordberg Award for Earth Sciences 192
Normal Lives for the Disabled (Gilbreth) 80
North Carolina State University 168
Northeast Utilities 102–103
Northwestern University 83
Notre Dame of Maryland 126
Novello, Antonia Coello **164**
nuclear medicine 177, 218
nuclear power 6, 102, 146–148, 197, 219
Nuclear Regulatory Commission 102–103
Nuclear Research Laboratory 6
nucleus
    cell 136–137, 195
    atomic 105, 142–143, 146, 148, 215–216
number theory 78, 182
Nuttall, Zelia Maria Magdalena **164–165**
Nystatin 86

O

Oak Ridge National Laboratory 6
Oberlin College 118
Ocampo-Friedmann, Roseli 166–167, 167
Office of War Information 18
Ohio State University 31
Ohta, Tomoko viii, **167–168**
Olduvai Gorge 117–118

On the Connexion of the Physical Sciences (Somerville) 194
O'Neill, Charles 84
Open University 17
opiate receptors in brain 175–176
Orangutan Foundation International 75
orangutans 73–75, 74, 81, 206
Order of Australia 159
Order of the British Empire 159
Order of Merit (Britain) 91
Order of Merit (France) 174
Ordway, John 180
Oregon State University 124
Orestes 99
organic chemistry 31–32, 70, 90–91, 125–126, 222
organ transplants 58–59, 100–101, 139–140, 164
Origins of Eukaryotic Cells (Margulis) 137
ornithology see birds
otters, river 49–50
Our Inner Conflicts (Horney) 95
overgrazing, ecological effects of 64–65
Oxford Survey of Childhood Cancers 196
Oxford University 31, 90–91, 168, 195, 196, 213–214

P

Pacific islands, geological maps of 75
Pacific Science Board 36
paleoneurology 56
Paleontological Society 75
Paris, University of 8, 44, 49–50, 103, 105
parity, conservation of 215–216
Park, Edwards 199
Park, W. H. 210
Passionibus Mulierum Curandorum (Trotula) 201
Pasteur, Louis 60
Pasteur Institute 212
pasteurization 60–61
Patrick, Ruth 169–170, 170
Patterns of Culture (Benedict) 18

Patterson, Francine 171, 171–172
PAWS Award 186
Payne-Gaposchkin, Cecilia Helena 65, 120, 173–174
Payne, Katharine 52, 157, 172–173
Payne, Roger 52, 172–173
Peabody Museum 165
Pebbles on the Hill of a Scientist (Seibert) 190
Peccei, Roberto 178
Peccei-Quinn symmetry 178
pediatric cardiology 199–201
Pell, Alexander 209
penicillin 89–91
Pennsylvania, University of 124, 143, 169, 190–191
Pennsylvania College 182
Pennsylvania College for Women 34
Pennsylvania Power and Light Co. 170
peptides 176
Peptide T 176
Perey, Margaret Catherine 174
Pert, Candace Beebe 175, 175–176
pesticides 33–35, 39, 110
Peter the Great 149
Philippines, University of 166
phocomelia 109, 201
phosphorus 222
Photographic Society of America 22
photometry 119–120
photosynthesis 203, 205
Physica (Hildegarde of Bingen) 89
Physical Geography (Somerville) 194
Piaget, Jean 23
Pickering, Edward C. 29–31, 65–66, 119–120, 140–141
Piedmont Mountains 13–14
Pinart, Alphonse Louis 164
Pittsburgh, University of 100, 130
Pius XII College 135
Planck, Max 146, 148
planisphere 99
plants
    collectors 24–25, 53–54, 150–151
    herbicide resistance 192

medicine, use in 88–89, 135–136
viruses affecting 71, 192
plasma (in physics) 4
Platearus, Joannes 201
plesiosaur 8
polio vaccine 54–55
pollution, effects of
    on animals 39
    on deep-sea ecology 205
    on freshwater ecology 169
    on hormones 39
    on humans 39, 181
polonium 44, 45, 105, 174
Poole, Joyce 157, 173
Popular Front 105
Population Study of the Song Sparrow (Nice) 160
Practica Brevis (Trotula) 201
President's Advisory Committee on Oceans and Atmosphere 52
Primack, Joel 178
Primer of Scientific Management (Gilbreth) 80
Princeton University 6, 47, 77, 154
Principia Mathematica (du Châtelet translation of Newton) 35–36
Prior, Fritz 42
probability theory 76
Proconsul africanus 117
protactinium 146
proteins, structure of 213–214
psychoanalysis 94–95, 112–113
Psychoanalysis of Children, The (Klein) 113
psychology
    of children 112–113, 160
    of parent-child relationships 95, 113
    of women 94–95
    of workers 79–80
Psychological Management (Gilbreth) 80
psychoneuroimmunology 176
pterosaur 8
public health reform 186–188
Public Health Service 54, 61, 164, 197

Public Health Special Recognition Award 163
Puerto Rico, University of 164
pulsar 17
Purdue University 80
Purposive Explanation in Psychology (Boden) 23
Putnam, Frederic W. 164–165
Putnam, Hilary 183

Q

QLT Phototherapies 125
quantum physics 46, 102, 141, 146, 161–162
quark, top 69
quasars 27–28
Quimby, Edith Hinckley **177–178**, 218
Quinn, Helen Rhoda Arnold **178**

R

rabies test 210
Rabson, Alan 55, 197
Race: Science and Politics (Benedict) 18
Races of Mankind, The (Benedict) 18
racism 18, 111
Radcliffe College 29, 48, 96, 118, 173–174, 199, 209
radiation
    health dangers 5–6, 110, 177, 196–197
    medical uses 126–127, 177
radiation physics 177, 218
radioactive decay 26, 142, 146, 174, 215–216
radioactivity 5, 25–26, 43–45, 104, 141, 146, 174
    artificial 104–106, 177
    from bomb tests 188–189
radio astronomy 16–17
radioimmunoassay 217–219
radioisotopes 217–219
Radiological Society of North America 177
radium 5, 25, 26, 44–45, 218

Radium Institute 26, 45, 105–106, 174
radon 5–6, 25
rainfall 191–192
Rajalakshmi, R. **179–180**
Ramakrishnan, C. V. 179
Rand Corp. 182
RCA 4
receptors
    on immune cells 139
    opiate, on brain cells 175–176
recoil of atoms 26
relativity 161
restriction fragment length polymorphisms 207–208
Revlon/UCLA Breast Center 127
ribozyme 212
Richards, Ellen Henrietta Swallow viii, x, 31, 153, **180–182**
Richards, Robert Hallowell 180–181
Ricketts Laboratory 190
Ricketts Prize 190, 193
Right Livelihood Award 131, 197
Rio de Janeiro, University of 106
rivers, ecology of *see* water—fresh, ecology
Rivers of the United States (Patrick) 170
Robinson, Julia Bowman xi, 182, **182–183**
Robinson, Raphael M. 182
Rockefeller Foundation 32, 192
Rockefeller Institute 187
rocks
    microorganisms in 166–167
    oil-bearing 75
Rogers-Low, Barbara 91
Rolex Award for Enterprise 172
Roots and Shoots 82
Royal Academy of Sciences (Berlin) 112
Royal Astronomical Society (Britain) 17, 31, 66, 88, 185, 194
Royal College of Physicians (Britain) 196
Royal Danish Geodetic Institute 120

Royal Danish Society of Science 120
Royal Geographic Society (Britain) 194
Royal Greenwich Observatory 27–28
Royal Institution (Britain) 125
Royal Society (Britain) ix, 10, 11, 87–88, 91, 126, 194
Royal Society of Canada 125
Royal Swaziland Society of Science and Technology 136
Royal Victoria College 25
Royal Zoological Society of New South Wales 19
Rubin, Vera 64, 120, **183–185**, *184*
Ruff, Michael 176
Russell, Henry 141
Rutgers University 39, 102, 203
Rutherford, Ernest 25

S

Sabin, Florence Rena x, **186–188**, *187*
Sachs, Robert G. 142
Sagan, Carl 136–137
Sagan, Lynn *see* Margulis, Lynn Alexander
Saint Mary's Dispensary for Women and Children 7
Salk, Jonas 54
Samoa, Mead research in 143–145
sand
    effect of waves on 11
    movement under vibration 78
San Diego, University of California at 27–28, 138, 139, 143, 211–212
sanitary chemistry 181
San Jose State College 68
Santa Barbara Breast Cancer Institute 127
Santa Clara, University of 172
Santa Cruz, University of California at 63–64, 135
Sarah Lawrence College 38
Saruhashi, Katsuko x, 168, *188*, **188–189**

Saruhashi Prize 168, 188–189
Saturn, rings of 114–115
scarlet fever 47, 210
Schaeffer, Howard 59
schizophrenia 113
Schwartz, Robert 58
Science Clinics 6
Science Council of Japan 189
Science Research Council 27
Science and Technology,
    University of 6
science, women in see women in
    science
Scientific Achievement Award 219
Scott, Charlotte Angas **189–190**, 209
Scottish Royal Observatory 17
Sea Around Us, The (Carson) 34
sea, deep 203–205
Segrè, Emilio 216
Seibert, Florence Barbara **190–191**
seismic gaps 134–135
Seismological Society of America 120
Self-Analysis (Horney) 95
semiconductors 5, 48–49
semimetals 48
Senckenberg Museum 56
SE polyoma virus 55, 197
serial endosymbiosis theory
    136–137
sex 21, 89, 90, 95, 96, 144–145, 202
*Sex and Temperament in Three
    Primitive Societies* (Mead) 145
Shapley, Harlow 29, 31, 141
sharks 36–37, 52
sheep breeding 159
shell theory 142–143
shock waves see waves in
    mathematics
Siberia 166–167
sickle-cell disease 162–163
signal, separating from noise 46–47
Silent Spring (Carson) 33, 35
Simpson, Joanne Malkus ix, xi,
    191–192
Simpson, Robert 191–192
Simpson Weather Associates 191
Sithole-Niang, Idah **192**
skin cells 38
Sloan Foundation 154

Slye, Maud Caroline **192–193**
Smadel, Joseph 55
Smith College 12, 85, 156–157,
    186, 212, 213–214, 215
Smith, Martha K. 162
Smithsonian Institution 151
Snyder, Solomon 175–176
Society to Aid Scientific Research
    by Women 31
Society of American Bacteriologists
    60
Society of Automotive Engineers 5
Society for the Diffusion of Useful
    Knowledge 194
Society of Industrial Engineers
    79–80
Society of Sea Water Sciences 189
Society of Vertebrate Paleontology
    56
Society of Women Engineers 49, 67
Society of Women Geographers
    52, 118, 145
sociobiology 96
Soil Conservation Board 64–65
solid-state physics 4–5, 48–49, 102
Somerville, Mary vii, 153,
    193–195
Somerville, William 194
Somerville College 90, 195
Sorbonne 43, 45, 105, 174
sounds, animal 172–173
Southampton University 17
South Dakota, University of 108,
    209
spectra
    of organic molecules 31–32
    of stars 30–31, 65–66, 140
Sperry, Roger 123
Sperry Corp. 94
Spirit of Achievement Award 212
split-brain research 123–124
Sprague Memorial Institute 190, 193
Squibb Award 86
Standard Model of Fundamental
    Particles and Interactions 178
Stanford Linear Accelerator 69,
    178
Stanford University 67, 69, 96,
    103, 111, 149, 172, 178, 195

stars
    binary (double) 140–141
    brightness 118–120, 173–174
    classification 29–31, 65–66,
        140–141, 173
    clusters 88
    creation of elements in 26–27,
        174
    evolution 141
    life cycle 26–27
    variable 66, 119–120, 173–174
State College for Women
    (Mississippi) 86
State University of New York 126,
    222
statistics 76, 109, 141, 159
Stevens, Nettie Maria viii, *195*,
    195–196
Stewart, Alice **196–197**
Stewart, Sarah 55, **197–198**
still *see* distillation
Stockholm, University of 114–115
Stone Age 117–118
"stones" in body organs 126
storms 191–192
Strasbourg University 174
Strassmann, Fritz 106, 147–148
streptococci 47, 61
stroke 123
Struve, Otto 173
subatomic particles 5, 6, 63, 69,
    102, 105, 142–143, 161–162,
    177, 215–216
submersibles 37, 52, 203–205, 204
sulfanilamide 57
superantigens 139
superconductors 48
supernova 17, 26
surgeon general (U.S.) 164
Surinam, wildlife of 50, 149
Susan G. Komen Foundation
    Award 110
Susquehanna Institute 60
Sussex University 23
Sustainable Sea Expeditions 52
SV40 55
Swarthmore College 63
Swaziland, University of 135–136
Sydney, University of 19, 159

syllogisms 116
Sylvania 4
Sylvester, James J. 116
Symbiosis in Cell Evolution (Margulis) 137
Synge, J. L. 153–154

T

Tales of the Cochiti Indians (Benedict) 18
Talladega College 38
Tanaka Prize 189
Taussig, Helen **199–201**, 200
Taylor, Frederick 79
T cells 100–101, 140, 211
Technische Hochschule of Hanover 67
Tektite (undersea habitat) 51
telescope 22, 27, 30, 87
    Hubble space 28, 63–64
    Keck 63–64
    radio 16
Teller, Edward 142
Terrestrial Magnetism, Department of 184–185
Teubner Memorial Prize 162
thalidomide 108–109, 199–201
Theon 99
Third World Organization of Women in Science 135–136
Thomas, Elizabeth Marshall 173
Thomas, M. Carey 13, 189
thorium 44
Three Mile Island Public Health Fund 197
time and motion study 79
tin mining, ancient 220–221
tissue culture 122, 130, 212
Toho University 188
Tokyo, University of 168, 188
tool use in chimpanzees 81
Toronto, University of 47, 69, 135, 153–154
toxins, bacterial 47, 210
transposition of genes 133
Transvaal Museum 205
tree planting 130–131
Trotula of Salerno x, **201–202**

Trudeau Medal 191
Trueblood, Kenneth 91, 125
Tsinghua University 222
Tswett, Michael S. 42
tuberculin 190–191
tuberculosis 106, 187, 190–191
Tübingen University 4
Tufts University Medical Center 58
Turin School of Medicine 121
Turkish Geological Research and Survey Directorate 220
Turner, John 64
turnover pulse hypothesis 206
Tyler Prize 75, 170
typhus fever 20

U

undersea exploration 36–37, 51–52, 203–205
Under the Sea Wind (Carson) 34
UNICEF 164
U.S. Agency for International Development Fellowship 192
U.S. Biological Survey 12, 34
U.S. Bureau of Fisheries 34
U.S. Congressional Antarctic Science Medal 167
U.S. Coast Survey 151
U.S. Department of Agriculture 60–61
U.S. Department of Commerce 5, 84, 192
U.S. Department of Defense 94, 129
U.S. Department of Energy 197
U.S. Department of Interior 75
U.S. Department of Labor 85
U.S. Fish and Wildlife Service 33–35
U.S. Geological Survey 13–14, 75
U.S. Navy 36, 92–94, 205
U.S. Office of Naval Research 19
UNIVAC 92, 93
universe
    distances in, measuring 118–120
    distribution of galaxies in 63–64, 76–77, 184
    formation of galaxies in 64, 77

mapping 76–77, 87–88, 118–120
    structure 77
University College (Nigeria) 2
University College, London 17, 26, 72, 125–126
uranium 5, 44, 106, 141, 147–148, 215
Uranus 87, 194
Utah, University of 110

V

vaccines, safety of 54–55
Vanderbilt University 122
Van Dover, Cindy Lee 203–205, *204*
van Lawick, Baron Hugo 81–82
Varian Associates 5
Vassar College viii, x, 18, 92, 116, 140, 152–153, 180, 183
Vassar, Matthew 153
vents, undersea 203–205
versed sine curve 1
Vetlesen Award 205
Vienna, University of 76, 146
Virginia, University of 169, 191
viruses 139, 219
    cancer-causing 54–55, 197–198, 211
    drugs against 59
    herpes 59
    potyvirus 192
    SE polyoma virus 55, 197
    structure 71
    tobacco mosaic 71
vision, color 116–117
vitamin B_{12} 89, 91
Voltaire 36
Vrba, Elisabeth **205–206**

W

Wadia College 179
Warner Prize 27
Washington University (St. Louis, Mo.) 40–41, 121–123
Washington, University of 4, 111
Watcher at the Nest, The (Nice) 160

water
   analysis 169, 180–181, 188–189
   bacteria in 190
   fresh, ecology of 155–156, 169–170
   sea, carbon dioxide in 188–189
   sea, radioactivity in 188–189
water bath 138
Watson, James 69, 71
wavelets 46–47
waves in mathematics 153–154
Weierstrass, Karl T. 114
Weinberg, Steven 178
Weldon Memorial Prize 168
Wellesley College 4, 29, 31, 86, 96, 156, 209
West Coast National Undersea Research Center 205
Westfield Normal School 195
Wexler, Milton 207
Wexler, Nancy Sabin **207–209**, 208
Weyl, Hermann 161–162
whales, humpback 52, 172–173
Wheaton College 76
Wheeler, Anna Johnson Pell viii, 189, **209–210**
Whitman, Charles Otis 193
Whitman College 177
Whitney, Mary V. 152
Whittaker, Robert H. 137
Wiener, Norbert 161
Wigner, Eugene 143
Wilkins, Maurice 70–71
William B. Coley Award 139
William and Mary, College of 205
Williams, Anna Wessels **210**
Williams College 13
Wilson, Allan C. 110–111
Wilson, Edmund B. 196
Windstar Award for the Environment 131
Wisconsin, University of 6, 13, 39, 60, 136
"witch of Agnesi" 1
With Love: Ten Heartwarming Stories of Chimpanzees (Goodall) 82
Wolf Prize 134

Woman of the World Award 131
Woman of the Year Award 131
Woman that Never Evolved, The (Hrdy) 97
women
   diseases of 201–202
   environmental protection, role in 130–131
   "natural sphere" of vii–viii
   psychoanalytic view of 94–95
   supposed intellectual inferiority of vii–viii, 78, 180, 193–194
   women physicians, wish for 2, 7, 20, 103, 201–202
women in science
   educational bars to viii, xi, 78, 87, 116, 123, 180, 189, 193–194
   employment bars to viii–x, 4, 27, 41, 123, 132, 141–142, 146, 161–162, 179
   family and career, bars to combining ix, xi, 4, 26
   financial bars to vii, 48, 104
   legal bars to vii, x, 2, 103
   men receiving credit for work of ix, x, 17, 80, 112, 117–118, 176, 196, 210, 219
   motivation and characteristics of xi, 59, 103–104, 111, 121–122, 123–124, 136, 183, 217
   social bars to vii–xi, 20–21, 70, 94, 96, 99, 128, 132
   success, reasons for x–xi
   support for x–xi, 49, 135–136, 153, 180–181, 188–189, 219
women's colleges x
Women's Hall of Fame 104
Women's Medical College 21, 210
Women's Social and Political Union 11
Wonderful Metamorphosis of Caterpillars (Merian) 149
Wong-Staal, Flossie 211, **211–212**
Woodman, A. G. 181
Woods Hole Oceanographic Institution 191, 203 *see also* Marine Biological Laboratory

workplaces
   design of 79, 84
   health risks in 83–85
   psychological needs in 79–80
World Academy of Arts and Sciences 52
World Environment Center 5
World War I 7, 11, 22, 45, 84, 85, 89, 104, 146, 162
World War II 15, 18–19, 34, 42, 54, 57, 64, 70, 73, 75, 76, 90, 92, 117, 121–122, 124, 141, 145, 159, 188, 191, 196, 209, 217–218
World Wildlife Fund 39, 50, 107
worms 98
Wright, Jane Cooke 38, **212–213**
Wrinch, Dorothy Maud **213–214**, 214
Wu, Chien-shiung xi, **214–216**, *215*

X

X chromosome 195
X-ray crystallography *see* crystallography, X-ray
X rays 133, 221
   health risks 6, 196
   in astronomy 16–17
   medical uses 6, 45, 104, 127, 146, 196, 199

Y

Yale University 92, 190, 206
Yalow, Rosalyn Sussman ix, x, 48, 49, **217–219**, 218
Yang, Chen Ning 215–216
Y chromosome 195–196
Yener, Kutlu Aslihan **219–221**, *220*
Yerkes Observatory 27, 173

Z

Zakrzewska, Marie 21
Zhao Yufen **222**
Zimbabwe, University of 192
Zinjanthropus 118